Goa

Marika McAdam

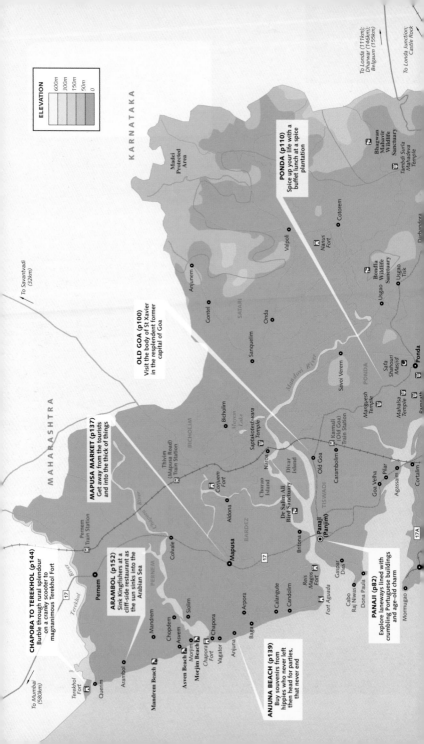

ELEVATION
600m
300m
150m
50m
0

CHAPORA TO TEREKHOL (p144)
Burble through rural splendour on a cranky scooter to magnanimous Terekhol Fort

ARAMBOL (p152)
Sink Kingfishers at a cliff-side restaurant as the sun sinks into the Arabian Sea

ANJUNA BEACH (p139)
Buy souvenirs from hippies who never left then head for parties, that never end

MAPUSA MARKET (p137)
Get away from the tourists and into the thick of things

OLD GOA (p100)
Visit the body of St Xavier in the resplendent former capital of Goa

PONDA (p110)
Spice up your life with a buffet lunch at a spice plantation

PANAJI (p82)
Explore laneways lined with crumbling Portuguese buildings and age-old charm

KARNATAKA

MAHARASHTRA

To Mumbai (580km)

To Savantvadi (32km)

To Londa (111km); Dharwar (146km); Belgaum (155km)

To Londa Junction; Castle Rock

Terekhol River
Chapora River
Mandovi River

Madei Protected Area

PERNEM
BARDEZ
BICHOLIM
SATARI
TISWADI
PONDA

Terekhol Fort
Querim
Arambol
Mandrem Beach
Mandrem
Chopdem
Asvem Beach
Asvem
Morjim
Morjim Beach
Siolim
Chapora
Chapora Fort
Vagator
Anjuna
Baga
Calangute
Candolim
Arpora
Fort Aguada
Reis Magos Fort
Cabo Raj Niwas
Dona Paula
Gaspar Dias
Panaji (Panjim)
Britona
Pernem
Pernem Train Station
Colvale
Mapusa
Dr Salim Ali Bird Sanctuary
Corjuem Fort
Aldona
Churao Island
Divar Island
Naroa
Thivim (Mapusa Road) Train Station
Moyem Lake
Bicholim
Saptakotesh-wara Temple
Sanquelim
Onda
Gontei
Anjunem
Valpoi
Nanus Fort
Cotorem
Madei Protected Area
Durbandora
Bhagwan Mahavir Wildlife Sanctuary
Tambdi Surla Mahadeva Temple
Usgao Tisk
Bondla Wildlife Sanctuary
Usgao
Savoi Verem
Safa Shahouri Masjid
Ponda
Manguesh Temple
Mahalsa Temple
Ramnath
Old Goa
Carambolim
Karmali (Old Goa) Train Station
Goa Velha
Pilar
Agassaim
Cortalim
Mormugao
17
17A
Savantvadi

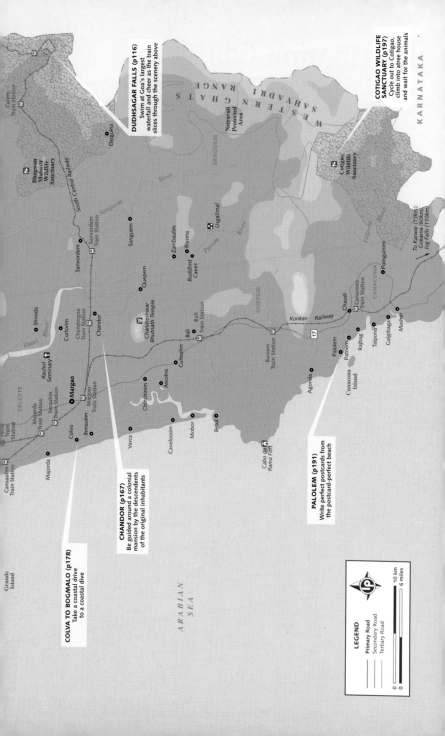

DUDHSAGAR FALLS (p116)
Swim at Goa's largest waterfall and cheer as the train slices through the scenery above

COTIGAO WILDLIFE SANCTUARY (p197)
Cycle out to Cotigao, climb into a tree house and wait for the animals

COLVA TO BOGMALO (p178)
Take a coastal drive to a coastal dive

CHANDOR (p167)
Be guided around a colonial mansion by the descendents of the original inhabitants

PALOLEM (p191)
Write perfect postcards from the postcard-perfect beach

WESTERN GHATS

SAHYADRI RANGE

KARNATAKA

Netravali
Protected
Area

Cotigao
Wildlife
Sanctuary

SANGUEM

QUEPEM

CANACONA

SALCETE

ARABIAN SEA

Grande Island

Cansaulim Train Station

Majorda Train Station

Seraulim Train Station

Margao Train Station

Rachol Seminary

Chandorga Train Station

Sanvordem Train Station

Canacona Train Station

Bali Train Station

Barcem Train Station

Colem Train Station

Bhagwan Mahavir Wildlife Sanctuary

Dudhsagar

South Central Railway

Chandreshwar Bhutnath Temple

Buddhist Caves

Usgalimal

Konkan Railway

To Karwar (13km); Gokarna (60km); Jog Falls (110km)

Majorda
Colva
Benaulim
Varca
Cavelossim
Mobor
Betul
Cabo da Rama Fort
Agonda
Palolem
Patnem
Rajbag
Talpona
Galgibaga
Masher
Poinguinim
Chaudi
Canacona Island
Sanvordem
Curtorim
Shiroda
Chandor
Quepem
Sanguem
Zambaulim
Rivona
Bali
Cuncolim
Assolna
Chinchinim

Zuari River

Sanguem River

Sanguem River

Pareda River

Talpona River

River

SANGUEM

QUEPEM

CANACONA

17

LEGEND
Primary Road
Secondary Road
Tertiary Road

0   10 km
0   6 miles

Destination Goa

Trying to describe Goa is like trying to bottle the Arabian Sea. For some, the state's best days are over; for others, they're just beginning. Goa is and always has been shaken and shaped by pilgrims, pioneers, warlords and wanderers. Its inhabitants, with their kaleidoscope of ancient cultures and edgy subcultures, exude pride in the distinctiveness of their homeland – a distinctiveness that is born of its diversity.

No wonder then that just about everybody wants to come here. Pink package tourists are blobbed along the beaches. Upwardly mobile Europeans disguise their clean-cut characters with tattoos and tattered clothing. Japanese backpackers shake off the orderliness of their upbringing, and packs of Israelis exorcise the frustrations of their recent military service. And then there are the foreign locals, whose time in Goa can be measured by the length of their dreadlocks.

Thrown into this milieu are Christian traditions, whitewashed churches and Portuguese houses. Head inland and you may stumble across a Roman Catholic wake held in honour of a Hindu deity. Visit a night bazaar on the coast and your assumptions about subcontinental travel will be inverted at the sight of Indian tourists buying handicrafts from white locals. This tiny state has got the X factor.

Spend any time trying to figure Goa out, and you'll get no closer to a tangible answer. Instead, surrender to the spirit of *susegad* – of relaxing and enjoying life while you can – by simply accepting that Goa is not so much a state of India but a state of mind… a state of simply 'being'.

PAUL BIGL

Highlights

CHRISTINE OSBORNE

Pay your respects at St Francis Xavier's tomb in the
Basilica of Bom Jesus (p105), Old Goa

Kick back and relax on Little Vagator Beach (p144)

NEIL SETCHFIELD

NEIL SETCHFIELD

Admire the intricate handicrafts
for sale at Goa's many markets
(p223)

NEIL SETCHFIELD

Perfect your haggling skills at the Anjuna flea market (p141)

OTHER HIGHLIGHTS

▪ Kite-surf by day and enjoy the live-music scene by night in laid-back Arambol (p152)

▪ Explore the coastline between Cavelossim (p187) and Agonda (p190) by motorcycle

▪ Experience Goa's renowned parties (p148) in Vagator and Anjuna

▪ Take a dip at Dudhsagar Falls (p116), Goa's tallest waterfall

Wander the picturesque streets of Fontainhas (p86), Panaji

PAUL BEINSSEN

CRAIG PERSH

Contemplate the soaring architecture of the Church of O Lady of the Immaculate Conception (p87), Panaji

Join local holiday-makers on
Vagator Beach (p144)

Discover Goa's unique cultural heritage (p30)

Let your worries fade away on picture-perfect Palolem Beach (p191)

MARK DU

Gaze at the detailed craftwork in the Church of St Francis of Assisi (p104), Old Goa

ANDREW MARSHALL & LEANNE WALKER

Catch a glimpse of local life in the rice fields around Old Goa (p100)

NEIL SETCHFIELD

Weave through cows and sun beds on Calangute Beach (p126)

Escape from everyday life on peaceful Benaulim Beach (p185)

GREG ELMS

Contents

East
Spice of life

Regional Map Contents

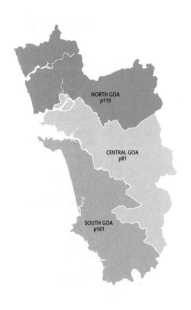

MUMBAI
pp62-3

NORTH GOA
p119

CENTRAL GOA
p81

SOUTH GOA
p161

The Authors

MARIKA McADAM

Marika is a lawyer who has spent the last few years travelling and writing in a bid to avoid practising law. Her quest has taken her to various parts of the globe, including the Indian subcontinent, where she penned her first Lonely Planet guide. After a short stint in East Timor volunteering for Lawyers Without Borders, and a longer stint in Melbourne as a Lawyer Without Employment, Marika headed to another former Portuguese colony – Goa.

Marika is the sole author of the 5th edition of *Bangladesh,* and has contributed to *Bluelist* and *The Lonely Planet Guide to Experimental Travel* (as if there's any other kind!).

My Goa

There's a reason north Goa has been done before; all the colour and contradictions of Goa are here. My Honda Kinetic has the heart of an Enfield and all the horsepower of a bicycle; it was born for this ride. Leaving the hippy heartland of Anjuna (p139), the coast road takes me through a montage of changing countryside and cultures. I pass fishermen in Siolim (p150) and Russians in Morjim (p150) as leather-clad bikies pass me. After an intermission at Arambol (p152) – a rendezvous point for global free spirits – I eventually find myself at the spot where the Arabian Sea meets the Terekhol River. A ferry takes me to the holiday holy grail of Terekhol Fort (p155) and its resplendent views southward over the expanse of Goa.

CONTRIBUTING AUTHOR

Dr Trish Batchelor wrote the Health chapter. She is a general practitioner and travel medicine specialist who works at the CIWEC Clinic in Kathmandu; she is also a medical advisor to the Travel Doctor New Zealand clinics. Trish teaches travel medicine through the University of Otago, and is interested in underwater and high-altitude medicine, and in the impact of tourism on host countries. She has travelled extensively through Southeast and East Asia and particularly loves high-altitude trekking in the Himalayas.

LONELY PLANET AUTHORS

Why is our travel information the best in the world? It's simple: our authors are independent, dedicated travellers. They don't research using just the Internet or phone, and they don't take freebies in exchange for positive coverage. They travel widely, to all the popular spots and off the beaten track. They personally visit thousands of hotels, restaurants, cafés, bars, galleries, palaces, museums and more – and they take pride in getting all the details right, and telling it how it is. For more, see the authors section on www.lonelyplanet.com.

Getting Started

The range of travellers who visit Goa, from first timers to package tourists to hard-core adventurers, is a testament to its widespread appeal and the relative ease of travelling here. Goa's size means that you don't have to stress about planning a route or slicing your days into units to see and do everything; if you don't like where you are, you can relocate to the other end of the state in a couple of hours.

Though Goa isn't as cheap as the rest of India, its range of facilities means that you can travel here on any budget; the only challenge comes during peak season when the crowds may force you to spend the occasional night in a pricier place.

Health and safety are considerations – as they are everywhere – but on the whole Goa couldn't be an easier place to visit.

WHEN TO GO

The best time to visit Goa is during the cooler months, from November to March. If you arrive in October, right at the start of the tourist season, you'll find the beaches pleasantly empty, but may also find that some of the facilities (such as beach shacks) aren't yet open for business.

See Climate Charts (p213) for more information.

April and May can be very humid, and swimming becomes less pleasant as the sea gets rougher. Some facilities may also be closed, as most beach shacks pack up after Easter.

Many Goans feel that the monsoon, which visits Goa between June and the end of September, is when the state is at its best. Parties and celebrations are held to welcome the rain, and the countryside turns lush and green almost overnight. In terms of tourism, Goa is virtually dead. Some guesthouses simply close up, and swimming in the sea is out of the question. The plus side to visiting at this time is that you will have the place to yourself at very little cost.

Without doubt the peak season for visitors to Goa is from 22 December to 5 January (give or take a couple of days on either side), and some people have been coming back annually for a decade or more. The massive influx of visitors allows hotels and guesthouses to charge exorbitant prices and many places are booked solid, but it's a great time to be in Goa. The weather is perfect, the place is buzzing and in typical Goan fashion there are parties most nights.

The high season covers the period from mid-December to late January (with the exception of the peak season over Christmas). The middle

---

DON'T LEAVE HOME WITHOUT...

- A light suitcase – there's so much to buy in Goa that you'll want space for shopping
- A light long-sleeved top in winter for slightly chilly evenings or early mornings
- A reliable padlock – it's an essential travel item for budget and even midrange travellers given that many guesthouses only offer a flimsy padlock for security
- A torch to navigate poorly lit streets
- Your driving licence (and copies) and sturdy closed-toe shoes so you can take in the countryside from the back of a motorcycle
- Shorts and tops of a respectable length

season, known in Goa simply as 'season', lasts from October to mid-December, and from February to June. The low season is from July to September.

The temperature throughout the year is fairly constant, varying from a maximum of 28°C or 29°C in July to a maximum of 33°C in May. Average minimums for the same months are 24°C and 26.5°C.

COSTS & MONEY

India as a whole is a very cheap country to visit. However, costs in Goa often depend on whether or not you're being charged as a rich foreign tourist. Some things seem ridiculously cheap: a haircut for US$1, a vegetarian thali (traditional all-you-can-eat meal) for 50c, a one-hour bus ride for 30c or a packet of Indian cigarettes for 50c. But souvenirs, many hotels, petrol and imported goods will seem relatively expensive in comparison.

By staying in rock-bottom budget hotels or guesthouses, eating fish curry rice (fish in a spicy sauce served over rice) at local restaurants and not moving around or partying too much, it's possible to get by in Goa on Rs 250 (US$6) a day. Outside the November to March high season, accommodation costs are substantially reduced. At the other end of the scale, staying at a five-star resort and living it up can easily cost US$250 a day or more.

Most visitors will opt for a middle ground. On a budget, but allowing for clean accommodation, meals in cheap restaurants or beach shacks, the occasional taxi or motorcycle hire and a bit of nightlife, expect to pay US$15 to US$25 a day. If you're on a midrange budget – staying in a decent hotel with a pool, eating seafood in touristy restaurants, taking taxis everywhere and buying souvenirs – set aside perhaps US$50 a day. If you're on a package deal with accommodation included, you should find that US$25 to US$30 is ample.

HOW MUCH?

Entry to club man/woman Rs 500/free!

20g chocolate Rs 5

10 cigarettes Rs 15

Sarong Rs 50

Shave Rs 40

See also Lonely Planet Index, inside front cover

TRAVEL LITERATURE

David Tomory's *Hello Goodnight: A Life of Goa,* published by Lonely Planet, explores Goa's relationship with travellers over the ages. It is a lushly written book that's sometimes too heavy on description but ultimately paints an in-depth picture of Goa and what it has meant to travellers. If you're looking for reasons to go to Goa, Tomory delves deep into the state and transcends the hackneyed notion of Goa as a mere beach destination.

Chasing the Monsoon, by Alexander Frater, is an Englishman's account of a journey north from Kovalam in Kerala all the way to Cherrapunji in Meghalaya, one of the wettest places on earth, following the onset of the monsoon as it moves north across the country. Frater does pass through Goa, but it is his exploration of the monsoon and its effect on people that is the real journey.

Richard Burton's *Goa and the Blue Mountains or Six Months of Sick Leave* is the earliest travelogue that is readily obtainable. Originally published in 1851, this account of his journey through Goa and southwards to Ootacamund makes great reading. The book is interesting for the historical perspective but is also highly enjoyable because of Burton's irreverent sense of humour. This book, in a beautiful blue hardback edition emblazoned with gold, is widely available all over Goa.

Goa Freaks: My Hippie Years in India, by Cleo Odzer, is a fascinating insider's account of the hippy heyday in Anjuna in the 1970s. Odzer unapologetically details her 'freak' life, which she sustained through

TOP FIVES

Best Beaches

The only generalisation you can make about visitors to Goa is that they all have some sort of interest in the beach. Beaches nibble along the entire coast of Goa, yet each is somehow different to the next.

- Palolem (p191) – the most popular beach in the south, and not saturated…yet
- Anjuna (p139) – chillum out at hippy central
- Arambol (p152) – kite-surf by day and retreat to cliffside guesthouses by night
- Vagator (p144) – small coves to enjoy before the parties begin
- Calangute and Baga (p126) – wall-to-wall sun beds and sun seekers

Top Markets

Markets are microcosms of the colour and contradictions of Goa; the image of Indian tourists buying pastries from German vendors is as Goan as that of fishermen selling their daily catch.

- Anjuna flea market (p141) – from humble hippy beginnings to a veritable carnival of infamy
- Ingo's Saturday Nite Bazaar (p129) – the best restaurants bring their offerings to the outdoor tables, and local fire-twirlers demonstrate their talent
- Mackie's Saturday Nite Bazaar (p129) – a rival of Ingo's, Mackie's is more of a low-key event but with has live music and outdoor bars set by the Baga River
- Mapusa market (p137) – traders come from all over the state to hawk their wares here
- Siolim markets (p150) – drink sugar-cane juice at the Chapora River market and watch women prying mussel shells apart with impressive skill, or head to St Anthony's Chapel at the crack of dawn to enjoy the flash market that appears each Wednesday

Favourite People-Watching Spots

Half of the experience of Goa is the other people who have come to experience Goa – this tiny state accommodates an enormous array of people.

- Chapora (p144) – immerse yourself in crowds of hippies and clouds of chillum
- Anjuna (p139) – watch English package tourists buy souvenirs from the hippies who never left
- Ingo's Saturday Nite Bazaar (p129) – pull up a bar stool and wonder at the origins of the eclectic passers-by
- Colva (p180) – get up early and grab your camera to witness fishermen bringing in their morning catch
- Calangute and Baga (p126) – gawk with camera-toting Indian tourists at touts and foreign tourists

drug-running scams. Her frank depiction of the drug scene is often confronting, but it is the character portraits she paints along the way that really linger.

Gregory David Roberts' *Shantaram* took the world by storm. This hefty travel tome is one man's account of his time in India. Set mainly in Mumbai (with detours to Goa), whether you like it or not this controversial 'fictional' work will stay with you long after you've read the final sentence and left India behind.

Not particularly about Goa but a fun Indian beach read nonetheless, William Sutcliffe's *Are You Experienced?* is a comical insight into the backpacker scene through the eyes of a reticent, insecure traveller.

Gita Mehta's *Karma Cola* is a good account of the natural healing culture that pervades Goa and a comically cynical account of the quest for enlightenment in India.

INTERNET RESOURCES

India in general, and Goa in particular, is very Internet savvy and you'll find countless excellent websites devoted to Goan travel, activities, culture, history, news and trance parties.

Findall-Goa (www.findall-goa.com) Up-to-the-minute website detailing what's happening around Goa and where. Also has flight information and maps.

Goa Tourism (www.goatourism.org, www.goa-tourism.com) The state tourism body, the Goa Tourism Development Corporation (GTDC), has two sites. The latter is particularly useful.

Goa World (www.goa-world.com) This site has information on everything from history and culture to recipes and Konkani; it also has links to some 300 Goa-related sites.

Goacom (www.goacom.com) This is one of the best websites for information on Goa for both tourists and residents; it features a monthly webzine.

Herald (www.oherald.com) This is the site of Goa's top-selling English-language daily.

Lonely Planet (www.lonelyplanet.com) It's not that we're biased, it's just that there's no better place to start your Internet explorations. Here you'll find succinct summaries of travel destinations, postcards from other travellers and the Thorn Tree Forum.

Itineraries

CLASSIC ROUTES

NORTHERN HIPPY TRAIL   Two Weeks

Start in crowded **Calangute** (p126), checking out **Fort Aguada** (p120) and the fort at **Reis Magos** (p120). Immerse yourself in the manic nightlife of **Baga** (p126), and visit Ingo's Saturday Nite Bazaar in **Arpora** (p129). When the high prices become too much, relocate to **Anjuna** (p139), hub of hippy. Party the nights away and spend days recovering on one of the beaches at **Vagator** (p144). While you're in the area, join the densely packed scene in **Chapora** (p144) and head to **Mapusa** (p136) for some market action.

Travel to **Arambol** (p152), where you can sleep in a cliffside guesthouse, toss a Frisbee or learn how to kite-surf. On the way stop off in **Siolim** (p150) and drive slowly by the beaches at **Morjim** (p150), **Asvem** (p150) and **Mandrem** (p151).

Finally, head up through picturesque countryside to **Terekhol** (p155). For a real treat, relocate to one of Goa's finest hotels, located in the fort. Or choose a more budget option and enjoy near-deserted **Querim Beach** (p155).

From Portuguese forts to traveller hang-outs that were made infamous in the 1960s when the first hippies paved the trail, this 50-odd-kilometre journey takes you through the dizzyingly diverse worlds of north Goa's beaches.

SOUTHERN SUN   Two Weeks

Get a feel for urban Indian life in the markets of **Vasco da Gama** (p177),
or do a trip down to **Bogmalo** (p178) if you're interested in starting easy
on a beach or getting right into it with a dive. From Vasco da Gama
you can catch a bus to **Margao** (p161) and stay as long as you like, or
jump in a bus or taxi and head to **Colva** (p180). Mix it up with the locals
for a day or two on this beach or the quieter neighbouring beach at
Benaulim (p185). Hire a scooter or motorcycle in Colva and travel up
the winding northern road, stopping at the beaches of **Majorda** (p179),
Utorda (p179), **Arossim** (p179) and **Velsao** (p179). Pick your favourite and
stay for a couple of nights, enjoying the laid-back beaches and under-
rated hidden restaurants. Head south again to explore **Varca** (p187) and
Cavelossim (p187).

Hand in your motorcycle and head back to Margao. If you have the
time and inclination, stay a while and do an excursion from here to
Chandor (p167) for some colonial atmosphere, or to **Loutolim** (p166) for
some ancestral exploration. When the beach calls again, move down
south to **Palolem** (p191), one of Goa's finest beaches. Soak up the sun, the
sand, the nightlife and the fine dining. If you get restless do a day trip to
Cotigao Wildlife Sanctuary (p197). Also be sure to explore nearby beaches of
Patnem (p195) and **Rajbag** (p196). If you're feeling adventurous, take a trip
towards the border of Karnataka state and seek out some undiscovered
beaches along the coast.

Take a detour off
the 70km route
from Vasco da
Gama to Palolem
to discover
postcard-perfect
Goa. Choose a
town that suits
and meander on a
scooter along the
surrounding coast.

ROADS LESS TRAVELLED

ANCESTRAL ADVENTURES, INLAND INTERLUDES   Three Weeks

Spend some time in **Panaji** (p82) exploring the Goa State Museum and the Latin Quarter. The following day, explore the famous churches of **Old Goa** (p100) in the morning and the Hindu temples around **Ponda** (p110) in the afternoon.

If you're interested in doing an adventurous inland trip, make for **Dudhsagar Falls** (p116), Goa's highest waterfall. On your way back to Panaji, stop off at the **Bhagwan Mahavir Wildlife Sanctuary** (p115), and be sure to visit **Tambdi Surla Mahadeva Temple** (p116). If you don't want to do an organised tour, hiring a motorcycle or chartering a taxi will speed things up.

Next, basing yourself at a beach anywhere between **Candolim** (p121) and **Chapora** (p144), explore inland Bardez; from the coast head to Betim, stopping off at the fort at **Reis Magos** (p120), then drive up to **Britona** (p156), past **Pomburpao** (p157) and cross the bridge at Aldona to visit **Corjuem Fort** (p156) in Bicholim taluka (district). Head back to Bardez, and at Pomburpao catch the ferry to **Chorao Island** (p100). Cross back over to Bicholim and head to **Mayem Lake** (p159) for a leisurely lunch (or romantic overnight stay). Visit **Saptakoteshwara Temple** (p158) while you're in the area.

For the last leg, head south to **Margao** (p161). Base yourself here or at one of the nearby beaches. From here, check out ancestral Portuguese colonial mansions at **Loutolim** (p166) and **Chandor** (p167). Finally, set yourself up at **Palolem** (p191) for a week or so of sun and sand.

Get an overview of the many Goas over three weeks and 250km. Explore the historical landmarks of central Goa, relax on south Goa's beaches and throw in an adventurous trip through the jungle to Goa's highest waterfall.

TAILORED TRIPS

TO MARKET, TO MARKET

Go on a Goan-style shopping tour. Start in Panaji with the **New Municipal Market** (p96) and wander down to the more atmospheric **Municipal Market** (p96) to drink chai amid the blur of bargaining. Step it up a notch with some upmarket shopping at the boutique shops of 18th June Rd.

In north Goa, base yourself at Candolim, Calangute or Baga and take a day trip out to sophisticated **Sangolda** (p135) to purchase a piece of colonial grandeur.

On Wednesday, take a deep breath and launch yourself into the chaos of the **Anjuna flea market** (p141), where the hippy days of old collide with everything that typifies Goa today.

For untouristy laughs, head to manic **Mapusa market** (p137) on Friday. Also, visit **Siolim** (p150), where crustaceans are sold along the Chapora River each morning and St Anthony's Chapel bursts to life every Wednesday morning as fresh-produce vendors pour in.

On a Saturday night in Arpora head to **Ingo's Saturday Nite Bazaar** (p129) and **Mackie's Saturday Nite Bazaar** (p129), which both layer on the atmosphere in a bid to win their preference.

Down in south Goa, where things still operate at a laid-back pace, take in the atmosphere of the **covered market** (p164) in Margao.

HOLISTIC HOLIDAY

Goa has long been a holistic holiday destination of choice. Natural healers, yogis and masseurs from all over the world are here, and it's worth rubbing shoulders with (or having your shoulders rubbed by) them.

Yogis staying in Anjuna should spend some tranquil time at **Yoga Magic** (p142) or visit the **Purple Valley Yoga Centre** (p140) for casual classes. As well as yoga classes, **Healing Here & Now** (p141) offers foot reflexology, naturopathy and colon cleansing for the more dedicated holistic holiday-maker. If you're interested in staying further north, book into the **Himalaya Iyengar Yoga Centre** (p153) in Arambol.

You can partake in an Ayurvedic massage or treatment through the **Ayurvedic Natural Health Centre** (p128) in Baga, which uses qualified Ayurvedic doctors. Or you could immerse yourself in the upmarket Ayurvedic world of **Pousada Tauma** (p128) in Calangute.

In Palolem, the **Palolem Ayurvedic Centre** (p192) offers Ayurvedic oil massages, and **Blue Planet** (p192) boasts massages and masseurs from all over the planet.

Spend a week or so at **Bhakti Kutir** (p193) at Patnem Beach to fully ensconce yourself in nature and natural healing. Or you could simply hang around the beach and look for signs advertising yoga, reiki, Bowen technique, t'ai chi…

Snapshot

Goa is unlike anywhere else in India – or the world for that matter. When the Portuguese left in the 1960s, everyone else arrived; the hedonistic hippies rolled up to build their brave new worlds on Goa's northern beaches, and India suddenly had a church-studded state to administer. The picture today is different only because Goa has learnt to embrace and enhance this diversity.

The extent to which Goa should be adopted and adapted by India remains a topic of conversation. There are still factions (albeit largely ignored ones) that campaign for the liberation of Goa from Indian 'occupation'. But the majority of the population is content to reinforce its Goan identity through the proud belief that while Goa is a part of India, it is also distinct from it.

NGOs battle to keep Goa free from the economic ills of the rest of the country and the social ills of the rest of the world. Meanwhile, the hippies who came in search of a remote paradise have left an indelible mark. The drugs they brought are still around and rave parties occasionally erupt. Furthermore, free love led to offspring who had Anglo ancestry but who were born and bred in Goa. And the diaspora continues to grow; there are children in Goa today whose genes are German or Japanese or American or English, but whose back yard is the beach and whose playground is the trance parties that their parents frequent. Yoga centres tout 'Yoga for Children' on their schedules, and roadside stalls sell preteen hippy wear.

Many of the hard-core hippies snub the influx of backpackers and package tourists (a trend they contributed to when their infamous lifestyle became a tourist attraction in its own right), but many are dependent on the tourist dollar to sustain their (one could say hippy-critical) lifestyle. Local Goans are similarly stuck; a significant number of them rely on the tourist season to sustain them through the rest of the year, but they also partly blame tourism for the desecration of the coastline, the depletion of natural resources such as fish and water, and the corruption of Goan youth through the introduction of drugs, promiscuity and AIDS.

In 1990, the state attracted 834,081 tourists. A decade later that annual figure had risen to 1.38 million. There are grave concerns about the economic implications if the boom ends, and there are grave concerns about the environmental and social implications if it doesn't.

These issues of economics, environment and identity have been pushed to the forefront of the Goan psyche today. As the government attempts to replace the budget traveller with the resort tourist – a move that would bring in more dollars, but not necessarily put them in the hands of more people – there is increasing discontent among the Goan people that politics continues to be fought on religious and caste lines, with ideology often taking a back seat to economics.

The challenge facing Goa is a new slant on an old struggle: that of reaping the benefits of foreign influence while protecting and promoting Goa's own distinct identity.

FAST FACTS

Population: 1.34 million

Income per capita: Rs 34,000

Largest town: Vasco da Gama (population 97,000)

Religion: Hindu 65%, Roman Catholic 30%, Muslim 5%

Size: length 105km, width 65km (you can drive from end to end in less than two hours)

Literacy rate: 82% (65% nationally)

Number of tourists annually: 1.38 million (12% of tourists to India)

History

PREHISTORY

Historians are at odds regarding the origins of the area's first semi-nomadic settlers. Some believe that the first Goans arrived as migrants from Africa, while others say that they were from eastern Asia, or perhaps were a northern tribe forced southwards by instability in their homeland.

As the lifestyle of the early Goans became more settled, formal agriculture developed and villages sprang up. The people became almost self-sufficient in food production and they soon began to look outwards from the confines of their coastal territory, establishing links with the other peoples of southern India. Around 2400 BC the society would have been profoundly altered, in particular by the arrival of Aryan migrants from the north, who brought with them the early strands of Hinduism. A second wave of Aryans, which may have included important groups – the Bhojas, Chediyas and Saraswat Brahmins – who came to precedence over the coming centuries, migrated southwards in around 700 BC.

> According to legend, Lord Krishna was enchanted by the land that is now Goa, and named it Govepuri, after the cows that belonged to charming milkmaids he encountered there.

EARLY HISTORY

During the Mauryan empire (321–184 BC), Goa became part of an administrative area known as Kuntala. During this period Buddhism arrived on India's west coast, brought by a monk named Punna, who resided near modern-day Zambaulim in south Goa. With the rapid demise of the Mauryans after the death of Emperor Ashoka in 232 BC, Goa came under the control of the Marathis, who ruled for about two centuries before being ousted in 50 BC by the temporarily powerful Anand-Chuttus.

Within a century Goa had changed hands again, this time becoming part of the powerful Satavahana empire, which controlled the whole of the west coast of India. During this period Goa emerged as an international trading centre, and evidence exists of regular trade with Africa, the Middle East and even the Romans.

Further dynastic upheaval during the 2nd century AD saw Goa passing to the Bhojas, who ruled from the city of Chandrapur, near the present

> Salcete taluka (district) derives its name from the Sanskrit word *sassast*, meaning '66', after the 66 Brahmin families who originally settled there. Similarly, Tiswadi (from *tis* or *tees*, meaning '30') is named for the 30 families who chose Tiswadi taluka as their home.

LET THERE BE GOA

According to Hindu legend, Goa and the Konkan coastline were created by the god Parasurama, the sixth incarnation of Vishnu. After many years of fighting to avenge the murder of his father, Parasurama finally came to the Sahyadri mountains (Western Ghats), that now form the border between Goa and Karnataka. In search of a completely pure piece of land on which to carry out sacrifices, Parasurama stood atop the Western Ghats and shot an arrow into the Arabian Sea below the mountains and commanded the waves to retreat to the point where the arrow landed. The arrow fell, it is said, at the point where Benaulim village now stands (*baan* meaning 'arrow', *ali* meaning 'village'), and the stretch of coastline that was revealed as the waves receded is the coastal plain of Goa. Parasurama performed his fire sacrifice in the north of the country (modern-day Pernem), and then peopled his new land with 96 Brahmin families.

TIMELINE

300 BC	AD 1050
Goa under Ashoka Mauryan rule	As the Kadambas rise to power, the capital shifts from Chandrapur to Govepuri (currently known as Goa Velha)

village of Chandor in south Goa, for nearly 300 years. Again, during the periods of peace, trade blossomed, but towards the end of the dynasty, power began to be ceded to other smaller states that had come to prominence in the area, including the Konkan Mauryans and the Kadambas. At the end of the 6th century the powerful Chalukyas of Badami succeeded in bringing the whole area under their control. Despite the change of power, the Kadambas managed to retain their position, administering the area as a feudatory state to the new Chalukya rulers.

In the middle of the 8th century the Chalukyas were defeated by the Shilaharas, who held on to power for the next 200 years. There was considerable infighting, but the Shilaharas appear to have thrived until eventually challenged in 973 by their old enemies, the Chalukyas. The ensuing struggle between the adversaries gave the Kadambas (who had served both of them as local chieftains) a chance to claim the area. After several attempts, the Kadamba leader Shastadeva captured the capital of Chandrapur in 979. The Chalukyas, although still the most powerful empire on the west coast, were content to let the Kadambas rule for them, and thus began one of the most glorious periods in the history of Goa.

> Konkani was recognised as one of the official languages of India in 1992. It is believed to have been the result of the impact of Prakrit (the language of the Mauryan empire) on the local Dravidian language that was spoken by early Goans.

THE GOLDEN AGE OF THE KADAMBAS

Finally, Goa had some stability, for although the Kadambas were feudatories to the Chalukyas, they succeeded in hanging on to power for 300 years. During this period Chandrapur grew into a large and beautiful city; it was used as the capital until around 1050, when a newer port on the Zuari River, known as Govepuri or Gopaka (now called Goa Velha), was adopted.

A unique mixture of cultural influences centred on Goa, with merchants coming from as far afield as Malabar, Bengal and Sumatra. In contrast with what was to come, this was a period of religious tolerance. Under the patronage of the Kadambas, Hinduism flourished and Goa became a pilgrimage destination with large temples and prestigious academic institutions. The only Kadamba structure to survive the eras that were to follow is Tambdi Surla Mahadeva Temple, which was saved by its remote jungle location.

> The Kadambas, whose name has become synonymous with main bus stations throughout Goa, were local feudatories of the Hoysala kingdom. They rose to power and ruled Goa for about 300 years.

THE MUSLIM RULE OF THE BAHMANIS

The peace was shattered at the beginning of the 14th century by a series of Muslim invasions from the north. In 1312 Govepuri, and much else along with it, was destroyed; 15 years later the Muslims returned under Mohammed Tughlaq and the old capital of Chandrapur was levelled. Raids continued until finally, in 1352, Goa came under the permanent Muslim rule of the Bahmanis.

Although the Bahmanis held Goa for a quarter of a century, they were in constant conflict with the mighty Vijayanagar empire, which had its capital at Hampi and controlled much of southern India. The persecution of Hindus in Goa at this time forced many to flee south until, in 1378, the Vijayanagar army finally succeeded in wresting Goa from the Bahmanis.

A period of peace followed, accompanied by excellent trade. In particular, Goa was used to import Arab horses for the Vijayanagar cavalry, while spices flowed as export goods back to the Arab countries.

1352	1498
Goa comes under rule of Muslim Bahmanis	Portuguese captain Vasco da Gama arrives in Goa; he is the first European to reach India via the Cape of Good Hope

In the early 15th century the ousted Bahmanis made concerted attempts to win back their old territory. In all, four expeditions were mounted, the last of which, under Mahmud Gawan, struck in 1469. Despite a lightning attack from land and sea, it took three years to bring Goa back under control, and it became part of the Bahmani kingdom again in 1472. As if in revenge for the effort that had been expended, the Bahmanis wreaked havoc; Hindu temples and the capital Govepuri caught the brunt of it. With Govepuri in ruins and the waters near it badly silted up, the Bahmanis established a new capital, Gove, near Ela, on the Mandovi River.

There was little time for the Bahmanis to celebrate their success, for within 20 years the kingdom had become riven by dispute and it split into four factions. One, the kingdom of Bijapur under its ruler Yussuf Adil Shah, inherited Gove. He was so impressed by the new city that he made it his second capital, and in Ponda constructed Safa Shahouri Masjid, which still stands today.

ARRIVAL OF THE PORTUGUESE

Almost before the city could adjust to its new-found prosperity, it was threatened again. In 1498 Vasco da Gama, a Portuguese sea captain, landed south of Goa at Calicut (present-day Kozhikode) on the Malabar Coast, 'seeking Christians and spices' with a view to undermining the Arab's monopoly of the spice trade. He didn't have much luck finding Christians, but there were spices in abundance.

A subsequent expedition managed to establish a small fortress in Cochin (present-day Kochi). In 1503 a nobleman named Afonso de Albuquerque sailed from Portugal to reinforce this base, and returned home full of enthusiasm for the opportunities on offer.

In 1506 Albuquerque was dispatched again with orders to take over as the second Portuguese viceroy of what amounted to little more than two fortresses, one at Cochin and the other at Cannanore (present-day Kannur). The voyage was long and it wasn't until 1508 that Albuquerque arrived in India. It was evident that a more permanent base was required on the Indian coastline and that the Portuguese needed to consolidate their presence in the area. Rumours were rife that the Arab rulers of the coastal states were concerned about Portuguese sea power and were planning to attack the Portuguese fleet.

Wasting little time, Albuquerque sailed for Goa, and in March 1510 attacked and occupied the main island in the river, where Panaji (formerly Panjim) and Old Goa stand today. Although the element of surprise had been on his side, his success was short-lived, for Yussuf Adil Shah soon recovered and counterattacked, driving him out barely two months later.

With the monsoon setting in, there was little that Albuquerque could do except withdraw his ships out of range of the enemy guns and find as much cover from the elements as possible. He and his men rode out the monsoon in miserable conditions before retreating down the coast to recover.

Albuquerque attacked again, and on 25 November (St Catherine's Day) he retook Goa. As a punishment to those who assisted the sultan in

During his time in Goa, Afonso de Albuquerque banned the Hindu practice of *sati,* the self-immolation of women on their husband's funeral pyre.

1510	1560
Portuguese nobleman Afonso de Albuquerque defeats the forces of Yusuf Adil Shah	The Inquisition begins its brutal 200 years of suppression of religious freedom

his defence of the city, Albuquerque ordered that all Muslim occupants of the city be put to death. He then set about fortifying the city and rebuilding the fort at Panaji.

Four months later, having put the new territory in order, Albuquerque departed on another voyage. During his absence there was a further attempt to recapture Goa, this time by Yussuf Adil Shah's son, Ismail Adil Shah. For several months the garrison managed to hold out until, reinforced by new arrivals from Portugal, they were able to establish a sound defence. In late 1512 Albuquerque returned victorious from having conquered Malacca and, organising the combined forces into two groups, attacked and defeated the Muslims.

After fortifying the colony, Albuquerque sailed west to consolidate his gains in the Gulf. He returned in 1513 in time to sign a treaty with the new ruler of Calicut and start on the serious work of laying out his new city.

Perhaps Albuquerque's greatest achievement during this period was the skilful political balancing act he performed. Both the Vijayanagar empire and the Bijapuris were potential threats, and Albuquerque played them off one against the other. The only bargaining tool he had was that both armies were keen to import horses (to use in attacks against each other); he turned this to financial as well as political advantage by making them promise that they would only buy their horses from him, thus making a tidy profit on the existing trade through Goa's ports.

In 1515 he was on the move again, this time to the Gulf, but it was his final voyage: he returned fatally ill. He died aboard his ship in Goa harbour on 15 December 1515, having been brought up on deck to see Goa one last time.

CONQUEST & EXPANSION

Although the initial threat to the Portuguese had been beaten off, their position was anything but secure. The conquistadors still held only the islands in the river estuary, while their enemies held the far banks to both the north and south.

An uncommonly good piece of luck fell to the Portuguese in 1520 when, after a spate of successes against the Muslims, the Hindus offered their conquests to the Portuguese. They swiftly occupied the areas of Ponda, Salcete and Bardez and, although the Muslims took most of the territory back fairly quickly, some parts, notably Rachol Fort, remained in Portuguese hands.

At this point political cunning did the trick; the Portuguese brought in Mir Ali, a rival for the Muslim throne, and threatened to support his bid. As a compromise, in 1543 the existing sultan ceded Bardez and Salcete permanently, on condition that Mir Ali was deported from the region. The areas that the Portuguese now held – Tiswadi, Bardez and Salcete – marked the extent of Portuguese territory in Goa for the next 250 years, and are now known as the Old Conquests (Velhas Conquistas).

In 1565 the balance of power that had existed in the region collapsed when a coalition of Muslim rulers finally crushed the Vijayanagar army at the Battle of Talikota. The subsequent sack of the Vijayanagar capital at Hampi is reputed to have taken several months.

The first printing press in India was established in Old Goa in 1556 by the Jesuits.

1664	1683
The Marathas, under the leadership of Shivaji, take Bicholem and Permen	The Marathas under the leadership of Sambhaji (Shivaji's son) come dangerously close to Old Goa

With the Muslim kingdoms in alliance and rid of their greatest enemy, it was inevitable that the Portuguese would come under threat. In 1570 the combined forces of Bijapur, Ahmednagar and Calicut besieged Goa with huge forces. Despite their overwhelming superiority in numbers, they failed to break the defence, and after a 10-month siege they gave up and withdrew.

CHRISTIANISATION OF GOA

Although a handful of priests had arrived in Goa with Albuquerque's fleet, and the Franciscans had managed to send a few friars in 1517, missionary work was relatively low-key in Goa for almost 30 years. Initially the approach was enlightened, and the religious conversion that did take place was unforced.

In 1541, following the arrival of a handful of zealots, laws were passed that all Hindu temples should be destroyed, along with strict laws forbidding the observance of Hindu rituals, and other regulations stating that only those who were baptised could retain the rights to their land.

In 1560 the Inquisition unleashed a period of nearly 200 years of brutal suppression and religious terrorism. During this period many Hindus fled across the Mandovi River into what is now Ponda, smuggling their religious statuary to safety and building temples to house them. Thousands died during this period at the whim of interrogators who sat around the 'Inquisition table', which is now kept at the Goa State Museum in Panaji.

Although the Roman Catholic Church had much to answer for, there were also undoubtedly many positive aspects to the work of the religious orders. By the middle of the 16th century, the Franciscans, Dominicans, Augustinians and Jesuits, among others, were present in Goa. The missionaries established hospitals and schools and taught alternative methods of farming and forestry. They also masterminded much of the building work that was taking place; work on the Se Cathedral was commenced in 1560, and the Basilica of Bom Jesus was built between 1594 and 1605.

At the first exposition of the Incorruptible Body in 1554, a Portuguese noblewoman by the name of Dona Isabel de Caron was so anxious to obtain a relic of St Francis Xavier that she bit off a toe on his right foot.

PORTUGAL FADES & THE MARATHAS ATTACK

At the same time that the most magnificent buildings of Old Goa were being constructed, Portugal's fortunes were beginning to wane.

In 1580, bankrupted by a disastrous campaign in North Africa, Portugal was annexed by Spain, and it was not until 1640 that the Portuguese regained independence. While this dealt an understandable blow to morale, finances and even manpower, a greater threat was the emergence of European rivals in the eastern oceans. In 1612 the Portuguese fleet was defeated off the coast of Surat, in western Gujarat, by the ships of the British East India Company, and the British suddenly became the power to be reckoned with in the Arabian Sea. The threat was eventually dealt with only by allowing the British to trade freely in all of Portugal's eastern ports, an agreement reached by the Convention of Goa in 1635.

By the early 1660s the Portuguese were also facing a threat from the east. Shivaji, the great leader of the Marathas, succeeded in taking the neighbouring territories of Bicholim and Pernem in 1664, before being

1737	1739
The Marathas, under the leadership of King Shahu (Shivaji's grandson!), finally capture Bardez and Salcete in 1737	The Portuguese and Marathas sign a peace treaty

forced to withdraw to deal with the Muslim leader Aurangzeb. His army was a constant worry around the Goan borders until his death in 1680.

In 1683 the Maratha army, now commanded by Shivaji's son, Sambhaji, got so close to Old Goa that defeat seemed inevitable. Ordering the coffin of St Francis Xavier to be opened, the viceroy laid the cane of office next to the saint's body and prayed for him to intercede. Miraculously, the Marathas withdrew at the last minute, again threatened by Mughal forces to their rear. The following year they took Chapora in Bardez taluka (district).

The Marathas returned again in 1737, taking the whole of Bardez, except for the forts at Aguada and Reis Magos, and the whole of Salcete, apart from Mormugao and Rachol. Finally a negotiated peace forced the Portuguese to hand over the territory of Bassein, near Mumbai (Bombay), in return for a Maratha withdrawal from Goa.

Goa's first newspaper, *O Heraldo*, was launched in 1900. It is now called *Herald* (www.oheraldo.in).

EXPANSION & DECLINE

The latter half of the 18th century saw both the expansion of the colony and the acceleration of its decline.

In 1764 the raja of Sonda, beset by his enemy Hyder Ali of Mysore, asked the Portuguese to occupy his lands in order to protect them. Although he intended the occupation to be temporary, the Portuguese obligingly moved into what today are Ponda, Sanguem, Quepem and Canacona, and the acquisition became permanent.

Between 1781 and 1788 the northern talukas of Pernem, Bicholim and Satari were also added to the colony, bringing under Portuguese control the entire area that Goa occupies today.

At the same time, the character of the colony was changing enormously because of the repression of the religious orders (the Jesuits were banned in 1759) and the effective end of the Inquisition in 1774. Thus the new territorial acquisitions were spared the forced conversions and crusading Christianity that had been imposed on the Old Conquests. By this stage too, Old Goa, once a city of more than 200,000 inhabitants, was practically abandoned because of recurring disease. The senate was formally moved to Panjim (present-day Panaji) in 1835, although it was another eight years before the city officially became the capital.

In 1787 there was a short-lived attempt at revolt from within Goa. The conspirators in the Pinto Revolt were mainly Goan churchmen, disaffected at the unequal status of Goans in the church hierarchy. The revolt was discovered while it was still in the planning stages, and several of the leaders were tortured and put to death, while others were imprisoned or shipped off to Portugal (see p125).

END OF EMPIRE

While many uneducated Goans accepted the status quo, among the educated classes there was already a nascent independence movement. The first manifestations of this were a series of uprisings by a clan called the Ranes, who came from Satari taluka in the northeast. For more than 50 years there was sporadic violence dealt with by Portuguese viceroys with a mixture of military suppression and concessions. Finally in 1912, after 14 rebellions, the movement was crushed by military force.

1781–1788	1787
Talukas of Pernem, Bicholim and Satari are added to the colony, completing the area that Goa occupies today	The unsuccessful Pinto revolt is attempted; its leaders are either tortured and executed, or shipped off to Portugal

---

THE POUND IS MIGHTIER THAN THE SWORD

Right at the end of the century, Goa was temporarily occupied without a shot being fired. The British, engaged in a struggle against the southern monarch Tipu Sultan (who had formed an alliance with the French), marched into Goa in 1797. Although they departed a year later, they were back in 1802, this time guarding against a possible invasion by the French. Despite repeated Portuguese protests, the British garrison remained in Goa until 1813. Although there was never any attempt to annex Goa, several years later (in 1839) the British government offered to buy Goa from the Portuguese for half a million pounds.

In 1910 when the Portuguese monarchy came to an end, it looked briefly as though the calls for self-determination were about to be answered. At the last moment, however, the proposed measures were withheld. The anger caused by this abrupt change in policy led to the emergence of a determined Goan independence movement, with figures like Luis de Menezes Braganza championing the cause. By the 1940s the Goan leaders were taking their example from the Independence movement across the border in British India.

On 18 June 1946 a demonstration in Margao (Madgaon) led to the public arrest of a prominent activist, Dr Ram Manohar Lohia, after he had been threatened at gunpoint to stop him addressing the crowd. The event provided the incentive needed to motivate the people, and large-scale demonstrations were held.

Many activists were arrested, and in all an estimated 1500 people were incarcerated. A militant wing of the Independence movement was formed, which called itself Azad Gomantak Dal, and carried out a number of raids on police stations, public industries and stray security patrols.

On 10 June 1947 the Portuguese Minister of Colonies, Captain Teofilo Duarte, warned that the 'Portuguese flag will not fall down in India without some thousands of Portuguese, white and coloured, shedding their blood in its defence'.

When overtures by the newly independent Indian government were made to the Portuguese in 1953, the lack of any formal response made it apparent that the Portuguese had no intention of withdrawing. Consequently, on 11 June 1953, diplomatic relations between the two countries were broken off. The same year, Dr TB Cunha (dubbed the Father of Goan Nationalism) formed the Goa Action Committee, which used *satyagraha* (nonviolent protest). On 15 August 1954 a huge *satyagraha* commenced. Many were arrested, beaten and imprisoned.

Exactly a year later, as a mark of indignation at the treatment of the Goan *satyagrahis,* a second protest was organised, this time to be conducted by Indians from outside Goa.

On the morning of the rally more than 3000 protesters, including women and children, entered Goa at various points along the border with India. In response to this openly peaceful protest, Portuguese security forces charged the protesters with batons and opened fire. Some of the protesters were killed and hundreds more injured.

During this period India manoeuvred for international support, and tried to exert pressure on more established members of the UN to persuade

On 18 June 1946, Indian socialist leader Dr Ram Manohar Lohia launched a mass movement for civil liberties at a public meeting in Margao – 18th of June Rd in Panjim is so called to commemorate this event.

1843	**1953**
Old Goa is abandoned and a new capital is officially established in Panjim	Diplomatic relationships between Portugal and India collapse

the Portuguese to leave peacefully. India's prime minister, Jawaharlal Nehru, in particular, was opposed to taking Goa by force, as he believed that this would jeopardise the whole ethos of achieving political aims by peaceful means. He also recognised that it was possible that Goans might not vote for independence if they were given a free choice.

In order to allay Goan fears, Nehru addressed the issue publicly:

> Goa has a distinct personality, and we have recognised it. It will be a pity to destroy that individuality, and we have decided to maintain it. With the influx of time, a change may come. But it will be gradual and will be made by the Goans themselves. We have decided to pre-serve the separate identity of Goa in the Union of India and we hold to it firmly. No agitation against it will be to any purpose.

Although the pledge to respect Goa's integrity was upheld, Nehru could not resist the forces pushing for India to take Goa by force. During the night of 17 December 1961, Operation Vijay began with Indian troops crossing the border. Little resistance was met and by the next evening, troops were outside Panjim. There was a brief gunfight at Fort Aguada when a 'rescue operation' attempted to liberate a number of political prisoners, but to all intents the surrender itself was a mere formality.

At 8.30am on 19 December, troops of the Punjab Regiment occupied the Secretariat Building and unfurled the Indian flag, signifying the end of the 450-year Portuguese occupation of Goa. The Portuguese left shortly afterwards, leaving most of their buildings intact, despite direct orders from Dr Antonio de Oliveira Salazar, the Portuguese dictator, that they should destroy everything before departing.

POST-INDEPENDENCE

When Portugal refused to relinquish control of Goa, the UN General Assembly ruled in favour of self-determination. When the Indian army moved in, the UN considered condemning the 'liberation' but was vetoed by the Soviet Union.

After the liberation, the commander of the expeditionary force, Major General Candeth, was appointed the military governor of Goa. Under the provisions of the Constitution 12th Amendment Act of 1962, the former Portuguese colonies of Goa, Daman and Diu were integrated with the Indian Union, effective from the first day of the liberation.

Towards the end of 1962, the new political system started to take root through a number of elections. In September an informal consultative council was formed and in October the first *panchayat* (local government council) elections were held. In December there were elections for the state assembly and Goa's two parliamentary seats, and the first proper state government was operating in Goa by the end of December 1962.

The major unanswered question was that of Goa's statehood. Neighbouring Maharashtra insisted that Goa be added to its own territory, and that Konkani, the language of the Goans, should not be recognised as an official language. The issue was finally settled on 16 January 1967 when, in an opinion poll, Goa, Daman and Diu opted to remain as a Union Territory, rather than be assimilated into their neighbouring states.

In May 1987 Goa split from Daman and Diu, and was officially recognised as the 25th state of the Indian Union. The struggle to retain Konkani had also been won; in 1992 it was recognised as one of the official languages of India.

1955	1961
Portuguese troops open fire on thousands of nonviolent protestors	Indian troops cross the border into Goa and the Portuguese leave soon after

GOA & WWII: SEA WOLVES

Although Portugal remained neutral throughout WWII, in 1943 Goa briefly became the location of one of the most important and little-known actions to take place in the Asian theatre. At the time the Germans were taking advantage of Goa's neutrality to use the small colony as a base for spying activities. Three German ships were sheltered in the harbour and a large amount of military intelligence was being collected by personnel on board. In particular, information on allied shipping was being passed from Mumbai to Goa and thence to German U-boats – nicknamed 'Sea Wolves' – which were then able to target the convoys accurately.

The Special Operations Executive (SOE) in British India needed to avoid violating neutral territory but at the same time had to take action. With an initial raid into Vasco da Gama they succeeded in abducting the German agent who they believed to be masterminding the operation, but the passage of information continued. The only solution, it was reasoned, was to sink the *Ehrenfels*, the ship on which the transmitter was hidden.

The way they went about it was less than conventional. Instead of using commandos, the SOE engaged the services of a territorial unit, the Calcutta Light Horse. After the volunteers were put through special training, they were loaded onto a tramp steamer for Goa. Nothing could have looked less threatening than the battered tub that entered Mormugao Harbour in the middle of the night. The soldiers attached mines to the German ships and then, having stealthily boarded the vessels, overcame the crews and destroyed the radio equipment as well, just for good measure.

All three German ships were destroyed in the raid and the passage of information about allied shipping effectively stopped. The raid was regarded as a great success, although it was several years before the details of what really happened were released. The story is recounted in James Leasor's book *Boarding Party* and the film, *Sea Wolves,* starring Gregory Peck and Roger Moore.

For most of the 1990s political instability, the bane of the country as a whole during this period, disrupted life in Goa. Goan politicians are notorious for 'floor-crossing' (switching parties). The political instability of the state is evident in the fact that during the 15 years between 1990 and 2005, Goa has had 14 governments.

The Congress Party held sway for much of the 1990s, but at the end of the decade the Hindu nationalist Bharatiya Janata Party (BJP) came to power after Congress was riven with defections. Under the leadership of Chief Minister Manohar Parrikar, the BJP ousted its rebellious Congress Party allies to ride to power in its own right in October 2000.

In mid-term elections in 2002 – hurriedly called because the government was reportedly close to collapse due to defections – the BJP failed to win an absolute majority, gaining 17 of the 40 seats. Cobbling together an alliance of the United Goans Democrat Party (UGDP), the Hindu Maharashtrawadi Gomantak Party (MGP) and an independent, Parrikar again won government.

However, the latest act of political randomness took place in March of 2005, when the governor (whose role is largely ceremonial) dissolved the assembly. The effect was to suspend legislature and declare President's rule. The dismissed Parrikar government declared that the 11.30pm ceremony swearing in the new Chief Minister was unconstitutional.

A by-election in June 2005 saw the Congress-led alliance come back to power after winning three of the five seats that went to polls. At the time of writing it held 18 seats on the legislative assembly, and the BJP 17.

The website www.freegoa.com promotes the independence of Goa from India. For more information on the free Goa movement, follow the links on www.geocities.com/prakashjm45/goa/ for the Goan Center, established to promote the liberation of Goa from Indian Independence.

1987	**2005**
Goa officially declared India's 25th state by Prime Minister Rajiv Gandhi	Governor dissolves assembly in March and President's rule is declared; Congress-led alliance comes back into power

The Culture

GOAN IDENTITY

Given that global interest in Goa is entrenched, Goans themselves have always had to assert and adapt their identity in relation to foreign influence. Resistance to Portuguese colonialism has morphed into historical pride at having Portuguese roots, while attempts to maintain the distinction between Goa and India reinforce a specifically 'Goan' identity that spurs on environmental, economic and social activism in a bid to keep Goa one of the most prosperous states in the country.

Today, the foreigners with whom Goa must engage are generalised into loose categories of backpackers, package or charter tourists and 'hippies'. The latter category is the most evocative. For some Goans, the term 'hippy' is synonymous with any unkempt and socially displaced foreigner who uses drugs, engages in wild orgies on the beach and seduces locals into similarly misguided ways. Some of those hippies, though, have thrown their chips in with this subcontinental state. Some of their children were born and educated here, and the future of Goa is of more consequence than the homeland from which they are displaced.

This is modern Goa, where a local hang-out means a hole-in-the-wall Indian restaurant where people speak Konkani and Hindi and drink chai. It also means a funky chill-out restaurant where the menu is German and patrons chillum out under banyan trees. It means a whitewash Catholic church alongside a Hindu temple, where Christian wakes are held in honour of Hindu deities.

The differences are evident but similarities pervade below the surface to unify different versions of Goa. Whether Catholic Goan, Hindu Goan or new Goan, all have an opinion about the changing face of Goa and nostalgic memories of 'the way it used to be', and all are eager to see that Goa doesn't lose its distinctiveness.

LIFESTYLE
Traditional Culture

The following information must be read in light of the fact that there are strong links and overlaps between the practices of the Christian and Hindu communities. Furthermore, the influences of the flood of visitors Goa receives every year means that many aspects of traditional Goan culture are disappearing or changing.

BIRTH

In Hindu communities it is considered the privilege of the young wife to go to her parents' house for confinement. After the birth the mother and child are rubbed with turmeric and oil, and the child is swathed in cloth bandages. The first ritual, albeit a declining one, comes on the sixth day after birth. Known as 'mother sixth' (sathi), a drum is beaten throughout the night and the family keeps a vigil to protect the child from evil spirits.

For 10 days after the birth the mother is considered impure and is not touched by anyone except the midwife. On the 11th day, mother and child are bathed, and the house is purified. On the 12th or 13th day the barse (naming) takes place. In Christian communities, the child is named at its baptism.

A good source of information for travellers to Goa is www.goacentral.com, with information sections about its history and culture.

If you're missing Goans when you leave Goa, tap into the global community of Goans living abroad. Young London Goans Society (www .ylgs.org.uk) and the UK and Canadian chapters of Goan Voice (www .goanvoice.org.uk; www .goanvoice.ca) are good places to start.

SUSEGAD

A term that crops up frequently in connection with Goans, *susegad* is an attitude along the lines of 'relax and enjoy life while you can'. It's a philosophy of not getting overwrought if work takes longer than planned, of making an appointment for 10am knowing full well that the other party won't turn up until at least 10.30am, and of taking time to sit and chat.

The original Portuguese word *socegado* (literally meaning 'quiet') may have been used more by the Catholic community than the Hindus, but Goans are alike in their understanding of *susegad*. On the 25th anniversary of Goan Independence, Prime Minister Rajiv Gandhi described how 'an inherent nonacquisitiveness and contentment with what one has, described by that uniquely Goan word *socegado,* has been an enduring strength of Goan character.'

It is *susegad* that makes a visit to Goa special; there are always people ready to smile and say hello, to let you onto a crowded bus or to sit and chat about whatever comes to mind.

MARRIAGE

Among both Christian and Hindu communities a similar process is undertaken to procure a suitable partner for a son or daughter. This generally begins with discreet inquiries among the community. Failing this, advertisements may be placed in local newspapers, emphasising the professional qualifications of the individual and the calmness of their character.

Dowries are still required to be paid by the bride's family in both Christian and Hindu weddings. This can either help facilitate a match or hinder it; a mixed-caste marriage will become much more acceptable if there's a good dowry, but a high-caste girl whose family has no money can find it very difficult to secure a partner from a similar background.

The wedding ceremony itself is a lengthy and noisy affair. Towards the end of the proceedings the bride and groom join hands in a ritual known as *kanyadana,* while water and silver coins are poured over their clasped hands. The final marriage ritual, *saptapadi,* takes place when the couple walks seven times around the sacred fire, thus making the marriage irrevocable.

Christian weddings are similar to those in the West, although some rituals are borrowed from Hindu traditions, such as the ritual bathing of the bride before the wedding. *Chuddo* (green bracelets traditionally worn by married women) are also worn by Christian brides. Tradition dictates that should her husband die before her, the widow should break the bangles on his coffin.

DEATH

Funeral ceremonies in the Hindu community are similar for all castes. Children below the age of eight are buried, while all others are cremated. In preparation, the body is washed, laid on a bier and covered with a shroud. The chief mourner (usually the eldest son) also bathes. The body is carried by family members or friends to the funeral pyre, the son lights it, then walks three times around it with a pot of water, finally standing at the head of the pyre.

On the third day after the cremation, the son, accompanied by a few friends and family, collects the ashes, which are then consigned to water – possibly the sea or a stream. Those who can afford it will travel north to scatter the ashes on the sacred Ganges River.

On the 10th day after the cremation, all members of the house take a purificatory bath, and on the 11th day, *panchagavya* (a liquid consisting

Teresa Albuquerque's *Anjuna: Profile of a Village in Goa* is a fascinating, in-depth look at the history of one Goan village through the years. Dr Albuquerque has both the academic background and the family connections in the community to be able to sketch an unrivalled portrait of the life of the village. History, architecture, folklore and traditions are all covered.

GAUDA GET OUT OF HERE

A traditional wedding among the minority Gauda people is unusual for the theatricality of the customs leading up to the ceremony. The day before the wedding, the groom is given a haircut and bathed. Then, he attempts to run away from his family and friends, refusing to marry the chosen bride. He is brought back to the house and the next day the ceremony takes place.

---

of cow's milk, cow's urine and other substances) is sprinkled over the house in a ritual purification.

In the Christian community, deaths are followed by burial. Personal items are placed with the deceased in the grave, including (depending on the habits of the deceased) cigarettes and a bottle of alcohol!

There are numerous superstitions in the Hindu and Christian communities about unrestful spirits – particularly of those who committed suicide or died before being given last rites. A number of measures are made at the funeral to discourage the spirit from returning. The clothing and funeral shroud are cut, and a needle and thread are placed in the coffin. The spirit of the deceased who wishes to come back must first repair its torn clothing, a task that takes until daylight, at which time departure from the grave is impossible.

Konkani does not have a script of its own; it is written mostly in the Roman script. The Portuguese language is now mostly confined to the rich, aristocratic families and the elder generation, particularly in Panaji's Latin Quarter.

Contemporary Issues
WOMEN IN SOCIETY

Generally, the position of women in Goa is better than that elsewhere in India. Not only do women in Goa have property rights that are not shared by women in other Indian states (thanks in part to the Uniform Civil Code), but Goan society has also been much more enlightened about the education of women.

A result of Goa's progressive policies has been that women are well represented in professions and positions of influence. While men undoubtedly still dominate, women fill large numbers of places as doctors, teachers and university lecturers, and 30% of *panchayat* (local government council) seats are reserved for women.

There are, however, aspects that still point to inbuilt prejudice – a trend that the discrepancy between male and female literacy in the state confirms (according to the 2001 consensus, 89% for men, 76% for women).

FEMALE FETICIDE

Among Hindus it is still considered preferable to have a boy rather than a girl. This is less important in Catholic families, but nonetheless the birth of a girl is greeted with less fanfare than that of a boy.

Robert S Newman's *Of Umbrellas, Goddesses & Dreams* is a series of essays on Goan culture and the changes of the past two decades by an American writer and regular visitor to Goa.

In a bid to counter the practice of aborting females, the determination of sex of the unborn child, with a view to terminating the pregnancy should it be female, has been made illegal by the Prohibition of Sex Selection Act. It is also illegal for medical practitioners to use prenatal diagnostics to determine the sex of foetuses. Nor can gynaecologists inform patients of the sex of their unborn child. Despite the law, the number of girls born continues to fall significantly short of the number of boys, because doctors who abide by the law lose business to those that don't.

Although in Goa girls do not suffer ill-treatment to the same extent that their sisters in other parts of India do, there are efforts to promote equality of the sexes here too. Posters declare 'Girl or boy small family is joy' and those geared towards the Catholic community remind people of God's equal love of males and females.

ECONOMY

Prior to Independence in 1961, Goa's economy was largely based on fishing, agriculture and the export of primary products such as timber and rubber. Because there was only a relatively small market for goods, industrialisation was minimal, and consisted only of small-scale fish- and fruit-canning plants and a few small factories. In 1961 the annual per capita income, assessed at current prices, was estimated at Rs 434. Today, the per capita income is Rs 34,000 – among the highest in India.

POPULATION

Goa's population has grown hugely since Independence. In 1961 the population was 590,000, at the last national census (2001) it had burgeoned to around 1.34 million. The spiralling figures reflect, more than anything else, the huge influx of Indians from elsewhere in the country.

The state's enormous migrant population predominantly consists of poor workers who arrive during the dry season in search of employment, mostly as labourers. There is another influx of visitors from as far afield as Nepal and Kashmir who come to sell goods to tourists. Whole families of women and children from Karnataka, Kerala and even Rajasthan travel to Goa to peddle handicrafts and fruit on the beaches. There are also the overlooked white expatriates (colloquially dubbed 'hippies'), some of whom would consider Goa to be their home.

RELIGION

Goa is often misunderstood as having a Catholic majority, perhaps because Christianity has had so predominant an influence on its history, culture and architecture. In fact, around 65% of Goans are Hindu and only 30% Christian. The remaining 5% is mostly Muslim.

A May 2003 survey by *India Today* magazine put Goa ahead of all other Indian states on parameters such as health, infrastructure and investment, while it came second in prosperity and consumer markets (only behind Delhi). Overall, Goa was ranked the best state of the country to live in.

BAKSHEESH

Though demands for baksheesh are not nearly as constant in Goa as in the rest of India, many find this a frustration. In keeping your cool, remember that it wasn't invented simply to extract money from tourists, but actually has some equitable and charitable underpinnings. Observe how Indians (even those who are obviously not excessively wealthy) often give something, and it's expected and accepted by both sides.

Whether or not you should give money to beggars has been a debate for as long as people have been travelling. The black-and-white school of 'No' justifies its policy with arguments that it is not always possible to know whether the money you give will be used for the betterment of the life of the person you hand it to, and that often it supports an evil industry whose victims are the beggars themselves. More moderate members of this camp argue that money is better given to charitable organisations. In contrast are those who simply look at individual situations for their individual merit and acknowledge that sometimes a beggar is simply a person in genuine need of help, which you have the capacity and opportunity to provide. Ultimately the choice is a personal one, but in making it there are various things to consider.

El Shaddai (www.childrescue.net) strongly discourages giving money to children who beg in Goa, given that they may have been harmed to illicit your sympathies and may be giving their money to an 'employer'. Instead, El Shaddai encourages you to buy them food or fruit, and direct them to an El Shaddai feeding programme. See p138 for more information about El Shaddai.

International Animal Rescue (www.iar.org.uk) is adamant that you not give money to people using snakes, monkeys or other animals for illegal begging. It is particularly firm on the cruelty involved in snake charming, and the environmental impact of removing them from the wild.

In making your decisions, be mindful of the fact that you do have the capacity to help people in Goa, and make responsible decisions accordingly.

However, statistical data does not reveal the religious diversity that typifies the state. During the imposition of Christianity by the Portuguese, some family members moved to Hindu-held areas, while others converted to the new faith and remained in Portuguese territory. Thus from the start, families contained members of different faiths.

The distinction was further blurred by the way the new religion was adapted to suit the local population. As early as 1616, the Bible was translated into Konkani. In 1623 Pope Gregory gave permission for Brahmin families converting to Catholicism to retain their caste, and a number of local festivals and traditions continued to be observed.

Even today, this fusion of these religions is evident. The countless whitewashed churches around the state demonstrate the splendid adaptation of Christianity; garlands often adorn Christ and the Virgin Mary, and Mass is often said in Konkani. Furthermore, Christians and Hindus often observe the same festivals, or at least pay respects to those of the other faith. In Mapusa, the Church of Our Lady of Miracles was built on the site of an old Hindu temple and the annual feast day sees crowds of Hindus and Christians paying tribute together. In Siolim, an annual wake is held in honour of the local deity. Every Christian and Hindu household in the community sends offerings to the shrine before a procession starts and prayers containing attributes of both faiths are offered in Konkani for the unity of the whole village.

At the time of research, a spate of robberies of relics from churches was shaking the complacency of religious tolerance that exists in the state, and ultimately reinvigorating the fervour with which the majority respect different faiths.

The geographical relationship with religion remains: Hindus are spread across the interior inland talukas (districts; Pernem, Bicholim, Satari, Ponda, Sanguem, Quepema and Canacona) and the far north of the state, while Christians tend to reside in the coastal regions, particularly in the central talukas (Tiswadi, Mormugao, Bardez and Salcete).

The largest Muslim community is in Ponda, where the state's oldest mosque is located.

> Goa's three English-daily newspapers are available online: *Herald* (www .oheraldo.in), *Navhind Times* (www.navindtimes .com) and *Gomantak Times* (www.gomantak times.com).

Hinduism

The essential Hindu belief is in Brahman, an infinite being from which everything derives and everything will return. One of the most common tenets deriving from this is karma. Hindus believe that life is cyclical and subject to reincarnations, eventually leading to moksha, a spiritual release. Karma is the law that determines an individual's progression towards that point; good karma (through positive actions) may result in being reborn into a higher caste and better circumstance, whereas bad karma (accumulated through bad deeds) may result in reincarnation in animal form. It is only as a human that one can acquire sufficient self-knowledge to achieve liberation from the cycle of reincarnation.

> The *Oxford Concise Dictionary of World Religions* is an excellent reference.

GODS & GODDESSES

The many gods and goddesses are merely manifestations of Brahman, who has three main representations (the Trimurti): Brahma, Vishnu and Shiva.

Brahman

Formless and eternal, Brahman is the source of all existence. Brahman is *nirguna* (without attributes), whereas other gods are manifestations of Brahman and therefore *saguna* (with attributes).

Brahma

Brahma, who is often depicted with four heads, plays an active role during the creation of the universe, but at other times is occupied meditating. Brahma is sometimes shown sitting on a lotus rising from Vishnu's navel; a symbol of the interdependence of the gods.

Vishnu

Vishnu, from whose feet the Ganges is said to flow, is often depicted with four arms holding a lotus, a conch shell, a discus and a mace. Vishnu is the preserver or sustainer of all that is good, and often associated with 'right action'. Vishnu has 22 incarnations, including Rama, Krishna and Buddha.

Shiva

Shiva is the destroyer, but without whom creation couldn't occur. The creative role played by Shiva is symbolised by his representation as the phallic lingam. Shiva has 1008 names and takes many forms, often depicted with four or five faces, draped with snakes, holding a trident while riding Nandi, his bull. Nandi symbolises power and potency, justice and moral order. Parvati, Shiva's consort can take many forms.

Ganesh

Elephant-headed Ganesh is the god of good fortune and the patron of scribes. There are many legends as to how Ganesh came to have an elephant's head. One is that he was born to Parvati in his father's (Shiva) absence. He was mistakenly beheaded by Shiva who, on discovering that he had decapitated his own son, vowed to replace Ganesh's head with that of the first creature he came across.

Krishna

An important incarnation of Vishnu, Krishna was sent to earth to combat evil. His seduction of milkmaids has inspired many paintings and songs.

Hanuman

The hero of Ramayana and the champion of acrobats, Hanuman is the monkey god who is capable of taking other forms.

The Shiva Movement

The Shaivite (followers of the Shiva movement) worship Shakti as mother and creator. The concept of Shakti is embodied in the ancient goddess Devi (mother and fierce destroyer), also known as Durga.

SACRED TEXTS

There are two categories of Hindu sacred text: those believed to be the word of god (*shruti,* meaning 'heard'), and those produced by people (smriti, meaning 'remembered').

The Vedas are regarded as *shruti,* and considered the basis for Hinduism; the oldest was compiled over 3000 years ago. The Vedas explain the universe and reflect on life and death.

The smriti texts are a collection of literature spanning centuries. They include expositions on domestic ceremonies, government, economics and religious law. Its best-known elements are Ramayana (the Ramayana centres on the conflict between gods and demons and is thought to be the work of one person, the poet Vilmike), the Mahabharata (focusing

A Classical Dictionary of Hindu Mythology & Religion, by John Dowson, is an Indian paperback reprint of an old English hardback. As the name suggests, it is in dictionary form and is one of the best sources for unravelling who's who in Hinduism.

Shiva is sometimes depicted as the lord of yoga: an ascetic with matted hair, an ash-smeared body and a third eye symbolising wisdom.

For easy-to-understand depictions of the Hindu holy texts, read Amar Chitra Katha's colourful comic-book-style versions of the Ramayana and the Mahabharata. Other titles in this children's series include Ganesh, Krishna and Hanuman.

on the exploits of Krishna) and Puranas, which promote the notion of Trimurti. The Vedas have popular appeal because, unlike the Puranas, they aren't limited to males of the higher castes.

SACRED ANIMALS & PLANTS

Healthy Living with Ayurveda, by Anuradha Singh, provides an understanding of one's constitution *(prakriti)* and tailoring a diet and exercise regime accordingly.

Hindus have long worshipped animals, particularly snakes and cows. The cow represents fertility and nurturing, while snakes are associated with fertility and welfare.

The Banyan tree symbolises the Trimurti and is symbolic of love; Shiva is believed to have married Parvati under one.

WORSHIP

Hindu homes often have a dedicated worship area. Beyond this, temples are the centre of religious life.

Puja is a focal point of worship and ranges from silent prayer to elaborate ceremonies. Devotees leave the temple with a handful of *prasad* (temple-blessed food). Other forms of worship include *aarti* (auspicious lighting of lamps) and bhajans (devotional songs).

ARTS

Goa's arts scene is dynamic and perpetually evolving. Goans celebrate at any opportunity and embellish their festivities with song and dance. The rich artistic and cultural heritage of Goa thrives today, and is entirely accessible to the foreign visitor who wants to find it.

Glance at the posters on notice boards and tree trunks and you will discover just how pervasive a love of arts is in this state; look for opportunities to learn the tabla, or for your kids to learn how to paint.

Music

The musical scene in Goa is as eclectic as they come. While you're here, be sure to get out and see some; even if you don't like the style, this is the perfect place to appreciate other peoples' appreciation of it.

THE CASTE SYSTEM IN GOA

Although the origins of the Hindu caste system are hazy, it seems to have been developed by the Brahmins (priest class) in order to maintain their superiority over indigenous Dravidians. Eventually, the caste system became formalised into four distinct classes, each with its own rules of conduct and behaviour.

These four castes are said to have come from Brahma's mouth (Brahmins; priest caste), arms (Kshatriyas; warrior caste), thighs (Vaisyas; caste of tradespeople and farmers), and feet (Sudras; caste of farmers and peasants). Beneath the four main castes is a fifth group, the Untouchables (Dalits; officially, Scheduled Castes), who literally have no caste and perform the most menial and degrading jobs. Hindus cannot change their caste – they're born into it and are stuck with it for the rest of their life.

The caste system does not play as large a part in Goa as elsewhere in India, but it is still recognised and treated in a uniquely Goan way. Interestingly, the Christian community follows the caste system too. This can be traced back to the Portuguese. As an incentive to convert to Catholicism, high caste Goan families were able to keep their caste privileges. Furthermore, when the religious orders were recruiting lay clergy from the local population, only Brahmins were considered suitable, as it was felt that only they would be able to command the respect of the rest of the people.

Today caste is considered important mainly when it comes to marriage; candidates are selected from appropriate castes.

Live musical events are regular occurrences attended by foreigners and locals alike. Performing musicians are sometimes foreigners who have come to Goa to fuse their music with Indian traditional elements. For example, Prem Joshua is a German performer whose take on Indian traditional sounds has been lapped up by the locals.

The Kala Academy has identified 27 forms of folk art in Goa.

CLASSICAL FOLK MUSIC

There's a strong tradition of classical music in Goa, from the labouring songs of Goa's poorest indigenous people, the Kunbis, to the formalised songs of the Christian community for singing at weddings and festivals.

The *mando* (p38) takes pride of place in the Catholic tradition, but there are plenty of other *zoitis,* songs common to both the Hindu and Christian communities sung at various stages of the marriage ceremonies. In fact there are folk songs for almost all occasions: children's lullabies *(piannos)*; songs for singing in the fields; songs for fishing; and even songs traditionally sung by the saltpan workers and toddy tappers.

The *fado* is a European-influenced form of Goan folk, and a dying art form. The *fado* (also known as *saudades* in Portuguese) still occasionally features on folk albums and is championed by artists like Oslando and Lucio Miranda.

For a real insight into traditional Goan music it might be worth getting any of the albums by Gavana, a cultural group formed to preserve and promote Goan music and dance.

Check out www .goatrance.de to find out where Goa trance parties are happening around the world.

KONKANI POP

To the untrained Western ear, one piece of Konkani pop is indistinguishable from the next. Konkani pop is an excitable onslaught of electric guitars and keyboards, with Konkani crooners and whining female singers.

GOA TRANCE

In the 1990s, Goan DJs developed their own brand of techno, now known as Goa trance (or psy-trance), and this is what you'll hear played at the infamous raves.

Difficult to describe but easily recognisable once you've heard it, Goa trance is a hypnotic mix of a heavy electronic beat (up to 170 beats per minute), with lighter levels said to be derived from classical Indian music. Though it has a heavy techno element, artists stress the spiritual side of the music, calling the style an 'interface between technology and spirituality'.

The site of acclaimed Goa trance DJ Goa Gil, www .goagil.com, includes tour dates.

Goa trance is performed by DJs and artists around the world, especially in Europe, Scandinavia, Israel and Japan, but probably the most famous artist is still Goa Gil, the dreadlocked and bearded maestro who started the full-moon parties in the early 1970s and developed the concept of Goa trance, along with fellow pioneer DJs Laurent, Fred Disko and Mark Allen. Gil came to India from San Francisco in 1969, studying yoga in the Himalaya before settling in Goa. He has released 13 albums and tours the world performing at raves, although his appearances in Goa are rare these days. The mainstreaming of Goa trance was helped along by the likes of Danny Rampling and Paul Oakenford. Today Goa trance labels largely originate in Europe or Japan, but there are still home-grown labels.

Accomplished Goa trance artists include Hallucinogen (*Twisted, The Lone Deranger),* Juno Reactor (*Transmissions, Beyond the Infinite, Bible of Dreams),* Man With No Name (*Moment of Truth, Earth Moving the Sun)* and Astral Projection (*Trust in Trance, Dancing Galaxy, Another World, Amen, Ten).*

LIVE MUSIC VENUES

The best place to catch a performance of Indian classical music and dance is at the Kerkar Art Complex in Calangute every Tuesday evening, or at the Kala Academy in Panaji. The Pop, Beat & Jazz Music Festival, held at the Kala Academy in February, provides opportunities to see performances of all types of music.

A good place to see local live acts is at the Saturday night markets in Baga and Arpora. Ingo's Saturday Nite Bazaar features everything from rock fusion bands to jazz and Goan folk music. For information on where to find Goa trance, see Party's a Goa?, p148.

Dance

Musical and dance arrangements generally have their origins in devotional practices. These days, however, both Hindus and Christians have appropriated and modified these traditions in such a way that music and dance now plays a significant role in the day-to-day life of Goans.

The most famous Goan song and dance form is the *mando*. Dubbed the 'love song of the people of Goa', the *mando* blends rhythms of Indian music with traces of Portuguese melody, and is accompanied by a *ghumot* (drum). The dance is highly stylised and the words of the songs are just as important as the movements. The theme of the *mando* is love, and its inherent deception, frustration, and union. The *mando* is often performed in honour of bridal couples. At weddings the *mando* is often followed by other traditional dances: the faster and more lively satirical *dulpod,* and sometimes the *dekhni,* which is performed by women, and known in Konkani as 'bewitching beauty'. It revolves around the story of a girl coaxing a boatman to take her across a river so she can sing at a wedding. In true Goan cross-cultural style, this traditionally Hindu song, is more often performed by Christian girls wearing Hindu dress.

Foogdi is another popular dance performed by women. There are numerous versions, but the most popular is in a circular formation, which begins slowly and gains speed towards the climax. The dance concerns domestic issues and contains fables to guide on family and societal issues.

Dances can be seen at tourist events and resorts, but the more authentic versions must be tracked down in villages on the eve of important events and during festivals.

While performing the *mando,* women sometimes wear Burmese-style skirts. These are presumed to have been introduced by upper-class Goans returning from the Portuguese colonies of Macau and Timor.

REMO FERNANDES

Known in the West and worshipped in India, Remo Fernandes is famous for his ability to fuse cultural influences in both his music and his image.

Remo was born in Siolim in 1953. After studying architecture in Bombay and hitchhiking around Europe and Africa (busking along the way), Remo returned to Goa. Several rejections from Indian labels made him record his first (and arguably one of his best) albums, *Goan Crazy,* at home in Siolim. From there, Remo shot to success with more hit albums, movie score offers, awards, product endorsements and titles like 'the Freddy Mercury of India'.

Remo is fondly loved in Goa, not only for the versatility of his talent but also for never cutting his Goan roots along his path to fame. When Remo turned 50 in May 2003, he celebrated with a 4½-hour free concert in Goa.

Look out for *Old Goan Gold* and *Forwards into the Past,* which has arrangements by Fernandes and vocals by Lucio Miranda. At the time of writing, a new album, *Muchacha Latina,* was due for imminent release. Remo still records in his studio at home.

Literature

Although it can sometimes be difficult to get hold of English-language Goan literature (books go out of print very quickly), Konkani literature is thriving and there is also some interesting writing by Goans in English.

Angela's Goan Identity, a fictional work by Carmo D'Souza, gives a fascinating insight into the struggle of Goan 'Anjali' (called 'Angela' by Portuguese priests) to define her Goan identity towards the final years of the Portuguese era in Goa.

Ferry Crossings, edited by Manohar Shetty, showcases Goan writing talent and highlights the diversity of cultural influences that have shaped the state. The short stories, translated into English from the four main languages used in Goa, deal with everyday subjects of Goan life.

Sorrowing Lies My Land, by Lambert Mascarenhas, first published in 1955, has since been reprinted. The subject is the struggle for Goan Independence launched in Margao in 1946. The book is held to be a classic of Goan literature. The subjects and settings of the short stories in his *In the Womb of Saudade* are drawn from Goan life.

Victor Rangel Ribeiro slowly weaves together Goan vignettes in his first and award-winning novel *Tivolem*. Mario Cabral E Sa's *Legends of Goa,* illustrated by one of Goa's best-known artists, Mario de Miranda, is a reworking of some of the best folktales of Goa. It lends extra colour to the state's traditions and history, and is an interesting read.

Dust: and Other Short Stories from Goa is a collection of short stories by Goan writer and conservationist Heta Pandit. The character-driven stories bring to life aspects of everyday life in Goa.

Architecture

The evolution of Goan architectural styles has run a parallel course with the evolution of Goa. The state's history of engagement with Europe has left an indelible imprint on almost every facet of cultural life. Architecture is no exception; it too has been appropriated and 'Goanised' over the years to such an extent that exploring churches, temples and palatial houses is one of the highlights of a visit to Goa.

TEMPLES

Goa's temples are interesting because they combine aspects of Muslim and Christian architecture into basically Hindu layouts. Domed roofs are a Muslim trait, while whitewashed octagonal towers and balustraded façades have been borrowed from Portuguese church architecture.

Of particular note are the *deepastambhas* (lamp towers) that are almost exclusive to Goan temples and are decorated with oil lamps at festival times. Early *deepastambhas,* such as the one at Saptakoteshwara Temple in Naroa, are distinctively eastern in shape and ornament, whereas later examples, such as the one at the Shantadurga Temple near Ponda, with its whitewashed pillars and baroque decoration, seem to have been lifted straight from the Catholic architecture of Old Goa.

Despite these unique aspects, Goa's temples share many common features with Hindu shrines throughout India, and the layout is pretty much standard to all. The pillared pavilion is known as the *mandapa*. Between the *mandapa* and the inner sanctum, where the deity resides, is the area known as the *antaralya,* and the sanctum itself is called the *garbhagriha*. On either side of the *antaralya* there are usually smaller shrines to the deities worshipped at the temple.

Outside the main building, the temple's courtyard is generally surrounded by *agarshalas* (accommodation blocks) for visiting pilgrims.

On a Goan Beach, by Remigio Botelho, tells the story of a young Goan returning to his homeland after many years in Kenya. It is a fascinating insight and fictional analysis of the complexities of Goan culture.

Well-known Goan poets include RV Pandit, Philip Furtado and Eunice D'Souza.

A Hindu house can be identified with the sacred *tulsi* plant growing in its forecourt in a *vrindavan* (ornamental container). According to Hindu mythology, the *tulsi* is actually one of Vishnu's lovers, who Lashmet (Vishnu's consort) turned into a shrub in a fit of jealousy.

Larger temples tend to have a storage area somewhere in these buildings where the *ratha* (ceremonial chariot) is stored. These carts are used to transport representations of deities around the village on feast days.

CHURCHES

Goa's churches owe the majority of their design features to the European traditions of their time, and some are openly copies of buildings in Rome or Lisbon (St Cajetan's in Old Goa is a replica of St Peter's in Rome). There are, however, some features that distinguish them from their European counterparts. In some cases these are practical modifications to suit the local climate. Large windows are set deep into the walls, for example, to allow plenty of light to penetrate, but to keep out direct sunlight.

The churches were constructed from the local rock laterite, which is porous, so there was a need to whitewash it regularly. The lime compound with which this was done was made from oyster shells. This had the effect of proofing the walls against moisture, although heavy monsoonal rain meant that the work had to be repeated every three or four years. Since laterite is coarse and unsuited to fine carving, the more important churches, such as the Basilica of Bom Jesus in Old Goa, have façades of basalt that had to be specially imported.

Other features that make the churches unique are the work of the local Indian artisans who built them. The floral decoration inside the Church of St Francis of Assisi in Old Goa is quintessentially Indian, as is some of the flamboyant woodcarving to be found in churches throughout Goa.

All churches in Goa share several common features, the most striking being the reredos (ornamented backdrop to the altar). Since most of Goa's large churches were built in the 16th and 17th centuries, the reredos' designs conform to the styles of the age – massive and ornate. In front of the reredos is the main altar and then the chancel, which is sometimes decorated with carvings or paintings. Many of Goa's churches are constructed in a cruciform design with side altars in the transepts.

HOUSES

There are still a few excellent examples of palatial houses throughout the Goan countryside. In the grandest houses, the layout allows for a huge frontage, often with floor to ceiling glass patio doors and tiny wrought-iron balconies in front of each window.

In the smaller houses the emphasis is on a wide veranda that almost encircles the house and provides plenty of shade. In almost all cases the central feature of the façade is the *balcao* (shady porch) that stands in front of the main entrance.

Within houses, the layout is generally dominated by a *saquão* (central courtyard) where the family carries out their affairs away from public scrutiny. Larger houses have a chapel or a family altar where daily prayers are said.

See p167 for information on two houses that are open to the public.

Painting

Although there is no style that is particularly distinctive to Goa, there is a long tradition of painting, evidence of which can be seen in the murals in the Rachol Seminary near the village of Raia. Today, Goa's budding artists are nurtured at the College of Art in Panaji, after which most opt to travel out of the state to study art at a higher level elsewhere.

In Goa, Odette Gonsalves is famous for her paintings of horses, and Dr Subodh Kerkar, who runs the Kerkar Gallery in Calangute and has

The Goa Heritage Action Group (www.goaheritage.org) is an NGO that aims to preserve and promote the natural and created heritage of Goa.

Before the availability of glass, windows were covered with translucent oyster shells. The 7cm to 10cm diameter discs were set in wooden frames and allowed a gentle, cool light to filter into the rooms.

Houses of Goa, by Heta Pandit and Anabel Mascaren, is an attractive in-depth coffee-table book that is available throughout Goa.

DOS & DON'TS

Goans are hospitable and friendly people, and visitors should not take advantage of the welcome they receive. Sadly, a number of tourists (domestic as well as foreign) see Goa's relatively liberal attitudes as an excuse to pay scant attention to the feelings of the local community.

Dress Sense

While most Goans are as modest as the rest of India in terms of dress, far too many travellers abuse Goan hospitality (and economic dependency) by wearing clothing that is entirely inappropriate and gives the rest of us a bad name. Nudism (which for Indians includes going topless) is illegal in Goa, although many foreigners continue to do it. Signs on some beaches warn of this and police occasionally patrol beaches (mainly to discourage illegal vendors), but there is generally a reluctance to enforce the law.

Though many Goans living along the beach have become resigned to it, many are offended by displays of nudity and some blame incidents of assault and harassment of foreign women on such behaviour. They won't say anything because, like everyone else, they are aware that their livelihoods depend on keeping tourists happy.

Much more worrying for tourists and locals is Goa's reputation throughout India as a place where women tourists are 'on show'. This has spawned a new and unwanted form of tourism, as Indian men from other states use Goa for a weekend's boozing and ogling. Free from family and community constraints, they can spend two or three days drinking (alcohol is much cheaper in Goa than elsewhere in India) and staring at sunbathers. If you wish to avoid this kind of unwanted attention and protect the next innocent traveller from negative assumptions, cover up while at the beach.

It goes without saying that it's appropriate to cover up in churches and temples, and in social situations.

It is also customary to take off your shoes before entering a Hindu temple, and a polite thing to do at a person's house. There is no hard and fast rule, but if there's a pile of shoes by the front door, or if your host or hostess removes their shoes upon entering the house, do likewise.

Religious Etiquette

It's important to behave respectfully when visiting religious sites, particularly when attending a service. Don't talk loudly or smoke, and dress conservatively (no shorts or singlet tops). Never touch a carving or statue of a deity. Religious etiquette advises against touching anyone on the head, or directing the soles of your feet at a person, religious shrine or image of a deity.

---

occasional exhibitions elsewhere, depicts typically Goan scenes in a variety of styles and disciplines. The work of artist and illustrator Mario Miranda adorns everything from books to billboards to the walls of Café Mondegar in Mumbai, and cartoonist Alexys Fernandes is well known for his contributions to many newspapers and magazines in Goa and elsewhere.

For those interested in the art scene, there are several galleries that can be visited. Between Calangute and Candolim, the Kerkar Gallery mostly shows work by Dr Kerkar himself, although there's also a small section of Goan handicrafts. In Panaji the Gitanjali Gallery at the Panjim Pousada has changing exhibitions of Goan and Indian artists.

Bollywood queen Aishwarya Rai is the first Indian woman to be immortalised in wax at Madame Tussaud's in London.

Cinema

The Indian film industry is the largest in the world with around 800 movies produced annually. It would seem though that quantity does not have a proportional relationship to quality. Bollywood movies have to be seen to be believed. They are formulaic and melodramatic montages that celebrate romance, violence and music, with lip-synched duets and dance routines, and skin-bleached stars who are worshipped like deities. There is little regard for details like plot and script, but the mainstream laps them up.

The other type of Indian movie is the one that has a basis in reality. These smaller-budget films grapple with real issues. Deepa Mehta, Arparna Sen and Mira Nair are some film-makers who dabble in this medium and bring home the awards.

While you'll have to hunt down the more alternative options, it's worth seeing a Bollywood movie while you're here.

The recently opened Inox Cinema in Panaji (p96) holds an annual film festival.

In addition to numerous Bollywood movies filmed in Goa throughout the year, parts of The Bourne Supremacy, starring Matt Damon and Franka Potente, were filmed in Palolem.

Theatre

Goa's active theatre scene is dominated by the unique local street plays known as *tiatr* and *kell tiatr*. The *tiatrs,* almost all of which are in Konkani, provide a platform for satire on politics, current affairs and day-to-day domestic issues. Each *tiatr* usually comprises seven acts of fifteen or so minutes each, with song and dance in between. The first ever *tiatr* was called 'Italian boy' and created by Lucasinho Ribeiro, a Goan living in Mumbai, who brought the art form back to Goa with him in 1894. An annual *tiatr* festival is held at the Kala Academy in Panaji, which showcases the work of well-known *tiatr* writers.

SPORT

While everyone knows how passionate Indians are about cricket, it may come as a surprise to learn that Goa's top sport is football (soccer), another legacy of the Portuguese. Every village has at least one football team – sometimes a team for each ward of the village – and league games are fiercely contested. The result of this keen following at village level has been the creation of several teams that regularly perform at national level; there are even Goan players in the national football squad. The main Goan teams are Salgaonkar, Dempo, Sesa Goa and Churchill Brothers, and major matches are played at the Nehru Stadium, Fatorda, near the Margao bus station. The season runs from October to April and tickets to the matches generally cost less than Rs 20.

While cricket is sometimes said to be a colonial imposition, football is believed to have been used by Goans in Mumbai to assert their distinctive identity within India during the 1960s and '70s.

Goans are also keen cricketers and games take place everywhere at local levels. Goa's English-language daily papers publish reports on matches and upcoming fixtures.

Environment

THE LAND

Goa occupies a narrow strip of the western Indian coastline, approximately 105km long and 65km wide, with a total area of 3701 sq km. It shares state borders to the north and northeast with Maharashtra, and to the south and southeast with Karnataka.

The state is divided up into two administrative districts – north and south Goa – with the major towns in each being Panaji (formerly Panjim, the state capital) and Margao (formerly Madgaon) respectively. Beyond this simple subdivision the state is further divided into 11 talukas (districts): Pernem, Bicholim, Satari, Bardez, Tiswadi and Ponda in north Goa, and Mormugao, Salcete, Sanguem, Quepem and Canacona in the south.

Topographically, Goa falls into three distinct areas: the Western Ghats, the midland region and the coastal region.

Goa's main rivers are the Mandovi, Zuari, Terekhol, Chapora, Sal and Talpona.

Western Ghats

In the east of the state lie the foothills and some of the peaks of the Western Ghats, the mountain range that runs along the west coast of India, separating the Deccan Plateau from the low-lying coastal areas. In Goa, the Western Ghats, made up locally of the Sahyadri Range, comprise about 600 sq km of the total area of the state. Some of the main peaks are Sonsagar (1166m), Catlanchimauli (1107m), Vaguerim (1067m) and Morlemchogor (1036m). The Ghats are the source of all seven of Goa's main rivers, the longest of which, the Mandovi, is 77km in length.

Midland Region

Goa's hinterland lies between the Ghats and the coast; it's a huge area mostly made up of laterite plateaus of between 30m and 100m in elevation. The laterite rock that comprises much of Goa is nearest to the surface on many of these plateaus. Since the plateaus are rich in both iron and manganese ores, they have become the scenes of large-scale open-cast mining.

Spice, fruit and areca nut plantations have become established in this region, particularly in the lower areas where soil is richer. Making efficient use of the water sources available, the terraced orchards support coconut palms and fruits such as jackfruit, pineapples and mangoes.

Goa – A View from the Heavens, by Gopal Bodhe, is a beautifully photographed book dedicated to Goa's environment and heritage.

Coastal Region

Though only a fraction of the total area of the state, the coastal region is its claim to fame.

Mangroves line many of Goa's tidal rivers and provide a unique habitat for birds and marine animals.

The inland areas, known to Goans as the *khazans,* are lands reclaimed by the building of bunds (embankments); the sluices and floodgates allows controlled use of land. While most of the land is irrigated using fresh water, many of the canals are allowed to fill at least partially with salt water, so that they can be used for fish farming. Other areas are flooded with salt water, which is then left to evaporate for the collection of salt.

WILDLIFE

Despite Goa's small size, the state's unique topographical and environmental variation allows for an impressive array of fauna, though some species now occur in only very small numbers. The forested areas of the

National Geographic has described Goa's Western Ghats as one of the richest ecosystems on the planet.

Western Ghats have traditionally provided a habitat for some extremely rare animals. In reality, unless you're prepared to spend days camped out in a wildlife sanctuary, the most interesting animals you are likely to see are those kept in captivity and some of the more common species that live in the wild. Bird enthusiasts have more success; Goa is particularly notable for its spectacular birdlife (see Chick It Out, p46).

Animals

MAMMALS

Although Goa Tourism's brochures would have you believe otherwise, wild elephants are rarely found in the state's forests nowadays. Most members of the cat family are extremely rare too, and sightings of tigers and leopards (known in India as panthers) are few and far between.

More common in this family is the jungle cat, which is about 60cm long excluding the tail. Notable for its long limbs and short tail, it is able to kill animals larger than itself. Also common are small Indian civets and common palm civets. Among the dog family, jackals, striped hyenas and wild dogs are occasionally sighted.

Goa has two common types of monkey that are frequently seen – bonnet macaques and common langurs. Much less commonly seen are slender loris, only occasionally found in the dense forests of Molem and Canacona. There are also very occasional sightings of sloth bears, which can grow up to 1.5m long and generally feed on bees and termites.

Other more frequently seen inhabitants are common mongooses, which are found near settlements, and common otters and smooth Indian otters, both of which are seen near water. The Western Ghats are also home to Indian giant squirrels, which are found in the forests of Molem, Valpoi and Canacona. Other relatives in Goa are three-striped palm squirrels, five-striped palm squirrels and flying squirrels.

Among the animals found at ground level are common Indian porcupines and the wild boar, both of which are notorious for damaging crops. Particularly common are the large gaurs (Indian bison). The animals you're most likely to see in Goa's wildlife sanctuaries are sambars and chitals, both species of deer. One of the rarer animals to inhabit Goa's forests is the nocturnal pangolin, otherwise known as the scaly anteater.

Common dolphins are found off the coastline and can often be seen on 'dolphin-spotting' boat tours.

REPTILES & AMPHIBIANS

The common house gecko is often seen in buildings at night feeding off insects attracted to light. Snakes are common in Goa but the only place you're likely to see one is in a snake charmer's basket at a market.

Among the nonpoisonous variety are common blind snakes. Much higher in the Ghats, locally named torava snakes grow up to 50cm in length and are notable for their yellowish colouring and rough tails. Indian pythons are undoubtedly the largest of the snakes found in Goa: they have been known to grow up to 4.5m in length.

There are relatively few venomous snakes in Goa. The most distinctive are cobras, which are found near the coast and inland. There are three common varieties, as well as the much larger (and now rare) king cobras. The common varieties can grow to more than 1.5m in length, and the venom is likely to be lethal if not treated quickly. Common Indian kraits are more poisonous still.

Kusadas (sea snakes) are common along the coastline, often seen dead on the beach; since they are completely adapted for water, they cannot

---

The Netravali 'bubble' lake in Sanguem taluka has continuous bubbles rising up to the surface. If you clap loudly, the bubbles increase in intensity. It's a mysterious phenomenon.

Rare sightings of the black panther have been reported from the jungles of Bhagwan Mahaveer Wildlife Sanctuary.

The bamboo poles sticking out of the banks of rivers are actually holding fishing nets below the water line. The fish are trapped during low tide when the water recedes through the nets.

move on land and die if stranded. *Kusadas* are extremely poisonous, but they are very timid and their fangs so far back that they rarely get enough grip to give a proper bite.

Goa has a small population of other reptiles including two species of crocodile. Although rare, it is still possible to see these along the banks of a few inland waterways, and several companies advertise 'crocodile-spotting' trips by motorboat along likely stretches.

Freshwater turtles are found throughout the state and Goa is also a traditional breeding ground for marine turtles, which struggle ashore between October and December to lay their eggs in the sand. Recent efforts have been stepped up to counter the threats posed to these remarkable animals by tourism and opportunistic locals (see Turtle Beaches, p151).

BIRDLIFE

Keen bird-watchers will be in seventh heaven in Goa, and even those who have previously had little interest in birds may find the rich variety at least a little bit enthralling.

A trip to the Dr Salim Ali Bird Sanctuary on Chorao Island is recommended. Other sites of interest are the wetlands at Carambolim (12km east of Panaji), at Shiroda (40km southeast of Panaji) and even the marshland south of the Baga River.

One of the best ways to see birds in Goa is to join an ecotour with **Southern Birdwing** (☎ 2402957; www.southernbirdwing.com); or contact locally based ornithologist and guide **Gordon Frost** (☎ 2275301).

Plants

The Western Ghats have the greatest diversity of plant life, including areas of jungle (around Dudhsagar Falls and the Bhagwan Mahavir Wildlife Sanctuary). The vegetation here is, for the most part, tropical evergreen, although there are large areas of cane, bamboo and semi-evergreen trees.

On the lower slopes of the Ghats, thinner, dry soil supports lateritic semi-evergreen forest. In many places (eg Cotigao Wildlife Sanctuary) the arid nature of the landscape leads to savanna-like vegetation. In the less dry patches of the lower slopes, timbers such as teak are grown.

In the midland region the lateritic rock is close to the surface and the soil is too thin in many places to support much more than coarse grass and scrub. Where possible, cashew trees, a significant cash crop that can withstand the hot dry conditions, have been laid out in plantations.

In the folds between the hills where shade and springs are found, the small valleys are often extremely fertile. Centuries-old methods are still followed in the cultivation of spices and fruits. Coconut palms are cultivated not only for the nuts and toddy (sap that is collected, fermented and distilled), but also to give shade to less hardy trees.

Beneath the canopy of coconut palms and mango trees, the tall, slender areca nut palms (which provide betel nuts for *paan*) are grown. These shelter an incredible variety of fruit trees and spice plants, ranging from pineapples to bananas, and pepper to cinnamon. Although many of these plants are indigenous to Goa, others were introduced by the Portuguese, including rubber trees, pineapples and chillies.

The coastal region has a similarly wide range of flora. The saline conditions support a substantial area of mangroves (estimated at a total area of 20 sq km).

Along the coast, coconut palms predominate. Another distinctive feature in the area is the large banyan trees that often provide shady meeting places.

In the village of Dhurbat, crocodiles on the canal are worshipped as the guardian spirits of the community.

Heinz Lainer's *The Goan Foundation* is a book for true bird enthusiasts. It is an overview of bird habitat, population, distribution, migration, breeding status and other information on the 420 bird species that have been recorded in Goa.

Ayurveda describes some 2000 species of plant, of which at least 550 are still in use.

CHICK IT OUT

Goa's climate and rich vegetation support an abundance of birds. Common varieties found in Goa include eagles and other birds of prey such as kites, buzzards, kestrels and ospreys. There are also many varieties of pigeons, doves, cuckoos, kingfishers and woodpeckers.

Out of Town

On the outskirts of town and in open spaces, a flash of colour between ruins may turn out to be a bee-eater. Indian rollers are related to bee-eaters, but are larger and bulkier; they are attractively patterned in mauve and blue.

Drongos are shiny black birds that have distinctively shaped tails and typically perch on a post or obliging cow. Pipits and wagtails strut among the stubble, sometimes in large flocks; wagtails can be recognised by their habit of pumping their tail up and down.

Common hoopoes, with their orange-brown bodies and black-and-white wings, tails and black-tipped crests, are seen in open country, around cultivated fields and villages.

Birds of prey such as harriers and buzzards soar over open spaces looking for unwary birds and small mammals on which they feed.

Kites and vultures can wheel on thermals for hours on end. Ospreys, another species of large hawk, feed almost exclusively on fish that they seize with their vicious, hooked talons; ospreys patrol large tanks (reservoirs) and other waterways.

Waterways

Stalking on long legs at the shallow edge of tanks and ponds are various species of egret, graceful white birds with long necks and daggerlike bills. Their elegant poise belies the deadly speed with which they spear frogs and fish. Cattle egrets stalk among livestock looking for large insects stirred up by their namesake.

Indian pond herons, also known as paddy birds, are small and well camouflaged in greys and browns. They are almost invisible until they take off, showing their pure white wings.

Colourful kingfishers, locally known as 'flying beers', wait patiently on overhanging branches before diving down for their prey. Several species are to be seen in the area, including black-and-white pied kingfishers, tiny but colourful common kingfishers (also known as river kingfishers) and the striking stork-billed kingfishers, which have massive red bills.

The water's edge is also home to smaller and drabber species, such as plovers, water hens and coots, which feed and nest among vegetation.

Forests

Patches of forest often support a richer variety of species, some of which pick grubs off the forest floor, while others forage among the branches and leaves.

Among those heard more often than seen are woodpeckers, whose drumming sound is made as they chisel grubs from under bark. Its colourful relatives include barbets, which habitually sit at the topmost branches of trees and call incessantly in the early morning; and Indian koels, whose loud, piercing cry in spring can be maddening.

Fruiting trees are a magnet for many bird species. Fruit eaters include a number of pigeons and doves, such as green pigeons and imperial pigeons; noisy flocks of colourful parrots; the minivets in splendid red-and-black or orange-and-black plumage; and various cuckoo-shrikes and mynahs, including hill mynahs, an all-black bird with a distinctive yellow 'wattle' about the face. Sadly, hill mynahs are sought-after as cage birds because they can be tamed and even learn to talk.

The jewels in the crown are the bizarre hornbills, which, with their massive down-curved bills, resemble the toucans of South America. At the other end of the spectrum in both size and colour, iridescent, nectar-feeding purple sunbirds could be called the jewels in the canopy.

A host of smaller birds, such as flycatchers, warblers, babblers and little tailorbirds (so-called because they make a neat little 'purse' of woven grass as a nest), forage for insects in all layers of vegetation from the ground up.

WILDLIFE SANCTUARIES & PROTECTED AREAS

In the late 1960s Goa established three wildlife sanctuaries: Bondla, Bhagwan Mahavir (which also contains Molem National Park) and Cotigao. There's also tiny Dr Salim Ali Bird Sanctuary on Chorao Island. In 1999 two new wildlife reserves – Madei (208 sq km) in Satari taluka and Netravali (211 sq km) in Sanguem taluka – were declared protected areas, but these lack infrastructure for visitors. The creation of these protected areas links the sanctuaries running along the Western Ghats, providing a corridor for wildlife.

Advance accommodation bookings and requests for further information can be made via the **Forest Department** (www.goaforest.com) or by contacting the **Conservator of Forests, Wildlife and Eco-Tourism** (☎ 2229701; 4th fl, Junta House, Swami Vivekanand Rd, Panaji 403001).

More than just being attractive and offering much needed shade, the banyan tree is a symbol of love for Hindus: Shiva and Parvati are believed to have been married under one.

Bhagwan Mahavir Wildlife Sanctuary

At 240 sq km, Bhagwan Mahavir (p115) is the largest wildlife sanctuaries in Goa. There are a couple of watchtowers from where it's possible to observe wildlife and there's accommodation at Molem. As with the other parks, visitors need to be patient to see much. The countryside and the forest inside the park are wonderful and it's worth a visit for the scenery alone. Within the sanctuary is Goa's highest waterfall, Dudhsagar.

Bondla Wildlife Sanctuary

Bondla Wildlife Sanctuary (p114) is the state's smallest, with an area of only 8 sq km, but is also the most accessible from Panaji or Margao. It has a basic forest watchtower overlooking a small water hole. Regular sightings in the sanctuary include gaurs, barking deer and sambars. The park has a nature interpretation centre, a small zoo, and basic accommodation at the park entrance.

Tourism has now overtaken mining in terms of industry importance. The contribution of mining to the state's GDP has declined from 40% to 15%.

Cotigao Wildlife Sanctuary

In the far south of the state, this 86-sq-km wildlife sanctuary (p197) offers regular sightings of sambars and gaurs from its tall tree-top watchtowers. There are also occasional sightings of large predators such as panthers, which have strayed into the park. There is a small nature interpretation centre and some accommodation, but it's an easy daytrip from Palolem.

Dr Salim Ali Bird Sanctuary

Named for India's most renowned ornithologist, this sanctuary (p100) is only 1.8 sq km, but an impressive repository of fascinating species. The network of channels through the sanctuary are best explored on a small canoe. The bird sanctuary is easily accessible from Panaji; a ferry

ECOFRIENDLY PIG OUT

You may never encounter one during your stay in Goa, but if you do there's something rather disconcerting about the traditional Goan toilet. Basically it's a normal squat-style toilet in which the pipe runs out of the building and straight into the pigsty behind the cubicle. The sound of contented snuffling is an unusual accompaniment to a normally solitary activity. However strange it may seem to Western eyes and ears, the pig loo is the perfect combination of environmental resources. The pig loo solves the problem of sewage disposal, wasted water and pig food all in one go and arguably does its bit to promote vegetarianism. By comparison, the sit-down flush loos now in use all over Goa are nothing but trouble.

from Ribindar (4km from of Panaji) takes you across the Mandovi onto Chorao Island where the sanctuary is located.

ENVIRONMENTAL ISSUES

In the February 1999 issue of *National Geographic* magazine, Goa was likened to the Amazon and Congo basins for its rich tropical biodiversity.

The greatest environmental threat facing Goa today comes as a result of the state's rush to develop economically, often to the detriment of its environmental development. While the tourist industry nibbles away at the coast, the mining industry is uprooting inland Goa, and there is simultaneous effort to counter the detrimental affects of industry.

Conservation

In addition to the wildlife sanctuaries that have been established, there are conservation activities underway. The **WWF** (www.wwfindia.org) has become increasingly active in Goa in recent years; visit its educational conservation exhibition at the Goa State Museum (p88).

The state government is still learning the language of conservation. The Wildlife Division of the Forest Department increasingly enforces the *Wildlife (Protection) Act 1972*; while there were only two instances of charges made in 1993–94, 24 charges were made in 2003–04.

The conservation of Goa's natural and man-made heritage is addressed by the **Goa Heritage Action Group** (www.goaheritage.org), which organises the annual Goa Heritage Festival and the Fontainhas Arts Festival.

The Book of Indian Birds has been revised many times since it was published in 1941, but still contains original text by Dr Salim Ali.

Green Goa Works (www.greengoaworks.com) is a nonprofit company chaired by Goan fashion designer Wendell Rodrigues has been established. It promotes the use of effective microorganisms (EM) in hotels, households and markets to reduce environmentally hazardous waste. EM is a highly concentrated liquid solution containing various naturally occurring organisms. When diluted, the liquid can be used as a household cleaning agent, without damaging the environment.

In 1964 the **Archaeological Survey of India** (http://asi.nic.in/main.html) assumed responsibility for conservation of the state's monuments, including buildings of Old Goa. This means there is some funding for maintenance and restoration work.

The **Goa Foundation** (www.goacom.com/goafoundation) is the state's leading environmental group. It works to maintain and protect Goa's environment by campaigning (often successfully) against mass developments, and runs a series of educational programs to inform people as to how they can

CARE FOR STRAY DOGS

Previous government policy was to shoot stray dogs; it was not unusual to see contractors (paid on a per-dog basis) roaming the streets and beaches taking pot-shots at hapless pooches. Thankfully, petitioning to courts put a stop to this, and the living conditions of Goa's strays have improved remarkably in recent years through the work of NGOs like **International Animal Rescue** (IAR; in UK ☎ 01825-767688; www.iar.org.uk), a UK-based NGO that has set up a shelter in Goa to care for sick animals and implement a sterilisation programme. Since it began operating in Goa in 1998, it has treated thousands of animals. A team of vets sterilises dogs (15 per week in Palolem alone), vaccinates them, and fits them with a blue IAR collar before releasing them back onto the streets.

Volunteers are needed to perform the arduous task of playing with the animals at the centre. Also, some timid dogs need to be befriended prior to sterilisation. Visitors are welcome (as are donations) to the centre near Mapusa. Visit IAR's Goa office, **Animal Tracks** (☎ 0832-2268328, 2268272; Madungo Waddo, Assagao, Bardez). Contact it if you see a sick or injured animal. If its vehicles are otherwise engaged, you may need to put the animal in a taxi to the centre.

RESPONSIBLE TRAVEL

■ Support those who support the environment – choose accommodation that has implemented ecofriendly approaches to waste management.

■ Dispose of items respectfully – minimise the waste you create by travelling with a water filter rather than buying bottled water, which will contribute to Goa's plastic waste problem.

■ Use water sparingly – water shortages usually occur at the end of the tourist season.

■ Goa is child-friendly, so make your children Goa-friendly – opt for reusable nappies over disposable ones.

■ Just because water-sports facilities are available, doesn't mean they should always be used – consider their impact on the habitat of plants, animals and people.

■ Many travellers in Goa don't know or don't care about their impact on Goa – perhaps a conversation about it can change this.

---

minimise their impact on the environment. For information about the work of the Goa Foundation and other NGOs, see p136.

Deforestation

Over-cutting of the forested Western Ghats started at the beginning of the 20th century, and by the time the Portuguese departed, considerable damage had been done. Shortly after Independence, licences were granted for further large-scale felling. In some cases the cleared land was replanted with imported crops such as eucalyptus and rubber plants. In many cases, however, the deforestation was permanent, with land being used for roads, open-cast mining and other development.

The construction of reservoirs in the hills near the Maharashtra border has been particularly damaging. Whole valleys are submerged under the new reservoirs, while neighbouring areas are deforested to rehouse the families made homeless.

Environmental groups estimate that more than 500 hectares of Goa's forests are disappearing every year, and that a mere 8% to 12% of the state is now under dense forest.

The damage caused by deforestation is far-reaching. The habitats of many of Goa's native animals are disappearing, as are the homelands of several of the minority peoples of the state. The Dhangars, Kunbis and Velips, whose way of life revolves around agriculture and animal husbandry, have been forced into smaller and smaller pockets of land.

The government seems to have stepped up its efforts to protect Goa's forests in recent years: felling fees now apply and licences must be issued. Also, it claims that since 1984, it has planted 4000 hectares of land under its Social Forestry scheme.

Mining

Nearly half of the iron ore exported annually from India comes from Goa. Goa's mines produce ore exclusively for export, and for eight months of the year huge barges ferry the ore along the Zuari and Mandovi Rivers to waiting ships.

Such large-scale extraction of ore has had a destructive effect on the Goan hinterland and the coastal region. Because no stipulation for environmental reconstruction was made when mining concessions were issued, many mines have simply been abandoned once extraction was complete.

Since it was first conceived, the Konkan railway outraged environmentalists, who are concerned about the interference of the railway with heritage sites in Goa, and its disturbance of irrigation channels.

Energy and Environment in India: A Handbook, by Bani P Banerjee, is a comprehensive and up-to-date academic account of the sustainability issues affecting India.

FADING FISHERIES

Goa's once-abundant waters are facing a very real threat from overfishing. Locals wistfully reminisce about their childhood days when *ramponkars* (fishermen) would give away 60cm-long kingfish because they had so many to spare. These days it's difficult to buy fish direct from boats, and even local markets offer slim pickings because much of the best fish is sold directly to upmarket hotels or shipped to interstate markets where the best prices are fetched. Much of the best shellfish (prawns, crabs and lobsters) is exported. Naturally this has driven up the price of seafood, not only for tourists, but for Goans who rely on their staple fish curry rice.

Overfishing has become a threat since modern motorised trawlers started to replace traditional fishing methods. Trawlers stay relatively close to the shore, adversely affecting the *ramponkars'* catch. The use of tighter nets, which do not allow juvenile fish to escape (these are either thrown away or used for fish fertiliser) has further dwindled fish stocks. Although the *ramponkars* have been agitating for some sort of restrictions on trawler fishing for a number of years, little has been done to avert what some ecologists believe will be a marine resource disaster.

Out of the 80 million tonnes of rock and soil extracted annually, only 13 million tonnes are saleable ore. Surplus is dumped on the spoil tips and a huge quantity of soil is washed away, smothering both river and marine life. Other side effects of mining have been the destruction of the local water table and the pollution of drinking water.

Tourism

Tourism has overtaken mining as Goa's most significant industry. In 2001, 1.38 million foreign and domestic tourists visited Goa – slightly more than the entire population of Goa. While many Goans welcome tourism as a valuable source of income, there is legitimate concern about the numbers involved, beyond mere pollution and overcrowding.

The Transforming of Goa is a collection of essays, edited by Norman Dantas, dealing with topics such as Goan identity, politics, language and religion. Although the scope is wider than merely environmental matters, the environment features prominently.

The changing face of tourism is bringing new environmental problems, and mass tourism is actively encouraged by the government. Hippies and backpackers are being replaced with higher-spending, short-term package tourists. Five-star hotels with lush grounds and golf courses and the proliferation of midrange hotels with swimming pools puts increasing strain on water resources. Many Goans question whether water from reservoirs built in deforested areas should be used to fill fountains and swimming pools, and maintain golf courses that will not even be used by the people of Goa.

Large-scale hoteliers have been known to violate environmental protection laws, acquiring water illegally and building within 200m of the high-water mark, resulting in the lowering of the water table. Local village wells frequently run dry weeks before the monsoon, and there is a danger that if saline intrusion occurs, ground water supplies could be ruined permanently.

While budget travellers pose social challenges to local Goans through nudity and drug use, there is little question that they have less environmental impact; bamboo and palm-thatch huts can be dismantled and put away at the end of a season.

Food & Drink

Goa has a unique cuisine that stems from the intermingling of the highly developed Goan culture and 450 years of Portuguese rule. The Portuguese were the first colonisers to arrive in India and the last to leave. Goa was kept in an isolated cocoon from the rest of the country, left to concoct an original cuisine that is as casual and vivacious as the Goans themselves. It's reflected in rich curries, roasts coated in masalas and marinated in palm vinegar, cakes made of semolina, jaggery and coconut, and bread that's leavened with *feni* (alcoholic drink; p54). Food and drink are integral to a lifestyle that revolves around dance, music and celebration – 'to enjoy' is the Goan instinct.

Check out *Savour the Flavour of India*, by Edna Fernandes, an authentic collection of Goan and Indian recipes.

STAPLES & SPECIALITIES

Given that Goa has the ocean on one side and is crisscrossed by a maze of canals, streams and rivers, it is little wonder that fish is the Goan staple, with over a hundred varieties of freshwater and saltwater fish and seafood. Along with those from Kashmir and Bengal, Goan Brahmins eat fish without the slightest qualms about polluting their 'holy status'.

In Goa, fish aside, chicken and pork are also favoured meats, and spicy Goan sausages – pickled in vinegar and red chillies – are a meaty must-try. Goan Hindus eat a lot of vegetables but the Christian diet is dominated by nonvegetarian foods (particularly on Sundays) with the occasional salad tossed in.

Goans specialise in elaborate puddings, cakes and sweet snacks. Don't miss *bathique* (a cake made of semolina, coconut and eggs), *dodol* (a black cake made of jaggery, rice flour and coconut cream) and famous *bebinca* (the layered 40-egg sweet that is rich with ghee and coconut milk).

Spices

Christopher Columbus was searching for the black pepper off Kerala's Malabar Coast when he stumbled upon America. South India still grows the finest quality of the world's favourite spice, and it is integral to most savoury dishes. Turmeric is the essence of most Indian curries, but coriander seeds are the most widely used spice and lend flavour and body to just about every savoury dish, while most Indian 'wet' dishes – commonly known as curries in the West – begin with the crackle of cumin seeds in hot oil. Tamarind is a popular souring agent in the south.

Because of the prices it can fetch, saffron is frequently adulterated, usually with safflower – dubbed (no doubt by disgruntled tourists) as 'bastard saffron'.

Goan cooking involves liberal amounts of spices, the most commonly used being cumin, coriander, chillies, garlic and turmeric. Another local ingredient used to flavour fish curries is *kokum* (a dried fruit that is used as a spice). Particular combinations of spices have led to a number of styles of cooking, which have subtly differing flavours – masala, vindaloo and the seafood dish *balchão* being some of the most famous.

NUTS ABOUT COCONUTS

The basic components of Goan cooking are, not surprisingly, local products. The claim that every part of the coconut is used for something is not an idle one. Coconut oil, milk and grated coconut flesh flavour many dishes, while toddy (the sap from the coconut palm), is also used to make vinegar and to act as a yeast substitute. Another important product of the palm is jaggery, a dark-coloured sweetener that is widely used in preparing Goan sweetmeats.

Rice

Rice is the most important staple in India; in South India, it turns up in every course. Long-grain white rice varieties are the most common, served piping hot with just about any 'wet' cooked dish. Rice is cooked up in a *pulao* (pilaf; aromatic rice casserole), as biryani in Muslim cuisine, or as masala rice in the South.

On average, Indians eat almost 2kg of rice a week.

Dhal

While their staples divide north and south, the whole of India is united in its love for dhal (lentils or pulses), from the thin *sambar* (vegetable and dhal stew) of the south to the thick *moong dhal* of the north. You may encounter up to 60 different pulses: the most common are *chana*, a slightly sweeter version of the yellow split pea; tiny yellow or green ovals called *moong dhal* (mung beans); salmon-coloured *masoor* (red lentils); the ochre-coloured southern favourite, *tuvar dhal* (yellow lentils; also known as *arhar*); *rajma* (kidney beans); *kabuli chana* (chickpeas); *urad* (black gram or lentils); and *lobhia* (black-eyed peas).

Meat

While India probably has more vegetarians than the rest of the world combined, it still has an extensive repertoire of carnivorous fare. Goat (known as mutton), lamb and chicken are the mainstays; religious taboos make beef forbidden to Hindus, and pork to Muslims.

Rice is used to symbolise purity and fertility in Hindu wedding ceremonies and is often used as *puja* (offering) in temples.

Sorpotel is one of Goa's most famous meat dishes, and is prepared from pork and pork liver, heart and kidneys. These are diced and cooked in a thick and very spicy sauce flavoured with *feni* to give it an added kick.

Xacuti is a traditional way of preparing meat, usually chicken, by cooking it in coconut milk, and adding grated coconut and a variety of spices. The result is a mild curry, but with a distinctive and delicious flavour.

Chouricos are spicy pork sausages that owe more than a passing debt to Portuguese culinary traditions. Goan sausages are prepared using well-salted and well-spiced cubes of pork. Once they have been made, the strings of sausages are dried in the sun and then hung above the fire where they are gradually smoked. Traditionally they are eaten during the monsoon, when fish is scarce. In preparation, they are soaked in water and then usually fried and served with a hot sauce and rice.

Cafrial is a method of preparation in which the meat (usually chicken) is marinated in a sauce of chillies, garlic and ginger and then dry-fried. The result is a rather dry but spicy dish.

Seafood

The Portuguese influence in Goan cooking extends to the sea. Seafood dishes such as *recheiado* (stuffed fish) and *caldeirada* (stewed fish) reflect the state's colonial heritage. But the true Goan staple dish is fish curry rice (fish in a spicy sauce served over rice).

Technically speaking, there is no such thing as an Indian 'curry' – the word, an anglicised derivative of the Tamil word *kari* (black pepper), was used by the British as a term for any dish including spices.

With the variety and range on offer, combined with the skills of the local cooks, there is a mouthwatering choice outside of this. Kingfish is probably the most common item on the menu, but there are many others including pomfret, shark, tuna and mackerel. Among the excellent shellfish available are crabs, tiger prawns and lobster. Other seafood includes squid and mussels.

For the sake of tourist tastebuds, many places present seafood lightly spiced, or without spices at all. In this case the food is generally fried, grilled or cooked in a garlic sauce. Traditional Goan cooking methods, however, usually involve seasoning the seafood in some way.

Among the most famous Goan dishes is *ambot tik,* a slightly sour curry dish that can be prepared with either fish or meat, but more usually fish. *Caldeirada* is a mildly flavoured offering in which fish or prawns are cooked into a kind of stew with vegetables, and often flavoured with wine. *Recheiado* is a delicious preparation in which a whole fish, usually a mackerel or pomfret, is slit down the centre and stuffed with a spicy red sauce, after which it is fried in hot oil. *Balchão* is a method of cooking either fish or prawns in a tangy tomato sauce. Because of the preservative qualities of the sauce, *balchão* can be cooked in advance and reheated up to four days after preparation. *Rissois* are snacks or starters that are made with prawns fried in pastry shells.

The Essential Goa Cookbook, by Maria Teresa Menezes, is an excellent, in-depth book focusing on this culinary hot spot.

Pickles, Chutneys & Relishes

No Indian meal is complete without one, and often all, of the above. A relish can be anything from a roughly chopped onion to a delicately crafted fusion of fruit, nuts and spices. The best known is raita (mildly spiced yogurt, often containing shredded or diced cucumber, carrot, tomato or pineapple; served chilled), which makes a delicious and refreshing counter to spicy meals. *Chatnis* can come in any number of varieties (such as sweet and salty) and can be made from many different vegetables, fruits, herbs and spices. But proceed with caution before polishing off that pickled speck on your thali; it'll quite possibly be the hottest thing you've ever tasted.

India has more than 500 varieties of mangoes, and supplies 60% of the world with what is regarded as the king of fruit.

Dairy

Milk and milk products make an enormous contribution to Indian cuisine: *dahi* (curd) is served with most meals and is handy for countering heat; *paneer* is a godsend for the vegetarian majority; popular lassi (yogurt drink) is just one in a host of nourishing sweet and savoury drinks; ghee (clarified butter) is the traditional and pure cooking medium (although it's not used nearly as much in India as in Indian restaurants abroad); and the best sweets are made with milk.

Sweets

The most famous of Goa's sweetmeats is *bebinca,* a wonderful concoction made from layer upon layer of coconut pancakes. Cooking the perfect *bebinca* is an art form, for not only does the cook have to get exactly the right mixture of egg yolk, flour, coconut milk and sugar, but the cooking has to be timed just right to ensure that all layers are cooked equally.

Dodol is another famous Goan sweet, traditionally eaten at Christmas, and made with rice flour, coconut milk, jaggery and cashew nuts. It is usually cooled in a flat pan and served in slices, and is very sweet. *Doce,* made with chickpeas and coconut, is another favourite.

Each year more than 13 tonnes of pure silver are converted into the edible foil that's added to sweets for decoration.

DRINKS
Nonalcoholic Drinks

Chai is the drink of the masses. It is made with more milk than water and more sugar than you want to know. A glass of steaming, sweet, milky and frothy chai is the perfect antidote to the heat; the disembodied voice droning 'chai, chai *garam*' (hot tea) will become one of the most familiar and welcome sounds of your trip.

While chai is the choice of the nation, coffee is available everywhere in Goa, although true coffee lovers are likely to be disappointed. The most widely produced brew is 'milk coffee', which is simply Nescafé made with boiled milk. Tourist hotels and restaurants have adapted to Western tastes, though, and most give you a pot of black coffee and a jug of milk. A number of restaurants and upmarket snack bars in Goa also offer freshly ground coffee – including cappuccino and espresso.

The highest quality Darjeeling tea is graded as SFTGFOP, which stands for Special Fine Tippy Golden Flowery Orange Pekoe.

Sweet and savoury lassi is popular all over India, although the best are made in the north. *Falooda* is a rose-flavoured Muslim speciality made with milk, cream, nuts and strands of vermicelli. Hot or cold *badam* (milk flavoured with saffron and almonds) is an invigorating breakfast drink.

On the streets there are multitudes of fresh-fruit vendors; if the juice is ridiculously cheap, then it's probably been adulterated and you might just get a combination of water, ice and essence. Restaurants think nothing of adding salt and sugar to juice to intensify the flavours; ask the waiter to leave them out if you don't want them.

Alcoholic Drinks

More than three quarters of India's drinking population quaffs 'country liquor' such as the notorious arak (liquor distilled from coconut palm sap, potatoes or rice) of the South. This is the poor-man's drink and millions of people are addicted to the stuff. It is cheap, gives an instant high and tastes ghastly. Each year, hundreds are blinded or even killed by the methyl alcohol in illegal arak.

Because beer is hit by government taxes when it's served in restaurants and bars in parts of India, a bottle can cost a few times more than your entire meal; not so in Goa – the cheap beer is indeed one of the draw-cards for domestic tourists. Most of the many local and national brands are straightforward Pilsners around the 5% alcohol mark; travellers' champion Kingfisher is available nationwide. Royal Challenge, Dansberg, Golden Eagle, London Pilsner and Sandpiper are good national brands.

FENI

It's as clear as water, it tastes like aromatic gasoline and it really packs a punch – Goa's most famous spirit is the double-distilled and fearfully potent *feni*. There are two types of *feni*, both of which are made from local ingredients.

Coconut or palm *feni* is made from the sap drawn from the severed shoots on a coconut tree. In Goa this is known as toddy, and the men who collect it are toddy tappers. Toddy can be collected year-round, so palm *feni* is in plentiful supply at all times.

Caju (cashew) *feni* can only be made during the cashew season in late March and early April. The cashew apple, when ripe, turns a yellow-orange colour and the nut ripens below it. When the fruit is harvested, the nuts are dried in the sun and the apples are trampled to collect the juice. Both palm toddy and *caju* juice can be drunk fresh immediately – but the juice only begins to ferment after it's left in the sun for a few hours.

After the fermentation process, the juice is placed in a large terracotta pot over a wood fire; the vapour exits through a tube that typically passes through an oil drum filled with water, below which the distillate is collected. The result is *uraq*, a medium-strength spirit (10% to 15% proof), some of which is kept and sold. The majority though, is distilled again to make *feni*. By the time it comes out of the second distillation, Goa's national drink has an alcoholic strength of around 30% to 35% proof.

Feni first-timers might be well advised to mix it with a soft drink like Limca or cola – or just close your eyes and shoot it. Goans are keen to offer advice to foreigners: don't drink it on an empty stomach; don't mix it with other spirits; and certainly don't swim after a couple of *fenis*. They're right; you don't realise how strong it is until you stand up.

A shot of *feni* in any bar or restaurant costs from Rs 20 to 40. You can also buy colourful decorative bottles from wine stores (between Rs 100 and 400), which make a good gift for friends you want to incapacitate.

Goa has several top-notch brews; look out for King in particular. These days a number of midrange to top-end restaurants offer imported beers such as Fosters, Heineken and Budweiser.

CELEBRATIONS

Goans need only the flimsiest excuse to celebrate and almost every month has a festival that requires feasting. Weddings are occasions to indulge gastronomic fantasies. Receptions begin with toasts, the cutting of an elaborate cake and ballroom dancing. The meal features roast suckling pig and other pork dishes such as *sorpotel* (pork and pig liver curry, to which pig's blood was traditionally added) and pork vindaloo (a pickled pork curry), so fiery that it has been nicknamed 'find a loo' by tourists taken by surprise. Seafood will also be prominent with dishes such as fish aspic (set in gelatine), oyster pie, stuffed and grilled *surmai* (mackerel) and curried or fried prawns. Desserts might include *bebinca,* crème caramel and *leitria* (an elaborate sweet made with coconut covered by a lacy filigree of egg yolks and sugar syrup).

Although Hindu festivals have the sheen of religious reverence, they are also occasions for feasting and each festival has its own special dishes. Sweets are considered the most luxurious of foods and almost every occasion is celebrated with a staggering range. *Karanjis,* crescent-shaped flour parcels stuffed with sweet *khoya* (milk solids) and nuts, are synonymous with Holi, the most boisterous Hindu festival, and it wouldn't be the same without *malpuas* (wheat pancakes dipped in syrup), *barfis* and *pedas* (multicoloured pieces of *khoya* and sugar). Pongal (Tamil for 'overflowing') is the major harvest festival of the south and is most closely associated with the dish of the same name, made with the season's first rice along with jaggery, nuts, raisins and spices. Diwali, the festival of lights, is the most widely celebrated national festival, and some regions have specific Diwali sweets; if you're in Mumbai, stuff your face with delicious *anarsa* (rice-flour cookies).

While the majority of the state marks its religious fervour by stuffing themselves, the most significant month for the other 5% is Ramadan, the Islamic month of fasting, when Muslims abstain from eating, smoking or drinking even water between sunrise and sunset. Each day's fast is often broken with dates – the most auspicious food in Islam – followed by fruit and fruit juices. On the final day of Ramadan, Eid al-Fitr, an extravagant feast celebrates the end of the fast with nonvegetarian biryanis and a huge proliferation of special sweets.

WHERE TO EAT & DRINK

There is a multitude of restaurants ('hotels'), their signage identifying them as either 'veg', 'pure veg' or 'nonveg'. Most midrange restaurants serve one of two basic genres: South Indian (which means the vegetarian food of Tamil Nadu and Karnataka) and North Indian (which comprises Punjabi–Mughlai food).

Not to be confused with burger joints and pizzerias, restaurants advertising 'fast food' are some of India's best. They serve the whole gamut of tiffin items and often have separate sweet counters. Some deluxe hotels have outstanding five-star restaurants, usually with pan-Indian menus so you can explore regional cuisines. Although outrageously expensive by Indian standards they're within splurging reach of most travellers.

Look out for bakeries, sweet shops and juice stores in the larger towns. Markets in larger towns can also be a treasure-trove of eatable delights; within the winding warrens are hole-in-the-wall eateries with authentic

A portal to websites about Indian wine, www .indianwine.com, has notes on manufacturers, information on growing regions and more.

Copra (dried coconut flesh) is pressed and made into coconut oil, a very popular cooking medium in Goa and the rest of South India.

For a comprehensive travellers' guide to India's cuisine, see Lonely Planet's *World Food India*.

fare for authentic (cheap!) prices. *Dhabas* (snack bars; literally 'wayside eateries') originally were the domain of North India, but you'll find versions of them throughout Goa. The rough-and-ready but extremely tasty food served in these hospitable shacks has become a genre of its own known as '*dhaba* food', though some moderately classy restaurants have appropriated the tag as a catchy title, and are far from shacks.

Goa has the best drinking in India. Several good locally brewed beers complement the free-flowing *feni*. Booze isn't subject to the exorbitant levies of other states and there are cosy bars. Some restaurants double as watering holes when the kitchen shuts down and can offer a more pleasant environment to sit and drink than the sometimes dingy bars.

The word balti (of the ubiquitous-in-England balti house) was created as a marketing ploy by clever restaurateurs – *balti* is the northwestern name for the common Indian wok, better known as a *kadhai*.

Quick Eats

Whatever the time of day, people are boiling, frying, roasting, peeling, juicing, simmering or baking food and drink to lure passers-by. Small operations usually have one special that they serve all day, while other vendors have different dishes for breakfast, lunch and dinner. The fare varies; it can be as simple as puffed rice or roasted peanuts, as unusual as a fried-egg sandwich, or as complex as the riot of different flavours known as *chaat* (any snack foods seasoned with *chaat* masala).

Deep-fried fare is the staple of the streets, and you'll find samosas (deep-fried pyramid-shaped pastries filled with spiced vegetables and less often meat), *aloo tikka* (mashed potato patty) and *bhajia* (vegetable fritter) in varying degrees of spiciness, along with *poori* (also spelt 'puri'; thin puffed balls of fried dough, often stuffed with a variety of yogurt-based fillings) and *kachori* (golden balls of thick dough served hot with a range of stuffings and condiments). Mouthwatering dosas (thin pancakes of rice and lentil batter, fried and folded, and often served with masala-spiced potato filling) are served up by discerning vendors throughout India, along with the other southern specialities of *idli* (round steamed rice cakes often eaten with *sambar* and chutney) and *vada* (also spelt 'wada'; potato and/or lentil savoury doughnut, deep-fried and served with *sambar* and chutney). Muslim-inspired kebabs have also found their way to Goa. Savvy street-side operators are beginning to fuse the Indian street-snack tradition with every cuisine imaginable; in Panaji you can stand on the side of the road and have a full Chinese meal.

Madhur Jaffrey is the West's foremost expert on Indian cookery; her books *Indian Cooking* and *A Taste of India* are bibles of subcontinental cuisine.

VEGETARIANS & VEGANS

India produces some of the best vegetarian food on the planet. There's little understanding of veganism (the term 'pure vegetarian' means without eggs), and animal products such as milk, butter, ghee and curd are included in most Indian dishes. If you are vegan, your first problem will be getting the cook to understand your requirements; street food might be your best option because at least there you can see how it is cooked.

Goan cuisine, however, does not naturally cater for the vegetarian, and as a compromise cooking styles such as *xacuti* and *caldinha* (dishes cooked in spices and coconut milk) are sometimes used in the preparation of vegetables. Two vegetable dishes, however, are *mergolho*, which is made from pumpkin and papaya, and breadfruit curry.

HABITS & CUSTOMS

Three main meals a day is the norm with as many tiffin as can be consumed without sabotaging the appetite. Breakfast is light, maybe *idlis* and *sambar*. A typical Goan lunch starts with a mildly spicy side dish such as *cafreal* (pieces of fried chicken coated in a green masala paste) or *caldeen* (fish simmered in coconut milk, ginger and cumin), both of which are normally served with soft, square-shaped little loaves called *pao*. The second and main course might be *caril de peixe* or *ambot-tik* (both fiery hot fish curries) along with the compulsory crisply fried fish eaten with rice. The alternative is often to have a thali; it's a great way to explore different flavours.

Few can wait until dinner before eating again so a substantial tiffin is often enjoyed at around 5pm. Dinner might not be until 10pm or 11pm. The Portuguese influence shows up more prominently in the evening meal. It might start with *sopa de camarao* (prawn soup, complete with heads and shells), followed by a side dish like chicken galantine or stuffed squid, to complement a main course like *assado de bife* (roast beef). Dessert could comprise coconut-filled crepes or a fool (mashed fruit and cream) made with mangoes.

Monisha Bharadwaj's The Indian Kitchen *is an excellent introduction to Indian staples and how to identify and store them, as well as 200 simple recipes.*

Food & Religion

Food in India is integral to spiritual advancement. Regardless of creed, Indians share the belief that food is just as important for fine-tuning the spirit as it is for sustaining the body.

Broadly speaking, Hindus avoid foods that are thought to inhibit physical and spiritual development, although there are few hard-and-fast rules. The taboo on eating beef is the most rigid restriction. Devout Hindus avoid alcohol and foods such as garlic and onions, which are thought to heat the blood and arouse passions. These items are universally banned from ashrams and temples and during most religious feasts. Some foods, such as dairy products, are considered innately pure and are eaten to cleanse the body, mind and spirit. Ayurveda, the ancient science of life, health and longevity, also heavily influences food customs (see p129).

For recipes online, go to www.indiaexpress.com /cooking; www.india curry.com; and www .thokalath.com/cuisine.

Food Etiquette

You should use your right hand for all social interactions, whether passing money, food or any other item. Eat with your right hand only; the left is considered unclean given its use in the bathroom. If you are invited to dine with a family, always take off your shoes and wash your hands before taking your meal. The hearth is the sacred centre of the home, so never approach it unless you have been invited to do so.

COOKING COURSES

For the moment, there isn't the prolific presence of cooking classes that you'd expect be advertised amid notices promoting music or massage or yoga or reiki. But keep your eyes open; more and more guesthouses and restaurants are starting to realise that there is a market for assisting

---

PAAN

Meals are polished off with *paan,* a sweet, spicy and fragrant mixture of betel nut (also called areca nut), lime paste, spices and condiments wrapped in an edible *paan* leaf and eaten as a digestive and mouth freshener, and peddled by the *paan*-wallahs you'll see everywhere. The betel nut is mildly narcotic and some aficionados eat them the same way heavy smokers consume cigarettes – over the years these people's teeth become rotted red and black.

There are two basic types: *mitha* (sweet) and *saadha* (with tobacco). A parcel of *mitha paan* is an excellent way to finish a satisfying meal. Pop the whole parcel in your mouth and chew slowly, letting the juices secrete around your gob. You're not doing it wrong; it really is supposed to be like this.

budding chefs. Some top-end hotels offer cooking classes, and there many operators based in Western countries operate package cooking courses. The **Oriental Thai Restaurant** (☎ 3092809) in Candolim offers Thai cooking courses on Wednesdays between 2pm and 5pm for a minimum of four people.

UK-based company **India on the Menu** (www.indiaonthemenu.com) runs week-long cooking courses in various locations around Goa; prices vary according to which accommodation option you choose.

Legend says that Buddha, after falling asleep during meditation, decided to cut his eyelids off in an act of penance. The lids grew into the tea plant, which, when brewed, banished sleep.

EAT YOUR WORDS

If you want to be able to say it before you eat it, turn to the Language chapter (p248) for help with pronunciation.

Useful Phrases

Do you accept credit cards?	*kyaa aap kredit kaard lete/letee haing?* (m/f)
What would you recommend?	*aap ke kyaal meng kyaa achchaa hogaa?*
Please show me the menu.	*mujheh minu dikhaiyeh*
I'm (a) vegetarian.	*maing hoong shaakaahaaree*
I'd like the ..., please.	*muje ... chaahiye*

Please bring a/the ...	*... laaiye*
bill	*bil*
fork	*kaangtaa*
glass	*glaas*
glass of wine	*sharaab kee kaa glaas*
knife	*chaakoo*
mineral water	*minral vaatar*
plate	*plet*
spoon	*chammach*

I don't eat ...	*maing ... naheeng kaataa/kaatee* (m/f)
Could you prepare a meal without ...?	*kyaa aap ... ke binaa kaanaa taiyaar kar sakte/saktee haing?* (m/f)
beef	*gaay ke gosht*
fish	*machlee*
meat stock	*gosht ke staak*
pork	*suar ke gosht*
poultry	*murgee*
red meat (goat)	*bakree*

I'm allergic to ...	*muje ... kee elarjee hai*
nuts	*meve*
seafood	*machlee*
shellfish	*shelfish*

Food Glossary

ambot tik	sour curry dish made with meat or fish and flavoured with tamarind
balchão	fish or prawns cooked in a rich, spicy tomato sauce; *balchão de peixe* is made with fish, *balchão de porco* is made with pork
bebinca	richly layered, pancake-like Goan dessert made from egg yolk and coconut
bhojanayalas	basic restaurant or snack bar serving vegetarian food
cabidela	a rich pork dish
cafrial	method of preparation in which meat, usually chicken, is marinated in a sauce of chillies, garlic and ginger and then dry-fried
caldeirada	a mild curry of fish or prawns layered in a vegetable stew

caldinha	meat or vegetable dish cooked in spices and coconut milk
chai	tea
chourico	spicy pork sausages, dried and smoked then cooked in hot sauce
dhaba	basic restaurant or snack bar
doce	sweet made with chickpeas and coconut
dodol	traditional Christmas sweet made with rice flour, coconut milk, jaggery and cashew nuts
dosa	paper-thin lentil-flour pancake
dudh	milk
feni	Goa's most famous drink, a liquor distilled from coconut toddy or juice of cashew apples
fish curry rice	Goa's staple dish, a simple concoction of fish or prawns in mild to hot curry and served with rice
fofos	fish rolls, spiced and fried in bread crumbs
jell	ice
kofi	coffee
kokum	dried fruit used as a spice
masko	butter
mergolho	vegetable dish made with coconut, cashews and raisins
phala	fruit
sakor	sugar
sanna	steamed rolls or cakes made with rice flour, ground coconut and toddy
sheet	rice
sorpotel	pork liver, heart or kidney cooked in thick, slightly sour, spicy sauce and flavoured with *feni*
tatee	egg
tiffin	lights meals or snacks eaten through the day; also stainless steel containers often with three or four tiers in which people carry their lunch
udok	water
uned	small, round, crusty rolls
uttapam	similar to a *dosa*
vindaloo	very hot curry, usually using pork, spiced with chillies, vinegar and garlic
xacuti	method of cooking where a very hot sauce of spices and coconut milk is used to marinate meat (usually chicken) until quite dry

Mumbai

Three centuries of development have transformed seven scrubby islands into a mighty metropolis of towering apartment blocks, colonial mansions, seafront promenades and air-conditioned shopping malls. If Delhi is the seat of history and Kolkata the seat of culture, Mumbai (Bombay) is the address of film and fashion – many leading designers are based here, where the Bollywood movie machine churns out more movies per year than Hollywood.

Mumbai is where Indian fantasies of wealth and glamour engage in a bizarre dance with poverty and slums, and where economic boom flirts with social collapse. More than 60% of Mumbaikers live in shantytowns, yet the city boasts some of the most expensive real estate in the country. Plans are afoot to build a futuristic new town of towering skyscrapers in the north of the city, transforming Mumbai into the Shanghai of India. From a visitor's perspective, Mumbai is easy to enjoy, and the longer you stay, the more you will.

Mumbai is the usual Indian gateway city for Goa, which is 600km south. Spend some time immersing yourself in the mayhem of Mumbai before seeking out the slower south, and your experiences will give you an appreciation of the juxtaposed worlds that comprise India.

HIGHLIGHTS

- Marvel at the triple-headed Shiva sculpture on **Elephanta Island** (p67)

- Put on some comfortable shoes and explore the madness and mayhem of Mumbai's markets– head to **Crawford Market** (p78) for great food

- Immerse yourself in the festive air at **Chowpatty Beach** (p67)

- Gawk in awe at the sight and sounds of early morning laundry at the **Mahalaxmi Dhobi Ghat** (p69)

- Spend a long afternoon slowly soaking up the atmosphere at the **Gateway of India** (p67)

■ POPULATION: 16.4 MILLION   ■ PHONE CODE: ☎ 022

HISTORY

The seven islands that form Mumbai were home to Koli fisherfolk as far back as the 2nd century BC; Koli shanties still occupy parts of Mumbai's shoreline today. The islands were ruled by a succession of Hindu dynasties from the 6th century AD, invaded by Muslims in the 14th century and ceded to Portugal by the sultan of Gujarat in 1534. The British government took possession of the islands in 1665, but leased them three years later to the East India Company – for UK£10!

During that era, Bombay developed as a major trading port, and within 20 years the presidency of the East India Company was transferred to Bombay from Surat. Although Bombay grew during the 18th century, it stayed isolated from its hinterland until the British defeated the Marathas (central Indians who controlled much of India) and annexed substantial portions of western India in 1818.

Mumbai's role in India's Independence was significant. It hosted the first Indian National Congress in 1885, launched the Quit India campaign in 1942 and was home to Mahatma Ghandi for many years. Post-Independence, the city became the capital of the Bombay presidency, but in 1960 was divided on linguistic grounds into Maharashtra and Gujarat. Bombay became the capital of Marathi-speaking Maharashtra.

The city's multicultural milieu was shattered by the pro-Maratha regionalist movement (spearheaded by the Hindu Shiv Sena party), which discriminated against Muslims and non-Maharashtrans. After the Shiv Sena won power in 1985, communalist tensions increased. Nearly 800 people died in riots following the destruction of Babri Masjib in Ayodhya in December 1992, and a bombing on 12 March 1993 killed another 300 people.

In 1996 the city officially changed its name to Mumbai, the original Marathi name derived from the goddess Mumba, who was worshipped by the early Koli residents.

ORIENTATION

Mumbai is an island connected by bridges to the mainland. The principal part of Mumbai is concentrated at the southern end of the island known as south Mumbai. The southernmost peninsula is Colaba, the travellers' nerve centre. Directly north of Colaba is the busy commercial area known as the Fort, where the old British fort once stood. It's bordered on the west by a series of interconnected grassed areas known as maidans. The island's eastern seaboard is dominated by the city's off-limits naval docks. Further north, across Mahim Creek are the suburbs of Greater Mumbai and the international and domestic airports. Many of Mumbai's best restaurants and night spots can be found here, particularly in the upmarket suburbs of Bandra and Juhu.

Maps

Eicher City Map Mumbai (Rs 250) is well worth picking up if you're going to be spending any significant length of time in town.

MUMBAI IN...

Three days

Kick off at the **Gateway of India** (p67), strolling south past the **Taj Mahal Palace & Tower** (p67) towards colourful **Colaba Street Market** (p78). Grab a cab back to Kala Ghoda and explore the museums and art galleries before tucking into lunch: try the excellent seafood at **Mahesh Lunch Home** (p73).

Head next for the old **Victoria Terminus** (Chhatrapati Shivaji Terminus; p67) and stroll back down Dr Dadabhai Naoroji Rd towards the Oval Maidan where the grand edifices of the High Court and Bombay University overlook impromptu cricket matches. Promenade in the early evening down Marine Dr towards **Chowpatty Beach** (p67), then return to Colaba for a chat over drinks at **Leopold's Cafe** (p72).

On the following day be sure to visit **Mani Bhavan** (p68): Ghandi's old home has been converted into an insightful and atmospheric museum.

Save the best till last: on your third day make the journey out to **Elephanta Island** (p67).

MUMBAI (BOMBAY)

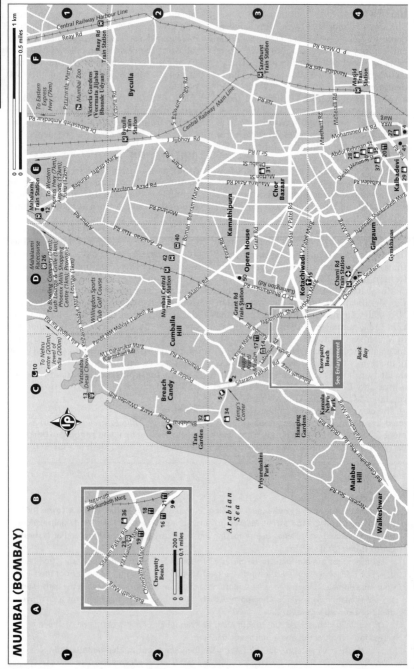

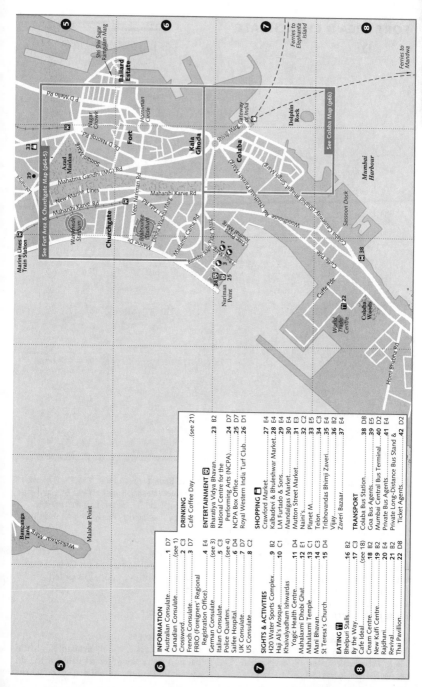

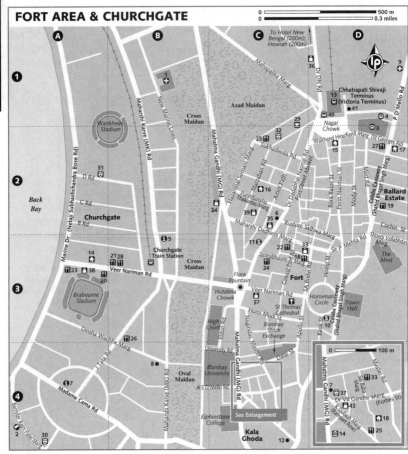

FORT AREA & CHURCHGATE

INFORMATION
Bookshops
In addition to the following, you can also find new and second-hand books at the roadside book market on the corner of MG Rd and Dr Dadabhai Naoroji Rd in Fort.

Crossword (Map pp62-3; ☎ 23842001; www.crossword bookstores.com; Sitaram Patkar Marg, Kemp's Corner, Breach Candy; ☺ 10am-9pm) A 'palace to reading' with a vast stock of novels, picture books, cookbooks, children's books, stationery, CDs and DVDs. There's a café.

Magna Book Gallery (Map p64; ☎ 22671763; 2nd fl, 143 MG Rd, Fort; ☺ 10am-8pm) A scholarly selection of titles on Indian culture and history.

Nalanda (Map p66; ☎ 22022514; Taj Mahal Palace & Tower, Apollo Bunder, Colaba; ☺ 8am-midnight) Imported and home-grown books and magazines.

Oxford Bookstore (Map p64; ☎ 56364477; www .oxfordbookstore.com; 3 Dinsha Wacha Rd, Churchgate; ☺ 10am-10pm) This is a two floor Western-style superstore. The 2nd-floor café is a popular student hang-out.

Emergency
There is a police station on Colaba Causeway, just south of Leopold's Cafe.
Ambulance (☎ 102)
Fire (☎ 101)
Police (☎ 100)

Internet Access
Internet access is widely available in Mumbai and there are Internet cafés at the domestic and international airports. Internet

INFORMATION		
ATM...(see 41)		
Bombay Hospital.............................**1** B1		
Bombay Hospital Pharmacy.........(see 1)		
French Consulate............................**2** A4		
General Post Office.........................**3** D2		
General Post Office Parcel		
Counter.....................................**4** D1		
German Consulate.........................(see 2)		
Government Dental College &		
Hospital.....................................(see 9)		
India Tourist...................................**5** B3		
Lawrence & Mayo...........................**6** C2		
Maharashtra Tourism Development		
Corporation.............................**7** A4		
Oxford Bookstore...........................**8** B4		
St George's Hospital......................**9** D1		
State Bank of India ATM.............**10** D3		
Thomas Cook...............................**11** C3		

SIGHTS & ACTIVITIES		
Bombay Natural History Society...**12** C4		
Victoria Terminus.........................**13** D1		

SLEEPING 🏠		
Ambassador..................................**14** A3		
Hotel City Palace.........................**15** D2		
Hotel Outram...............................**16** C2		
Welcome Hotel.............................**17** D2		

EATING 🍴		
Apoorva.......................................**18** C3		
Bharat Lunch Home.....................**19** D2		
Gaylord.......................................**20** A3		
Indian Summer............................**21** B3		
Mahesh Lunch Home....................**22** C3		
Pearl of the Orient...................(see 14)		
Pizzeria.......................................**23** A3		
Pratap Lunch Home.....................**24** C3		
Relish......................................(see 26)		
Royal China.................................**25** C2		
Samrat..**26** B3		
Sher-e-Punjab.............................**27** D2		
Tea Centre...................................**28** B3		

DRINKING 🍸		
Café Cofee Day............................**29** C1		

ENTERTAINMENT 🎭		
Inox Cinema.................................**30** A4		
Mumbai Cricket Association.....**31** A2		
Not Just Jazz By The Bay.........(see 23)		
Sterling Cinema...........................**32** C2		

SHOPPING 🛍		
Bombay Store...............................**33** C3		
Fashion Street Market..................**34** C2		
Khadi & Village Industries		
Emporium..................................**35** C2		
Planet M......................................**36** D1		
Reid & Taylor...............................**37** C3		
Tanishq..**38** A3		
Trafford House.............................**39** C2		

TRANSPORT		
Bus Stand....................................**40** D1		
Central Railways Reservation		
Centre......................................**41** D1		
Western Railways Reservation		
Centre.......................................(see 5)		

cafés in Mumbai charge Rs 20 to 40 per hour. Reliable options:

Satyam i-way (Map p66; Colaba Causeway; 🕙 8am-11pm; per hr Rs 40) Entrance on JA Allana Marg.

Waghela Communications Centre (Map p66; ☎ 22048718; 23B Narowji F Rd, Colaba; 🕙 8.30am-midnight; per hr Rs 30)

Media

English-language publications:

City Info Free monthly listings booklet available in many hotels and guesthouses.

Indian Express (www.indianexpress.com) Has a Mumbai edition.

Mid-Day (www.mid-day.com) The main local English-language paper.

Time Out Mumbai (www.timeout.com/travel/mumbai) Published every two weeks, this is the best round-up of what's going on the city.

Times of India (http://timesofindia.indiatimes.com/) Has a Mumbai edition.

Medical Services

For minor health problems, visit a pharmacist or contact India Tourism (p66) for a list of doctors. Consultations normally cost Rs 100 to 200. There are pharmacies all over Mumbai where you can buy common medicines without a prescription.

Bombay Hospital (Map p64; ☎ 22067676; New Marine Lines, Churchgate; 🕙 24hr) Close to Fort and Colaba.

Bombay Hospital Pharmacy (Map p64; ☎ 22067676; Bombay Hospital, New Marine Lines, Churchgate; 🕙 24hr)

Government Dental College & Hospital (Map p64; ☎ 22620668; St George's Hospital Compound,

P D'Mello Rd, Fort; 🕙 8.30am-4pm Mon-Fri & 2nd & 4th Sat)

Lawrence & Mayo (☎ 22076049; 274 Dr Dadabhai Naoroji Rd, Fort; 🕙 10am-7.30pm Mon-Sat) For replacement glasses and contact lenses.

Saifee Hospital (Map pp62-3; ☎ 23861418; Charni Rd, Girgaum; 🕙 24hr)

St George's Hospital (Map p64; ☎ 22620344; P D'Mello Rd, Fort; 🕙 24hr)

Money

Bank head offices are on Dr Dadabhai Naoroji Rd in Fort. Most banks have ATMs that accept major international credit cards. Banks and foreign exchange offices offer similar rates and commissions – typically 1% on each. Rates are similar for cash and cheques.

American Express (Map p66; ☎ 56385404; Regal Cinema Bldg, Shivaji Marg, Colaba; 🕙 9.30am-6.30pm Mon-Fri, 9.30am-2.30pm Sat)

Citibank ATM (Map p66; SP Mukherji Chowk/Regal Circle, Colaba)

State Bank of India (Map pp62-3; ☎ 22661765; Bank St, Fort; 🕙 10.30am-4.30pm Mon-Fri, 10.30am-1.30pm Sat) Changes cash and travellers cheques.

State Bank of India ATM (Map p66; Mandlik Rd, Colaba)

Thomas Cook (Map p64; ☎ 22048556; Dr Dadabhai Naoroji Rd, Fort; 🕙 9.30am-6.30am Mon-Sat)

Post

General Post Office (GPO; Map p64; Walchand Hirachand Marg, Fort; 🕙 10am-8pm Mon-Sat) Parcels are handled by the parcel office on the 3rd floor of the annexe behind the GPO.

Tourist information

India Tourism (Map p64; ☎ 22074333, domestic terminal ☎ 26156920, international terminal ☎ 28325331; www.india-tourism.com; 2nd fl, Western Railway Reservations Office, Maharshi Karve Rd, Churchgate; ⏱ 8.30am-6pm Mon-Fri, 8.30am-2pm Sat) Stacks of information about India and Mumbai. Has counters at the domestic and international terminals of Mumbai airport.

Maharashtra Tourism Development Corporation
(MTDC; Map p64; ☎ 22024482; www.maharashtratourism.gov.in; Express Towers, 9th fl, Nariman Point; ⏱ 9.45am-5.30pm Mon-Sat) Provides basic local advice.

DANGERS & ANNOYANCES

Crime is not a major problem for visitors to Mumbai, though petty theft and scams

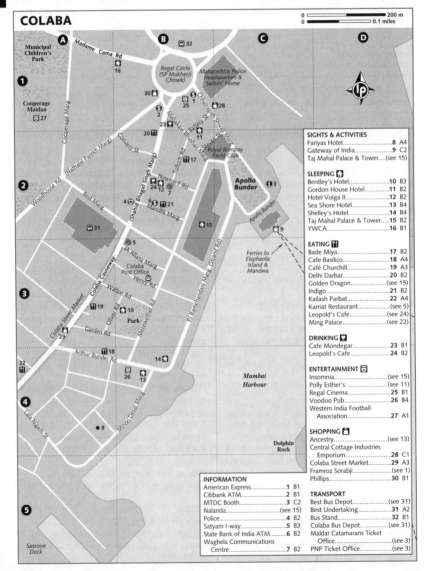

COLABA

0 ————————— 200 m
0 ————————— 0.1 miles

SIGHTS & ACTIVITIES
Fariyas Hotel.....................**8** A4
Gateway of India...............**9** C2
Taj Mahal Palace & Tower....(see 15)

SLEEPING 🛏
Bentley's Hotel..................**10** B3
Gordon House Hotel............**11** B2
Hotel Volga II....................**12** B2
Sea Shore Hotel.................**13** B4
Shelley's Hotel..................**14** B2
Taj Mahal Palace & Tower....**15** B2
YWCA.............................**16** B1

EATING 🍴
Bade Miya........................**17** B2
Cafe Basilico....................**18** A4
Café Churchill...................**19** A3
Delhi Darbar.....................**20** B2
Golden Dragon................(see 15)
Indigo............................**21** B2
Kailash Parbat..................**22** A4
Kamat Restaurant.............(see 5)
Leopold's Cafe.................(see 24)
Ming Palace...................(see 22)

DRINKING 🍷
Cafe Mondegar..................**23** B1
Leopold's Cafe..................**24** B2

ENTERTAINMENT 🎭
Insomnia..........................(see 15)
Polly Esther's...................(see 11)
Regal Cinema....................**25** B1
Voodoo Pub......................**26** B4
Western India Football
    Association....................**27** A1

SHOPPING 🛍
Ancestry..........................(see 13)
Central Cottage Industries
    Emporium......................**28** C1
Colaba Street Market...........**29** A3
Framroz Sorabji................(see 1)
Phillips...........................**30** B1

INFORMATION
American Express.................**1** B1
Citibank ATM......................**2** B1
MTDC Booth........................**3** C2
Nalanda..........................(see 15)
Police..............................**4** B2
Satyam I-way......................**5** B3
State Bank of India ATM........**6** B2
Waghela Communications
    Centre..........................**7** B2

TRANSPORT
Best Bus Depot..................(see 31)
Best Undertaking.................**31** A2
Bus Stand.........................**32** B1
Colaba Bus Depot..............(see 31)
Maldar Catamarans Ticket
    Office...........................(see 3)
PNP Ticket Office...............(see 3)

are reasonably common. Pickpockets can be a problem on public transport and at crowded tourist attractions. As in any big city, women should avoid walking around alone late at night. Avoid demonstrations and other potential flashpoints of violence.

For information about scams, see p215.

SIGHTS
Gateway of India

An exaggerated colonial marker conceived of after the visit of King George V in 1911, the **Gateway of India** (Map p66) was the point of arrival for thousands of British sahibs and memsahibs (gentlemen and gentlewomen). Facing out to Mumbai Harbour, the yellow basalt arch of triumph derives from the Muslim styles of 16th-century Gujarat. Officially opened in 1924, it was redundant just 24 years later when the last British regiment ceremoniously departed India through its archway, marking India's movement towards Independence. Try to visit in the late afternoon, when the light brings out the colours of the yellow basalt. Boats to Elephanta Island leave from nearby.

Taj Mahal Palace & Tower

Behind the Gateway is another famous landmark, the **Taj Mahal Palace & Tower** (Map p66), commonly referred to as the Taj Mahal Hotel. Even if you can't afford to stay here, it's worth popping inside for a peek at the sumptuous interior and magnificent central stairwell.

The Taj Mahal Palace & Tower stands with Singapore's Raffles as one of the classic colonial hotels, so you might be surprised to learn that this grand building was built as a challenge to foreign prejudice. The founder of the Taj was the Parsi industrialist JN Tata, who embarked on this grand endeavour after being refused entry to one of Mumbai's British-owned hotels, al legedly for being 'a native'. Tata had the last laugh – the Taj is still going strong after more than a century, while British hotels have faded into obscurity.

Elephanta Island

This **island** (admission Rs 250; ⏱ 9am-5.30pm Tue-Sun) is easily the most popular sight in Mumbai. Carved into the basalt bedrock of the island is a series of Hindu caves containing some of the finest temple carvings in India.

The main temple on Elephanta is a honeycomb of shrines, caverns, open courtyards and prayer halls, created by the Maurya civilisation in the 6th century. The centrepiece is a massive statue of **Mahesh-Murti** (Trimurti), depicting Shiva as the creator, preserver and destroyer of the universe. Many carvings around the cave temple were damaged by the Portuguese, but the statue of Shiva as **Nataraja**, dancing the divine dance that created the universe, is still impressive. Uphill from the main temple are three smaller caves with unfinished carvings.

By the entrance to the archaeological zone is a small **museum** containing sculptures rescued from around the island. Local guides offering their services in exchange for tips hang around here.

Ferries to the island leave from the Gateway of India between 9am and 2.30pm, the last returning at 5.30pm. Boats (economy/deluxe Rs 90/110) pool their profits, so there's no advantage in choosing one over the other. Take advantage of the deluxe boat, which includes a guided tour.

Chowpatty Beach

When India rebelled against British rule, this was where the crowds gathered to chant 'Jai Hind' (Victory to India). The **beach** (Map pp62–3) received a thorough makeover in the late 1990s and the new Chowpatty boasts a litter-free strip of golden sand, patrolled by lifeguards and lit by giant strip lights at night. The liveliest time to visit Chowpatty is during the annual **Ganesh Chaturthi festival** (p70), when clay effigies of the elephant-headed god are ritually immersed in the ocean, accompanied by water throwing, dancing and music. The 10th day sees millions descending on Chowpatty Beach to submerge the largest statues.

Visiting carnivalesque Chowpatty Beach at night, eating *bhelpuri* (a sweet and sour concoction of puffed rice with tomatoes, onions and chilli, eaten with chutney), and getting a vigorous head rub from a *malishwallah* (head masseur) is an essential part of any trip to Mumbai.

Victoria Terminus

Travel writer Jan Morris once described **Victoria Terminus** (Map p64) as 'the central building of the entire British Empire' – not

MUMBAI

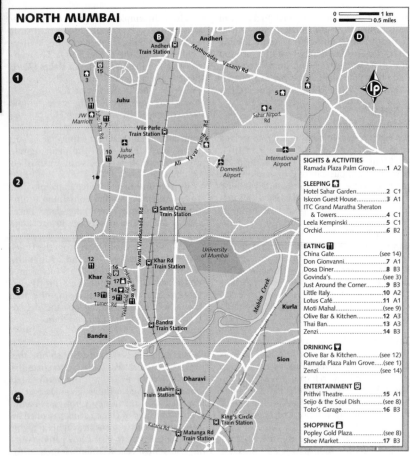

NORTH MUMBAI

SIGHTS & ACTIVITIES	
Ramada Plaza Palm Grove	**1** A2
SLEEPING	
Hotel Sahar Garden	**2** C1
Iskcon Guest House	**3** A1
ITC Grand Maratha Sheraton	
& Towers	**4** C1
Leela Kempinski	**5** C1
Orchid	**6** B2
EATING	
China Gate	(see 14)
Don Giovanni	**7** A1
Dosa Diner	**8** B3
Govinda's	(see 3)
Just Around the Corner	**9** B3
Little Italy	**10** A2
Lotus Café	**11** A1
Moti Mahal	(see 9)
Olive Bar & Kitchen	**12** A3
Thai Ban	**13** A3
Zenzi	**14** B3
DRINKING	
Olive Bar & Kitchen	(see 12)
Ramada Plaza Palm Grove	(see 1)
Zenzi	(see 14)
ENTERTAINMENT	
Prithvi Theatre	**15** A1
Seijo & the Soul Dish	(see 8)
Toto's Garage	**16** B3
SHOPPING	
Popley Gold Plaza	(see 8)
Shoe Market	**17** B3

bad for a municipal train station in the middle of Mumbai.

This glorious Victorian-gothic structure was created in 1887 by architect Frederick Stevens, a pioneer of the so-called 'hybrid' style, which fused mosque and temple architecture. Victoria Terminus is still Mumbai's largest and busiest train station, though many long-distance services now leave from Mumbai Central. After Independence, the station was renamed Chhatrapati Shivaji Terminus (CST) in honour of the Maratha hero, but most locals still refer to it as 'VT'.

Get up close and admire the detail: the exterior is covered with carvings, statues, turrets and domes. Try to visit at lunch, when hundreds of tiffin-wallahs arrive from the suburbs carrying packed lunches for Mumbai's office workers.

Mani Bhavan

Many of Mahatma Gandhi's core philosophies were conceived in a small room on the 2nd floor of this small but moving **museum** (Map pp62–3; ☎ 23805864; www.gandhi-manibhavan; 19 Laburnam Rd, Breach Candy; admission free; ☉ 9.30am-5.30pm), created in the building Gandhi stayed in during visits to Mumbai.

Inside is a diverse collection of objects relating to Gandhi, from photos and letters to the spartan room where he sat with his spinning wheel. On the lower level you'll see a letter Gandhi wrote to Hitler, calling for him to exercise restraint. Although some exhibits are crumbling, it's a profound and evocative place that shows why Gandhi's words still resonate today.

Haji Ali's Mosque

At the end of a causeway snaking into the Arabian Sea is a whitewashed mosque (Map pp62–3) containing the tomb of Muslim saint Haji Ali. According to one story, Haji Ali was a wealthy Mumbai businessman who renounced material possessions and devoted himself to meditation after a pilgrimage to Mecca. In another version, he is said to have died en route to Mecca, his body thrown overboard with a message requesting that it be buried wherever it washed ashore.

The mosque becomes an island at high tide, but is accessible at other times via the concrete causeway. If you get stuck, there's nothing to do but sit and wait.

Mahalaxmi Dhobi Ghat

If you've recently handed in any laundry, it may well be down there somewhere among the tubs, troughs and washing lines. The sight of some 5000 dhobi-wallahs (washermen and washerwomen) soaking, scouring and beating Mumbai's washing is one of the most memorable images you'll take home from this city.

The causeway next to Mahalaxmi station offers a panoramic view of the dhobi ghat (Map pp62–3); or follow the concrete steps down from the causeway for a closer look. Officially, visitors are discouraged from the compound, but enterprising launderers offer unofficial tours for around Rs 100. Photography is prohibited inside the compound, but you may be permitted to take a few shots if a launderer is showing you around.

Mumbai's original dhobi ghats were located on the site of Victoria Terminus, but the British preferred not to air their dirty laundry in public.

ACTIVITIES
Swimming

A few hotel pools accept nonguests for a fee of around Rs 500:

Fariyas Hotel (Map p66; ☎ 22042911; D Vyas Marg, Colaba)

Orchid (Map p68; ☎ 26164040; Nehru Rd, Domestic Airport, Andheri)

Ramada Plaza Palm Grove (Map p68; ☎ 26112323; Juhu-Tara Rd, Juhu)

Yoga
Dr Kataria's School of Laughter Yoga

(☎ 26316426; www.laughteryoga.com) Contact the school if you fancy joining one of 50 laughter clubs that meet at parks and beaches across Mumbai every morning.

Kaivalyadhama Khaivalyadham Ishwardas Yogic Health Centre (Map pp62-3; ☎ 22818417; www .kdham.com; 43 Netaji Subhash Rd, Chowpatty)

A renowned yoga institute that may accept experienced practitioners at some of its weekly classes – call for details.

WALKING TOUR

Mumbai's sprawling market quarter between Lokmanya Tilak and Grant Roads is crammed with stalls selling everything from sequins and saris to toothpaste and tin boxes. Start your walking tour at the **Crawford Market (1**; p78) and investigate the

---

WALK FACTS

Start Crawford Market
Finish Mutton Street Market
Distance 2.5km
Duration 3.5 hours

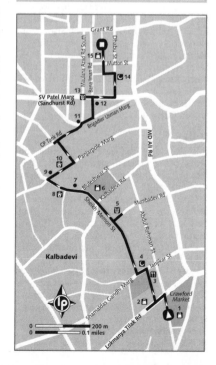

wonderful **steel-pot shops (2)** on Lokmanya Tilak Rd.

Next walk up Sheikh Memon St for a tasty thali at **Rajdhani (3**; p74), stopping for a peek at the eye-catching **Jumma Masjid (4)**, the most important religious site for Muslim Mumbaikers. This multidomed mosque was built in 1770 and is distinct for its many arches. On Fridays it is filled with and surrounded by devotees. Continue walking north along Sheikh Memon St to Mumbadevi Rd, ducking down the alley to atmospheric **Mumbadevi Mandir (5)**. Cross the next junction to Bhuleshwar St, passing by the ancient **Kalbadevi & Bhuleshwar Markets (6**; p78). Just north is a series of fragrant lanes packed with **flower vendors (7)** and a **kabutar khana (8**; Jain pigeon-feeding station). Visit the **religious market (9)** and **Jain Mandir (10)** on Panjarpole Marg, turn left onto Panjarpole First St, then right onto CP Tank Rd to reach **Yadnik Chowk (11)**, where plumbers and painters wait for customers on the roadside.

Walk east along Brigadier Usman Marg and turn left into Bara Iman Rd, passing a bustling **wet-and-dry market (12)**. Just west of the junction with SV Patel Marg (Sandhurst Rd) is a colourful **Shiv Mandir (13**; Shiva temple), which is allegedly protected by supernatural snakes. Next walk east along SV Patel Marg and turn left on Dhabu St to reach the stately **Raudat Tahera Mausoleum (14)**. Turn left at the next junction and then turn right to finish off at the **Mutton St Market (15)**. Hail a taxi on Grant Rd to take you home.

TOURS

Taxi drivers by the Gateway of India run tours of downtown sights for Rs 550, though they often include a visit to a pushy souvenir shop.

Go to the Elephanta cruise booking desks by the Gateway of India for information on group bus tours and tours to Mumbai theme parks.

Other recommended tour operators include the following:

Bombay Heritage Walks (☎ 26055756; heritage walks@hotmail.com) Hour-long walking tours of old Mumbai run by two female architects, on the third Sunday of every month (Rs 100). Tailored tours can be arranged for Rs 500.

Bombay Natural History Society (BNHS; Map p64; ☎ 22821811; www.bnhs.org; Hornbill House, Shahid Bhagat Singh Marg, Fort; Rs 10-20, plus membership for yr Rs 400; ☉ 10am-5.30pm Mon-Fri & 2nd & 4th Sat) Nature tours around Mumbai, including Sanjay Gandhi National Park. There are weekend tours for members. Dr Salim Ali (of Goan bird sanctuary fame) was the president of the BNHS.

H20 Water Sports Complex (Map pp62-3; ☎ 23677546; Chowpatty Seaface, Chowpatty; ☉ 10am-10pm, closed during monsoon) Short boat cruises around Back Bay (Rs 70). Groups of six or more can enjoy longer harbour cruises and night cruises (day/night Rs 150/250 per person).

India Tourism (Map p64; ☎ 22074333; 2nd fl, Western Railway Reservations Office, Maharshi Karve Rd, Churchgate; ☉ 8.30am-6pm Mon-Fri, 8.30am-2pm Sat) A half-/full-day tour for up to five people costs Rs 350/500.

MTDC (Map p64; ☎ 22026713; www.maharastratourism.gov.in; MTDC Booth, Gateway of India, Apollo Bunder, Colaba; upper/lower deck Rs 40/90; ☉ at 7pm & 8.15pm Sat & Sun) Hour-long open-topped bus tours of downtown Mumbai between October and June. Book in advance.

FESTIVALS & EVENTS

Almost every week of the year there's a festival happening somewhere in Mumbai.

Banganga Festival Classical music festival held over two days in January at the Banganga Tank (reservoir).

Elephanta Festival Classical music and dance on Elephanta Island in February.

Indian Derby India's most popular horse race since it started in 1942. Held in February

Kala Ghoda Festival Two weeks of arts performances and exhibitions in February.

Nariyal Poornima Celebration of the start of the fishing season after the monsoon. Held in August.

Ganesh Chaturthi Held in August/September, this is Mumbai's biggest annual festival: a 10-day celebration of the elephant-headed deity Ganesh (see p67).

Colaba Festival Arts festival in Colaba, held in October; merges with Diwali festivities, depending on the year.

Prithvi Theatre Festival Contemporary Indian theatre and performances by international troupes and artists in November.

Larzish Festival Daring celebration of queer film-making in November.

SLEEPING

At the top end of the market you can find real luxury, and Mumbai has no shortage of comfortable midrange accommodation, but the city is surprisingly bereft of cheap accommodation.

Budget hotels in Mumbai mostly have a bed in a box-room with a ceiling fan and a choice of shared or private bathrooms; few cost less than Rs 500 and many charge more than Rs 1000. Midrange hotels are usually a better bet with spacious rooms, air-con, cable TV, phones, room service and attached bathrooms with hot showers.

The range of top-end hotels is infinite. All have expected features like Internet connections, minibars, and top restaurants, but some are far-out special.

Advanced bookings are recommended, especially from September to March. There's a useful **hotel booking service** (☎ 56048772) at the airport's international terminal.

Budget

Hotel New Bengal (Map p64; ☎ 23401951; www .biryas.com; Sitaram Bldg, Dr Dadabhai Naoroji Rd, Fort; s/d/ tr with bathroom Rs 260/380/500, s/d deluxe Rs 1000/1150) Probably the best bargain in Mumbai, this neat Bengal-owned hotel has a Bengali restaurant on site. Choose a clean box-room without a bathroom, or a private room with a small bathroom. Beware of the 8am checkout time.

Hotel Lawrence (Map p64; ☎ 22843618; 33 Sai Baba Marg, Fort; s/d without bathroom Rs 400/500) This hotel is simple, clean and cheap as chapatis. Bathrooms are shared but all rooms have fans and windows. Eateries on K Dubash Marg are seconds away.

Sea Shore Hotel (Map p66; ☎ 22874237; Kamal Mansion, Arthur Bunder Rd, Colaba; s/d Rs 400/550) An enthusiastic team of Game Boy junkies run this clean hotel with good harbour views and the occasional sea breeze. Two rooms have air-con for an extra Rs 100.

Hotel Outram (Map p64; ☎ 22094937; Marzaban Rd; small s/d without bathroom Rs 460/520, r with bathroom & AC Rs 1200; 🔀) A plain but welcoming establishment in a quiet location between Victoria Terminus and the maidans. Rooms with a bathroom are passably clean but lack sunlight.

Midrange

Bentley's Hotel (Map p66; ☎ 22882890; www.bentleyshotel.com; 17 Oliver Rd, Colaba; smaller/larger r Rs 1028/ 1308, AC extra Rs 200; 🔀) A Colaba institution, spread over several apartment buildings. Rooms are spick-and-span with TVs and optional air-con. It's breezy and calm, and the staff are genuinely friendly.

YWCA (Map p66; ☎ 22826814; www.ywcaic.info; 18 Madame Cama Rd, Fort; dm Rs 625, s/d Rs 725/1360,

d/t with AC Rs 1590/2225) Perky staff, immaculate rooms, and free breakfast and newspaper in the morning make the YWCA one of the better choices in Fort. Men and women are welcome.

Welcome Hotel (Map p64; ☎ 56314488; welcome _hotel@vsnl.com; 2nd fl, 257 Shahid Bhagat Singh Marg, Fort; s with/without AC 980/676, d Rs 1320/936) Handy for Victoria Terminus and the GPO, the Welcome has pristine rooms with breakfast and snacks included in the rate. Book ahead.

Iskcon Guest House (Map p68; ☎ 26206860; guest .house.bombay@pamho.net; Hare Krishna Land, Juhu Church Rd; s with/without AC Rs 1432/1320, d Rs 2000/ 1600) This mock-Mughal guesthouse is over the top, but rooms have Gujarati furniture and massive balconies. There's also a top-notch veg restaurant.

Shelley's Hotel (Map p66; ☎ 22840229; www .shelleyshotel.com; 30 PJ Ramchandani Marg; r standard/ deluxe/deluxe sea view Rs 1442/1622/1935) Shelley's is a charming leftover from the British Raj. Rooms are unashamedly old fashioned, with tasteful hardwood furniture and miles of open floor space. Occupants of inland-facing rooms can enjoy communal balconies with sea views.

Hotel Volga II (Map p66; ☎ 22885341; 1st fl, Rustam Manzil, Nawroji F Rd; s without bathroom Rs 400, d with/ without bathroom Rs 900/600; 🔀) Just around the corner from the travellers' haunt Leopold's, the Volga II's tiny but clean rooms will do for a few nights. Its central location often means it's full. Doubles with a bathroom have air-con and TV.

Well-located while you wait for your train or plane:

Hotel City Palace (Map p64; ☎ 22615515; www .hotelcitypalace.net; 121 City Tce, Walchand Hirachand Marg; s/d without bathroom Rs 750/950, with AC & bathroom Rs 1175/1375; 🔀) Cramped but spotlessly clean rooms directly opposite VT.

Hotel Sahar Garden (Map p68; ☎ 28500409; sahargarden@indiainfo.com; MM Rd, Andheri; s/d 850/2000) Chintzy but cheerful rooms with TVs, black-marble bathtubs and easy airport access.

Top End

Taj Mahal Palace & Tower (Map p66); ☎ 56653366; tmhresv.bom@tajhotels.com; Apollo Bunder, Colaba; tower r US$300-370, palace r US$420-580) Mumbai's finest Raj hotel since 1903 is comprised of an old building, a magnificent fantasy of arches, domes and towers, and the modernist Taj

Tower, which looms high above Mumbai Harbour. Service runs to free afternoon cocktails and a complimentary bottle of wine in your room.

ITC Grand Maratha Sheraton (Map p68; ☎ 28303030; itcgrandmaratha.sales@welcomgroup.com; Sahar Airport Rd, Sahar; d US$250-375) The ultimate in luxury, the ITC boasts the best spa, the best restaurants and the best interior designer in Mumbai. Rooms feature wi-fi, subtle lighting and sumptuous fabrics.

Leela Kempinski (Map p68; ☎ 56911234; www .theleela.com; Sahar Airport Rd, Sahar; d US$175-385) The Leela was always the grandest hotel in Mumbai, and recent refurbishments have only lifted it higher. Traditional musicians play in a Mughal pavilion in the foyer and rooms contain every imaginable luxury, including plasma-screen TVs.

Orchid (Map p68; ☎ 26164040; www.orchidhotel .com; Nehru Rd, Domestic Airport, Vile Parle; d US$270-435; 🖃) Built according to ecological principles, Orchid is surrounded by lush gardens, and is close to the domestic airport. This modern and understated place also has a rooftop pool and restaurant.

Ambassador (Map p64; ☎ 22041131; www.ambas sadorindia.com; Veer Nariman Rd, Churchgate; s/d Rs 7000/7800, ste Rs 25,000) A Mumbai icon and home to Mumbai's only revolving restaurant. The glittering interior of the Ambassador could have been designed by an Indian Versace.

Gordon House Hotel (Map p66; ☎ 22871122; www .ghhotel.com; 5 Battery St, Colaba; s/d Rs 5500/6000) The most boutique of Mumbai's boutique hotels, Gordon House offers three floors of stylish rooms with Scandinavian, Mediterranean and 'country cottage' themes. Rooms are memorable and facilities, including Polly Esther's nightclub (p76), and the fresh and creative All Stir Fry Chinese restaurant, are excellent.

EATING & DRINKING

An incredible variety of restaurants, cafés and snack stands line the streets of Mumbai. Street vendors at Chowpatty, Juhu and Nariman Point close the gap between rich and poor by serving cheap, cheerful snacks to office workers and rickshaw-wallahs alike. At the other end of the scale are ostentatious luxury restaurants, where a meal can cost as much as many Mumbaikers earn in a month. In between are hundreds of relaxed cafés and

family restaurants. At certain hours, restaurants double as drinking holes.

The most popular eats in Mumbai are North Indian kebabs and curries, Mangalorean seafood and Chinese rice and noodles. You'll also find Parsi food and indigenous dishes from the Koli people. Many places serve interpretations of Western cuisine, which vary from unconvincing to sublime. Vegetarians are widely catered for.

The following reviews are divided into area and categorised as budget (mains for under Rs 150), midrange (between Rs 150 and 300) and top end (more than Rs 300). For more information on Mumbai restaurants, pick up the *Times Food Guide* from any bookshop.

Colaba

Colaba is the most popular place to stay and eat, with dozens of options. Try some of the cheaper *dhabas* (snack restaurants) – many serve excellent and hygienic food!

BUDGET

Leopold's Cafe (Map p66; ☎ 22020131; Colaba Causeway; ⊙ 8am-midnight) Almost every traveller to Colaba visits the fan-cooled dining room at Leopold's for a quick meal or chilled Kingfisher. The laid-back ambience is conducive to striking up conversations with strangers, and the menu features memorable Indian and Chinese dishes.

Cafe Mondegar (Map p66; ☎ 22020591; 5A Colaba Causeway; ⊙ 8am-12.30am) Café by day, bar by night, Mondy's is popular with international visitors. The interior has 1950s charm and a cartoon mural by Goan cartoonist Mario Miranda. The menu is classic foreigner fare: breakfasts are hearty and there are chips aplenty. Good as the continental dishes and fresh juice concoctions are, however, it's the beer which is the highlight.

Bade Miya (Map p66; ☎ 22848038; Tulloch Rd; ⊙ 7-11pm) Every evening tables are set up along a narrow road near the Taj Mahal Palace & Tower and dozens of diners materialise from nowhere to feast on *seekh* kebabs and tandoori chicken.

The following are also noteworthy:
Kailash Parbat (Map p66; ☎ 22046079; 1st Pasta Lane; ⊙ 8am-11pm) Childhood haunt for many Mumbaikers. Pure veg dishes from Sind are the highlight.
Kamat Restaurant (Map p66; ☎ 22874734; Colaba Causeway; ⊙ 8.30am-10.30pm) Simple veg *dhaba*.

MIDRANGE

Ming Palace (Map p66; ☎ 22872820; 73 Apsara Bldg, Colaba Causeway; ☼ 11am-3.30pm & 7-11pm) A solid Chinese restaurant with a gregarious doorman. Serves huge portions of Korean, Chinese and Japanese food under a glittering golden roof.

Café Basilico (Map p66; ☎ 56345670; www.cafe basilico.com; Sentinel House, Arthur Bunder Rd; ☼ 7.30am-1.30am) Fork-twizzlingly good pasta, gourmet sandwiches and home-baked bread in a smart wooden dining room.

Also recommended:

Cafe Churchill (Map p66; ☎ 22844689; Colaba Causeway; ☼ 11am-midnight) European-inspired dishes. Opposite Cusrow Baug.

Delhi Darbar (Map p66; ☎ 22020235; Holland House, Colaba Causeway; ☼ 11.30am-midnight) Meaty Mughlai meals.

TOP END

Golden Dragon (Map p66; ☎ 56653366; Taj Mahal Palace & Tower, Apollo Bunder; ☼ noon-2.45pm & 7-11.45pm) This ostentatious Chinese restaurant at the Taj is all dark wood and ornamental screens. Dishes run the gamut from sweet-and-sour pomfret to beggars' chicken – a whole chicken cooked inside lotus leaves (24 hours' notice required).

Indigo (Map p66; ☎ 56368980; 4 Mandlik Marg; ☼ noon-3pm & 7.30pm-midnight) Mumbai's best European restaurant, Indigo serves intoxicatingly good food backed by a global wine list in stylish surroundings. Bill Clinton ate here and loved it.

Thai Pavilion (Map pp62-3; ☎ 56650808; Taj President Hotel, 90 Cuffe Pde; ☼ 12.30-2.45pm & 7-11.45pm) For fine Royal Thai food, head to this gem of a restaurant at the Taj President Hotel. The dining room resembles a Thai royal palace, and dishes are decorated with carved flower garnishes.

Fort Area & Churchgate

Fort is busy by day, but empty by night – the busiest areas after hours are Kala Ghoda and around Victoria Terminus.

In Churchgate, the centre of the action is Veer Nariman Rd, so much so that you might need to wait for a table.

BUDGET

Pratap Lunch Home (Map p64; ☎ 22871101; MB House, Janmabhoomi Marg; ☼ 11.30am-4pm & 5.30-11.45pm) Pratap Lunch Home has a similar seafood menu to the posher 'lunch homes' in the area, but at half the price.

Howrah (Map p64; ☎ 23401976; Sitaram Bldg, Dr Dadabhai Naoroji Rd; ☼ 11.45am-3.45pm & 7pm-midnight) Chicken, mutton and seafood in Bengali sauces under a scale model of Kolkata's Howrah Bridge. From the Victoria Terminus, head north along Dr Dadabhai Naoroji Rd for a couple of hundred metres and you'll find it at Hotel New Bengal, on the right-hand side of the road.

Tea Centre (Map p64; ☎ 22819142; Resham Bhawan, 78 Veer Nariman Rd; ☼ 8am-11pm) A real culinary character, where waiters in turbans serve tea in silver pots. This lovely spot, run by the Indian Tea Board, is a perfectly civilised place for afternoon tea.

For a fuss-free feed:

Pizzeria (Map p64; ☎ 22856115; 143 Marine Dr; ☼ noon-12.30am) Pizza served pronto. Overlooking the sea.

Café Coffee Day (Map p64; ☎ 39515909; Capital Cinema Bldg, Marzaban Rd; ☼ 8am-midnight) There are branches all over town including at Chowpatty Beach.

Mocha Bar (Map p64; ☎ 56336070; Veer Nariman Rd; ☼ 9am-1.30pm) For caffeinated concoctions and a puff on a hookah.

MIDRANGE

Mahesh Lunch Home (Map p64; ☎ 22870938; www.maheshlunchhome.com; 8B Cawasji Patel St; ☼ noon-4pm & 6pm-midnight) A perennial favourite of Mumbai seafood buffs, Mahesh serves top-notch Mangalorean coastal cuisine. The house speciality is *gassi*, a rich seafood curry with coconut and tamarind.

Indian Summer (Map p64; ☎ 22835445; www.indiansummerindia.com; 80 Veer Nariman Rd; ☼ noon-3.30pm & 7pm-midnight) Indian Summer, with its smartly dressed waiters, is a relaxing place to enjoy veg and nonveg cuisine. The lunchtime buffet (Rs 270) is worth every paisa.

Other good Indian options:

Bharat Lunch Home (Map p64; ☎ 22618991; 317 Bharat House, Shahid Bhagat Singh Marg; ☼ 11.30am-4pm & 5.30pm-midnight) Mainly Mangalorean, with refreshingly cheap Bombay duck.

Sher-E-Punjab (Map p64; ☎ 22621188; 264 Shahid Bhagat Singh Marg; ☼ noon-11.30pm) Punjabi specialities.

Apoorva (Map p64; ☎ 22870335; SA Brelvi Rd; ☼ 11.30am-4pm & 6pm-midnight) Classy seafood.

Samrat (Map p64; ☎ 22820022; Prem Court, J Tata Rd; ☼ noon-10.30pm) Smart vegetarian.

TOP END

Khyber (Map p64; ☎ 22673227; 145 MG Rd; ⌚ 12.30-3.30pm & 7.30-11.30pm) One of the finest places to dine in the whole of Mumbai, Khyber is styled like an Afghan palace. This atmospheric eatery is a maze of winding stairs, arched doorways and perforated marble screens. The exciting menu covers a fabulous range of Mughlai and North-West Frontier Province cuisine. Reservations are essential.

Joss (Map p64; ☎ 56356908; 30 K Dubash Marg; ⌚ 12.30-3.30pm & 7.30-11.30pm) At Joss you can eat spicy beef with chillies and garlic in a room decorated like a gilded Thai temple. The Chinese, Thai and Southeast Asian menu is rewarding.

Trishna (Map p64; ☎ 22614991; 4 Sai Baba Marg; ⌚ noon-3.30pm & 6.30pm-midnight) This commendable seafood restaurant keeps getting better. Try the Hyderabadi pomfret and *koliwala* (fisherman's style) prawns.

Pearl of the Orient (Map p64; ☎ 22041131; Ambassador Hotel, Veer Nariman Rd; ⌚ 1.30-3.30pm & 7.30-11.30pm) Take a spin at the revolving restaurant atop the Ambassador Hotel (and spin out when the bill mounts up on luxury taxes).

Royal China (Map p64; ☎ 56355310; Hazarimal Somani Marg; ⌚ noon-3.15pm & 7-11.15pm) Shine your shoes, don your best outfit and enjoy lunch-time dim sum, or a dinner of duck with plum sauce, surrounded by flickering candles.

Gaylord (Map p64; ☎ 22871101; Mayfair Bldg, Veer Nariman Rd; ⌚ 11.30am 4pm & 5.30-11.45pm) Wrought iron, potted palms and waiters in cummerbunds add a touch of the Raj to this 1950s Mumbai institution. The Indian and continental food is consistently reliable.

Chowpatty Beach & Around

As well as Chowpatty's famous *bhelpuri* stands, there are several excellent cafés and restaurants close to the beach.

BUDGET

By the Way (Map pp62-3; ☎ 23803532; Pandita Ramabhai Rd; ⌚ 11am-11pm) Run by Seva Sadan, a charitable organisation that cares for disadvantaged women, this budget canteen-style café serves fast food, including Western and Parsi dishes, and big slices of apple pie.

Cafe Ideal (Map pp62-3; ☎ 23630943; Chowpatty Seaface; ⌚ 10am-10pm) North Indian staples and cold beers by the beach. The food isn't as splendid as the sea breeze is.

New Kulfi Centre (Map pp62-3; Chowpatty Sea face; ⌚ 10am-10pm) A tiny ice creamery serving up freshly churned *kulfi* (Indian rice-cream flavoured with cardamom).

Rajdhani (Map pp62-3; ☎ 23449014; Sheikh Memon St; ⌚ noon-4pm & 7-10.30pm) Tiny thali restaurant in an alley north of Crawford Market.

MIDRANGE

There are some good midrange to top-end options.

Cream Centre (Map pp62-3; ☎ 23679222; www .creamcentre.com; 25B Chowpatty Seaface; ⌚ noon-midnight) Queue at this imminently popular place, where you can feast on everything from nachos to Russian salad.

Revival (Map pp62-3; ☎ 23637834; Chowpatty Sea-face; ⌚ noon-3.30pm & 7-11.30pm) This upmarket vegetarian restaurant has a swish dining room, and generous Sunday lunch buffet (Rs 325).

North Mumbai

Culinary activity and nightlife is spreading north to Bandra and Juhu. Bandra is notoriously faddish; the restaurants that have been recommended here are well established, but ask locally if any must-visit restaurants have opened up. In Juhu, don't forget to head to the beach for *bhelpuri*.

BUDGET

Dosa Diner (Map p68; ☎ 26404488; cnr Turner & Waterfield Rds; ⌚ 11.30am-11.30pm) For quality cheap eats head here, where there are tasty dosas (paper-thin lentil-flour pancakes) and a special kids menu.

Just Around the Corner (Map p68; ☎ 26006717; cnr 24th & 30th Rds; ⌚ 8am-12.45am) Quality pizzas, burgers, pasta and salads, plus Indian or Chinese concoctions scooped into foot-long subs.

MIDRANGE

China Gate (Map p68; ☎ 26432570; 155 Waterfield Rd; ⌚ noon-4pm & 7pm-12.30am) A swish Chinese restaurant with tiled pagoda roof. Reservations on weekends are essential.

Thai Ban (Map p68; ☎ 26458176; Gaspar Enclave, Dr Ambedkar Rd; ⌚ noon-4.30pm & 7-11.45pm) Tasty Thai curries, salads and stir fries more than compensate for the plain interior of this friendly restaurant.

Moti Mahal (Map p68; ☎ 26408577; cnr Turner & Waterfield Rds; ♥ noon-4pm & 7-11pm) Moti Mahal dishes up Mughlai delights in tidy surrounds. Starched white tablecloths and suited waiters put this place above the competition. There's an interesting array of tandoori kebabs on offer.

Govinda's (Map p68; ☎ 26200337; Hare Krishna Land, Juhu Church Rd; ♥ 12.30-3.30pm & 7.30-10.30pm) A midrange Indian establishment serving vegetarian lunch and dinner buffets accompanied by fresh juices, buttermilk and *jal jeera* (lemon water flavoured with cumin).

TOP END

Lotus Café (Map p68; ☎ 56933277; JW Marriott, Juhu-Tara Rd; ♥ 6.30am-12.30am) Set in the huge, airy foyer of the top-end Marriott hotel, Lotus Café offers one of the best buffets in Mumbai. Come for breakfast, lunch or dinner.

Don Giovanni (Map p68; ☎ 26153125; www.don giovanniristorante.com; Hotel Bawa Continental, Juhu-Tara Rd; ♥ 12.30-2.40pm & 7.30-11.40pm) Homemade pastas and hearty village stews by an Italian immigrant family.

Little Italy (Map p68; ☎ 56923266; www.littleitaly -india.com; 18B Juhu-Tara Rd; ♥ noon-3pm & 7-11.30pm) Vegetarian pastas and pizzas made with imported Italian cheeses. Slightly more expensive than Don Giovanni.

To see and be seen with the It girls and in boys of Mumbai:

Olive Bar & Kitchen (Map p68; ☎ 26058228; Pali Hill Tourist Hotel, 14 Union Park; ♥ 12.30-6pm & 7.30pm-2am) Mediterranean dishes drizzled with olive oil. Dress to impress.

Zenzi (Map p68; ☎ 56430670; www.zenzi-india.com; 183 Waterfield Rd; ♥ noon-1.30am) Gourmet French and Indochinese food for trendy yuppies.

ENTERTAINMENT

Mumbai has a laid-back attitude to alcohol. Officially, alcohol can only be served to over 21s, but foreigners are rarely asked for ID. City regulations prohibit the sale of alcohol after 1.30am, but many bars and clubs push on till 3am at weekends. A large beer costs anything from Rs 80 to 120, though more in glamorous venues. Set aside at least Rs 1000 for nightclub and lounge-bar entry fees.

Colaba has noisy cafés, smart nightclubs and sophisticated lounge bars that attract a mixed local and foreign crowd. The action in Churchgate is at Veer Nariman Rd and there are several drinking holes hidden away in Fort. Recently, attention has shifted to the edgy venues of Bandra and Juhu.

Nightlife in Mumbai is frenetic; new places open in a trice and go under just as quickly. For the latest listings and entertainment news, pick up *Mid-Day*, the *Times of India* or the Mumbai edition of *Time Out*. The *Times Nightlife & Leisure Guide* sold with the *Times Food Guide* is another good source of information.

Bars & Pubs

Leopold's Cafe (Map p66; ☎ 22020131; Colaba Causeway, Colaba; admission free; ♥ 8am-midnight) Leopold's (of *Shantaram* fame) is the most popular drinking hole in Colaba. Beer and local wines are served in a nostalgic fan-cooled dining room.

Cafe Mondegar (Map p66; ☎ 22020591; 5A Colaba Causeway, Colaba; admission free; ♥ 8am-12.30am) Chilled beer served to chilled locals and foreigners every evening. There's a tiny air-conditioned room out the back for a more chilled-out (ahem) drinking experience.

Olive Bar & Kitchen (Map p68; ☎ 26058228; Pali Hill Tourist Hotel, 14 Union Park, Bandra; admission free; ♥ 12.30-6pm & 7.30pm-2am) Mediterranean restaurant by day, bustling terrace bar by night, this is where Mumbai's elite go to rub noses with the bright lights of Bollywood. Scruffy drinkers won't make it past the style police.

Zenzi (Map p68; ☎ 56430670; 183 Waterfield Rd, Bandra; admission free; ♥ noon-1.30am) Futuristic orange-and-grey décor and a 'sit back and chill' attitude have made Zenzi one of Bandra's favourite bars. Park by the indoor lounge bar or on an easy chair on the terrace.

Other interesting choices:

Lush Lounge & Grille (☎ 56634601; Phoenix Mills Shopping Centre, 462 Senapati Bhapat Marg, Lower Parel; admission Sun-Thu Rs 800, Fri & Sat Rs 1000; ♥ 7pm-1.30am) New York–style lounge bar full of steel surfaces and air-kissing socialites. From the Mahalaxmi Race Course, head northeast, parallel to the train track. After a kilometre or so you'll find it at the other end of the queue.

Provogue Lounge (☎ 24972525; High Street Phoenix, 462 Senapati Bhapat Marg, Lower Parel; admission before/ after 11pm Rs 500/1000; ♥ 10.30pm-1.30am Mon-Sat) This designer clothing store packs away the clothes and pulls out the cocktails after hours. A kilometre out of town beyond Mahalaxmi Racecourse; in the heart of the trendy Phoenix area.

Seijo & the Soul Dish (Map p68; ☎ 26405555; 2nd fl, 206 Krystal, Waterfield Rd, Bandra; admission Fri/Sat

---

GAY MUMBAI

Although Mumbai has the busiest gay scene in India, don't expect Soho or Chelsea on Chowpatty Beach. Sex between men is still illegal in India and the only openly gay night in Mumbai is Saturday night at Voodoo Pub (below) in Colaba. However, **Gay Bombay** (www.gaybombay.org) organises occasional low-key events around town. Be warned that AIDS rates are soaring – around one in five gay men in Mumbai now carry the virus.

Rs 200/500; ⊙ 7pm-1.30am) Futuristic Japanese-style bar with Manga cartoons on the walls.

Toto's Garage (Map p68; ☎ 26005494; 30th Rd, Bandra; admission free; ⊙ 6pm-12.30am) Former auto-repair shop decorated with tools and engine parts. There's a VW above the bar.

Voodoo Pub (Map p66; ☎ 22841959; Kamal Mansion, Arthur Bunder Rd, Colaba; admission Rs 250; ⊙ 8.30pm-1.30am) Hosts the only gay night in Mumbai on Saturdays.

Nightclubs

Most of Mumbai's nightclubs are inside luxury hotels so smart dress is a prerequisite for a big night out. Couples are preferred, but most clubs admit well-behaved stags and she-stags.

Enigma (Map p68; ☎ 56933000; JW Marriott, Juhu-Tara Rd, Juhu; couple Rs 1000; ⊙ 9pm-3am Wed-Sun) Dominated by a sparkling crystal chandelier, the JW Marriott's nightclub shakes to house and Hindi pop.

Insomnia (Map p66; ☎ 56653366; Taj Mahal Palace & Tower, Apollo Bunder, Colaba; admission Mon-Fri Rs 600, Sat & Sun Rs 1000; ⊙ 9.30pm-1.30am Tue-Sun) Deeply cool and knows it, this glitzy nightclub at the Taj Mahal Palace & Tower attracts the cream of the cream. Taj guests are spared the hefty cover charge.

Polly Esther's (Map p66; ☎ 22871122; Gordon House Hotel, 5 Battery St, Colaba; admission Rs 600-900; ⊙ 9pm-1.30am Tue-Sat) Cocktail umbrellas, lava lamps and waiters in Afro wigs – Polly Esther's proudly embraces the 1970s, and Mumbai loves her for it. Stags are admitted on Thursday.

Red Light (Map p64; ☎ 56346249; cnr K Dubash Marg & MG Rd, Fort; couple/male/female Mon-Sat Rs 800/800/400, Sun Rs 600/600/300; ⊙ 7pm-1.30am) A single red traffic light out the front, and dance, trance and hip-hop inside.

Cinemas

Mumbai has dozens of cinemas. The following screen Hollywood blockbusters as well as the latest Bollywood offerings.

Eros Cinema (Map p64; ☎ 22822335; cnr J Tata & Maharshi Karve Rds, Churchgate; tickets Rs 40-80) Art Deco cinema with a glorious façade.

Inox Cinema (Map p64; ☎ 56595959; 2nd fl, CR-2 Centre, Barrister Rajni Patel Marg, Nariman Point; tickets Rs 180-200) Mumbai's flashest cinema.

Regal Cinema (Map p66; ☎ 22021017; SP Mukherji Chowk/Regal Circle, Colaba; tickets Rs 40-150) Classic Art Deco cinema.

Sterling Cinema (Map p64; ☎ 22075187; Marzaban Rd, Fort; tickets Rs 40-125) Smart air-conditioned cinema near Victoria Terminus.

Performing Arts

You can find listings of theatrical performances, concerts and dance in the free pamphlet *This Fortnight* in Mumbai, available from the India Tourism office near Churchgate station. Contact the following organisations for information about their current programmes.

Bharatiya Vidya Bhavan (Map pp62-3; ☎ 236 31261; KM Munshi Marg, Chowpatty) A philanthropic organisation striving to preserve traditional Indian arts. Hosts lectures on Indian culture and philosophy.

National Centre for the Performing Arts (NCPA; Map pp62-3; ☎ 22833737 iwwsw.ncpamumbai.com; cnr Marine Dr & Shri V Saha Rd, Nariman Point; tickets Rs 100-320) Government-sponsored organisation with a fast-changing schedule of theatre, music and performing arts. Performances are at 6.30pm or 7pm.

Nehru Centre (☎ 24964680; Nehru Centre Auditorium, Dr Annie Besant Rd, Worli) Mostly free dance, theatre and music performances. Follow Lala Lajpatrai Marg Rd north along the coast.

LIVE IN MUMBAI

Live music is fairly thin on the ground in Mumbai, but local bands strut their stuff at **Not Just Jazz by the Bay** (Map p64; ☎ 22851876; Veer Nariman Rd; Wed-Thu Rs 150, Fri-Sun Rs 200; ⊙ 6pm-2am) in Churchgate. From Wednesday to Saturday, live bands play everything from Bollywood pop to Western rock, and you can sing along to your favourite *masti* (fun) hits on the karaoke machine from Sunday to Tuesday.

BOLLYWOOD OR BUST

The Bollywood movie industry, based in the suburbs of north Mumbai, is the largest in the world, producing a staggering 1000 movies a year. Bollywood stars – such as Amitabh Bachchan, Shah Rukh Khan and Aishwarya Rai – are adored by one-sixth of the world's population. Their faces are used to promote everything from Coke to politics – some temples even sell medallions with gods on one side and Bollywood stars on the other.

Until recently, behind-the-scenes Bollywood was off limits to mere mortals, but salvation has come in the form of **Bollywood Tourism** (☎ 5666 2777; www.bollywoodtourism.com), a private Bollywood tour run by senior figures from the movie industry. The day-long tour (adult/child US$100/US$75) starts with an visit to a purpose-built set (where visitors learn about acting, stunts, dance routines, directing and editing), followed by a visit to a working Bollywood studio.

Alternatively, you can pay Rs 50 to watch the Bollywood magic on the nearest big screen.

Take the inward bound fork at Patel Stadium; the Nehru Centre is about 100m down.

Prithvi Theatre (Map p68; ☎ 26149546; www .prithvitheatre.org; Janvi Kutir, Juhu Church Rd, Juhu; tickets Rs 50-100, Sun Rs 150; ☺ shows 6pm & 9pm most evenings) Leading performance space for Hindi and Marathi theatre in Mumbai.

Sport

As elsewhere on the subcontinent, Mumbaikers are sports fanatics. Contact the **Mumbai Cricket Association** (Map p64; ☎ 22819910; Wankhede Stadium, D Rd, Churchgate; local matches free, interstate matches Rs 20, test matches Rs 50-10,000; ☺ 10am-5.30pm) to try to obtain tickets. You can also do some punting at the **Royal Western India Turf Club** (Map pp62-3; ☎ 23071401; www .rwitc.com; Mahalaxmi Race Course, Keshavrao Khadye Marg, Mahalaxmi; admission Rs 20-150; ☺ 2-5pm race days) or catch a game of amateur football through the **Western India Football Association** (Map p66; ☎ 22024020; Cooperage Football Ground, Maharshi Karve Rd, Colaba; admission free; ☺ 4-6pm).

SHOPPING

In addition to government emporiums selling village-made souvenirs, this shopping mecca has manic markets, air-conditioned malls and designer-label boutique stores that rival those in Paris and Milan.

Colaba Causeway is lined with stalls selling clothing. Electronics, pirated CDs and DVDs and leather goods can be found on Dr Dadabhai Naoroji Rd between Victoria Terminus and Flora Fountain, and MG Rd from Flora Fountain to Kala Ghoda.

Antiques

Mumbai's antique shops are concentrated around the Taj Mahal Palace & Tower.

Prices can be high and much of the stock is about as old as an iPod.

Ancestry (Map p66; ☎ 22831358; Kamal Mansion, Arthur Bunder Rd, Colaba; ☺ 10am-7pm Mon-Sat) It's hard to trace the genealogy of the miscellaneous ceramics and glassware of Ancestry.

Framroz Sorabji (Map p66; ☎ 22021638; Shivaji Marg, Colaba; ☺ 11am-6pm Mon-Sat) Rummage through bits and bobs from Victorian jewellery to old Mughal coins.

Natesan's (Map p64; ☎ 22852700; www.natesans antiqarts.com; Jehangir Art Gallery, MG Rd, Fort; ☺ 10.30am-6.30pm) There is rare furniture, brassware and religious art to be perused at Natesan's, in the basement of Jehangir Art Gallery.

Phillips (Map p66; ☎ 22020564; www.phillipsan tiques.com; SP Mukherji Chowk, Colaba; ☺ 10am-7pm Mon-Sat) Wooden carvings, Victoriana, brassware and genuine antiques in the heart of this heritage precinct.

Trafford House (Map p64; ☎ 22090129; 6 Prescott Rd, Fort; ☺ 10.30am-7.30pm) Antiques, as well as modern furnishings made from antique materials can be found here.

Emporiums

There are some fantastic government-run and private emporiums selling classic Indian souvenirs and handicrafts.

Bombay Store (Map p64; ☎ 22885048; www .thebombaystore.com; Western India House, Sir P Mehta Rd, Fort; ☺ 10.30am-7.30pm Mon-Sat, 10.30am-6.30pm Sun) Indulge in Indian arts and handicrafts, ranging from incense and sandalwood to table lamps and T-shirts.

Central Cottage Industries Emporium (CCIE; Map p66; ☎ 22027537; www.cottageemporiumindia.com; 34 Shivaji Marg, Colaba; ☺ 10am-7pm) Established by the government in 1948 to increase the

MUMBAI

profile of Indian crafts. Sells Indian ornaments for fair prices.

Khadi & Village Industries Emporium (Map
p64; ☎ 22073280; 286 Dr Dadabhai Naoroji Rd, Fort;
⊙ 10.30am-6.30pm) Charitable emporium
inspired by the teachings of Ghandi. Sells
handmade fabrics, knick-knacks and crafts
produced by rural communities.

Jewellery
Expect no subtlety from classical Indian
jewellery. Mughal-inspired creations dripping with gemstones are breathtaking but a
tad over the top for everyday wear. Indian
pearls are particularly good value at state-
government emporiums.

Popley Gold Plaza (Map p68; ☎ 26511349; 118A
Turner Rd, Bandra; ⊙ 10.30am-8.30pm) An Aladdin's
cave of glittering gems.

Tanishq (Map p64; ☎ 22821621; 7 Brabourne Stadium, Veer Nariman Rd, Churchgate; ⊙ 11am-8pm) Distinguished designer jewellery.

Tribovandas Bhimji Zaveri (Map pp62-3;
☎ 23425001; www.tbztheoriginal.com; 241/3 Sheikh
Memon Rd, Kalbadevi; ⊙ 11am-7.30pm Mon-Sat) Three
floors of gold.

Vijay (Map pp62-3; ☎ 23639050; www.vijay-jewel
lers.com; 67 Hughes Rd, Chowpatty; ⊙ 11.15am-7.30pm
Mon-Sat) Specialises in heavy gold Mughal-
style necklaces.

Markets
Have a poke in these interesting markets:

Colaba Street Market (Map p66; Colaba Causeway, Colaba) Mock antiques, T-shirts, knick-
knacks and silk scarves.

Crawford Market (Map pp62-3; Dr Dadabhai Naoroji
Rd, Fort) Household products, luggage, dried
fruit and bulk mangoes.

Fashion Street (Map p64; MG Rd, Fort) Dis-
counted casual clothing, work shirts and
baseball caps.

Fort Street Market (Map p64; Dr Dadabhai Naoroji
Rd, Fort) Electronics, pirated DVDs, software
and (curiously) marital aids.

Kalbadevi & Bhuleshwar Markets (Map pp62-3;
Lokmanya Tilak Rd to SV Patel Marg, Kalbadevi & Bhuleshwar)
Everything from flowers to temple statues.

Mangaldas Market (Map pp62-3; Sheikh Memon St,
Kalbadevi) Kitchenware, bulk fabric and cheap
saris.

Mutton Street Market (Map pp62-3; Mutton St, Nag-
para) Rare antiques, among the junk.

Shoe Market (Map p68; Linking Rd, Bandra) Shoes
of every shape and hue.

Music
Indian pop and Bollywood soundtracks are
the choice of most local shoppers, but you
can also find Indian classical music and instruments at the following stores.

LM Furtado & Co (Map pp62-3; ☎ 22013163;
www.furtadosmusic.com; 540/4 Kalbadevi Rd, Kalbadevi;
⊙ 10am-8pm Mon-Sat) Fiddles, guitars, drums
and sitars are all on sale here.

Planet M (Map p64; ☎ 56353874; Times of India
Bldg, Dr Dadabhai Naoroji Rd, Fort; ⊙ 11am-9pm Mon-
Sat, noon-8pm Sun) Come here for movie sound-
tracks, Bollywood DVDs and Western pop.
You can listen before you buy.

Rhythm House (Map p64; ☎ 22842835; www
.rhythmhouseindia.com; 40 K Dubash Marg, Fort; ⊙ 10am-
8.30pm Mon-Sat, 11am-8.30pm Sun) This place features modern and classical Indian music.

Tailors
Mumbai has dozens of tailors who can knock
up a suit or gown for a fraction of the price
you would pay in Europe or the USA.

Naina's (Map pp62-3; ☎ 23613613; www.nain
ashah.com; Khatau Mansion, 95 Bhulabhai Desai Marg,
Breach Candy; ⊙ 10am-8pm Mon-Sat) This couture
fashion house of designer Naina Shah sells
off-the-rack designer gear and made-to-
measure items.

Reid & Taylor (Map p64; ☎ 22042630; 55A
Veer Nariman Rd, Fort; ⊙ 10.30am-7.30pm Mon-Sat)
Reid & Taylor can turn out magnificent
three-piece suits in 24 hours. Prices range
from Rs 7000 for lightweight cotton to Rs
20,000 for the best-quality woollen worsted.

Telon (Map pp62-3; ☎ 22042630; 55A Veer Nariman
Rd, Fort; ⊙ 10.30am-7.30pm Mon-Sat) Head to
Telon for Bollywood-meets-Versace designs
for men.

GETTING THERE & AWAY
Mumbai is a major hub for domestic and
international flights and plenty of cheap
deals are available. Trains and buses connect Mumbai to towns across India. There
are numerous private operators and state
government–run long-distance buses to/
from Mumbai. Buses to almost everywhere
leave from Dr Anadrao Nair Rd near Mumbai Central train station, including some
sleeper buses to Goa. Travel to Goa and
other southern destinations can also be
arranged with the private bus agents near
MG Rd or the cluster situated just west of
Crawford market, near MRA Marg.

Long-distance state-run buses depart from Mumbai Central bus terminal close to Mumbai Central train station. Buses service major towns in Maharashtra and neighbouring states. They're marginally cheaper and more frequent than the private services, but they're not nearly as comfortable.

For more information on getting to and from Mumbai, see p230.

GETTING AROUND
To/From the Airports
INTERNATIONAL

The prepaid taxi desk in the arrivals hall charges fixed rates (Rs 110 to Juhu, Rs 200 to Bandra, Rs 325 to Colaba; plus Rs 10 per bag and Rs 5 service tax). You could try to negotiate a lower rate with a private taxi, but it's not really worth the hassle. Air-con rates are 20% higher. A 5% or 10% tip is appreciated.

Don't catch an autorickshaw from the airport to the city: they're prohibited from entering downtown Mumbai and can only take you as far as Mahim Creek. The cheap alternative is to catch an autorickshaw to Andheri train station (around Rs 25) and a suburban train to Churchgate or Victoria Terminus (Rs 9, 45 minutes). Don't try this during rush hours.

DOMESTIC AIRPORT

Taxis outside the domestic airport charge meter rates, plus Rs 10 per item of luggage. The journey to the centre of town should cost around Rs 300. Make sure your driver uses the meter and conversion card.

A taxi from the city centre (say Victoria Terminus) to either of the airports costs around Rs 300 with a bit of bargaining, plus extra for baggage. Taxi drivers in Colaba ask for Rs 350 (around 30% more between midnight and 5am). Alternatively, catch a suburban train to Vile Parle and an autorickshaw from there (Rs 50).

Boat

Both **PNP** (Map p66; ☎ 22885220) and **Maldar Catamarans** (Map p66; ☎ 22829695) run regular ferries to Mandwa (Rs 100 one way), useful for accessing Murud-Janjira and other parts of the Konkan coast, avoiding the long bus trip out of Mumbai. Their ticket offices are beside the Gateway of India.

Bus

Single- and double-decker buses run all over Mumbai. Routes can be confusing and there's a mad rush to get off at every stop. Route numbers are signed in English on the side of buses. Short journeys are only a few rupees; simply jumping on a double-decker bus can be an entertaining and inexpensive way of seeing the city (bus 103 passes some interesting spots).

For more information about bus routes, contact **Best Undertaking** (Map p66; ☎ 22185541; www.bestundertaking.com; Colaba Bus Depot, Colaba Causeway, Colaba).

Taxi

The most convenient way to get around the city is the black-and-yellow Premier taxi, India's version of a 1950s Fiat. In south Mumbai drivers almost always use the meter without prompting and give the correct change. The minimum fare is usually Rs 13 for the first 1.6km and Rs 7 per kilometre thereafter. Note that taxis hanging around tourist attractions are usually hoping for a longer fare; flag down a moving taxi for shorter trips.

North of Mahim Creek, autorickshaws do the job of taxis. Rates are similar but you may have to bargain as drivers are less inclined to use the meter. Ask to see conversion charts at the end of the journey.

Train

There are three main lines, making Mumbai's train network relatively easy to navigate. The most useful service operates from Churchgate heading north to stations such as Charni Rd (for Chowpatty Beach), Mumbai Central, Mahalaxmi (for the dhobi ghat), Vile Parle (for the domestic airport), Andheri (for the international airport) and Borivali (for Sanjay Gandhi National Park).

Commuter trains to the suburbs leave from **Victoria Terminus** (Chhatrapati Shivaji Terminus; CST; ☎ 22620746; Nagar Chowk, Fort) and **Churchgate** (☎ 22039840; Veer Nariman Rd, Churchgate). Passengers have a choice of padded 1st-class seats and bench seats in 2nd. Women should take advantage of the ladies-only carriages and there are areas for disabled commuters. Trains only pause at suburban train stations for a moment, so be ready to jump off. Watch your valuables.

Central Goa

Travellers often make a beeline for the beaches of north or south Goa, but some of the highlights of the state are in central Goa. By exploring this region, you will easily find the pulse of Goa.

Panaji (Panjim) is Goa's most interesting town (calling it a city would be something of an overstatement) and, with its Portuguese Old Quarter (also called the Latin Quarter), a repository of historical and architectural splendour. It is a melting pot of old and new, and a meeting point for culture and commerce – alleyways wind their way between whitewashed churches and boutiques selling international brand-name products. The state capital is idyllically located on the Mandovi River, and cruises (despite their noise and nonsense) offer an opportunity to see Panaji from another perspective. This understated town is one of Goa's highlights.

About 9km to the east of Panaji is Old Goa, one of the finest attractions in the state, and the reason that Goa was known in the 17th century as the Rome of the East. Here, laterite churches and cathedrals (including the basilica containing the almost 500-year-old body of St Francis Xavier) are all that remain of the former Portuguese capital. Old Goa is now a Unesco World Heritage site that travellers and pilgrims are enamoured with.

The temples and spice gardens around Ponda make an interesting day trip from Panaji. Two of Goa's wildlife sanctuaries are also in this part of the state. Bondla Wildlife Sanctuary is well set up for wildlife-spotting, while a 4WD trip through Bhagwan Mahavir Wildlife Sanctuary will take you to Dudhsagar, Goa's highest waterfall.

HIGHLIGHTS

- Stay in a colonial heritage hotel and eat out in the Old Quarter in **Panaji** (p82), Goa's most elegant city

- Explore the magnificent churches of **Old Goa** (p100), a bike ride and an era away from modern-day Panaji

- Learn how spices can change your life and dine on a traditional lunch at a **spice farm** (p114) near Ponda

- Take a 4WD trip through the jungle and swim at the base of **Dudhsagar Falls** (p116)

- Float through mangroves in a dugout canoe and look for cranes and kingfishers at **Dr Salim Ali Bird Sanctuary** (p100).

CENTRAL GOA

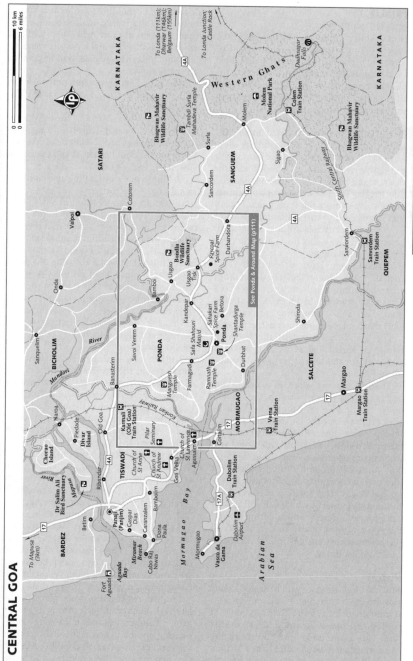

PANAJI

☎ 0832 / pop 93,000

In a country composed of unique cities, Panaji (Panjim) boasts its own brand of originality. The Portuguese left an indelible mark on this small, neat town and their Indian descendants are proud to be continually maintaining and adapting that legacy to suit their ever changing capital.

The architecture of Panaji is the most blatant sign that Goa evolved independently of the rest of India; winding alleyways are lined with Portuguese houses with distinctive red-tiled roofs, wooden window shutters and rickety balconies overhanging tidy streets. The old quarter of Fontainhas particularly evinces the Portuguese history that is spliced into the Indian milieu; plain whitewashed churches are tucked in small laneways that are a short walk from not-so-subtle Hindu temples.

Across Ourem Creek is the business district of Patto, where the tallest buildings are to be found. It is here where the state's prosperity comes into focus as the traffic gets busier and old buildings are replaced with sharp-edged modern constructions.

The Mandovi River laps the northern border of Panaji and at night it becomes a catwalk for the tourist boats that parade up and down.

Though tourists often dart off to the beaches of the north or south, they would do well to linger a little longer in this laid-back capital where the Goan spirit of taking it easy is alive and well. Opening hours are lazy in this slow-paced, low-rise capital and its compact size makes everything comfortably accessible on foot. Panjim makes for a nice prelude or ending to lackadaisical days on the beach. The bustling markets, busy restaurants (some of which will still be surprised to see a foreigner wandering in) and the ebb and flow of day-to-day municipal life offer an easy insight into the life and times of Goa today.

History

Much of the area on which Panaji stands was originally marshland, and for centuries it contained little more than a couple of fishing settlements. In around 1500, shortly after Goa came under the control of the Muslim sultan Yussuf Adil Shah, a fortress was built here to guard the entrance to the

Mandovi. The building later became known as the Idalcao's Palace, Idalcao being a Portuguese corruption of Adil Khan. Little, if anything, of the original structure remains, although today's Secretariat Building stands on the same site.

When the Portuguese nobleman Afonso de Albuquerque arrived in March 1510 he soon took the fort and set about reinforcing it. His efforts were in vain, for in May he was forced by Yussuf Adil Shah to abandon the position and had to wait until November before he could retake it and the city of Govepuri (today's Old Goa). Having done so, Albuquerque personally supervised the rebuilding of the fortress to his own specifications. Accounts of the time say that he was in such a hurry to complete the work before the next Muslim attack that even his officers were pressed into manual labour.

The only other bit of building that took place at this time was the raising of a small church in around 1540 on the site where the huge Church of Our Lady of the Immaculate Conception now stands. Since all ships had to call in at the fortress on arrival in Goa, the church was the first stop for the Portuguese sailors celebrating their safe arrival in India.

The first large-scale land reclamation was completed in 1634 when, under the orders of the viceroy, the count of Linhares, a causeway was built to join Panjim (the Portuguese name for the settlement) and Old Goa, which until that time had been separated by marshland. The 3km route, known as the Ribandar Causeway (from the name of the village at its eastern end), was a far-sighted piece of planning. It made Panjim a feasible alternative as the capital when, years later, Old Goa had to be abandoned because of the repeated cholera epidemics that were decimating the population.

As you drive east from Panaji towards Old Goa today, you can see that the ground is still marshy. The area south of the road is used for saltpans; sea water floods the area and evaporates, leaving yellow-brown deposits of sea salt.

Limited reclamation took place in the late 17th century, though mostly as private projects undertaken by a few wealthy land-owners who had chosen the area for their own estates. However, as conditions in Old Goa became more desperate, the land began

THE GOA INQUISITION

When Vasco da Gama sailed for India 'seeking spices and Christians' it was perhaps inevitable that the worst excesses of European religious zeal should reach Goa sooner or later. As it turned out, they arrived sooner.

The Inquisition was re-established in Spain and Portugal in the late 15th century against a background of rumours that many new Christians, including those who had been converted from Judaism, were secretly still observing their old faith. Many escaped the oppression in Portugal by relocating to the colonies overseas.

It wasn't long before the accusations followed them and missionaries began to be scandalised at the lax behaviour of both the new Christians and the other Portuguese settlers. At the request of the missionaries, a deposition of the Inquisition arrived in Goa in 1560. The new tribunal was known as the Goa Inquisition, but its jurisdiction spread across the whole of the Portuguese eastern empire.

Having established itself in the sultan's old palace in Old Goa, the tribunal set about imposing its will. Hindus were forbidden to practise their faith and even the Christian population lived in fear. The tribunal sat regularly in judgment before the long carved table that today is in the Goa State Museum in Panaji, and below the crucifix that now hangs in the Chapel of St Sebastian in Panaji. The more fortunate victims were stripped of their possessions; those who were less lucky were detained indefinitely in the dungeons beneath the Palace of the Inquisition.

Those who were judged guilty underwent the notorious auto-da-fé (act of the faith), a public ceremony, which was conducted in the square outside the Se Cathedral and accompanied by the tolling of the great bell in the cathedral tower. If they failed the test of faith they would usually be burned at the stake. Those who were willing to admit their heresy at the last moment were strangled before the pyre was lit.

The Inquisition was suppressed in Goa in 1774.

CENTRAL GOA

to support increasing numbers of refugees from the capital. At first the viceroy and most of the noblemen moved to Panelim, near present-day Ribandar, to escape the epidemics, but when that too became unhealthy a new location was sought.

In 1759 the viceroy moved to Panjim, where he took over the fortress as his own residence. Although Mormugao had already been selected as the best location for a new capital, the fact that the viceroy had chosen to live in Panjim rather sealed the issue. Those who could afford it moved to Panjim, and more land was reclaimed.

By the early 19th century the city was taking shape. In 1834, Panjim became known as Nova Goa, and in 1843 it was finally recognised by the Portuguese government as capital of Goa. A spate of building took place to make the new capital worthy of its title. Among the public buildings erected were the army barracks (now the police headquarters and government offices) and the library. In essence though, Goa was a forgotten corner of the Portuguese empire, and lack of money and political interest meant that building work was low-key.

In effect there was little change to the size and shape of the town until Goa's independence from Portugal in 1961. After the departure of the Portuguese, the city was renamed Panaji and a few superficial changes were made. The Secretariat Building became home to the State Assembly and a couple of statues were erected to heroes of the Goan Independence movement. As a sign of Panaji's progressiveness, the flash new Assembly Complex was built on the hill just north of Panaji and inaugurated in 2000. However, not a lot has altered in Panaji. Over the years, new building and road work has taken place, but locals and authorities are aware of retaining the city's unique atmosphere and colonial heritage.

Orientation

Despite the numerous tiny backstreets, Panaji is not a difficult place to find your way around; it's interesting just to wander about and explore at leisure. The main part of the town is sandwiched between the Mandovi River to the north and the high ground of the quaint Altinho district to the south. Dayanand Bandodkar (DB) Marg is

PANAJI

CENTRAL GOA

0   300 m
0   0.2 miles

INFORMATION

American Express................................(see 88)
British Tourist Assistance Office............1 F4
Broadway Book Centre...........................(see 65)
Cell Tone...2 D3
Central Telegraph Office.........................3 D3
Centurion Bank ATM................................4 B3
Conservator of Forest, Wildlife &
   Ecotourism...5 C4
Cyberjoint..(see 83)
E-zzy Travels...6 C4
Foreigners Registration Office............(see 20)
Forest Department.....................................7 C4
German Honorary Consulate....................8 E3
Goa Medical College.................................9 A3
Goa Tourism Development
   Corporation (GTDC) Office................10 F3
Goa Tourism Development
   Corporation (GTDC) Tourist
   Information Centre..............................(see 87)

Government of India Tourist Office...11 D3
HDFC Bank ATM.......................................12 B4
HDFC Bank ATM.......................................13 B4
ICICI Bank ATM..14 C4
ICICI Bank ATM..15 C4
Income Tax Office....................................16 F3
Italian Honorary Consulate....................17 E3
Iway business centre...........................(see 87)
KTC (Katamda Transport
   Coporation)..18 C3
Log Inn..19 E3
Main Post Office......................................20 C2

Menezes Air Travel................................(see 88)
Police Headquarters...............................21 C3
Portuguese Honorary Consulate.......22 F5
Shruti Communications.....................(see 63)
Singbal's Book House.............................23 D3
State Bank of India.................................24 B2
Thomas Cook...25 F3
UTI Bank ATM..26 C5

SIGHTS & ACTIVITIES
Bishop's Palace..27 C2
Caravela Casino..28 E4

Chapel of St Sebastian..........................29 C5
Chief Minister's Residence....................30 D3
Church of Our Lady of the
   Immaculate Conception.....................31 E5
Goa State Museum..................................32 C2
Institute Menezes Braganza.................33 D4
Jama Masjid...(see 5)
Junta House..34 C4
Mahalaxmi Temple..................................35 D5
Maruti Temple.......................................(see 32)
Panaji Central Library.............................36 E3
Pedro Fernandez Music.......................(see 5)
Public Observatory..................................37 F3
Santa Monica Jetty.................................38 D2
Secretariat Building.................................39 D2
Statue of Abbé Faria...............................

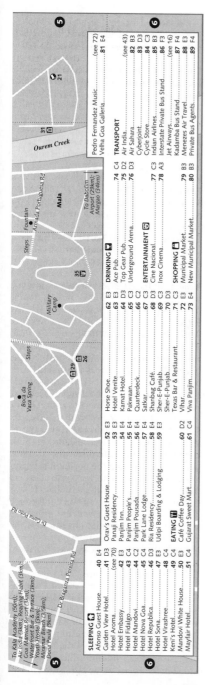

CENTRAL GOA

a major boulevard that skirts the Mandovi all the way to the Secretariat Building before becoming Avenida Dom Joao Castro and continuing to the New Pato Bridge in the east and to Campal and Miramar in the west. The Kadamba bus stand is on the eastern side of the town, across Ourem Creek.

Information

BOOKSHOPS

There are some very decent bookshops to be found in the Panaji area.

Broadway Book Centre (☎ 5647038; 1st fl, Ashirwad Bldg, 18th June Rd; ⏲ 9.30am-8pm) Has a good collection of English fiction and books on Goa. Next to Rizvi Tower.

Reading Habit (☎ 2463057; Dayanand Bandodkar Marg, Miramar; ⏲ 10am-7.30pm Mon-Sat) Offers a good collection of fiction, particularly Indian literature. There is also a comprehensive travel section selling various guides to the region and many titles focused on Goan history. There's also a small selection of clothing for sale upstairs. It's diagonally opposite the turn-off to the Marriot Hotel on Dayanand Bandodkar Marg.

Singbal's Book House (☎ 2425747; singalbookhouse36@rediffmail.com; Church Square) A modest collection of mostly educational books. There are a few novels and a collection of language guides.

EMERGENCY

Ambulance (☎ 102)
Fire (☎ 101)
Police (☎ 100)

INTERNET ACCESS

Cyberjoint (☎ 5640190, 2435905, 9822131835; Jose Falcao Rd; per hr Rs 30) About five computers overseen by a nice family.

Iway Business Centre (MG Rd; ⏲ 7am-midnight; per hr Rs 40) Pricier than other places but flashier and with more computers.

Log Inn (Login; ☎ 2228477, 5643708; 1st fl, Durga Chambers; per hr Rs 30; ⏲ 9am-11pm) In the same building as Check Inn Hotel, just off 18th June Rd. Also has scanning facilities.

Shruti Communications (per hr Rs 30) Phone calls can be made from here; it's off 31st January Rd, under Hotel Venite.

INTERNET RESOURCES

Corporation of the City of Panaji (www.panjim.org) Maintained by the city council, this is a useful website, for information on all things Panaji.

LIBRARIES

Panaji Central Library (☎ 2436327; Institute Menezes Braganza, Malaca Rd; ⏲ 9.30am-1.15pm & 2-5.45pm

Mon-Fri) On the west side of the Azad Maidan, next to the police headquarters.

MEDICAL SERVICES

Goa Medical College (☎ 2458700; Dayanand Bandodkar Marg) About 500m west of the Hotel Mandovi, this has the nearest medical facilities to Panaji. It has a casualty department.

Goa Medical College Hospital (☎ 2458725, 2458700) In Bambolim, 9km south of Panaji on the National Highway (NH) 17. Most of the departments and specialisations of the Goa Medical College are now based here.

MONEY

There are plenty of efficient foreign-exchange places in Panaji. By comparison, visiting the local banks (even the State Bank of India) for foreign exchange is a waste of time. There are a number of ATMs, including a UTI Bank ATM near the Kandamba bus stand.

American Express (AmEx; ☎ 2432960; Menezes Air Travel, Ourem Rd)

Centurion (MG Rd) Its 24-hour ATM accepts international cards.

HFDC (18th June Rd) Its 24-hour ATM accepts international cards.

ICICI (Dr Atmaram Borkar Rd) Its 24-hour ATM accepts international cards.

Menezes Air Travel (☎ 2432960; Ourem Rd) An agent for Amex if you need replacement cheques.

State Bank of India (Dayanand Bandodkar Marg; ☻ 10am-4pm Mon-Fri, 10am-1pm Sat & Sun) Changes cash and travellers cheques.

Thomas Cook (☎ 2221312; www.thomascook.co.in; 8 Alcon Chambers, Dayanand Bandodkar Marg; ☻ 9.30am-6pm Mon-Sat year-round, 10am-5pm Sun Oct-Mar) Pristine and professional, this is the best foreign-exchange place in Panjim. Changes all brands of travellers cheques commission free and gives cash advances on Visa and MasterCard.

POST

Hidden in the lanes around the main post office, there are privately run parcel-wrapping services that charge reasonable prices for their artistic services.

Main post office (MG Rd; ☻ 9.30am-5.30pm Mon-Fri, 9am-5pm Sat, poste restante 9.30am-4pm Mon-Sat) Has a Speedpost parcel service and reliable poste restante. Some services close early so try to get there before 4pm to be on the safe side.

TELEPHONE & FAX

Central Telegraph Office (Dr Atmaram Borkar Rd; ☻ 7am-8.30pm) You can make international telephone calls from here, but there are plenty of private STD/ISD offices throughout the city charging similar rates. Fax facilities are widely available at the same places.

TOURIST INFORMATION

Goa Tourism Development Corporation (GTDC; www.goa-tourism.com; Church Square ☎ 223412; Communidade Bldg; head office ☎ 2224132, 2226728, 2226515, 2436666; Alvaro Costas Rd; Panaji Residency ☎ 2227103; MG Rd) The head office is the most helpful out of all of the offices; staff actually seems happy that you've dropped by. To book tours you will need to go to the GTDC-run Panaji Residency (p93).

TRAVEL AGENCIES

There are several travel agencies where you can book and confirm flights; many are along 18th June Rd.

E-zy Travels (☎ 2435300, 2425742, 2424378; www .ezytravels.com; Shop 8-9, Durga Chambers, 18th June Rd) A professionally run travel agent that books international flights.

Menezes Air Travel (☎ 2432960; www.interserve travel.com; Ourem Rd)

Sights

FONTAINHAS & SAO TOME

The old districts of Panaji are squeezed between the hillside of Altinho and Ourem Creek. The Old Quarter is an attractive area to walk around, with narrow streets, overhanging balconies and a bygone Mediterranean atmosphere.

Fontainhas, which is said to takes its name from the Fountain of Phoenix spring near the Maruti temple, is the further south of the two districts. Originally this area was accessible only from the northern side and was a tangle of buildings constructed on land reclaimed from the marshes. It was not until Emidio Gracia Rd was cut through the hillside from the town centre that the district was joined more directly with the rest of Panaji. The construction of Ourem Rd, which for many years was the main thoroughfare out of Panaji to the south, also helped to open up the area.

Apart from its old-world charm, Fontainhas is notable for the **Chapel of St Sebastian** (St Sebastian Rd), built in 1818. This small whitewashed church at the end of a lovely street contains a number of interesting features – in particular, at the end of the right-hand aisle, a striking **crucifix**, which originally stood in the Palace of the Inquisition in Old

Goa (see The Goa Inquisition, p83). Also worth a look is the building now used by cultural organisation **Fundacao Oriente** (p96). It has been beautifully restored, and in an area where most of the traditional houses are looking a bit battered, this one really stands out.

Located to the north of Fontainhas, the tiny area around the main post office is known as Sao Tomé. The post office was once the tobacco-trading house for Panaji, and the building to the right of it was the mint. The square that these buildings face once housed the town pillory, where justice turned into spectacle when executions took place. It was here that several conspirators involved in the Pinto Revolt (p125) were put to death.

SECRETARIAT BUILDING

The oldest colonial building in Goa, the present-day Secretariat stands where Yussuf Adil Shah, the Muslim sultan who gained control of Goa at the end of the 15th century, had his fortress palace. Before the Portuguese built the main road, this palace was on an island surrounded by the waters of the Mandovi.

After the Portuguese arrived, the palace was reinforced and used as a customs post; it also served as temporary accommodation for incoming and outgoing viceroys. The tradition was that the new viceroy was handed the ceremonial keys to the city of Old Goa under the Viceroy's Arch, and so, while waiting for the ceremony, the new appointee had to stay in Panaji or Reis Magos. Similarly, after handing over responsibility, the outgoing viceroy had to wait outside the capital for his ship home.

After the viceroys abandoned Old Goa, the building was adopted as their official residence from 1759 until 1918, when it was moved to the buildings on the Cabo Raj Niwas instead. From this time onwards the building was used for government offices, and until recently it housed the State Assembly. The assembly now meets in the new **Assembly Complex**, located on the hill across the river.

In a small triangle of lawn next to the Secretariat Building is an unusual **statue** of a man apparently about to strangle a woman. It's a tribute to hypnotist Abbé Faria, one of Goa's most famous sons (p110).

CHURCH OF OUR LADY OF THE IMMACULATE CONCEPTION

This stunning whitewashed church lords it over the Municipal Gardens in the town centre. Although there has been a church on this site since about 1540, the present building dates from 1619; it's a surprisingly large church considering the area was practically uninhabited back then.

Panaji was the first port of call for ships from Lisbon, so Portuguese sailors would visit this church to give thanks for a safe crossing before continuing to Old Goa. By the 1850s the land in front of the church was being reclaimed and the distinctive crisscrossing staircases were added in the late 19th century. It was at about this time that the huge bell that now hangs in the central belfry was brought here. It had previously hung in the tower of the Church of St Augustine in Old Goa, but was removed when the tower started to crumble. The bell is the second largest in Goa (after the Golden Bell in the Se Cathedral in Old Goa).

The church is beautifully illuminated in the lead up to Christmas and during the Feast of Our Lady of Immaculate Conception, which culminates on 8 December.

Mass is held here daily in English, Konkani and Portuguese.

MUNICIPAL GARDENS & JAMA MASJID

Panaji's central square is the leafy but unkempt **Municipal Gardens**, also called Church Square (Largo da Igreja). The **Ashokan Pillar** in the centre once had a statue of Vasco da Gama as its crowning glory, but is now topped by the seal of present-day India, four lions sitting back to back atop an abacus decorated with a frieze and the inscription 'Truth Alone Triumphs'. Three relief busts once set into the walls around the garden can now be seen in the Goa State Museum.

The tiny **Jama Masjid**, barely 100m south of the Municipal Gardens, is said to have been built about two centuries ago. It was comprehensively renovated in 1959, though you can still walk past it without even realising it's there. The exterior of the building is a standard square and the entrance blends in with the small shops on either side, but the interior is extremely ornate in the classic Islamic white-marble style.

The grassy **Azad Maidan** (Freedom Park) wouldn't win any prizes at a flower show. It

CENTRAL GOA

is centred on a small pavilion, which houses a modern sculpture dedicated to freedom fighter and 'Father of Goan Nationalism' Dr Tristao de Braganza Cunha (1891–1958). The domed edifice formerly held the statue of Afonso de Albuquerque that now stands in the museum in Old Goa.

INSTITUTE MENEZES BRAGANZA & PANAJI CENTRAL LIBRARY

At the northwest corner of the Azad Maidan, the Institute Menezes Braganza and the Central Library occupy a part of the old buildings that used to be the army headquarters. It's worth poking your head through the door, at least to see the entrance hall, which is decorated with four large blue-and-white pictures that cover the whole wall. The scenes depicted on these *azulejos* (painted tiles) are taken from *Os Lusíadas,* an epic poem by Luís Vaz de Camões (p103).

Much of the upper floor of the building is given over to the Institute Menezes Braganza, which was founded in 1871 as a scientific and literary institution. Originally called the Institute Vasco da Gama, it was renamed in 1963 in honour of the champion of the Goan Independence movement, Luís de Menezes Braganza. The institute has a small **art gallery** that contains some rare prints and paintings.

On the lower floor of the building is the **Panaji Central Library** (☎ 2436327; ☽ 9.30am-1.15pm & 2-5.45pm Mon-Fri), the oldest public library in India. Founded in 1832 as the Publica Livraria, it is surprisingly rich in old texts, having inherited a substantial amount from the religious institutions of Old Goa when they were forced to close down.

GOA STATE MUSEUM

This large, roomy **museum** (☎ 2458006; www.goa museum.nic.in; admission free; ☽ 9.30am-5.30pm Mon-Fri), in a rather forlorn area near the Kadamba bus stand, has a dozen or so galleries featuring Christian art, Hindu and Jain sculpture and bronzes, and paintings (including miniatures) from all over India. The collection is gradually expanding and interesting exhibits include an elaborately carved 16th-century table used in the Goa Inquisition, a pair of huge rotary lottery machines containing thousands of wooden balls (the first lottery draw was in 1947),

and a large wooden chariot used in Hindu fairs during the 18th century.

The first room is a **sculpture gallery** containing Hindu carvings and bronzes dating from the 4th to 8th centuries AD. The second area is a **Christian art gallery** with a variety of wooden sculptures of saints, devotional paintings and some colonial wooden furniture. Also on display are some Jain busts, and three huge relief busts of Luís Vaz de Camões, Afonso de Albuquerque and Dom João de Castro, which originally stood in the Municipal Gardens. Upstairs there's a gallery containing cultural exhibits from various Goan villages, and a gallery of contemporary art from Goa and India.

The WWF has also established a **conservation gallery** in the museum, which provides information about conservation in Goa.

You can ask for a free guided tour; otherwise the uniformed staff will silently follow you around to make sure you don't touch anything.

MARUTI TEMPLE

Dedicated to the monkey god Hanuman, this modern temple is resplendently lit at night. Admire it as you're crossing the Mandovi River from Pato, and enjoy the view over the Old Quarter from its veranda. This temple will get better with age; the new finish of everything means that it is far more spectacular from afar.

The Maruti temple is the epicentre of a four-day festival celebrated in February. The festival usually lingers for 10 days and lasts well into the night. Enormous and colourful statues of Hanuman are placed in the street, and stalls set up all around the Hindu quarter of Mala.

MAHALAXMI TEMPLE

This modern temple off Dr Dada Vaidya Rd is not particularly imposing, or even very interesting, but if you've never visited a Hindu temple before it's worth a look inside and amply demonstrates that among Panaji's ubiquitous whitewashed churches there is a thriving Hindu community. The temple was built in 1818 and is devoted to the goddess Mahalaxmi, the deity of Panaji.

ALTINHO

On the hillside above Panaji is the district known as Altinho. Apart from good views

DETOUR: PEDALLING AROUND PANAJI

If you can get past the insane traffic on the highway between the Mandovi Bridge and the Kadamba bus stand, the area around Panaji offers some enjoyable bicycle touring.

One of the best rides in the state is the 9km trip out to **Old Goa**. The pancake-flat road follows the Ribandar Causeway along the south bank of the Mandovi River; it's a scenic ride passing through the village of Ribandar. Having a bicycle is very handy for exploring Old Goa itself, since the churches and ruins are quite scattered. Ride down to the Mandovi through the Viceroy's Arch and take the ferry across to **Divar Island**; a couple of hours spent exploring this absorbing rural outpost is perfect on a bicycle. You can ride to the southwest corner of the island where there's another ferry back across to Ribandar. Riding back towards Panaji there's yet another ferry point from where you can cross to **Chorao Island** and cycle through the fringes of the **Dr Salim Ali Bird Sanctuary**.

Another rewarding day ride from Panaji is to head west along the Mandovi River (along Dayanand Bandodkar Marg) through the Campal district, then southwest past Miramar Beach and out to **Dona Paula**, the small peninsula at the mouth of the Zuari River. There's a small hill approaching the peninsula but generally this road is flat and wide and the traffic is light. At the roundabout at Dona Paula, turning right (coming from Panaji) takes you up to Cabo Raj Niwas, while turning left takes you across the elevated suburban area behind Panaji. You can ride all the way east to **Bambolim** on the main highway and then back to Panaji (a round trip of about 22km), although the highway is busy and accident prone. It's also possible to detour north through the suburb at the back of Altinho, emerging on Ourem Rd in Fontainhas – ask locals for directions.

over the city and river, the main attraction here is the **Bishop's Palace**, a huge and imposing building completed in 1893.

The archbishop of Goa came to reside in Panaji early in the 20th century. He initially laid claim to the residence on Cabo Raj Niwas, the promontory that looks out over the confluence of the Mandovi and Zuari Rivers. However, it was not to be. When the Portuguese governor general realised that it was the best property in Goa, the archbishop had to change his plans and move back to Panaji.

Today, Altinho is the most prestigious place to live in Panaji; the pope stayed here during his visit to Goa in 1999.

CAMPAL

The road to Miramar from Panaji runs through the Campal district. Just before you reach the Kala Academy, on the seaward side of the road are the **Campal Gardens**, also known as the Children's Park. The Gardens offer a view over Reis Margo Fort and the boats that cruise along the Mandovi River each evening. Art and music events are also held here.

PUBLIC OBSERVATORY

For anyone interested in checking out the incredibly clear night skies over Goa, the local branch of the Association of Friends of Astronomy has a **public observatory** (☎ 2425547; 7th fl, Junta House, Swami Vivekanand Rd; ☽ 7-9pm 14 Nov-31 May). The local enthusiasts are only too happy to welcome visitors and explain what you're looking at. The view of Panaji by night is lovely, especially around dusk.

Activities

Panaji is perfect for walking and shopping but if you're here for a while and want to be more active, consider the following options.

CYCLING

Panaji is a great base for cycling trips. Head east to Old Goa and spend a day exploring the sites, or head southwest to Ponda, pausing on your way at Miramar. See above for details of rides around Panaji.

DIVING

Interestingly enough, Panaji is also a good base to launch a diving trip. The well-organised **Barracuda Diving** (☎ 2437001; www.barracudadiving.com) is based at the Goa Marriot Resort in Miramar. Most open-water dives are around Grande and Devbagh Islands. Courses include a noncertificate introductory course (Rs 3500), and a PADI introductory course (Rs 8000), both of which are run over two mornings and involve pool training and two shallow dives. A four-day PADI open-water course is Rs 15,000; a two-day advanced open-water course costs Rs 10,000; and a 14-day dive master course is Rs 25,000. For qualified divers, two boat dives (departing 8am) costs Rs 2250, including all equipment, snacks and guide supervision.

Walking Tours

NEW PANAJI

From the city's most notable landmark, the **Church of Our Lady of the Immaculate Conception** (**1**; p87), walk west to the **Municipal Gardens** (**2**; p87), then north along Dr RS Rd to MG Rd, a busy thoroughfare. On your right is the **Statue of Abbé Faria** (**3**; p110).

Also to your right you will see the **Secretariat Building** (**4**; p87), believed to be the oldest Portuguese building in Goa.

Crossing the road to Dayanand Bandodkar Marg, walk east towards **Panaji jetty** (**5**), used by old steamers. Continue along the river until you come to the Betim ferry. Opposite this, a short detour southeast brings you to **Institute Menezes Braganza** (**6**; p88), with its gallery and library. Continue along the riverfront until you reach the bustling **Municipal Market** (**7**; p96), which makes for an atmospheric detour. Head back to DB Marg via the **New Municipal Market** (**8**; p96). If you don't want to see a movie at the glitzy **Inox Cinema** (**9**; p96), continue past the **Campal Gardens** (**10**; p89) and call in on the **Kala Academy** (**11**; p95) to find out what's going on.

If you're not too tired, walk back to the start by turning left onto Dr Braganza Pereira Rd and taking the first major left after 200m. This will take you to a roundabout, where you can turn right onto 18th June Rd for street stalls and boutiques.

WALK FACTS

Start Church of Our Lady of the Immaculate Conception
Finish Kala Academy
Distance 3.5km
Duration 1.5 hours

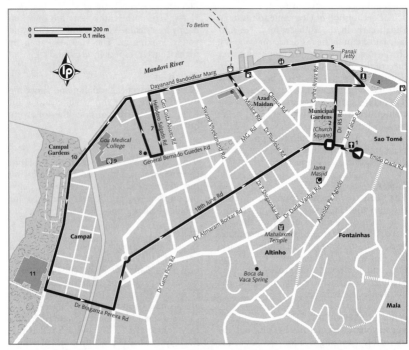

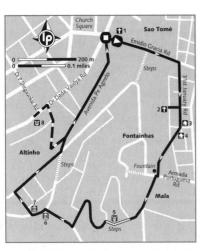

CENTRAL GOA

WALK FACTS

Start Church of Our Lady of Immaculate Conception
Finish Mahalaxmi Temple
Distance 4.5km
Duration 2 hours

OLD PANAJI
Start at the **Church of Our Lady of Immaculate Conception** (**1**; p87) and walk east up the hill along Emidio Gracia Rd. At the four-way junction, where you will find food vendors, turn right onto 31st January Rd. After about 150m, turn right to the quaint **Chapel of St Sebastian** (**2**; p86). There are many picturesque old buildings down these laneways. Take some time to explore the area.

Continuing down to 31st January Rd, at the very centre of the intersection you will pass the **Panjim Inn** (**3**; p93) on your left. Break for a drink on the balcony here or at Café Gitanjali in **Panjim Peoples** (**4**; p93). Continue down the right fork of the road, past Fontainhas' namesake fountain. Continue along this pleasant street until you come across steps on your right leading to **Maruti temple** (**5**; p88). The balcony of the temple is the ideal place to catch your breath and admire the view over the Old Quarter.

Follow the road behind the temple into the Altinho district. When you reach a junction with a red 'stop and proceed' sign, turn right and continue around to the

Bishop's Palace (**6**; p89). The building towers over its neighbour, the less grand **Chief Minister's Residence** (**7**). At the next junction, turn right and wander back downhill to Church Square, or detour down through the more humble residencies of Altinho to **Mahalaxmi temple** (**8**; p88).

Tours
The GTDC (p86) operates manic hour-long cruises along the Mandovi River aboard the *Santa Monica*. You'll see this and other boats – lit up like Christmas trees – swanning around the river every evening trying to outdo each other with the volume of their music. There's a sunset cruise (6pm) and a sundown cruise (7.15pm), both of which cost Rs 100. They include a live band performing Goan folk songs and dances. Drinks and snacks are available at an extra charge. On full-moon nights there is a two-hour cruise at 8.30pm (Rs 150). All cruises depart from the **Santa Monica jetty** (2438754, 2437496), next to the huge Mandovi Bridge, and tickets can be purchased here or at any GTDC offices.

A couple of private operators, **Paradise Cruises** (Emerald Cruises; 2431192, 2431215; fax 2223126) and **Royal Cruises** (2435599), have virtually identical hour-long trips from Santa Monica jetty each evening (Rs 100; 6.15pm, 7.30pm and 8.45pm). Their boats are bigger and rowdier than the *Santa Monica*. Paradise also operates open-sea 'dolphin cruises' (Rs 300, including snacks and drinks) from 10am to noon.

When the GTDC gets the numbers (about 15 people), it also runs a Goa By Night bus tour (Rs 140, including a river cruise and tour of illuminated sights), leaving at 6.30pm from the Santa Monica jetty.

Festivals & Events
Panaji is a city renowned for festivals in a state that is renowned for festivals. Taking part in cultural and religious events is a wonderful way to access a city, so if you can manage it try to time your visit to coincide with something – though do be warned that accommodation becomes more rare and more expensive. The following are some of the highlights in Panaji:
Fontainhas Arts Festival Old homes in the old quarter are converted into galleries. Held between January and March.

Pop, Beat & Jazz Music Festival A two-day festival at the Kala Academy in February.

Maruti Zatra Procession of the monkey god Hanuman and a festive fair. It's held in February at the base of the Maruti temple.

Carnival Started by the Catholics, appropriated by everyone, Carnival is the biggest thing to happen all year in Panaji. The mock King Momo kicks it off with a decree ordering his loyal and obedient subjects to relax and enjoy life. Held in February/March.

Shigmotsav Celebrated all over the state in March/April, but special celebrations are held in Panaji on the full-moon day of March, marked by a float through the streets.

Feast of Our Lady of the Immaculate Conception Fireworks, a fair and a procession of the long-named lady though the streets on 8 December.

The Kala Academy (p95) seems to be busy all year organising various classical dance, folk music, drama, singing, food and culture events. They really kick into action around November and December. Contact the Kala Academy if you want to find out what's happening when you're in Panaji.

Sleeping

BUDGET

Hotel Republica (☎ 2224630; Jose Falcao Rd; d Rs 300) There is no air-conditioning, no hot water and only squat toilets, but there is a great elevated balcony and years worth of character. If Harry Potter books were set in Goa, this would be the Weasleys' house. What it lacks in cleanliness and courtesy it makes up for in quirkiness.

Mandovi White House (☎ 2223928; 5552004 @yahoo.com; 31st January Rd; s/d with AC Rs 350/450, without AC Rs 300/400; ✷) Slightly off the road and slightly off the rails is the White House. The personality of the proprietor, Mr Vincent de Souza, is glued to the walls in the form of random newspaper clippings and various paraphernalia – a testament to the subjectivity of taste. His business card boasts a '10am cutout time'…perhaps when guests are required to help assemble newspaper clippings. Prices can more than double over peak season.

Hotel Embassy (☎ 2226019, 5622054; Emidio Garcia Rd; s/d/tr Rs 375/550/750) Rooms here are far nicer then the building's exterior would suggest. Bathrooms have hot water and are tiled, though not all have sit-down toilets. Some of the rooms at the front of the building are bright and comfortable. All rooms

are Rs 1000 in peak season but discounts are cheerfully forthcoming outside of that.

Orav's Guest House (☎ 2426128, 5640103; 31st January Rd; s/d Rs 250/450) Rooms are not as rickety as you would expect in this price range. All have a bathroom with hot water and are good value.

Park Lane Lodge (☎ 2227154; d without bathroom Rs 515) This seems like too elegant a building to be included in a budget section, but it fits. Unfortunately the cluttered character of the Park Lane Lodge doesn't spill into the rooms themselves, which are quite bland. Though the rooms are makeshift and overpriced, they are clean and the family that runs the lodge is great. It also boasts a lovely location in Fontainhas.

If you're really on a budget then consider these absolute shoestring options:

Youth Hostel (☎ 225433; Baywatch, Dona Paula Jetty Rd; dm member/nonmember Rs 40/60) Cheap but an 11pm lights-out rule gives it a boarding-school feel. It's 3km outside of Panaji in Miramar.

Udipi Boarding & Lodging (☎ 2228047; Sao Tome; d without bathroom Rs 100) Close to the centre of town but it's a tad grimy.

MIDRANGE

Afonso Guest House (☎ 2222359; d with bathroom Rs 800) Afonso looks like hotels are supposed to look in the beautiful Old Quarter. Its namesake is an extremely houseproud manager, who has put a great deal of care and effort into creating this place. Rooms with hot-water bathrooms are extremely good value and there is a lovely rooftop terrace with a tiled mosaic floor, where you can sit and enjoy a drink in early mornings and late afternoons. There isn't a speck of dust to detract from the elegant design.

Mayfair Hotel (☎ 223317, 2230457, 2225772; mayfair@sancharnet.in; Dr Dada Vaidya Rd; s Rs 650, d with/without AC Rs 950/800, s/d/tr deluxe Rs 750/900/1000; ✷) The standard rooms here are light and airy; all rooms have bathrooms and some even have balconies overlooking the street. Be warned though that the street noise can be unrelenting and you might be better off with a room opening onto the garden at the back. The reception area has a mosaic on the wall depicting life in rural Goa.

Hotel Sona (☎ 2222226, 2223973, 2420240; www.hotelsona.com; Ourem Rd; s without bathroom Rs 250, d with bathroom Rs 600, r deluxe Rs 960) Prettily located near the river in a nice part of town. Not all of the 30 rooms of this four-storey building face the river, so make sure you check it out first. Cheaper rooms have a common bathroom with spacious showers, some of which have a coloured glass window that makes you feel as though you are bathing in the attic of a cathedral.

Hotel Virashree (☎ 2226656; tchaitanya@hotmail .com, virashree@hotmail.com; Dr Dada Vaidya Rd; s/d standard without AC Rs 400/425, deluxe with AC Rs 775/795; ☒) Across the road from Mahalaxmi Temple, rooms at Hotel Virashree are cleaner and more modern than the exterior of the building would lead you to believe. It's hard to beat the value of the standard rooms with a bathroom and TV. Windows are also quite large and let in natural light, but there isn't the same smooth service you'll find at the nearby Mayfair.

Keni's Hotel (☎ 2224581, 2224582; fax 2435227; 18th June Rd; s Rs 412, d Rs 541-644, ste Rs 670) This is good value, particularly given its location. Keni's Hotel is old but well kept, with no dank, crusty smells. Rooms are spacious and have TV and hot water. The hotel is accessed from a tiny lane off 18th June Rd.

Ria Residency (☎ 2220002, 2420002, 2430002; prajakt@hotmail.com; r Rs 800) The linear design of the brand new Ria Residency lacks the charm of the Panjim Inn across the road. However, given the facilities, cleanliness and location, this is a well-priced option. The outdoor terrace is a nice touch too. Diagonally opposite Panjim Inn, off 31st January Rd.

Panaji Residency (☎ 2227103; MG Rd; d with/without AC Rs 1050/790, r deluxe Rs 1400; ☒) Run by the GTDC, this is an unremarkable place

but it's centrally located and has a decent restaurant. This is also the starting point of many GTDC tours.

Why anyone would want a bird's-eye view of the Municipal Gardens is a mystery, but if you're after accommodation at this central location you could try the following places:

Hotel Aroma (☎ 2423519; Cunha-Rivara Rd; d with AC Rs 650) Spacious and airy rooms. Buckets of hot water for washing are brought on request.

Garden View Hotel (☎ 2227844; Municipal Gardens; d with/without AC Rs 500/400; ☒) Though the rooms are tired, they have the full gamut of facilities and are well priced. Discounts are forthcoming during quiet times.

TOP END

Panjim Inn (☎ 2226523, 2435628, 2228136; www.pan jiminn.com; E212 31st January Rd, Fontainhas; s/d Rs 1440/1620, r deluxe Rs 1845, ste Rs 2610) One of the most charming places to stay in Panaji, this beautiful mansion from the 19th century has a large 1st-floor veranda with the fragile elegance of a Chinese pavilion. Some of the spacious rooms have four-poster beds, and all of them have colonial furniture and individual character. If you're interested in staying at the Panjim Pousada or the Panjim People's, you can also come here; they're all run by the same aesthetically gifted people.

Panjim Pousada (☎ 2226523, 2435628, 2228136; www.panjiminn.com; 31st January Rd, Fontainhas; s/d Rs 1440/1620, r deluxe Rs 1845, ste Rs 2610) Down the road from the Panjim Inn, the nine divine, colonial fantasy rooms at Panjim Pousada are set off a stunning central courtyard that displays (and sells) art. Various doorways

---

THE AUTHOR'S CHOICE

Panjim People's (☎ 0832-2226523, 0832-2435628, 0832-2228136; www.panjiminn.com; E212 31st January Rd, Fontainhas; d standard/slightly larger Rs 4950/5400; ☒) From the people who brought the Panjim Inn to the Old Quarter comes Panjim People's, the most decadent of them all. With the same intention of old-world revival, the People's is a step up in elegance from other options in the area.

If you're lucky enough to get one of the four bright and airy rooms in this landmark of Fontainhas, you're in for a travel treat. Rooms truly do justice to the proud exterior of this converted heritage building. Decadent four-poster beds, colonial-era furniture and tiled mosaic bathrooms allow you to immerse yourself in luxury away from the entire modern world, despite modern amenities like a fridge and TV. The larger room at the back of the building has an ornately carved antique rosewood bed head, which is an elegant centrepiece. Each of the four rooms has a slightly different character, though all have private balconies overlooking picturesque fragments of the Old Quarter. Downstairs is Café Gitanjali, where you can enjoy romantic art over a romantic drink.

and spiral staircases lead to the rooms; those on the upper level are by far the best.

Goa Marriot Resort (☎ 2463333; fax 2463300; Miramar Beach; d US$150-340; 🖳 🖭) Unquestionably one of the best places to stay in Goa, the Marriot Resort is expertly choreographed from the word go, with the five-star fantasy beginning with the foyer. The pool and garden area isn't enormous, but it is enticing. Another asset of the Marriot is the Waterfront Terrace & Bar (opposite), which is perfectly integrated into the design of the pool area.

Hotel Fidalgo (☎ 2226291; info@hotelfidalgo-goa .com; 18th June Rd; s/d/ste Rs 1800/2300/8000; 🖳 🖭) After a complete revamp, Hotel Fidalgo has become the most modern hotel in central Panaji. There is a food 'enclave' with various restaurants, a swimming pool, an Ayurvedic health spa and various shops. It's polished and professional without being hoity-toity. Add a luxury tax of 10%.

Hotel Mandovi (☎ 2426270, 2224405; www.hotel mandovigoa.com; DB Marg; r standard Rs 1550-2000, s with river views Rs 2650-4000, d with river views Rs 3050-5000) In the spirit of former colonial capitals that have an old-style hotel facing the river (think the Raffles in Singapore and the Strand in Rangoon), the Mandovi is Panaji's not-so-grand contribution. Its 53-year-old charm is starting to wither to the point that its location is really the drawcard. However, the on-site facilities such as restaurants, a bakery and a small bookshop also give it a point of distinction from its newer rivals.

Hotel Nova Goa (☎ 2226231, 2226237; www.hotel novagoa.com; Dr Atmaram Borkar Rd; s/d Rs 1600/2100, ste Rs 2500-3000; 🖭) There are 88 rooms at the Nova Goa and a pool hidden away behind the main building, which is done in the style of a giant concrete toilet block. The rooms are quality cookie cutter.

Eating

Panaji is great for eating out, mainly because it doesn't have the strips of tourist-oriented places that are rife along the coast. Here instead are quality restaurants that the locals love. With some exceptions, most places only start serving dinner at around 7pm so try not to work up an appetite too much earlier.

Hotel Venite (☎ 2425537; 31st January Rd; mains Rs 80-125; ⏲ Tue-Sat) This elegant affair has both Australian and Portuguese wines, and a versatile food menu that ranges from pepper steak to Portuguese fish and spaghetti Napolitaine. Drinks are reasonable; a Kingfisher is the standard Rs 30. Be drawn in through the shell-mosaic entrance, then step upstairs to the seven rickety candlelit balconies overhanging the street (though you won't be comfortable if you're a large person). The whole restaurant is basked in the warm orange glow that all good meals should be garnished with. The food isn't as sublime as the atmosphere makes you anticipate, though.

Vihar (MG Rd; mains Rs 15-80, juices Rs 25-30; ⏲ 7am-10pm) Vihar is a justifiably popular place serving South and North Indian food and Chinese to a constant stream of locals and clued-in backpackers. A big plus is the juice bar that cranks out some winning concoctions. The whole menu is vegetarian.

Viva Panjim (☎ 2422405; 178 31st January Rd, Fontainhas; mains Rs 100; ⏲ noon-3pm & 7-10.30pm) This is a long-standing favourite located behind Mary Immaculate High School. Despite its popularity it has thus far resisted the urge to spill out onto the street. There are only very limited tables, the nicest being the three outside in the picturesque laneway on which the restaurant cosily sits. The restaurant dishes out elegant Indian and Chinese fare.

Horse Shoe (☎ 2431788; E245 Ourem Rd; mains Rs 60-195; ⏲ noon-4.30pm & 7-10.30pm) Reservations are recommended at this stylish Portuguese-Goan restaurant. The elegant but simple atmosphere is presided over by the owner-manager-chef who takes great personal pride in this project.

Shanbag Café (Municipal Gardens; mains Rs 10-35; ⏲ 7am-8pm) This small vegetarian restaurant with orange décor is very friendly. It's clean and well organised, and the locals love it. This is the perfect place to sample Goan fare because the straightforward menu has handy photos and the friendly staff are good picking out food for confused foreigners. Try *idli* (round steamed rice cakes) for breakfast with chai; it will set you back around Rs 20. A full *paratha* meal, where the flat bread is served with an array of dishes or stuffed with meat and vegetables, costs around Rs 30.

Sher-e-Punjab (☎ 2425657; www.sher-e-punjab .com; 18th June Rd; mains Rs 40-100; ⏲ 11.30am-3pm,

6.30-10pm) This is where local families go when they want to dine out. It has a great selection of food for reasonable prices. There is another branch on the first floor of the Hotel Aroma, though the courtyard at the one on 18th June Rd is a perfect accompaniment to a meal.

Satkar (18th June Rd; mains Rs 20-50; ⏰ 11am-3pm & 6.30-10pm). A favourite among locals, Satkar is a great place to dine. Its vegetarian meals are splendidly cheap and tasty, and you won't find a better veg thali (traditional all-you-can-eat meal; Rs 25) in Panaji. Even the Chinese dishes are comparatively good and there is an interesting array of *faloodas* (rose-flavoured milk drinks).

Pakwaan (☎ 2421442; Vagle Vision, 18th June Rd; dosas Rs 35, mains Rs 30-80) A great budget restaurant that local families adore, Pakwaan has all the classic Indian fare plus sandwiches, salads and pizzas. There are some unusual fusions on the menu, such as 'American chopsuey' dosa (paper-thin lentil-flour pancake) and dried-fruit pizza!

Quarterdeck (☎ 2432904, 2432905; mandovi_goa@sancharnet.in; Dayanand Bandodkar Marg, Mandovi Riveria; ⏰ 3-11pm) This is a great place to sit and watch the party boats doof-doof by. The self-proclaimed 'Super Multicuisine Restaurant' has a fantastically laid-back atmosphere, and the food is fantastic and not too shamefully priced. The Goan prawn curry (Rs 125) is recommended.

Texas Bar & Restaurant (☎ 5643130, 2226077; 1st fl, Hotel Neptune; mains 80-150; ⏰ 11am-3pm & 7-9pm) There is some heavy meat-based fare here, and a lengthy cocktail list that doesn't suit the Wild West theme as well as the mutton does. It offers a diverting respite from the streets and, for your further displacement, waiters wear tasselled leather waistcoats and sometimes even cowboy hats.

Waterfront Terrace & Bar (☎ 2463333; Goa Marriot Resort; buffet breakfast/lunch/dinner Rs 375/500/849; ⏰ 24hr) The design of this splash-out coffee shop and restaurant cleverly uses glass so that the indoor eating area blends to the outside pool area of the Goa Marriot Resort (opposite). For true indulgence, try a buffet or Sunday brunch.

Café Coffee Day (Arthur Viegas Bldg; ⏰ 9am-11pm) This popular chain café is not too far from the Municipal Gardens, and has a small balcony where you can sit lazily, drink your iced coffee and eat your chocolate cake.

Gujarat Sweet Mart (Gujarat Lodge; ☎ 2224367, 2224567; 18 June Rd; drinks Rs 10-30) With the perfect atmosphere to educate yourself in the world of Indian sweets, Gujarat Sweet Mart is a great place to point at and eat an overwhelming array of treats, some freshly made on the premises. There's also a great array of drinks such as sweet lassis and thick milk shakes, which range in flavour from basic varieties through to mocha almond and ginger lemon.

Kamat Hotel (5 Church Square; mains from Rs 10-60; ⏰ 8am till late) Kamat is a popular choice for locals. The vegetarian menu is enormous, with mostly Indian and a selection of Chinese dishes; there are also some sandwiches on the menu, plenty of ice cream, and a great drink selection. The upstairs eating area is an air-conditioned spotless cocoon away from the streets.

Drinking

There isn't much of a drinking scene in Panaji; rather than heading for pubs, the trend seems to be to linger at restaurants that stay open quite late. For those who are craving a more active atmosphere, the joy-riding boats that thump their way up and down the Mandovi are as close as you'll get; see p91 for more information. There are a few hole-in-the-wall pubs around town, though many have a very seedy feel to them. The following pubs all have a slightly dark, predominantly male, but ultimately comfortable atmosphere.

Top Gear Pub (Dayanand Bandodkar Marg; ⏰ 11am-3pm & 7pm-midnight) Don't take more than 10 friends or you won't fit inside. This nano-pub, with all the detail of a real-live Irish drinking hole, has possibly been designed with real-live leprechauns in mind.

Ace's Pub (Swami Vivekanand Rd; ⏰ 7pm-11pm) A two-tier place, opposite Junta House, with the vibe of a dingy cocktail bar.

Underground Arena (☎ 2228305; Hotel Manvin's, Church Square; ⏰ 8.30pm-11pm) This is the most spacious place for a drink, with a big TV that implies that if there are sports to be watched, they should be watched here.

Entertainment

Kala Academy (☎ 2223280; www.kalaacademy.org; Dayanand Bandodkar Marg) On the west side of the city at Campal, the Kala Academy is Goa's premier cultural centre, with a programme of dance, theatre, music and art exhibitions throughout the year. Many performances are in Konkani, but there are occasional English-language productions. Kala Academy is reputed to be a prestigious place to study; see p214 for more information.

Fundacao Oriente (☎ 2230728; 175 Filipe Neri Xavier Rd, Fontainhas; ⏰ 9.30am-1pm & 2.30-6pm Mon-Fri) Holds arts exhibitions and musical events in a bid to promote cultural exchange between Portugal and Goa.

Caravela Casino (☎ 2234044/7, 5642844/7, 2439160; goacas@sancharnet.in; Fisheries Jetty, Dayanand Bandodkar Marg) This floating casino makes for an interesting night out. There is a sunset cruise (adult/child Rs 500/250, 5.30pm to 8pm) and a dinner cruise (9pm to 10pm), as wee as a daytime cruise (Rs 1800). Entering the gambling section of the boat costs an extra Rs 200. Be warned there is a dress code: no shorts, sandals or three-quarter pants are allowed. Prices include domestically produced drinks, though imported drinks cost more. Disembarking is easy, with row boats taking people on and off on the boat.

Inox Cinema (☎ 2420999; www.inoxmovies.com; Old GMC Heritage Precinct, Campal; tickets Rs 50-120) Congratulations movie buffs, you have come to *the* best place in Goa. This recently built cinema is behind Goa Medical College and screens both Bollywood and Hollywood movies (in English). It's one of those by-products of globalisation that makes you think you could be anywhere in the world. And just when you thought the seats couldn't get any more comfortable, you realise that they recline. Go crazy at the snack bar (at last popcorn that doesn't cost more than the movie!) and enjoy.

Waterfront Terrace & Bar (☎ 2463333; Goa Marriot Resort; ⏰ 7am till late) The very indulgent, though comfortable, Waterfront Terrace & Bar has theme nights every Monday, Wednesday and Thursday. These are often musical evenings that stretch on long after dinner has ended. At the time of research, Saturday night was the designated jazz night (Rs 800). Contact the Marriot to find out what's on.

For a raw cinema experience you could go to Cine Nacional, which plays mostly 'adult' movies and has a seedy feeling to match. Movies are shown at 10am, 3pm, 6.15pm and 9.45pm.

Shopping

The main shopping strip for more upmarket shopping is 18th June Rd; it is livelier at night, when the touts and the shoppers come out. Here you will find high-class souvenirs and boutique clothing stores, as well as shops selling dried fruits and nuts. On MG Rd near Delhi Darbar are shops selling imported brands, including Levis, Lacoste, Wrangler, Nike and Benetton, for about a third of the price you would pay in Europe.

Municipal Market (⏰ from 7.30am) The atmospheric place, where narrow streets have been converted into covered markets, is relatively ordered. There's a fresh produce area, in addition to clothing stalls and some very small eateries. The fish market is a particularly interesting strip of activity.

New Municipal Market (⏰ from 7.30am) Near the Muncipal Market is this recently established market. You'll find everything from fruit and vegetables to tailors, but you won't find as much atmosphere as at the Municipal Market. Give it a few years and perhaps all the shops will be occupied.

Pedro Fernandez Music (19 D Joao Castro Rd) This lovingly filled shop, next to Vihar restaurant, sells traditional Indian instruments such as drums and sitars.

Velha Goa Galeria (☎ 2426628; www.constavin .com; ⏰ 9.30am-1pm & 3-7.30pm) Head here for some very high-class souvenirs. The gallery has beautiful mosaic and pottery items, none of which are cheap but most of which are lovely.

Getting There & Away
AIR

For travel agencies that handle ticketing and flight confirmation, see p86. The following airlines have offices in Panaji:

Air India (☎ 224081; 18th June Rd) Next to Hotel Fidalgo.

Air Sahara (☎ 2230237; General Bernado Guedes Rd)

Indian Airlines (☎ 2237821; ground fl, Dempo Bldg, Dayanand Bandodkar Marg; ⏰ 10am-1pm & 2-5pm Mon-Sat) On the road out to Miramar.

Jet Airways (☎ 2438792; Shop 7-9, Sesa Ghor, Patto Plaza, Dr Alvaro Costa Rd) Near the GTDC office.

BOAT

The passenger-vehicle ferry across the Mandovi River to the fishing village of Betim is a useful ferry service for the northern beaches. It departs from the jetty on Dayanand Bandodkar Rd roughly every 15 minutes between

6am and 10pm (passenger/motorcycle free/ Rs 4). From Betim there are buses to Calangute and Candolim via Reis Magos.

BUS
State-run bus services operate out of Panaji's **Kadamba bus stand** (☎ 2438256). Fares vary depending on the type of bus, but the destinations include Hospet (Rs 165, nine hours), Bangalore (Rs 390, 14 hours), Mangalore (Rs 263, 11 hours), Mumbai (15 to 18 hours), Mysore (Rs 345, 17 hours) and Pune (Rs 326, 12 hours). There are also services to Londa (Rs 35), from where you can get a daily direct train connection to Mysore and Bangalore, and services to Hubli (Rs 65, six hours) and Belgaum (Rs 55, five hours). For Hampi, you're better off taking the bus rather than a bus-train combination. You can take the daily government-run bus to Hospet (9km from Hampi) and then a local bus to Hampi from there, but there are plenty of private buses, including overnight sleepers, on this route.

Many private operators – with luxury and air-con buses to Mumbai, Bangalore, Hampi and other destinations – have offices outside the entrance to the Kadamba bus stand. Most private interstate buses arrive and depart from the separate interstate bus stand next to the Mandovi Bridge, although some arrive and depart from the actual ticketing offices.

A reliable booking service is **Paulo Tours & Travel** (☎ 2438531; www.paulotravels.com; G1, Cardoza Bldg), just north of the Kadamba bus stand. It has sleeper coaches to Hampi (Rs 450), Mumbai (Rs 600) and Bangalore (Rs 375), though the prices rise for the peak season. The buses aren't the pinnacle of comfort – they can be cramped, and typically erratic Indian driving and rough roads make sleep a lottery. If you're on a sleeper, check whether you're sharing with anyone. Ordinary buses (without air-con) cost Rs 275 to Mumbai and Rs 350 to Hampi.

Luxury buses can also be booked through agents in Margao, Mapusa and the beach resorts, but they still depart from Panaji.

It's possible to get buses to destinations further afield, including to Cochin and Chennai, but they are infrequent and these trips are better tackled by a combination of train and bus or by breaking the journey and changing buses.

Panaji is also a hub for local buses heading in all directions. For the southern beach resorts you'll have to change in Margao, and for points north of Calangute, you'll generally have to change in Mapusa. Some of the more popular bus routes within Goa include the following:

Calangute Frequent services throughout the day and evening (Rs 7, 45 minutes).
Mapusa Frequent buses run to Mapusa (Rs 7, 25 minutes), and there's a separate ticket booth at the Kadamba bus stand for express services.
Margao Minibuses to Margao (ordinary/express Rs 12/17, 45 minutes) leave from platform 11. Change at Margao for the southern beaches.
Miramar & Dona Paula Frequent buses ply this route (Rs 4, 20 minutes).
Old Goa Direct buses to Old Goa (Rs 4, 25 minutes) leave constantly.
Ponda Regular buses to Ponda (Rs 8, 55 minutes) run via Old Goa.
Vasco da Gama Minibuses to Vasco da Gama (Rs 17, 45 minutes) leave from platform 10.

TAXI
Autorickshaws, taxis and motorcycle taxis gather at several places in Panaji, including the Kadamba bus stand and around the Municipal Gardens. Typical taxi fares from Panaji include Rs 200 to Calangute, Rs 200 for a return trip to Old Goa with waiting time, and Rs 450 to Margao.

TRAIN
The train is a far more comfortable and faster option than the bus for Mumbai and Mangalore. Panaji's nearest train station is Karmali (Old Goa), 12km to the east. You can catch a bus to Old Goa and then an autorickshaw. Otherwise, taxis charge around Rs 80 to/from the station, and autorickshaws charge Rs 50. The **Konkan Railway reservation office** (◷ 8am-8pm Mon-Sat) is on the 1st floor of the Kadamba bus stand. The travel agencies just north of the bus stand can also make train bookings.

Getting Around
Given the frequently one-way flow of the traffic, it's often more efficient to walk than to take a taxi or autorickshaw. Distances aren't great and this is one of the nicest towns in Goa to walk through. However, if you do want to hire a motorcycle or scooter, Panaji is a good place to do so.

CENTRAL GOA

TO/FROM THE AIRPORT

There are no bus services from the airport to Panaji, other than those for upmarket hotel guests. Prepaid taxis from Dabolim Airport cost Rs 390 and take around 40 minutes. It will work out cheaper if you can arrange to share the taxi with others. Alternatively, when you step out of the airport building, turn left and walk to the main road, where you can catch a bus to Vasco de Gama (Rs 4, every 15 minutes or so). From the minibus stand at Vasco you can take a direct bus to Panaji (Rs 17, 45 minutes) or Margao (Rs 15, 45 minutes). Queues for the tickets can be long but are orderly. Buses leave between 7.20am and 7pm when they are full (every 10 to 15 minutes).

BICYCLE

Opposite Cine National there's a **cycle store** (☎ 2222670, 2226569; fax 5640219), which rents out old Chinese push-bikes. Prices start at Rs 6 per hour and Rs 60 per day.

MOTORCYCLE

The most prolific rental presence in town is Queen Paulo Travels, which can actually advertise because it is registered (ie legally operating). You'll see signs outside their various agents. Two reliable places to go are Hotel Aroma (p93) and Mayfair Hotel (p92), which both organise Queen Paulo bikes. A Honda Activa will cost around Rs 250, and an Enfield around Rs 400. At busier times prices will fluctuate by Rs 50 or so. Another choice is friendly **Cyberjoint** (☎ 5640190, 2435905, 9822131835; Jose Falcao Rd), which rents out Hondas for Rs 250 per day. The other option is to ask around on the street; try the Municipal Garden area or near the general post office – one of the taxi drivers should be able to help you.

AROUND PANAJI

Miramar
☎ 0832

Miramar, 3km southwest of the city (follow Dayanand Bandodkar Marg along the Mandovi waterfront), is Panaji's nearest beach. The couple of kilometres of exposed sand facing Aguada Bay is hardly inspiring compared to other Goan beaches, but this is a popular place to watch the sun sink into the Arabian Sea, and it's an easy bicycle ride from the centre of Panaji.

While there is good swimming to be had at **Miramar Beach**, be warned that the experience might not be an altogether relaxing one. Not many foreigners venture down to Miramar Beach so you'll be something of an attraction – and in a less than modest bathing suit, an absolute spectacle.

Along the seafront road, at the start of Miramar Beach, is **Gaspar Dias**. Originally a fort stood here, directly opposite the fort at Reis Magos. They were designed to defend the entrance to the Mandovi, although they were of limited use; in 1639 the Dutch attacked Goa and managed to destroy a number of ships before being driven off. There's no fort here now, but the most prominent position on the beachfront is taken up by a **statue** representing Hindu and Christian unity.

If the kids get bored of the beach you could take them to the **Goa Science Centre** (☎ 2463426; New Marine Hwy; admission Rs 10; ⏱ 10.30am-6.30pm). Even though the centre only opened in December 2001, it is already looking tired. The science park in the centre grounds is a collection of play equipment that 'explain the laws of physics due to their intrinsic quality'. The centre focuses on interactive exhibits; kids can engage with the extensive oceanographic section and get more of an appreciation for the sea than just sun and sand. It's a few minutes' walk south along the New Marine Hwy from the Miramar roundabout.

There are many food stands lining the road if you continue from the roundabout towards Dona Paula. There is also a very well-placed Café Coffee Day. A reputable place for a seafood meal is **Martin's Beach Corner** (☎ 2464877; mains Rs 40-100; ⏱ 11am-3pm & 6.30-11pm) at Caranzalem, near Blue Bay Hotel. This is an unassuming spot but is well known to locals and the food is genuinely good. It also has a claim to fame – Roger Moore and Gregory Peck ate here during the filming of *The Sea Wolves*.

There are frequent buses to Miramar from Panaji (Rs 4, 20 minutes).

Dona Paula
☎ 0832

Continuing south past Miramar, the coast road leads to Dona Paula, a small peninsula with several resort complexes that have grown up around a fishing village. Although everyone agrees that the area is named after Dona Paula de Menezes, the woman whose tombstone can be found in the chapel in the Cabo Raj Bhavan, there are numerous variations of the story about her. In one story she was the viceroy's heart-broken daughter who hurled herself from the nearby cliffs. Others have it that she was the virtuous wife of a nobleman, while still others claim that she was a lady-in-waiting to the viceroy's wife and also that she was the mistress of the viceroy himself. The only thing that seems certain is that she bequeathed the land on which the village is now built to the church.

SIGHTS & ACTIVITIES

On the westernmost point of the peninsula stands an old fortress, **Cabo Raj Bhavan** (also known as Cabo Ray Niwas). Today the large estate on this headland is the residence of the governor of Goa. The double-storey structure is full of antique artefacts.

Plans to build a fort to guard the entrance to the Mandovi and Zuari Rivers were first proposed in 1540 and, although it was some years before work began, a chapel was raised on the spot almost immediately. The fort was subsequently completed and the chapel was extended by the Portuguese viceroy to include a Franciscan friary or convent. The fort, which was equipped with several cannons, was never actually used in anger, and from the 1650s the buildings were requisitioned as a temporary residence for the archbishop. In 1798 it was taken over by British troops, who remained in residence (apart from a brief break) until 1813.

On the southern side of the access road to the fort is the **British cemetery**, which is the last reminder of the British troops' presence. After their departure, the buildings were once again taken over by the archbishop of Goa as his private residence. They didn't remain long in his possession, however, for in 1866 the viceroy took a shine to the buildings, and had them refurbished and converted into the governor's palace.

You can drive up to the entrance gates (turn right at the roundabout if coming from Panaji), where there's a parking area and viewpoint with good views back across Miramar Beach, the Mandovi estuary and Fort Aguada. The chapel is open to the public for Sunday-morning service and at Christmas and Easter.

Continuing through the roundabout brings you to Dona Paula's small bay, where there are water sports and souvenir stalls. The **Dona Paula Sports Club** (☎ 2453278) – a fancy name for a shack on the beach – hires out jet skis; for Rs 70 you can jet-ski for a kilometre.

At the end of the road is a pier and small outcrop of rock, on which stands a **sculpture** designed by Baroness Yrsa von Leistner called 'Images of India'.

SLEEPING

Across from the harbour, on the peninsula facing the sea and the mouth of the Zuari River, are a couple of small resort hotels that are quite secluded and reasonably good value outside the high season.

Goan Delicacy (☎ 2453265; goandelicacy@yahoo .com; Hawaii Beach; r Rs 600-1000) If you're interested in staying in the 'real Goa', far from the mayhem of Dona Paula, then the obvious choice is Goan Delicacy, which has two spacious rooms (one upstairs, one down) both with a separate sitting room complete with satellite TV, a clean hot-water bathroom, a small kitchenette and a balcony where you can really make yourself at home. The rooms sleep up to four people. It's right across the road from a quiet patch of beach, from where you can pity the poor souls in the crowds across the way.

Zauri View (☎ 2456545; zuariview@yahoo.co.in; B3 Baywatch, Jetty Rd; d with bathroom Rs 1200) Opposite Hawaii Beach, Zauri View has four pleasant rooms overlooking the sea, and facilities such as hot water and satellite TV to keep you comfortable.

Cidade de Goa (☎ 2454545; www.cadadedegoa .com; d US$200; 🖭) Absolute indulgence is on offer at this opulent hotel 1km down the coast by Vaniguinim Beach. This is an exclusive world of opulence with all the usual five-star requirements including beachfront pool, health club and casino.

There are some miniresort-style accommodation options, both of which have a patch of beach and their own pool:

O Pescador (☎ 2453863; www.opescador.com; s/d with AC Rs 1200/2000, without AC Rs 1100/1400; 🖭 🖭) Space has been well used to create a nice view of the private beach. Full payment is required up front.

Prainha (☎ 2453881-3; www.prainha.com; d Rs 2000-2500; 🖭 🖭) Lovely, though slightly overpriced, beachside cottages and pleasant rooms in peaceful gardens.

EATING

Goan Delicacy (☎ 2453265; Hawaii Beach) A well-hidden gem down one of Dona Paula's most delightful roads, Goan Delicacy is a friendly, airy and immaculate place that cooks up delicious and imaginative fare such as lemon fish soup, steaks and ice cream. It's right next to the beach.

Nautica (vegetable thalis Rs 30; 🕑 8am-10pm) Nautica is a popular multitiered restaurant with good views over the bay. It's also surprisingly well priced given its attempt at class; a vegetable thali is Rs 30, as is a beer. It's near Dona Paula Jetty.

Menino's Bar and Restaurant (☎ 2452702; mains Rs 30-100; breakfast, lunch & dinner) This low-key restaurant at the Jetty is a popular spot for Indian tourists, and serves Indian, Chinese and Goan dishes. The terrace is an ideal place to sit and admire the view.

GETTING THERE & AWAY

Frequent buses to Miramar and Dona Paula leave from the Kadamba bus stand in Panaji (Rs 4, 20), and run along riverfront Dayanand Bandodkar Marg. There are several stops along this road.

Dr Salim Ali Bird Sanctuary

Named after the late Dr Salim Moizzudin Abdul Ali, India's best-known ornithologist, this sanctuary on Chorao Island was proclaimed by the Forest Department in 1988 to protect the birdlife that thrives here and the mangroves that had grown around reclaimed marshland. Apart from the ubiquitous white egrets and purple herons, you can expect to see colourful kingfishers, eagles, cormorants, kites, woodpeckers, sandpipers, curlews, drongos and mynahs, to name a few. Marsh crocodiles and otters have also been spotted by some visitors, along with the mudskipper fish that skim across the water's surface at low tide. There's a bird-watching tower in the sanctuary that can be reached by boat when the water level is not too low.

Dr Salim Ali Bird Sanctuary is portrayed by cynics as having little to offer those who are not interested in birds. This is a great shame given that getting to the island is easy and a leisurely drift through its mangrove swamps offers a fascinating insight into life on this fragile terrain. Seeing the farming and fishing activities of the island is a fascinating contrast to nearby Panaji.

The best time to visit is either in the early morning (about 8am) or in the evening (a couple of hours before sunset), but since the Mandovi is a tidal river, boat trips depend somewhat on tide times. A trip to the sanctuary allows you to get waterborne and see Goa from a new perspective, and to that end the best way to cruise the waterways is in a dugout canoe with a local boatman, many of whom will be waiting on the mainland side of the ferry to the island. The going rate is anywhere between Rs 350 and Rs 500 for a 90-minute trip. Once you arrive on the island, you will have to pay the forest officer Rs 50 to enter the sanctuary.

A particularly good guide is **Paresh Sawant** (☎ 0832-2239141, 9822489611), a Chorao Island local and a bird-lover since his school days. Paresh will take you for a 1½-hour guided tour of the mangroves in a dugout canoe and excitedly point out the going-ons of the sanctuary, both human and animal. To find him, ask around at the ferry crossing or call him after 9pm to arrange a meeting time.

To get to Chorao Island, take a bus bound for Old Goa and ask to be let off at the Ribandar ferry crossing. Ferries go back and forth from 6.30am into the night, and are free for pedestrians (motorcycle/car Rs 4/20).

OLD GOA
☎ 0832

About 9km east of Panaji, a handful of imposing churches and convents remain in a city that was once so grand and so powerful it was said to rival Lisbon in magnificence. Known as the Rome of the East, Old Goa is without doubt Goa's premier historical attraction and you should put aside at least a morning or afternoon to explore it.

DETOUR: CHORAO ISLAND

Chorao Island can be explored by bicycle or motorcycle, and you can also walk around the marshlands skirting the Dr Salim Ali Bird Sanctuary (above). Although there's not much to see on the island, the village of **Chorao** has a number of Portuguese houses and is a typical Goan backwater where many locals are still pleasantly surprised to see you there – which is unexpected when you're so close to the capital.

Old Goa was not only the capital of the new Portuguese colony but also the principal city of the Portuguese eastern empire. Its rise was meteoric: over the course of the hundred years following the arrival of the Portuguese in Goa, the city became famed throughout the world. One Dutch visitor compared it with Amsterdam for volume of trade and wealth. Its fall, however, was just as swift, and eventually the city was completely abandoned.

Today, although some of the churches are still in use (the tomb of St Francis Xavier is in the Basilica of Bom Jesus), many of the old buildings have become museums maintained by the Archaeological Survey of India.

Old Goa can get very crowded on weekends and feast days. The best time to visit is weekday mornings, when you can take in mass at the Se Cathedral or Basilica Bom Jesus and explore the rest of the site before the afternoon heat sets in.

When visiting Old Goa do not come dressed in beach wear or sleeveless shirts. As a basilica, Bom Jesus is particularly sacred to Christians. Indian tourists visiting the churches show much more respect than many Westerners – even (unnecessarily) leaving their shoes outside as they would at a Hindu temple.

History

The first large-scale settlement in the area took place in the 15th century, when a port sprang up on the banks of the Mandovi near the tiny village of Ela. While the capital of the state was still officially to the south (at the site known today as Goa Velha), it had started to lose importance, both because of its vulnerability (it was sacked by Muslim invaders from the north in 1312 and 1470) and because the Zuari River, Goa Velha's port, had started to silt up. Shortly after the arrival of the Muslim Bahmani sultanate in 1470, the status of capital and the name Govepuri were transferred to the new site on the north of the main island, opposite Divar Island.

Within a short time the new capital was a thriving city. When the Bahmani sultanate disintegrated and Govepuri came into

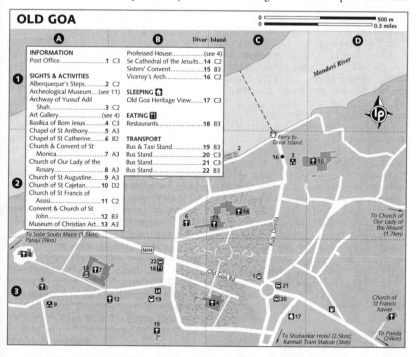

OLD GOA

0 _____ 500 m
0 _____ 0.3 miles

INFORMATION
Post Office..........................1 C3

SIGHTS & ACTIVITIES
Alberqueque's Steps............2 C2
Archeological Museum....(see 11)
Archway of Yussuf Adil
  Shah..................................3 C2
Art Gallery.........................(see 4)
Basilica of Bom Jesus...........4 C3
Chapel of St Anthony............5 A3
Chapel of St Catherine.........6 B2
Church & Convent of St
  Monica..............................7 A3
Church of Our Lady of the
  Rosary...............................8 A3
Church of St Augustine.........9 A3
Church of St Cajetan...........10 D2
Church of St Francis of
  Assisi................................11 C2
Convent & Church of St
  John.................................12 B3
Museum of Christian Art......13 A3

Professed House...............(see 4)
Se Cathedral of the Jesuits...14 C2
Sisters' Convent.................15 B3
Viceroy's Arch....................16 B3

SLEEPING
Old Goa Heritage View........17 C3

EATING
Restaurants........................18 B3

TRANSPORT
Bus & Taxi Stand.................19 B3
Bus Stand..........................20 C3
Bus Stand..........................21 C3
Bus Stand..........................22 B3

Divar Island

Mandovi River

Ferry to
Divar Island

To Church of
Our Lady of
the Mount
(1.7km)

To Solar Souto Maior (1.5km);
Panaji (9km)

NH4

Old Goa Rd

Rua Direita

Church of
St Francis
Xavier

To Shubankar Hotel (2.5km);
Karmali Train Station (3km)

To Ponda
(24km)

the hands of the Muslim Bijapur sultanate, Gove was so favoured by Yussuf Adil Shah that it became his second capital. Contemporary accounts tell of the magnificence of the city and of the grandeur of the royal palace. In the years following his takeover, the city was enlarged and strengthened with ramparts and a moat. It became a major trading centre and a departure point for pilgrims to Mecca, and gained prominence for its shipbuilding.

In 1510, with the arrival of the Portuguese, Gove (which was known to the Portuguese as Goa) was the scene of not one but two takeovers. Afonso de Albuquerque managed to gain control of the entire island briefly in March, but was then evicted by Yussuf Adil Shah two months later. Having ridden out the monsoon in his ships, the indomitable Albuquerque attacked again in the autumn, and on 25 November (St Catherine's Day) recaptured Gove.

With Gove now firmly under control, the new rulers started to build. A major impetus was the arrival of the religious orders. Although the first missionaries arrived with Albuquerque as chaplains to his fleet, the real influx began in 1542 with the arrival of (among others) the young Francis Xavier.

In the following year the city experienced its first taste of the problems that were to lead to its eventual abandonment, when a cholera epidemic wiped out an estimated 200,000 inhabitants. Undeterred, the missionaries built churches, hospitals and seminaries, vying with each other to produce the most splendid buildings. All were modelled on European counterparts and consequently there are domes, pilasters, barrel arches and flying buttresses by the dozen.

By the late 16th century the city had expanded hugely; the city walls were removed and the moat filled in to allow for the spread. Goa at this time had an estimated population of around 250,000.

Ironically it was also at this time that Goa's fortunes began to turn. By the end of the 16th century, Portuguese supremacy on the seas had been usurped by the British, Dutch and French. The city's decline was accelerated by another devastating cholera epidemic, which struck in 1635. Bouts of disease recurred in the following years and eventually led to plans to abandon the city.

In 1684, against considerable opposition, the viceroy ordered work to begin on a new capital in Mormugao. His successor abandoned the project and then restarted work when ordered to do so by Lisbon, but the plan never really got off the ground.

In 1695, however, the viceroy himself decided to move to Panelim (then a village outside Old Goa). Although Old Goa remained the capital, everybody who could afford to do so followed his example to escape the appalling health problems. In this same year the population of the city was 20,000 – less than a 10th of what it had been a century before. By 1759, Panelim too had been struck by the same problems and the viceroy again moved his residence, this time to Panjim.

Despite Old Goa's virtual abandonment, in 1777 the government in Lisbon ordered the city be rebuilt, arguing that if the water supply and drainage could be thoroughly cleaned and reconstructed the city would be healthy. Work was abandoned five years later when the death toll among the workers from cholera and malaria became too high to continue.

The final blow came in 1835 when the Portuguese government ordered the repression of the religious societies and most of the missionaries were shipped home. By 1846 only the convent of Santa Monica was in regular use. When that was abandoned the ruins of the great city were left all but empty.

From the late 19th century until the mid-20th century the city remained empty, apart from one or two buildings used as military barracks. When archaeological interest started to increase, work was done to clear the area and some buildings were returned to their former uses. But for many of the buildings, which had been plundered for building materials or had simply fallen down, the reprieve came too late. The starkest reminder of this is the ruined tower of the Church of St Augustine, which can be seen from miles around.

Information

There's no tourist office but guides are available at the main churches. You can also inquire at the Archaeological Museum, which has books on Old Goa, including S Rajagopalan's excellent booklet *Old Goa*,

LUÍS VAZ DE CAMÕES

Luís Vaz de Camões (1524–80) is regarded as Portugal's greatest poet. The young man was banished to Goa in 1553 at the age of 29, after being accused of fighting with and wounding a magistrate in Lisbon. He was obviously no soft touch, for he enlisted in the army and fought with some distinction before attracting further official disapproval for publicly criticising the administration.

His reward this time was to be exiled to the Moluccas, and he returned to Goa only in 1562. Written at this time was his most famous work, *Os Lusíadas,* an epic poem glorifying the adventures of Vasco da Gama. Classical in style and imperialist in sentiment, the poem became an icon of Portuguese nationalism.

A statue of Camões, erected in 1960, stood in the centre of Old Goa until 1983, when many Goans decided that it was an unacceptable relic of colonialism. An attempt by radicals to blow it up met with only partial success, but the authorities took the hint and removed the statue. It now stands in the Archaeological Museum in Old Goa.

published by the Archaeological Survey of India. One of the most comprehensive books is *Old Goa the Complete Guide* by Oscar de Noronha (2004).

Sights

SE CATHEDRAL

At over 76m long and 55m wide, this is the largest church in Asia. The cathedral was begun in 1562, on the orders of King Dom Sebastiao of Portugal, to replace the older church of St Catherine, which had served as a cathedral up to this time. Progress was slow. Work on the building wasn't completed until 1619 and the altars weren't finished until 1652, some 90 years after the building's construction had first been ordered.

The cathedral stands on what was the main square of the city, and looking east from the main entrance it's possible to visualise something of the city's former layout. The grassy area in front of the doors was the large market square, to the left was the Senate House and to the right was the notorious Palace of the Inquisition.

The exterior of the cathedral is notable for its plain style, after the Tuscan tradition, and for the rather lopsided look that the loss of one bell tower, which collapsed in 1776, has given it. The remaining tower houses the famous **Golden Bell**, which is the largest bell in Asia and is renowned for its rich tone.

The huge interior of the cathedral is also plain. To the right as you enter is a small, locked area that contains a font that was made in 1532 and is said to have been used by St Francis Xavier. The two small statuettes, which are inset into the main pillars, are of St Francis Xavier and St Ignatius Loyola. There are four chapels on either side of the nave, two of which have screens across the entrance. Of these, the **Chapel of the Blessed Sacrament** is quite outstanding, with every inch of wall and ceiling gilded and beautifully decorated – a complete contrast to the austerity of the cathedral interior.

Opposite, on the right of the nave, is the other screened chapel, the **Chapel of the Cross of Miracles**. The story goes that in 1619 a simple cross made by local shepherds was erected on a hillside near Old Goa. The cross grew bigger and several witnesses saw an apparition of Christ hanging on it. A church was planned on the spot where the vision had appeared and while this was being built the cross was stored nearby. When it came time to move the cross into the new church it was found that it had grown again and that the doors of the church had to be widened to accommodate it. The cross was moved to the cathedral in 1845.

Towering above the main altar is the huge gilded reredos (ornamental screen behind the altar in Goan churches). Its six main panels are carved with scenes from the life of St Catherine, to whom the cathedral is dedicated. She was beheaded in Alexandria, and among the images here are those showing her awaiting execution and being carried to Mt Sinai by angels.

Mass takes place from Monday to Saturday at 7am and 6pm; on Sunday it's at 7.15am, 10am (high mass) and 4pm.

THE INCORRUPT BODY OF ST FRANCIS XAVIER

Goa's patron saint, Francis Xavier, was born into a wealthy and aristocratic family in Navarre, Spain, on 7 April 1506. A brilliant scholar, he studied at Paris University, where he met Ignatius Loyola and thus came to the turning point in his life. Together with five others, they formed the Society of Jesus (the Jesuits) in 1534 and almost immediately hatched plans to travel to the Holy Land, where they hoped to convert the Muslims. Although the plans fell through, there was plenty to be done in other areas, and when missionaries were requested for the eastern empire, it seemed an ideal opportunity.

In April 1541, Xavier sailed from Portugal, arriving in Goa in May 1542. After a brief spell teaching, he commenced his travels, which took him to Ceylon, Malacca and Japan, among other places. In February 1552 he persuaded the viceroy to allow him to plan an embassy to China, a mission that his death cut short. He died on the island of Sancian, off the Chinese coast, on 2 December 1552.

After his death his servant is said to have emptied four sacks of quicklime into his coffin to consume his flesh in case the order came to return the remains to Goa. Two months later, the body was transferred to Malacca, where it was seen to be still in perfect condition – refusing to rot despite the quicklime. The following year, Francis Xavier's body was returned to Goa, where people declared its preservation to be a miracle.

The church was slower to acknowledge it, requiring a medical examination to establish that the body had not been embalmed. This was performed in 1556 by the viceroy's physician, who declared that all the internal organs were still intact and that no preservative agents had been used. He noticed a small wound in the chest and asked two Jesuits to put their fingers into it. He noted, 'When they withdrew them, they were covered with the blood which I smelt and found to be absolutely untainted.'

It was not until 1622 that canonisation took place. By then, holy relic hunters decided to corrupt the incorrupt body. In 1614 the right arm was removed and divided between Jesuits in Japan and Rome, and by 1636 parts of one shoulder blade and all the internal organs had been scattered through Southeast Asia. By the end of the 17th century the body was in an advanced state of desiccation and the miracle appeared to be over. The Jesuits decided to enclose the corpse in a glass coffin out of view, and it was not until the mid-19th century that the current cycle of expositions began.

Every 10 years, the glass coffin containing the body is brought out so the masses can see the 450-year-old remains. The exposition takes place around Xavier's feast day – 3 December – with the next event taking place in 2014.

CHURCH OF ST FRANCIS OF ASSISI

West of Se Cathedral, the Church of St Francis of Assisi is one of the most interesting buildings in Old Goa. A small chapel was built on this site by eight Franciscan friars on their arrival in 1517. In 1521 it was replaced by a church consecrated to the Holy Ghost. This church was subsequently rebuilt in 1661, and only the doorway of the old building was incorporated into the new structure. This original doorway, in ornate Manueline style, contrasts strongly with the rest of the façade, the plainness of which had by that time become the fashion.

The interior of the church is particularly beautiful – perhaps because the local artisans were given greater freedom with their skills here than elsewhere. The walls and ceiling are heavily gilded and covered with carved wood panels, and there are a number of large paintings on the walls of the chancel. A huge arch that supports the choir, painted vividly with floral designs, and the intricately carved pulpit are worth looking out for. The reredos again dominates, although it is different from others in Old Goa, with a deep recess for the tabernacle. The four statues in the lower part of the reredos are of the apostles, and above the reredos is Christ on the cross. The symbolism of this scene is unmistakable: Jesus has his right arm free to embrace St Francis, who is standing on the three vows of the Franciscan order – poverty, humility and obedience.

Like many other churches in Old Goa, this church has the tombstones of many of the Portuguese gentry laid into the floor. The font, situated just beside the door, is made partly from a fragment of an old pillar from a Hindu temple.

ARCHAEOLOGICAL MUSEUM

The convent at the back of the Church of St Francis of Assisi is now the **Archaeological Museum** (admission Rs 5; ☻ 9am-6.30pm Sat-Thu). It houses fragments of sculpture from Hindu temple sites in Goa, which show Chalukyan and Hoysala influences, and stone Vetal images from the animist cult that flourished in this part of India centuries ago. Also here are two large bronze statues: one of the Portuguese poet Luís Vaz de Camões (p103), which once stood in the area between the Se Cathedral and the Basilica of Bom Jesus, and one of Afonso de Albuquerque, the first governor, which stood at Miramar.

Upstairs, a gallery contains portraits of the Portuguese viceroys. These paintings were housed in random locations around the state until they were finally collected and displayed here.

CHAPEL OF ST CATHERINE

About 100m to the west of the Church of St Francis stands the Chapel of St Catherine. An earlier chapel was erected on this site by Afonso de Albuquerque in 1510 to commemorate his entry into the city on St Catherine's Day. In 1534 the chapel was granted cathedral status by Pope Paul III and in 1550 it was rebuilt. The inscribed stone that was added during the rebuilding states that Afonso de Albuquerque actually entered the city at this spot, and hence it is believed that the chapel is built on what used to be the main gate of the Muslim city. The Chapel of St Catherine was rebuilt in laterite in 1952. The chapel remains empty and is rarely open to visitors.

BASILICA OF BOM JESUS

This basilica is famous throughout the Roman Catholic world. It contains the tomb and mortal remains of St Francis Xavier, the so-called Apostle of the Indies (opposite). A former pupil of St Ignatius Loyola, the founder of the Society of Jesus (the Jesuits), St Francis Xavier's missionary voyages became legendary – considering the state of transport at the time, they were nothing short of miraculous.

This is the only church in Old Goa that is not plastered on the outside, the lime plaster having been stripped off by a zealous Portuguese conservationist in 1950. Apparently the idea was that, exposed to the elements, the laterite would become more durable and thus the building would be strengthened. Despite proof to the contrary, no-one has got around to putting the plaster back yet.

Construction began in 1594 and the church was completed in 1605. The façade has elements of Doric, Ionic and Corinthian design, and the pillars and detail are carved from basalt that was brought from Bassein, some 300km away. Prominent in the design of the façade is the Jesuit emblem 'IHS', which is the abbreviation of the words for 'Jesus' in Greek.

Inside the basilica the layout is simple but grand. The original vaulted ceiling has now been replaced by a simple wooden one. To the left of the door as you enter the basilica is a statue of St Francis Xavier, but yet again the huge and ornate gilded reredos that stretches from floor to ceiling behind the altar takes pride of place. The baroque detail of the ornament contrasts strongly with the classical, plain layout of the cathedral itself. As in the Church of St Francis of Assisi, the symbolism of the figures depicted is important. The reredos shows St Ignatius Loyola protecting a tiny figure of the Christ child. St Ignatius' eyes are raised to a huge gilded sun above his head, on which IHS is emblazoned. Above the sun is a depiction of the Trinity.

To the right of the altar, however, is the highlight for the vast majority of visitors, for it is here that the body of St Francis Xavier is kept. The body was moved into the church in 1622, and in the late 1680s the duke of Tuscany financed the building of the marble catafalque. In exchange for his contribution he was given the pillow on which St Francis' head had been resting. The duke engaged the Florentine sculptor Giovanni Batista Foggini and finally, after 10 years' work, the three-tiered structure was erected in the basilica in 1698. The catafalque is constructed of jasper and marble. On each side of the second tier are bronze plaques that depict scenes from the saint's life. Atop the structure is the casket, which was designed by Italian Jesuit

Marcelo Mastrili and constructed by local silversmiths in 1637.

Passing from the chapel towards the sacristy there are a couple of items relating to St Francis' remains and, slightly further on, the stairs to a **gallery**. Even if the paintings are not to your taste, a visit to the gallery is still worthwhile, as there's a small window that looks down on the tomb of St Francis Xavier, allowing you a different perspective.

Next to the basilica is the **Professed House of the Jesuits**, a two-storey laterite building covered with lime plaster. It actually predates the basilica, having been completed in 1585. It was from here that Jesuit missions to the east were organised. Part of the building burned down in 1633 and was partially rebuilt in 1783.

Mass is held in the basilica at 7am and 8am Monday to Saturday, and at 8am and 9.15am on Sunday.

CHURCH OF ST CAJETAN

Modelled on the original design of St Peter's in Rome, this church was built by Italian friars of the Order of Theatines, who were sent by Pope Urban VIII to preach Christianity in the kingdom of Golconda (near Hyderabad). The friars were not permitted to work in Golconda, so they settled at Old Goa in 1640. The construction of the church began in 1655, and although it's perhaps less interesting than the other churches, it's still a beautiful building and the only truly domed church remaining in Goa. The altar is dedicated to Our Lady of Divine Providence, but the church is more popularly named after the founder of the Theatine order, St Cajetan (1480–1547), a contemporary of St Francis Xavier. Born in Vicenza, St Cajetan spent all of his life in Italy, establishing the Order of Theatines in Rome in 1524. He was known for his work in hospitals and with 'incurables', and for his high moral stance in an increasingly corrupt Roman Catholic church. He was canonised in 1671.

The façade of the church is classical in design and the four niches on the front contain statues of apostles. Inside, clever use of internal buttresses and four huge pillars have turned the interior into a cruciform, above the centre of which is the towering dome. The inscription around the inside of the base of the dome is a verse from St Matthew's Gospel. The largest of the altars

on the right side of the church is dedicated to St Cajetan himself. On the left side are paintings illustrating episodes in the life of St Cajetan; in one it appears that he is being breast-fed at some distance by an angel whose aim is remarkably accurate.

RUINS OF THE CHURCH OF ST AUGUSTINE

All that is really left of this church is the 46m-high tower, which served as a belfry and formed part of the façade of the church. The few other remnants are choked with creepers and weeds, and access is difficult.

The church was constructed in 1602 by Augustinian friars who arrived at Old Goa in 1587. It was abandoned in 1835 because of the repressive policies of the Portuguese government, which resulted in the eviction of many religious orders from Goa. The church fell into neglect and the vault collapsed in 1842. In 1931 the façade and half the tower fell down, followed by more sections in 1938. The tower's huge bell was moved in 1871 to the Church of Our Lady of the Immaculate Conception in Panjim, where it can be seen (and heard) today.

CHURCH & CONVENT OF ST MONICA

Work on this three-storey laterite building commenced in 1606 and was completed in 1627, only to burn down nine years later. Reconstruction started the following year and it's from this time that the buildings date. Once known as the Royal Monastery because of the royal patronage that it enjoyed, the building was the first nunnery in the east. Like the other religious institutions, it was crippled by the banning of the religious orders, but did not immediately close, although it was forbidden to recruit any further. It was finally abandoned when the last sister died in 1885. During the 1950s and '60s the buildings housed first Portuguese and then Indian troops, before being returned to the church in 1968.

The building is now used by the Mater Dei Institute as a theological centre. Visitors are allowed in if they are reasonably dressed. There are fading murals on the inside of the western walls of the chapel.

MUSEUM OF CHRISTIAN ART

Adjacent to the Convent of St Monica, this **museum** (adult/child Rs 15/free; ⏱ 9.30am-5pm) contains a collection of statuary, paintings and sculptures, most of it transferred here from the Rachol Seminary. Many of the works of Goan Christian art made during the Portuguese era, including some of those on display here, were produced by local Hindu artists. Among the items on show are richly embroidered priest vestments, a number of devotional paintings and carvings, and a fair amount of silverware, including crucifixes, salvers and crowns.

CHURCH OF OUR LADY OF THE ROSARY

Passing beneath the flying buttresses of the Convent of St Monica, about 250m further along the road is the Church of Our Lady of the Rosary, which stands on the top of a high bluff. It is one of the earliest churches in Goa – the legend has it that Albuquerque surveyed the attack on the Muslim city from the bluff and vowed to build a church there in thanks for his victory.

The church, which has been beautifully restored, is Manueline in style, and refreshingly simple in design. There are excellent views of the Mandovi River and Divar Island from the church's dramatic position, but unfortunately the building is frequently locked.

The only ornaments on the outside of the church are simple rope-twist devices, which bear testimony to Portugal's reliance on the sea. Inside the same is true; the reredos is wonderfully plain after all the gold of those in the churches below, and the roof consists simply of a layer of tiles. Set into the floor in front of the altar is the tombstone of one of the governors, Garcia de Sa, and set into the northern wall of the chancel is that of his wife, Caterina a Piro, who was the first Portuguese woman to arrive in Goa. According to legend they were married by St Francis Xavier as she lay dying.

CHAPEL OF ST ANTHONY

Opposite the ruins of the Church of St Augustine is the Chapel of St Anthony, which is now in use as part of a convent. The chapel, dedicated to the saint of the Portuguese army and navy, was one of the earliest to be built in Goa, again on the directions of Albuquerque in order to celebrate the assault on the city. Like the other institutions around it, St Anthony's was abandoned in 1835 but was brought back into use at the end of the 19th century.

VICEROY'S ARCH

Perhaps the best way to arrive in Old Goa is in the same way that visitors did in the city's heyday. Approaching along the river (and probably giving thanks for having made it at all), the visitors would have first glimpsed the busy wharf just in front of the entrance to the city. Although the city's fortifications were demolished to make way for new buildings, on the road up from the dock there was nonetheless an archway to symbolise entry.

This archway, called the Viceroy's Arch, was erected by Vasco da Gama's grandson, who became viceroy in 1597. On the side facing the river, the arch (which was restored in 1954 after collapsing) is ornamented with the deer emblem of Vasco da Gama's coat of arms. Above it in the centre of the archway is a statue of da Gama himself. On the side facing the city is a sculpture of a European woman wielding a sword over an Indian, who is lying under her feet. No prizes for guessing what the message is here. The arch originally had a third storey with a statue of St Catherine.

If you take a moment here, it's possible to imagine something of the layout of the old city. Looking towards the ferry dock, the main docks at which the newly arrived ships were unloaded were to the left. The arsenal and mint were here too, although they were dismantled for building materials after the city was abandoned. To the right, the quay led into one of the busiest market areas in the city. If you face the Viceroy's Arch, just to the left was the Muslim ruler Yussuf Adil Shah's palace, which was eventually taken over as the viceroy's residence. All that remains of the palace now is the **gateway**, which can be seen on the left as you approach the entrance to the Church of St Cajetan. The road running from the dock through the Viceroy's Arch and into the city was known as the Rua Direita, and was lined with shops and businesses.

CHURCH OF OUR LADY OF THE MOUNT

There is one other church in Old Goa, which often gets overlooked as it is some 2km east of the central area. Approached by a long and overgrown flight of steps, the hill on which the church stands commands an excellent view of the whole of Old Goa below. This is reputedly where Yussuf

Adil Shah placed his artillery during the assault to recapture the city in May 1510, and again when he was defending the city in November. The church was built shortly after, completed in 1519, and has been rebuilt twice since.

Festivals & Events

Procession of All Saints On the fifth Monday of Lent, this is the only procession of its sort outside Rome. Thirty statues of saints are brought out from storage and paraded around Old Goa's neighbouring villages.

Feast of St Francis Xavier Held on 3 December and preceded by a nine-day novena, this is the biggest festival of the year. There are lots of festivities and huge crowds here over this period, especially for the exposition of St Francis Xavier's body, held once every 10 years – the next expo is in 2014.

Sleeping

There are only a couple of hotels in the vicinity of Old Goa – not that there's much reason to stay there given its proximity to Panaji.

Old Goa Heritage View (Old Goa Residency; ☎ 228 5327, 2285013; d with/without AC Rs 600/440; 🌂) The GTDC's offering has reasonably good-value rooms and is a comfortable distance from everything you're in Old Goa to see.

Shubhankar Hotel (☎ 2284619, 2285920; Karmali; s/d with bathroom Rs 300/500, without bathroom Rs 100/200, with AC Rs 400/600; 🌂) The cheapest option is Shubhankar Hotel, which has clean (sterile) rooms that are good value. This hotel mainly caters to people using the Karmali train station, which is immediately around the corner.

Eating

Solar Souto Maior (☎ 5614524; www.solargoa.in) For a culinary and historical experience, come to this restored part of a Portuguese palace that has been converted into a café and a series of shops and gallery rooms. The building itself is 420 years old, but has only recently been restored with enormous taste and care. Solar Souto Maior also hosts cultural events and art exhibitions. It's only 1.5km from Old Goa in the district of St Pedro – taxi drivers will know where it is.

Tourist Inn (curries around Rs 80) Although there are a few basic restaurants scattered around the sites of Old Goa, at Tourist Inn you can enjoy a cold beer and the view over St Xavier's. Its menu does warn of a 15-minute wait but it's well located for a pit stop between sites.

There are random street stalls scattered throughout the area that sell drinks and snacks.

Getting There & Away

There are frequent buses to Old Goa (Rs 4, 25 minutes) from the Kadamba bus stand at Panaji; buses from Panaji to Ponda also pass through Old Goa. Buses to Panaji or Ponda leave when full (around every 10 minutes) from either the main roundabout or the bus stand in front of the Basilica Bom Jesus. Alternatively, Old Goa makes a nice bicycle or motorcycle excursion.

DIVAR ISLAND

The small island of Divar, which lies to the southeast of Chorao Island and to the north of Old Goa, is not only a useful short cut on the route from Panaji to Bicholim taluka (district), but is also worth a visit in its own right. Somehow Divar Island, separated from the rest of the state by the forked waters of the Mandovi, seems even quieter and more picturesque than the villages on the mainland. The largest settlement on the island, **Piedade**, is sleepy but picturesque; it's well maintained but also has hints of crumbling Portuguese architecture.

Divar Island was sacred to the Hindus and it contained two particularly important temples – the Saptakoteshwara Temple (which was moved across the river to Bicholim when the Portuguese began to persecute the Hindus), as well as a Ganesh temple that stood on the solitary hill in Piedade. It's likely that the Ganesh temple was destroyed by Muslim troops near the end of the 15th century, since the first church on this site was built in around 1515.

The church that occupies the hill today, the **Church of Our Lady of Compassion**, is in fine condition. It combines an impressive façade with an engagingly simple interior. The ceiling is picked out in plain white stucco designs, and the windows are set well back into the walls, allowing only a dim light to penetrate into the church.

From the small park near the church there are excellent views to the north, west and south. Across the river to the south, the whitewashed towers of the churches of Old Goa are clearly visible.

Divar Island can only be reached by ferry. A boat from Old Goa (near the Viceroy's Arch) runs to the south of the island, and the east end of the island is connected by ferry to Naroa in Bicholim taluka. A less frequent ferry operates to Ribandar from the southwest of the island.

Divar makes a good outing by bicycle, especially combined with a trip to Old Goa. Most of the island is flat, but it's a tough slog getting up the hill to the church. Although buses run between the ferry and Piedade, it would be a frustrating exercise trying to get around here by public transport – even taxis are scant.

At the time of research, **Deevaya A Resort** (☎ 0832-5641936), a huge five-star resort, was in the process of being built on Divar Island, at the rather unlikely northern end of the road. To find it, keep on driving straight through the intersection when you get off the ferry. When the road peters out and you feel as though you're lost, keep going and the resort will appear before you like a mirage.

GOA VELHA
☎ 0832

Before the establishment of Old Goa as the Muslim capital, the major port and capital city under the Kadambas had been on the south side of Tiswadi Island, on the banks of the Zuari River. The Kadambas knew this city as Govepuri, but the Portuguese, distinguishing between the new capital, Goa, and the old site, called it Goa Velha.

In its heyday, Govepuri was an international port, attracting Arab traders who began to settle in the area. In 1312 the city was almost totally destroyed by Muslim invaders from the north, and over the following years repeated invasions by the Muslims caused havoc. It wasn't until Goa was taken into the Vijayanagar empire in 1378 that trade revived, but by this time the fortunes of the old capital had begun to decline anyway, due to both the crushing blow of its destruction and the fact that the waters on which it based its livelihood were silting up.

In 1470 the Muslim Bahmani sultanate took Goa, destroyed what was left of the old city, and moved the capital to the new site in the north, which they also called Govepuri but which is now known as Old Goa.

Little remains of Goa Velha, the site of which lies 3km north of the small village of Agassaim, on the northern side of the Zuari bridge. There are, however, some interesting sights nearby, and since the Panaji–Margao road runs straight through the centre of this area, the sites are easily accessible.

However, this whole area is a good place to come for a leisurely day out on a motorcycle. The countryside is lovely and, among other things, you can see the traditional methods of salt collection, which are practised in saltpans all around here. The saltpans are man-made rectangular 'fields' in which water is caught and channelled. As the water evaporates, a crystallisation process occurs and the salt is harvested.

Sights
CHURCH OF ST ANDREW

Just off the main road at the northern extent of Goa Velha is the Church of St Andrew, which hosts an annual festival. On the Monday a fortnight before Easter, 30 statues of saints are taken from their storage place and paraded around the roads of the village. The festivities include a small fair, and the crowds that attend this festival are so big, the police have to restrict movement on the national highway that runs past the village.

The procession has its origins in the 17th century when, at the prompting of the Franciscans, a number of life-size statues were paraded as a reminder to the local people of the lives of the saints. Originally the processions started and ended at Pilar, but in 1834 the religious orders were forced to leave Goa and the statues were transferred to the Church of St Andrew. Processions lapsed and many of the original sculptures were lost or broken, but in 1895 subscriptions were raised to obtain a new set.

CHURCH OF ST ANNE

About 5km north of Goa Velha, the Church of St Anne (known to the local people simply as Santana) is one place that has really suffered from neglect over the past few years. A hand-painted sign by the side door still boasts the claim made by some observers that this is one of the greatest churches of its type (baroque with Indian influences). However, it's now hard to feel anything other than sorry for the appalling state it's in now. Even so, blackened as it is, with vegetation growing out of the façade and broken shutters hanging down, the place is still undeniably impressive. The massive front of the chapel is set off by the large cross before the building, and if you peep through the doors you can see that the interior is still intact. The whole thing has a rather ghostly air about it.

PILAR SEMINARY

North of Agassaim, set on a hill high above the surrounding countryside, is the Pilar Seminary, one of four seminaries built by the Portuguese; only two of the seminaries still survive, the other being Rachol Seminary, near Margao. The hill on which the seminary stands was once the site of a large Hindu temple that overlooked Goa Velha. The original church on the site was built in 1613 by Capuchin monks. They established a centre of learning there and named the seminary Our Lady of Pilar, after the statue they had brought from Spain.

Abandoned in 1835, the seminary was rescued by the Carmelites in 1858 and became the headquarters of the Missionary Society of St Francis Xavier in 1890. The movement gradually petered out and in 1936 the buildings were handed over to the Xaverian League. Today the seminary is still in use, and is also the site of local pilgrimages by those who come to give thanks for the life of Father Agnelo de Souza, a director of the seminary in the early 20th century who was beatified after his death.

The old Church of Our Lady of Pilar has an original statue brought from Spain and also some attractive paintings in an alcove at the rear of the chapel. Just up the hill, in the seminary itself, there is a small museum containing some religious paintings and carvings, and some of the relics of the Hindu temples that were on or near this site.

CHURCH OF ST LAWRENCE

About 3km south of Goa Velha, at the south end of Agassaim, is the Church of St Lawrence, a plain and battered-looking building that houses one of the most flamboyantly decorated reredos in Goa. The heavily gilded construction behind the altar is unique not only for its wealth of detail but also for its peculiar design, which has multitudes of candlesticks projecting from the reredos itself. The panelled blue-and-white ceiling of the chancel sets the scene. Also interesting are the Jesuit IHS symbols set into the tiled walls.

Getting There & Away

All buses running between Panaji and Margao pass through Goa Velha and Agassaim. Buses will drop you at the entrance to the Pilar Seminary. To reach the Church of St Anne you really need your own transport.

PONDA & AROUND
☎ 0832

Ponda taluka is something of a Hindu heartland; the dense terrain of the hills hides Goa's most renowned temples, which have distinct architectural styles and histories, as well as Goa's oldest remaining mosque, Safa Shahouri Masjid (Safa Masjid).

ABBÉ FARIA

A pioneer in the field of hypnosis and a favourite son of Goa, Jose Custodia Faria studied under Franz Anton Mesmer – the famous hypnotist whose name led to the word 'mesmerise' – and was the first to assert that the subject's will and expectations were crucial to the success of the hypnosis.

Faria was born in Candolim, Goa, in 1756. His father was Portuguese and his mother Indian. When he was eight years old they were seized with religious fervour and separated; his mother became a nun and his father a monk. He was sent from Goa to Lisbon to study for the church, was ordained in Rome and then moved to Paris, where he was involved in the French Revolution.

In Paris his interest in hypnosis developed under Mesmer. He began to practise as a hypnotic medium, but his séances, though they attracted a considerable following, were roundly condemned by the church and he was publicly denounced. Just before he died in 1819, Faria published a seminal text on hypnosis, *On the Cause of Lucid Sleep*.

Alexander Dumas was so intrigued by the story of Abbé Faria's life and work that he based the mad monk in *The Count of Monte Cristo* on him.

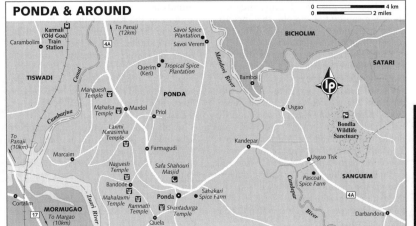

PONDA & AROUND

CENTRAL GOA

For nearly 250 years after the arrival of the Portuguese, Ponda remained under the control of Muslim or Hindu rulers, and many of the temples came to exist when Hindus were forced to escape from Portuguese persecution by fleeing across the waterway that marked the border of Ponda. Upon reaching safety, they built temples in which to securely install the deities they took with them. There the temples remained, safe from the destruction that occurred in the Velhas Conquistas (Old Conquests). By the time that Ponda itself came under Portuguese control, increased religious tolerance meant that no threat was posed to the temples.

Despite the temples' history, true temple junkies may be disappointed with Ponda's collection. Because most had to be built from scratch, or at least rebuilt since the arrival of the Portuguese, these are modern in appearance compared to India's other temples. But don't let unfair comparisons detract from the contrast of an inland trip away from the famous coastline.

The other reason to visit Ponda taluka is to visit one of the spice plantations that wait on the other side of a winding drive, welcoming you with lavish lunches and tours of their grounds (p114).

The capital of Ponda taluka is the town of Ponda. Given its central location in Goa, several large companies established themselves here as an effective base from which to distribute their goods. It didn't take long for commerce to colonise the town, so that now its centre feels like an overcrowded slice of city – a stark contrast to the relative peace and quiet of its surrounds.

Sights

MANGUESH TEMPLE

This temple admirably demonstrates two features of Goan Hinduism – it is dedicated to a deity recognised only in Goa, Manguesh, and it exhibits a mix of architectural styles.

Manguesh was an incarnation of Shiva. Legend has it that Shiva, having lost everything to his wife Parvati in a game of dice, came to Goa in a self-imposed exile. When Parvati eventually came looking for him, he decided to frighten her and disguised himself as a tiger. In horror, Parvati cried out *'trahi mam girisha'* (O lord of mountains save me), whereupon Shiva turned back into his normal form. The words *mam girisha* became associated with the tale and thus the form in which he appeared at the time came to be known as Manguesh. A lingam (phallic symbol of Shiva) left to mark the spot where all this had occurred was eventually discovered by a shepherd, and a temple was built to house it.

Originally the temple was based on the south side of the Zuari River, near the place where the village of Cortalim stands today. When the Portuguese took control, however, the lingam was brought to Priol and installed in a new temple. The grounds were enlarged in the mid-18th century and today there is a substantial complex that includes accommodation for pilgrims and the temple administrative offices.

Architecturally, the temple is distinctly Goan; it shows the influences of both Christian and Muslim styles. Evidence of Christian influence is in the octagonal tower above the sanctum, the pillared façade of the seven-storey *deepastambha* (lamp tower) and the balustrade design around the roof. The domed roofs indicate the Muslim influence. The tank (reservoir) in front of the temple is the oldest part of the complex. If you walk down to the right side of the temple, you can also see the chariots that are used to parade the deities during the temple's festival, which takes place in the last week of January or the first week of February.

MAHALSA TEMPLE

The Mahalsa Temple, 1km down the road from the Manguesh Temple, is in the tiny village of Mardol. This temple's deity originally resided in an ancient shrine in the village of Verna in Salcete taluka. The buildings were reputedly so beautiful that even the Portuguese priest whose job it was to oversee their destruction requested that they should be preserved and converted into a church. Permission was refused, but before the work began in 1543 the deity was smuggled away to safety.

Again, Mahalsa is a uniquely Goan incarnation, this time of Vishnu in a female form. Various legends suggest how Mahalsa came into being. In one, Vishnu, who was in a particularly tight corner during a struggle with the forces of evil, disguised himself as Mohini, the most beautiful woman ever seen, in order to distract his enemies. The trick worked and Mohini, with her name corrupted to Mahalsa, was born. To complicate matters, Mahalsa also fits into the pantheon as an incarnation of Shiva. In general, however, she is regarded by her devotees as a representative of peace; for this, and for her multifaceted identity, she has many devotees.

Once you pass through the entrance gate and out of the busy side street, the temple is pleasantly peaceful. The inner area is impressive, with huge wooden pillars and slatted windows, and like the other temples in this area, an ornamented silver frame surrounds the doorway to the sanctum. Walk around to the back of the main building and peer through the archway to the water tank; the combination of the ancient stonework, palm trees and paddy fields beyond is quite a sight.

In front of the temple stands a large *deepastambha* and a 12.5m-high brass oil lamp that is lit during festivals; it is thought to be the largest such lamp in the world.

In addition to the annual chariot procession held in February for the **Zatra festival**, the temple is also famous for two other festivals. Jasmine flowers are offered in tribute to the god Mahalsa during the **Zaiyanchi Puja festival** in August or September. The full-moon festival of **Kojagiri Purnima** is also celebrated here; the goddess Lakshmi (Laxmi) descends on the earth on this particular night (usually in September) to bestow wealth and prosperity on those who stayed awake to observe the night vigil.

LAXMI NARASIMHA TEMPLE

Almost immediately after leaving the village of Mardol on the main road, a side road to the right takes you up a hill towards the Laxmi Narasimha Temple. This is one of the most attractive temples around Ponda. It's dedicated to an incarnation of Vishnu, half lion and half man, that he created to defeat a formidable adversary. The deity was moved here from the area of the Old Conquests in the mid-16th century. The best part of the temple is the ancient-looking water tank, which is to the left of the compound as you enter. Although the temple has a sign by the door announcing that entry is for the 'devoted and believers only', nonbelievers will probably be allowed to have a look. Otherwise you get the best overall view of the place from the gateway to the tank, looking through the *mandapa* (pillared pavilion) to the inner area and the sanctum beyond.

NAGUESH TEMPLE

A short distance further south, in the village of Bandode, is the small and peaceful Naguesh Temple. The most striking part of the temple is the ancient water tank, where the overhanging palms and the weathered stone make an attractive scene. Also of note are colourful images in relief around the base of the *deepastambha*. Unlike its neighbours, this temple was in existence well before Albuquerque ever set foot in Goa, but the buildings you see today are newish and rather uninteresting. The temple is dedicated to Shiva.

MAHALAXMI TEMPLE
Only 4km outside Ponda, and a stone's throw from the Naguesh Temple, is the relatively uninspiring Mahalaxmi Temple. The goddess Mahalaxmi, looked upon as the mother of the world, was particularly worshipped by the Shilahara rulers and by the Kadambas, and thus has featured prominently in the Hindu pantheon in southern India. Here she wears a lingam on her head, symbolising her connection with Shiva.

RAMNATH TEMPLE
This temple is notable mainly for the impressive silver frame of the door to the sanctum. Although other temples have similar finery, the work here is exceptional, particularly the two unusual scenes depicted at the top of the lintel. The lower of the two depicts kneeling figures worshipping a lingam, while the upper one shows Vishnu lying with Lakshmi, his consort, on a couch made up of the coils of a snake. The lingam installed in the sanctum was brought from Loutolim in Salcete taluka.

SHANTADURGA TEMPLE
The Shantadurga Temple is one of the most famous shrines in Goa. Consequently, it is not only packed with those who come to worship, but also with tourists brought here by the bus load.

The goddess Shantadurga is another form taken by Parvati, Shiva's consort. As the most powerful of the goddesses, Parvati could either adopt a violent form, Durga, or she could help to bring peace, as Shanta. The legend goes that during a particularly savage quarrel between Shiva and Vishnu she appeared in her Durga form and helped to make peace between the two gods – thus embodying the contradiction that the name Shantadurga implies. In Goa, she has come to be worshipped as the goddess of peace and has traditionally had a large following.

The temple, which was built in 1738 during the reign of Shahu Raja of Satara, stands on a hillside facing the road from Ponda and makes an impressive sight.

SAFA SHAHOURI MASJID
The oldest mosque remaining in Goa, the Safa Shahouri Masjid, is right by the NH4A on the outskirts of Ponda. Built by Ali Adil Shah in 1560, it was originally surrounded by gardens and fountains, and matched the mosques at Bijapur in size and quality. The buildings were damaged and then left to decay when the Portuguese moved into the area. Today little remains of its former grandeur, although the Archaeological Survey of India has undertaken limited restoration.

The mosque, a tiny white building set on a stone platform well back from the road, is usually kept locked. In front of it is an ancient water tank, constructed of laterite; unusually, the tank is on the south side of the building, rather than to the east in front of the entrance. Apart from the tiny mosque and the dilapidated tank, there are only a few broken pillars and random blocks of stone to mark the extent of the old buildings.

Sleeping & Eating
Given that Ponda is a mere 30 km from Panaji and has little to offer other than a few decent restaurants and logistical convenience to the sights of interest, few travellers opt to stay overnight.

Farmagudi Hill Retreat (☎ 2335122, 2335037; dm Rs 100, r with/without AC Rs 650/500, r deluxe Rs 1050; 🛪) Farmagudi is Ponda's GTDC residency and is by far the best place to stay in Ponda. Rooms are cottage style and quite private, which makes a nice change from the concrete blocks that comprise most GTDC establishments. There are 39 rooms and some dorm beds, though solo female travellers are unlikely to be allowed to use one. There is also an Indian-and-Chinese restaurant on site.

Hotel Prakash Heritage (☎ 2317794, 2317796; Super Market Complex; d with/without AC Rs 500/450, ste Rs 900; 🛪) This decent option is more centrally located in the busy heart of Ponda. Rooms are plain but reasonably sized and have hot water. If you want more space, ask for a special rate on the suite.

Café Bhonsee (☎ 2318725; thalis around Rs 30) This all-vegetarian restaurant is a highlight of Ponda and takes a lot of pride in the way it looks and the food it serves. The environment is clean and warm, and there is something in the air that says the local families look forward to coming here. It's just across the road from Hotel Prakash Heritage.

Sumudra Pub (☎ 2316779; ◷ 11am-3pm & 7-11pm) This is another place that refreshingly doesn't have tourists in mind. It has a spacious and airy eating area above the street, and boasts seafood specials plus a prawn curry (around Rs 50).

Getting There & Away

Buses to Ponda (Rs 15) leave from the Kadamba station in Panaji. There are three major places to get off the bus when arriving in Ponda. The first (and probably easiest) is the roundabout just outside the Farmagudi Hill Retreat. The others are the Kadamba bus station, which is impractical given that it's either an uphill walk or an autorickshaw ride to town, and the busier bus stop in the middle of town.

BONDLA WILDLIFE SANCTUARY

The drive out to the **Bondla Wildlife Sanctuary** (adult/child Rs 5/2, motorcycle/car Rs 10/50, camera/video camera Rs 25/100; ◷ 9am-5pm, Fri-Wed) is a pleasant one; the roads wind through villages, lush vegetation and rice fields – a dense, green contrast to the terrain closer to the coast.

You're unlikely to see animals just by wandering around the sanctuary, and in-

deed it can even be difficult finding them in the zoo, which is 1.5km into the park and was established to ensure that animal enthusiasts don't leave the park too disappointed. Entry to the zoo is included in your entrance fee into the sanctuary. There are various animals in enclosures here, and you can even have a ride on an elephant (Rs 80). The presence of numerous signs warning people not to tease, touch or throw stones at the animals is a happy addition. This place isn't as bad as many subcontinental zoos, and the animals seem fairly content to laze around. It's a pleasant sort of spot to walk around for half an hour.

There is pleasant **chalet accommodation** (☎ 0832-2229701; dm/s/d Rs 75/250/350) at the entrance to the sanctuary. The interior of these quaint huts is nothing to rave (nor complain) about, but the exteriors, complete with small balcony, wouldn't look out of place housing a hobbit. Call ahead to reserve because it's a long way to drive to find the place is full.

Getting to Bondla is easiest with your own transport, and it makes a pleasant motorcycle ride from Panaji, Margao or Ponda. By public transport there are buses from Ponda to Usgao village (Rs 5), from where you'll need to take a taxi (Rs 150) for the

---

SPICE UP YOUR LIFE

Spice farms are one of the main reasons to come to Ponda. There are four major spice farms in the Ponda region, each with a slightly different character but all offering an interesting tour for Rs 300, including a traditional lunch. Both Sahakari Spice Farm and Savoi Plantation are favoured by tour companies and charter buses, and the latter is visited by GTDC on its Backwater Thrills tour (p227).

Sahakari Spice Farm (☎ 0832-2312394, 9422057312; www.sahakarifarms.com) enjoys the closest position to Ponda, only 2km away. It also offers the longest tour (2½ hours). When you arrive, you will be attacked with flowers by brightly dressed and enthusiastic staff. There are added attractions such as elephant feeding.

Savoi Plantation (☎ 0832-2340272, 0832-2340243; www.savoiplantations.com) is a long-running and well-organised spice farm. In addition to its spices, Savoi has crops of betel nuts, coconuts and pineapples. There are also two rooms available, both with a bathroom and balcony (Rs 2000, including breakfast, lunch and dinner). The Savoi Plantation also has special cultural nights from Monday to Thursday (Rs 450).

Pascoal Spice Farm (☎ 9422055455, 9422643449; www.pascoalspicevillage.com) is in a secluded area of Khandepar. Its tour takes around 45 minutes. There is also some accommodation (room with/ without air-con Rs 1050/550) on this 58-acre property; the rooms are not too fancy, but the farm is a very peaceful place to while away a day or two.

Only 6km from Ponda, **Tropical Spice Plantation** (☎ 0832-2340329; H No A14, Arla Bazar, Keri) is at first sight far more photogenic than the others, with a small bridge leading to the restaurant area, which might afford a glimpse of some birdlife. Its tour takes 45 minutes.

DETOUR: INDIAN(A) JONES AND THE CAVES OF KHANDEPAR

For archaeological enthusiasts and spelunkers, a trip out to the small village of Khandepar will prove rewarding.

Khandepar is 5km northeast of Ponda on the NH (National Highway) 4A. Set back in the dense forest behind the Mandovi River you will find (with some asking around) four rock-cut caves believed to have been created in the laterite around the 12th century, though some archaeologists date their origin back as early as the 9th century. The first of the caves is the largest and the details that remain suggest the caves were probably used by a community of Buddhist monks. The fourth cave confirms this theory; it contains a pedestal used for prayer and meditation. The motif carved onto the ceiling of the first cave is typical of the Kadambas, confirming the popular theory that some time in the 10th or 11th century the Kadambas appropriated the caves and turned them into Hindu temples.

These are amongst Goa's oldest remaining historical treasures, and yet (herein lies the excitement) they were only rediscovered in 1970.

Don't be surprised if no-one knows what you're talking about when you get to the Khandepar junction. Be persistent and ask around until you find someone knowledgeable enough to take you to the site; it's worth the effort to get here before it becomes a prime tourist attraction. Bring a torch. And perhaps a whip.

remaining 10km to the park. Another alternative is to catch any eastbound bus from Ponda along the main highway (NH4A) to the turn-off known as Usgao Tisk, and hope there's a taxi there to take you the 15km to the park or at least to Usgao village.

MOLEM & BHAGWAN MAHAVIR WILDLIFE SANCTUARY

☎ 0832

The town of Molem seems to be entirely devoted to serving the stream of tourists who come to visit Dudhsagar Falls and the sanctuary – there are wall-to-wall stalls.

The village of Molem is the gateway to the **Bhagwan Mahavir Wildlife Sanctuary** (admission Rs 5, motorcycle/car Rs 10/30, camera/video camera Rs 30/130; 🕒 8.30am-5.30pm). With an area of 240 sq km, this is the largest of Goa's four protected wildlife areas; it also contains the 107 sq km Molem National Park. The sanctuary is situated on the eastern border of the state, 53km from Panaji and 54km from Margao, but it is easily reached by both road and rail.

If you're heading to Dudhsagar Falls you probably won't see much wildlife, but there are some well-fed tourist-savvy monkeys hanging around near the falls. As with other Goan wildlife sanctuaries, unless you stay for at least a couple of days you're unlikely to catch a glimpse of many of the animals that inhabit the forest here, including gaurs (Indian bison), sambars, leopards,

chitals (spotted deer), slender loris, jungle cats, Malayan giant squirrels, pythons and cobras. There is an observation platform a few kilometres into the park; the best time to see wildlife is in the early morning or late evening.

The sanctuary's setting in the foothills of the Western Ghats is beautiful and the countryside is some of the most peaceful that you'll find in Goa, so it's a lovely place to spend a day or two. Nearby are also a couple of sights that are definitely worth taking in – notably the ancient temple remains at Tambdi Surla and the cascading waterfall at Dudhsagar.

About 100m west of the GTDC Dudhsagar Resort is the Nature Education Centre, where you can contact the forest officer about the keys for vehicle access through the main park gate, which is about 3km east along the NH4A.

GTDC Dudhsagar Resort (Molem Jungle Resort; ☎ 2612238, 2612319; d with/without AC Rs 650/500; 🍴) is just to the east of the police checkpoint in Molem. The resort is a loud staged affair where the gardens around the restaurant are filled with package-holiday tourists all watching other tourists ride a shackled Indian elephant around the yard.

The main entrance to the park is on the NH4A, which heads eastwards out of Goa towards Belgaum and Londa. It's easy enough to get by public transport to the little truck stop that constitutes the village of

Molem; take any bus to Ponda and change to any bus for Belgaum or Londa. Molem is 28km east of Ponda (Rs 10, 45 minutes).

However, it's far better to travel out here under your own steam on a hired motorcycle, as Molem itself is depressing and all the sights are several kilometres away from the main road. It is extremely hard to find anyone willing to rent you a motorcycle once you get to Molem, and taxis are few and far between.

AROUND MOLEM
Tambdi Surla Mahadeva Temple

The 13th-century Mahadeva Temple found at Tambdi Surla is the only surviving structure of the glorious Kadamba dynasty in Goa. As such, it is not only historically interesting but also visually striking, quite unlike anything else in the state.

The temple appears to have survived the ravages of both the Muslim and Portuguese invaders purely by reason of its incredibly isolated position. No-one quite knows why this spot was chosen; there was no road past here and there's no evidence of there having been any major settlement nearby. Furthermore, the high-quality black basalt of which the temple is constructed must have been brought a considerable distance – perhaps from across the Western Ghats themselves, as the rock is nowhere to be found in Goa. All in all, the origins of the temple are something of a mystery. Although it hasn't survived completely unscathed (the headless Nandi bull in the *mandapa* is evidence of some desecration), it has been preserved by the fact that until recently it was only accessible after a trek through the jungle.

The temple itself is very small. At the eastern end, the open-sided *mandapa* is reached via doorways on three sides. The eastern of these entrances faces a set of steps down to the river, where ritual cleansing was carried out before worship. Inside the *mandapa* the plain slab ceiling is supported by four huge **carved pillars**. The clarity of the designs on the stone is testimony not only to the skill of the artisans, but also to the quality of the rock that was imported for the construction. At about head height on each pillar there is a deeply carved groove, which is thought to have once contained small balls carved from the same piece of stone.

Above the groove, the symmetrical discus-shaped section is symbolic of the cymbals used in Hindu services. The best examples of the carvers' skills, however, are the superb **relief panel** depicting a lotus flower, set in the centre of the ceiling, and the finely carved **screen** that separates the outer hall from the *antaralya* (inner area). On either side of the entrance to this area is a slab carving and two niches containing carvings of minor deities. Finally, beyond the inner hall is the *garbhagriha* (sanctum) where the lingam resides.

The outside of the temple is plain. On the tower itself (which appears to have lost its top section) there are three relief carvings depicting the three most important deities in the Hindu pantheon; on the north side (facing towards the access road) is Vishnu, to the west is Shiva and on the south is Brahma. On the level above these three carvings are three more, depicting each of the deities' consorts.

The temple is about 13km north of Molem and the trip out to it along quiet country lanes is wonderful. You need your own transport.

From the Molem crossroads, take the road running north towards Sancordem. After 3km or 4km there's a fork with the remains of an old stone road sign. It's almost invisible, but you need to take the right-hand fork, which, according to the sign, goes to 'Bolkondo'. About 3km on there's a further fork, which is signposted to Tambdi Surla. At the end of this road is a small car park and a short path leading to the temple.

Dudhsagar Falls

Goa's most impressive waterfalls are on the eastern border with Karnataka; at 603m the falls are the second highest in India after Jog Falls. Though the falls are apparently at their best in the monsoon season (when they're inaccessible), even in the winter months they are an impressive sight, enhanced by the train line that skirts quite close to them. The crowds admiring the sight from the foot of the falls often burst into cheers and applause as a train slices through the view. However, reaching them is expensive and time consuming. Getting to Dudhsagar (the name means 'Sea of Milk') will take the best part of a day, which doesn't leave a great deal of time at the falls themselves.

It's possible to stop at the **Devil's Canyon** en route to the base of the falls. Despite the dramatic name, it's an attractive spot with a deep pool formed between the steep-sided rocks. Locals say that it got its name through being a dangerous spot to swim – reputedly it's extremely deep, with strong underwater currents.

The best way to reach the falls independently is by local train, but with the closing of the Dudhsagar station it's no longer as simple as getting off and walking there. There's a local train at 7.20am from Margao to Colem; check return train times at Margao station. You have to get off at Colem station, where locally controlled 4WDs ferry groups for Rs 1800 per jeep (Rs 300 per head for a group of six) for the approximately 45-minute journey. The views as the train line disappears up into the Western Ghats are undeniably fine.

The jeep takes you through the heart of the wildlife sanctuary, past a number of extremely scenic jungle and forest areas that would otherwise be inaccessible (there are three rivers to be forded, which would make this trip tricky by motorcycle). Swimming is possible, but don't picture yourself taking a romantic swim on your own – there will be other people here. Many of them. Some people walk the distance to the falls, which would certainly enhance the pleasure of a swim at the base of the waterfalls at the end.

An easier alternative to taking the train is to charter a taxi (or ride a motorcycle) to Molem village (15km from the falls) or Colem station, and pick up a jeep from here. The jeep will cost as much from here as from the station.

The even easier option is to take a GTDC tour, which includes a detour out to Tambdi Surla Mahadeva Temple. It runs on Wednesdays and Sundays from 9am to 6pm (Rs 600), and leaves from both Panaji and Calangute. It also takes you to the Molem Jungle Retreat (p115) for lunch, which isn't included in the tour price.

CENTRAL GOA

North Goa

North Goa has the most developed, dynamic and diverse coastline of the state. Candolim and Calangute, by far the most tourist-populated beaches, are lined with hundreds of beach shacks, hotels and restaurants. Further north, Anjuna and Vagator Beaches are home to hippies and the curious folk who wander through to meet them and to dip their toe into the melting pot of subcultures and alternative lifestyles that have permeated here. North of the Chapora River are the quieter beaches of Morjim, Asvem and Mandrem, which are taking their time to develop individual character. Further north still is Arambol, which in recent years has provided respite for party people seeking refuge from the more saturated southern beaches.

The high point of the week is Wednesday, where tourists, local foreigners and traders from all over the country converge on the atmospheric Anjuna flea market. Saturday night is also a big event; the night bazaars of Baga and Arpora attract everyone, making for an eclectic and therefore quintessentially Goan experience.

Head away from the hype to the less discovered inland areas of Bardez, Pernem, Bicholim and Satari, and you will find villages, farmland and a scattering of temples that have retained their authenticity despite all the morphing and mayhem of the coastal areas. Whether explored on a motorcycle or just enjoyed from the beach, this region of Goa must be experienced.

NORTH GOA

HIGHLIGHTS

- Shop at **Anjuna flea market** (p141) till the sun goes down, then head to a happening beach shack

- Grab a cliffside guesthouse with a balcony overhanging the ocean at **Arambol** (p153)

- Sample local cuisine and purchase items from all over India at the **Saturday night markets** (p129) of Arpora and Baga

- Spend a night on the town with kids from Britain and Bombay in **Baga** (p134)

- Immerse yourself in the surreal world of **Goan parties** (p148) in Anjuna or Vagator

NORTH GOA

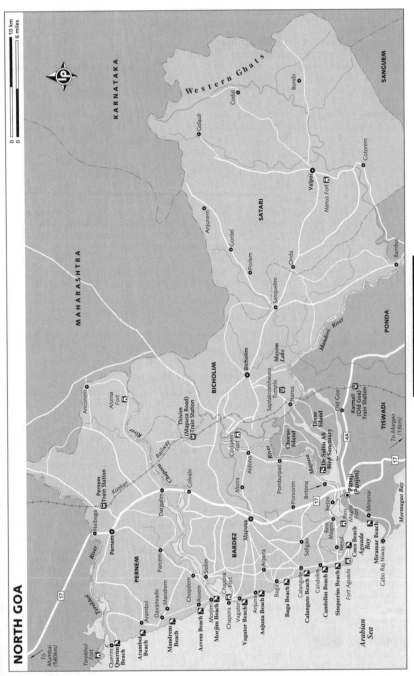

NORTH GOA

PANAJI TO FORT AGUADA

Reis Magos

A classic Portuguese **fort** and **Reis Magos Church**, dedicated to St Jerome, make the small village of Reis Magos worthy of a stop on the way to the beaches. It's not difficult to appreciate the importance of the site that this fort occupies, as it offers protection at the narrowest part of the Mandovi River. The fort was built in 1551 after the north bank of the river came under Portuguese control. It was rebuilt in 1703, in time to assist the desperate defence against the Marathas (1737–39), during which the whole of Bardez, with the exception of the Reis Magos and Aguada forts, was occupied.

Although Reis Magos had the distinction of never being captured by the enemy, it was occupied by a foreign army in 1799 when the British requisitioned both it and Fort Aguada in anticipation of a possible attack by the French. After the British withdrawal in 1813 the Reis Magos fort gradually lost importance, and was eventually abandoned by the military and converted into a jail. It's not open to the public, but it's still worth coming up here for the excellent views.

The little church standing below the fortress walls is made all the more attractive by the imposing black bastions that loom above it. The first church was built in 1555, shortly after the fort itself. A seminary was later added, and over the years it became a significant seat of learning.

Only the church remains, with its steep steps up from the road and fine views of the Mandovi River from the main doors. Outside the church, the lions portrayed in relief at the foot of the steps show signs of Hindu influence, and a crown tops off the façade. The interior of the church is impressively colourful and contains the tombs of three viceroys. Reis Magos is the scene of a colourful **festival** on 6 January, when the story of the three kings is recreated with young local boys acting the parts of the Magi.

Buses run regularly between Betim and Candolim or Calangute, so coming from either direction you can be let off at the Reis Magos junction and then walk the short distance to the church and fort.

Nerul & Coco Beach

Coco Beach is a lot quieter than other nearby beaches and affords a great view across the water to Miramar and Panaji (Panjim). One thing that has contributed to the relative quietness of Coco Beach is the fact that there are no water sports here; local fishermen successfully brought an end to them after complaining that the commotion had a negative impact on their livelihood.

In recent years, there has been an increase in the range of accommodation available.

Albert's Odyssey (☎ 0832-2401518; r Rs 500) is a great place to stay. Rooms have lots of storage space and hot-water bathrooms. Albert's also organises boat and fishing trips and turns out good food. If you can't find a room here, staff may be able to suggest another place nearby.

Behind Nerul church, **Bai Tereza Beach Camp** (☎ 9890694138/58; www.goabeachcamp.com; 1-/2-/3-/4-person tent incl full board Rs 1300/2200/2900/3600, 1-/2-/3-/4-person tent incl breakfast Rs 795/1190/1385/1580) is a newly established Danish-run camp consisting of iglooesque tents on the far end of the beach, which is probably the most secluded point you can get. Meals are provided by the Danish chef, and the bonfire is lit at night. There is a young and international vibe to this place, though the high prices keep it a tad exclusive.

Fort Aguada

Standing on the headland overlooking the mouth of the Mandovi River, Fort Aguada (Map p122) occupies a magnificent position, confirmed by the fact that it was never taken by force. This is a very popular spot to watch the sunset, with uninterrupted views north and south. The motivation for building the fort came from the increasing threat of attacks by the Dutch, among others, and work was commenced in 1612.

The fort covers the entire headland, and the river was once connected with the seashore at Candolim to form a moat, entirely cutting off the headland. One of the great advantages of the site was the abundance of water from natural springs on the hillside, which meant that the fort became an important watering point for ships; the spring also led the fort to be named Aguada (*àgua* is Portuguese for 'water'). The British occupied the fort in 1799 to protect Goa from the French.

Today the main point of interest is the bastion that stands on the hilltop, although when compared with the overall area surrounded by defences, you realise that this is only a fraction of the fort. The buildings below the bastion on the waterfront now house the state prison, but the old bastion on the hilltop can be visited. In the main courtyard of the fort are the underground water tanks. These huge echoing chambers indicate just how seriously the architects took the threat of a long siege.

The **old lighthouse**, which stands in the middle of the fort, was built in 1864 and once housed the great bell from the Church of St Augustine in Old Goa before it was moved to the Church of Our Lady of the Immaculate Conception in Panaji. Unfortunately, at the time of research they weren't letting anyone up to the top.

Nearby, the **new lighthouse** (adult/child Rs 5/3; 4-5.30pm) can also be visited; cameras are not allowed inside.

A short way to the east of the bastion is the pretty **Church of St Lawrence**, which also occupies a magnificent viewpoint. The Church was built in 1643 to honour St Lawrence, the patron saint of sailors.

South of the church and at the end of the road is **Aguada Jail**, which houses a number of Westerners, mostly on drug charges.

To get to Fort Aguada you can ride a bike or motorcycle or take a taxi along the 4km winding road that heads east from Sinquerim Beach and loops up around the headland. It's an enjoyable motorcycle ride, with good views along the top of the headland. By bicycle there's a steep initial climb, best done in the early morning. Otherwise there's a steep 2km walking trail to the fort that starts just past Marbella guesthouse.

CANDOLIM & SINQUERIM
☎ 0832 / pop 8600

Candolim Beach and Sinquerim, the beach immediately below Fort Aguada, are now almost entirely the domain of the package-tour companies, although independent travellers can still find some relatively cheap rooms here, especially outside the peak season. Sinquerim Beach is a small curve of sand dominated by the five-star Taj Holiday Village and Aguada Hermitage. For the past couple of years the *River Princess*, a grounded tanker that no-one wants to take responsibility for, has sat forlornly about 500m offshore.

Candolim Beach is a clean, straight stretch of sand running north to Calangute. It's a little quieter, with fewer beach shacks, and tends to attract a slightly older crowd, as well as the few travellers who find Calangute and Baga too busy and Anjuna and Vagator too much of a scene.

Orientation & Information

The main drag, roughly between Sinquerim in the south and St Anthony's Chapel in the north, is lined with souvenir shops, restaurants, hotels, travel agencies and places to make phone calls or read email. **Davidair** (☎ 2277007; www.com2goa.com) is a reputable travel agency specialising in flights out of Goa and organised tours.

There are numerous currency exchanges offices and travel agencies where you can change money and get cash advances on credit cards. HFDC (near Acron Arcade) and UTI Bank (near Dona Alcino Resorts) have ATMs, and you can change cash and travellers cheques at the State Bank of India. A useful multipurpose place is Archana Complex (often called the Elephant Shop because of its carved elephants); on the main road, it changes money at good rates, provides tourist information and sells a wide range of carvings and souvenirs.

The post office is near the north end of the village.

Activities
BOAT TRIPS

John's Boat Tours (☎ 2497450, 9822386050, 5620190) has earned its good reputation by providing a decent service, and through a BBC plug that it has milked for all its worth since. It has dolphin-watching trips (Rs 795) and boat rides to the Anjuna flea market (Rs 395), and also does a tour through backwater mangroves (Rs 995). Its dolphin trips operate with a policy of 'no dolphins, no pay'. There are also overnight trips on a Keralan houseboat (Rs 4000). John's is now branching out with 4WD tours covering Dudhsagar Falls (Rs 995) and spice plantations (Rs 850). John's also arranges fishing and snorkelling trips. There are numerous booking agents around town.

DIVING

There is a **Goa Dive Center** (☎ 9822157094; 4-9pm) operating out of Candolim, where you

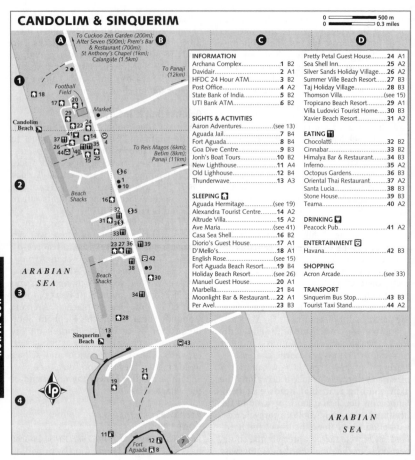

CANDOLIM & SINQUERIM

can sign up for advanced or beginner PADI-certified courses. It also organises snorkelling trips. For more information visit the Goa Dive Center in Calangute (p128).

WATER SPORTS
The place to go if you are looking to paraglide, jet-ski, dolphin-watch or banana-boat-ride is in front of Fort Aguada Beach Resort and the Taj Holiday Village on Sinquerim Beach. There are a collection of adventure-sport operators who openly compete with each other; make sure you let them know that you're not staying at one of the nearby resorts. A few choices are **Aaron Adventures** (2479749), Thunderwave, which is popular with Indian tourists, and Hi-Tide, which also

does return trips to the Anjuna flea market on Wednesday (Rs 350). Prices fluctuate but you can expect to pay around Rs 800 for a jet ski, Rs 1000 for parasailing and between Rs 250 and 450 for a dolphin-watching trip, depending on what's included and how long the tour goes for.

Sleeping
BUDGET
Though Candolim really doesn't have the budget traveller in mind, there are a few pleasant options. Look in areas away from the beach, such as the quiet backstreets.
Villa Ludovici Tourist Home (2479684; d Rs 500) This is a lovely family home with five rooms. The house and its owners have real

WARNING

The beach might look calm but as many as 50 tourists die every year in the lovely Arabian Sea. In fact, capsizing boats are so common that little is done other than a respectful few days where boats don't operate. Then it's back to business. Those who can't swim are particularly vulnerable but strong undertows have killed many experienced swimmers. If you're heading out on a boat, check that there are adequate life jackets. Also take note of warning signs at beaches and don't assume that a lifeguard will be able to assist you.

character, which makes for a lovely Goan experience. Some guests get so attached they come back year after year.

Tropicano Beach Resort (☎ 2489732; d Rs 500) This spot is run by the very hospitable Flossy Vaz. Her rooms are the downstairs ones, which are wrapped around a pleasant garden.

Dioros Guest House (☎ 3090713; diorosgoa@yahoo.com; r Rs 500) This is in a striking white building and is run by a hospitable family. Rooms have hot water and private balconies overlooking the well-maintained gardens.

Manuel Guest House (☎ 2489729; r Rs 300) This is another decent option, and it's run by a friendly family. Rooms are good value. Discounts flow freely for long-stayers.

The **Altrude Villa** (☎ 2489703) and **Thomson Villa** (☎ 2489297) sit opposite each other, and both have rooms competitively priced at around Rs 400. Choose the one that feels the more hospitable to you.

MIDRANGE

Most of the accommodation in the Candolim-Sinquerim area is dedicated to the midrange traveller. Repeat visitors often book months in advance, and it might be worth doing the same.

Pretty Petal Guest House (☎ 2489184; www.prettypetalsgoa.com/accom.htm; s/d from Rs 500/700) Pretty Petal is a beacon of cleanliness down an unpaved road. Its grounds and rooms are spectacularly clean and neat, and the women who run the place are wonderfully friendly. There is a security guard posted on the gates and the place feels entirely comfortable and secure.

Alexandra Tourist Centre (☎ 2489097, 2489230, 2489250; d with/without AC Rs 1320/880; 🔀) With a prime location in the thick of things on Candolim Beach road, this is a good midrange option with a popular restaurant downstairs and obliging staff.

Xavier's Beach Resort (☎ 2479489; xavierbeachresort@yahoo.com; s/d Rs 900/1200) This very pleasant place off a side street has an airy beachside feel. There is a pleasant restaurant, which makes good use of the grounds. Some of the rooms (particularly the singles) can feel a bit like concrete cells so make sure you choose one that's comfortable.

Per Avel (☎ 2479074; www.peravelgoa.com; d with/without AC Rs 1200/1000; 🔀) A pleasant midrange option. The exterior of the buildings, which accommodate 21 rooms, are painted happy colours, and staff are friendly. Rooms are nothing flash but are cosy enough and reasonable value outside season, when they cost Rs 600. There are various areas that are well suited to idling.

A couple of long-running options are the **Sea Shell Inn** (☎ 2276131; Candolim-Aguada Rd; d incl breakfast Rs 950), the best of the affiliated Sea Shell hotels, and the **Casa Sea Shell** (☎ 2479879; seashellgoa@hotmail.com; Candolim-Aguaga Rd; r incl breakfast Rs 850), an unattractive concrete block from the outside. The former is a pleasant white house that displays an old-style charm and is charmingly out of place in this built-up area. There is a restaurant at the front of the Sea Shell Inn that is very popular at night, more for the atmosphere than the food.

Some other options, which all claim (with varying degrees of justification) to be resorts, perhaps on account of their swimming pools:

Summer Ville Beach Resort (☎ 2479075; www.summervillebeachresort.com; d Rs 900-1800; 🏊) Clean spotless rooms within comfortable reach of the beach.

Silver Sands Holiday Village (☎ 2489744; r Rs 1500; 🏊) A range of rooms and cottages, with an enticing swimming pool. It sometimes feels a tad deserted.

Holiday Beach Resort (☎ 2489088; www.holidaybeachresortgoa.com; d Rs 700; 🏊) Basic, adequately clean rooms, each with a fridge and bathroom. Some even have a small patio. Despite the swimming pool, calling this a resort is a stretch.

TOP END

Marbella (☎ 2479551; marbella_goa@yahoo.com; d Rs 1600-2850) Marbella is an old-style place where new-style people set up for weeks.

Hidden down a quiet lane, it's a beautifully restored Portuguese villa with only six rooms. All rooms are fully equipped, though some with more luxury than others. The penthouse suite is the prime choice, though even the ground-floor garden rooms deliver the colonial fantasy.

Fort Aguada Beach Resort (☎ 5645858; reservations.goa@tajhotels.com; d Rs 10,000-45,000; ☎) A five-star Taj Hotel, with a foyer and pool that overlooks a long stretch of beach stretching infinitely north, the Fort Aguada Beach Resort is a good choice for its facilities and location.

Taj Holiday Village (☎ 5645858; www.tajhotels.com; r Rs 8500-24,000; ☎) This is a five-star option without the onerous block-style buildings that come with many multiple-star establishments. Rooms are individual cottages and the grounds are immaculately maintained while still being usable. Beach chairs and umbrella-bedecked tables are strategically placed, and there is a small bar in the swimming pool.

Eating

Down on the beach are dozens of shacks serving the obligatory Western breakfasts, seafood dishes and cold drinks. There's a good selection of beach shacks on Candolim Beach at the end of Candolim Beach road, opposite the post office. At night though, the beach shacks tend to give way to their competition on the streets unless there is a party going on.

Despite the fact that Candolim is at virtual saturation point with tourist-oriented restaurants, there are still some quiet restaurants that foreigners rarely notice, let alone venture into. If you're up for some real Goan cuisine with real Goans, keep your eyes open and follow your nose.

There are a couple of top-end eating options that are worth splashing out on.

Banyan Tree (☎ 276201-10, ext 582; Taj Holiday Village; mains Rs 150-460) Meals at this elegant Thai restaurant are not cheap, but the atmosphere is simply gorgeous; tables are wrapped around the small building, which is dwarfed by thebanyan tree next to it. In the evenings, the lighting is so superb that you can feel the romance even if you're just passing on the street.

After Seven (☎ 2297957; aftersevenrestaurant@yahoo.com; H No 1/274B, Chapel Lane; mains Rs 400; ☼ from 7pm) Known as After Eight until Nestlé stretched its legal tentacles to Candolim, After Seven (which has consequently had to open an hour earlier to justify the name change!) serves decadent seafood dishes such as king prawns (around Rs 850).

Stone House (☎ 2470090; Fort Aguada Rd; mains Rs 150) The food here is great: lots of grilled steaks and seafood (from Rs 300) with random Chinese or pasta dishes thrown in. Music is always well-chosen jazz and blues, and the setting out the front of the solid laterite house is very atmospheric. Sometimes there's live music.

Inferno (☎ 9822140130; mains Rs 50-180) Inferno fires up at night (pun very much intended). The décor has a flame theme, and the occasional sizzler that is ordered from the barbecue menu attracts attention as a waiter carries the blazing meal across the open-air restaurant. The menu is quite a stressful thing to work through; there are clay-oven specials such as stuffed naan (flat bread), grilled steaks, lobster and tiger prawns. The vegetarian options don't skimp on flavour.

Oriental Thai Restaurant (☎ 3092809; mains Rs 40-200; ☼ noon-2pm & from 6pm Sun-Fri) Next to Candolim Beach car park, the Oriental has wonderful Thai dishes. It also has Thai cooking classes every Wednesday between 2pm and 5pm (Rs 1200 including dinner; call to confirm).

Cuckoo Zen Garden (☎ 2489570; www.cuckoozen.com; ☼ 7-11pm) With its Taiwanese-Japanese chef, Taiwanese staff, and Taiwanese, Japanese and Chinese food, clean and fresh Cuckoo Zen Garden is one of Candolim's leaders in Asian authenticity.

Chocolatti (☎ 2479340; rrebelo@sancharnet.in; mains Rs 25-150; ☼ Mon-Sat) The freshly packaged goodies (cakes, biscuits and, of course, home-made chocolates) are pleasant takeaway treats, but if one of the few garden tables is free order yourself whatever muffin the ovens happen to baking (Rs 25) or, if you're feeling outlandish, try a piece of cake (Rs 60).

Prem's Bar & Restaurant (☎ 5616773; 3951086; mains Rs 80-140) Not as pricey as it looks, this place has a great breakfast menu to wake up to. The atmosphere lends it class; tables under umbrellas in a green patch of garden make it feel a world away from the road. At night it's lit up in a way that seems to boost it up a rung on the style ladder.

Teama (☎ 2489774; 5625870; www.teamagoa.com) This is a proper restaurant with the laid-back feel of a beach shack. There's a pleasant rooftop eating area, but at night the thing to do is grab a table by the side of t he street and watch passers-by. It's near the Candolim Beach car park.

Other options worth mentioning:

Santa Lucia (☎ 9822104134; mains Rs 130-240; ☽ from 6.30pm) Primarily Italian, with some 'European' style concoctions thrown in. A 'Zurich-style veal' will set you back Rs 200.

English Rose (mains Rs 40-100) Laid-back crowd and English fare. It's down the lane from Teama.

Octopus Garden (mains Rs 70-200) A pleasant 'seafood-and-steak house' with attentive service, opposite the Stone House.

Himalya Bar & Restaurant (mains Rs 50-80) This small Tibetan restaurant (formerly Hue Lan's Tibetan Kitchen) is one of the most low-key budget places to eat in these parts. Vegetarian fried *momos* (Tibetan dumplings) cost Rs 80.

Cinnabar (☎ 5643671; Acron Arcade; ☽ 8am-midnight) A popular spot for its real coffee and extensive outdoor seating in comfortable cane chairs. The only interruption to your newspaper perusal will be the excellent service.

Drinking

Almost every restaurant in Candolim stays open late and becomes predominantly a drinking venue with food on the side. In light of the fact that restaurants are now doubling as late-night drinking venues, most of the pubs that were in town have closed down under the weight of competition.

Still in the game is the **Peacock Pub** (☎ 323090217), which is claimed by its proprietors, the Johnsons, to be 'Goa's only real English pub'.

Entertainment

Around the festive season, the beach shacks get into party mode with dance floors and pumping music. At other times though, the shacks wind down when it gets dark and the crowds move away from the beach to the busy streets or the clubs of Calangute.

Havana (☎ 3952973; Havana_goa@yahoo.co.in; ☽ from 7pm) is a recently opened Latino restaurant. The chairs scattered around the garden give off more of a lounge-bar than restaurant feel. There is live music and various theme nights. Some nights are more alive than others; at times staff outnumber customers.

Shopping

Along the roads leading to the beach (particularly Candolim Beach road) there are wall-to-wall tourist shops selling clothes, jewellery and other trinkets. Along Fort Aguada Rd there are plenty of shops; heading towards the fort you'll even find boutique furniture and homeware shops. Recent years have seen a rise in the number of shopping arcades in the area.

Acron Arcade (☎ 5643671; www.acronarcade.com; 283 Fort Aguada Rd) This shopping arcade has a Sankars bookshop, clothing, jewellery, art and other stores as well as a Cinnabar, where you can indulge in overpriced coffee and cakes.

Ashoka Jewellers (☎ 2489996; www.ashokajewellers.com; Shop 5-6 Magnum Resorts, Candolim) This store gets high praise from return customers.

Getting There & Around

There are frequent buses between Sinquerim and Calangute or Mapusa (Rs 12). The buses stop at the T-junction at the

---

THE PINTO REVOLT

In 1787, Candolim was the scene of the first serious attempt to overthrow the Portuguese. The founders of the conspiracy were mostly churchmen, angry at the racial discrimination that meant they were not allowed to occupy the highest clerical positions. Two of them, Caetano Francisco Conto and Jose Antonio Gonsalves, travelled to Portugal to plead their case in the court at Lisbon. Unsuccessful in their attempts to remove the injustice, they returned to Goa and started plotting at the home of the Pinto family in Candolim. Gradually the number of conspirators grew as army officers and others joined the cause.

The plans were near enough to completion for a date to have been fixed when the plot was discovered by the Portuguese authorities. A total of 47 conspirators, including 17 priests and seven army officers, were arrested. The lucky ones were sentenced to the galleys or deported, while 15 of the less fortunate were executed in Panaji and their heads mounted on stakes.

southern end of the main road. There are also a few buses from Panaji (Rs 7, 20 minutes) via Betim and Nerul. If you're headed to Panaji it's easy enough to flag down a bus as it passes every 10 to 15 minutes.

The Candolim Beach tourist taxi stand, near Silver Sands Holiday Village, has a list of 'set' prices for trips. A taxi to Dabolim Airport costs Rs 540.

You can hire bicycles near the taxi stand and there's another stall renting out bikes on the road to the Aguada Hermitage.

CALANGUTE & BAGA

☎ 0832 / pop 15,800

This is the package tourist's heaven and the cynical backpacker's hell. This broad stretch of sand was the first beach where overland travellers settled in the 1960s before moving on to Anjuna and further afield, but Calangute managed to evolve and retain the title of most popular beach in the state, becoming the epicentre of Goa's rapidly expanding package-tourist market. This is India's answer to Ibiza and, in the high season at least, is the most overhyped, overpriced, overcrowded strip of mayhem in the state.

The village, once nestled between marshland and sand dunes among a sea of coconut palms, is now a mass of concrete hotels and guesthouses stretching almost without a break from Calangute to Baga. Calangute Beach itself is dotted with sun beds, spit-roasting tourists and meandering cows.

So, why do people keep coming? There's no denying there's plenty going on. There is a range of places to stay, some of the best restaurants in Goa, glitzy shopping malls, and all the touts, taxis, trinkets and beach bars you'll ever need. Up at the northern Baga end, the beach is a less crowded and the landscape more interesting.

Orientation

The actual town of Calangute is urban sprawl, and on the main roads you couldn't feel further from the beach. The advantage to all this development is that Calangute is not all about tourists; if you look hard down side streets you'll find a whole other world – where it feels more like India than the UK, and where locals are genuinely surprised to find you.

South Calangute isn't yet as developed as central Calangute to the north and even

once-quiet Candolim to its south. Give it time though; any space these days is being snapped up Monopoly-style by property developers looking to cram in another hotel or shopping arcade.

The covered bridge that crosses Baga river is aptly dubbed the 'bomb shelter'. It's a notorious place for traffic accidents so take particular care whether you're crossing on wheels or by foot.

Information

BOOKSHOPS

Literati (☎ 2277740; books@literati-goa.com; E/1282, Gaura Vaddo, Calangute; ☺ 10am-7pm Thu-Tue) A lovely bookshop café off the road towards Candolim. It serves basic drinks and snacks that you can enjoy in the enclosed courtyard while browsing through a pile of books. There is an interesting selection of second-hand books, and a good new book section with a strong focus on Indian writers.

Oxford Bookstore (☎ 09326060647; www.oxford bookstore.com; ☺ 10am-7pm) Just at St Anthony's Chapel; this place looks glitzier on the outside than its books do on the inside.

Rama Books (☎ 2279544) You can buy and trade books here. It has a collection of English, German, French and some Italian, Dutch, Swedish, Spanish and Japanese titles – in no particular order beyond that. Literary gems are few and far between. Prices are random but consistently high. Located at the roundabout.

INTERNET ACCESS

At the time of research, many of the numerous Internet cafés in the area were charging Rs 60 per hour. The further away from the tourists you get, the cheaper rates become; shop around down the alleyways and you may find access for Rs 40 or 50.

Mubli (per hr Rs 60; ☺ 9am till late) You can order basic food and drinks while you surf at this Internet café. There are only five computers but the pleasant rooftop terrace makes it a nice place to email your friends about emailing from a rooftop terrace in Goa.

MONEY

There are plenty of exchange offices in both Calangute and Baga. It's also convenient to use the foreign-exchange and credit-card services of a reputable travel agency.

Centurion Bank ATM (Calangute-Anjuna Rd)

ICICI Bank ATM (☺ 24hr) Near the market.

State Bank of India (Calangute) Will change cash and travellers cheques.

UTI Bank ATM (☺ 24hr) Near the market; accepts international cards.

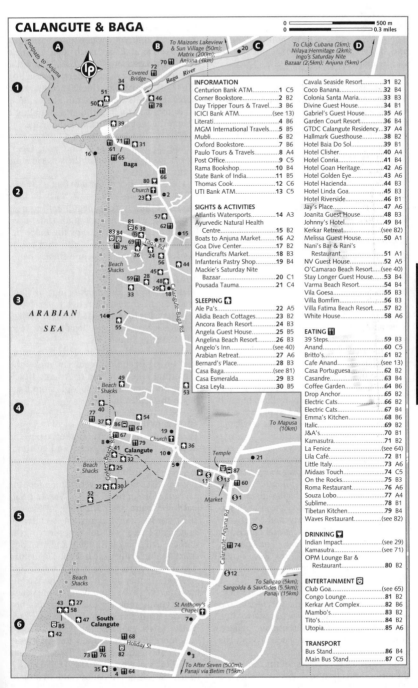

CALANGUTE & BAGA

0 ———— 500 m
0 ———— 0.3 miles

To Maizons Lakeview
& Sun Village (50m);
Matrix (200m);
Anjuna (4km)

To Club Cubana (2km);
Nilaya:Hermitage (2km);
Ingo's Saturday Nite
Bazaar (2;5km); Anjuna (5km)

ARABIAN
SEA

INFORMATION

Centurion Bank ATM	**1** C5
Corner Bookstore	**2** B2
Day Tripper Tours & Travel	**3** B6
ICICI Bank ATM	(see 13)
Literati	**4** B6
MGM International Travels	**5** B5
Mubli	**6** B2
Oxford Bookstore	**7** B6
Paulo Tours & Travels	**8** A4
Post Office	**9** C5
Rama Bookshop	**10** B4
State Bank of India	**11** B5
Thomas Cook	**12** C6
UTI Bank ATM	**13** C5

SIGHTS & ACTIVITIES

Atlantis Watersports	**14** A3
Ayurvedic Natural Health Centre	**15** B2
Boats to Anjuna Market	**16** A2
Goa Dive Center	**17** B2
Handicrafts Market	**18** B3
Infanteria Pastry Shop	**19** B4
Mackie's Saturday Nite Bazaar	**20** C1
Pousada Tauma	**21** C4

SLEEPING

Ale Pa's	**22** A5
Alidia Beach Cottages	**23** B2
Ancora Beach Resort	**24** B3
Angela Guest House	**25** B5
Angelina Beach Resort	**26** B3
Angelo's Inn	(see 40)
Arabian Retreat	**27** A6
Bernard's Place	**28** B3
Casa Baga	(see 81)
Casa Esmeralda	**29** B3
Casa Leyla	**30** B5

Cavala Seaside Resort	**31** B2
Coco Banana	**32** B4
Colonia Santa Maria	**33** B3
Divine Guest House	**34** B1
Gabriel's Guest House	**35** A6
Garden Court Resort	**36** B4
GTDC Calangute Residency	**37** A4
Hallmark Guesthouse	**38** B2
Hotel Baia Do Sol	**39** B1
Hotel Clisher	**40** A4
Hotel Conria	**41** B4
Hotel Goan Heritage	**42** A6
Hotel Golden Eye	**43** A6
Hotel Hacienda	**44** B3
Hotel Linda Goa	**45** B3
Hotel Riverside	**46** B1
Jay's Place	**47** A6
Joanita Guest House	**48** B3
Johnny's Hotel	**49** B4
Kerkar Retreat	(see 82)
Melissa Guest House	**50** A1
Nani's Bar & Rani's Restaurant	**51** A1
NV Guest House	**52** A5
O'Camarao Beach Resort	(see 40)
Stay Longer Guest House	**53** B4
Varma Beach Resort	**54** B4
Vila Goesa	**55** B3
Villa Bomfim	**56** B3
Villa Fatima Beach Resort	**57** B2
White House	**58** A6

EATING

39 Steps	**59** B3
Anand	**60** C5
Britto's	**61** B2
Cafe Anand	(see 13)
Casa Portuguesa	**62** B4
Casandre	**63** B4
Coffee Garden	**64** B6
Drop Anchor	**65** B2
Electric Cats	**66** B2
Electric Cats	**67** B4
Emma's Kitchen	**68** B6
Italic	**69** B2
J&A's	**70** B1
Kamasutra	**71** B2
La Fenice	(see 64)
Lila Café	**72** B1
Little Italy	**73** A6
Midaas Touch	**74** C5
On the Rocks	**75** B3
Roma Restaurant	**76** A6
Souza Lobo	**77** A4
Sublime	**78** B1
Tibetan Kitchen	**79** B4
Waves Restaurant	(see 82)

DRINKING

Indian Impact	(see 29)
Kamasutra	(see 71)
OPM Lounge Bar & Restaurant	**80** B2

ENTERTAINMENT

Club Goa	(see 65)
Congo Lounge	**81** B2
Kerkar Art Complex	**82** B6
Mambo's	**83** B2
Tito's	**84** B2
Utopia	**85** A6

TRANSPORT

Bus Stand	**86** B4
Main Bus Stand	**87** C5

To Mapusa
(10km)

To Saligao (5km);
Sangolda & Saudades (5.5km);
Panaji (15km)

To After Seven (500m);
Panaji via Betim (15km)

NORTH GOA

TELEPHONE

There are many places in both Calangute and Baga where international phone calls can be made quickly and easily.

TOURIST INFORMATION

GTDC Residency (☎ 2276109; Calangute) There is no tourist office as such, but the staff at this hotel (p131), run by the Goa Tourist Development Corporation (GTDC), can usually help out with specific queries or with booking GTDC tours.

TRAVEL AGENCIES

Day Tripper Tours & Travel (☎ 2276726; www .daytrippergoa.com) On the main Calangute–Candolim road, this is a good travel agency specialising in trips within Goa and interstate, as well as flights.
MGM International Travels (☎ 2276249; www .mgmtravel.com) Near the roundabout in the market area, MGM is the most established travel agency in Calangute. Good for booking long-distance buses.

Sights & Activities
BEACHES

The main activity in Calangute is lazing on the beach, and there's no shortage of sun beds and umbrellas on this crowded strip. Most beach shacks will let you use their sun beds for free if you're eating or drinking at their shack, although if it's busy there's a charge of around Rs 50. Vendors are restricted from working on the beach and police often make a show of patrolling, but that doesn't stop people selling sunglasses, sarongs, massages and ear-cleaning services.

ART GALLERIES

A real asset in south Calangute is the **Kerkar Art Complex** (☎ 2276017, 2276509; www.subodhkerkar .com). It is primarily the gallery of Subodh Kerkar, whose work is displayed in every nook and cranny, but is also a well-used cultural space. Every Tuesday night, between 6.45pm and 8.30pm, is a classical dance and music performance (Rs 600). The complex also has the fantastic Waves Rest-aurant (p132) and there are a few rooms at Kerkar Retreat (opposite).

If you're interested in art, see what's happening at **Sangolda** (p135), a spectacular old building converted into a decadent shop that looks more like a museum and gallery. Sometimes the exquisite space around the café is used for exhibitions.

There are a few 'galleries' around town, but the term is often synonymous with 'shop'.

WATER SPORTS

There are numerous water-sport businesses that operate at Baga Beach. One example is **Atlantis Watersports** (☎ 9890047272; www.atlan tiswatersports.com), which offers parasailing (Rs 1300), windsurfing (Rs 400 per hour) and water-skiing (Rs 700 per 10 minutes), among other things. You'll find that negotiating a discount is not an enormous challenge.

It's not difficult to find an operator on Calangute Beach; they'll find you. Operators usually hang around the steps leading to the sand.

The main office of **Goa Dive Center** (☎ 9822 157094; www.goadivecenter.com; Tito's Rd) is here on Tito's Rd. It runs beginners' courses (Rs 2700), which include pool time, class time and an ocean dive. For the more benign sportsperson there is also snorkelling (Rs 1000 including mask and fins).

BOAT TRIPS

Boat trips to see dolphins or out to Coco Beach can be arranged through water-sports operators, **Day Tripper Tours & Travel** (☎ 2276726; www.daytrippergoa.com) or **John's Boat Tours** (☎ 2479780) in Sinquerim.

On market day (Wednesday), motorised outrigger boats regularly make the trip around the headland to Anjuna Beach (Rs 50 one way), ferrying people from Baga Beach to the flea market.

YOGA & AYURVEDA

There is an extraordinary range of Ayurvedic treatment centres in Baga and around, and it's nigh-on impossible to know where to start. Ask around.

One that has been recommended for its range of services is the **Ayurvedic Natural Health Centre** (ANHC; ☎ 2409275, 2409036; www .healthandayurveda.com), set on 1.4 hectares of land. Don't be shy about dropping in; the staff are extremely hospitable and are good at explaining Ayurvedic health. The centre runs free guided tours between 10.30am and 5.30pm, Monday to Saturday. The ANHC has concocted a 2½-hour programme where you get to sample a gamut of treatments, and can arrange pick-up from your hotel. It also runs yoga classes.

A more upmarket option for Ayurvedic treatment is the exclusive **Pousada Tauma** (☎ 2279061; www.pousada-tauma.com; r €215-330; 🖳), which has accommodation and treatment

AYURVEDA

With its roots in Sanskrit, the word Ayurveda is derived from *ayu* (life) and *veda* (knowledge); it is the knowledge or science of life. The principles of Ayurvedic medicine were first documented in the Vedas some 2000 years ago, but it is reputed to have been practised for centuries prior to its documentation.

Ayurveda sees the world as having an intrinsic order. Illness is a departure from this, a loss of balance or equilibrium. Fundamental to Ayurvedic philosophy is the belief that we all possess three *doshas* (humours): *vata* (wind or air); *pitta* (fire); and *kapha* (water and earth). Together these are known as the *tridoshas,* and disease is the result of imbalance among them. Each individual may express various aspects of each, but usually one type predominates. If there is deficiency or excess of any *dosha,* disease can result – an excess of *vata* may result in dizziness and debility; an increase in *pitta* may lead to fever, inflammation and infection. *Kapha* is essential for hydration and lubrication; a deficiency here could produce painful limbs and influenza-type illness.

Ayurvedic treatment aims to restore the balance of the *doshas,* and hence good health, principally through two methods: *panchakarama* (internal purification) and massage. The body can be purified through the elimination of toxins orally, nasally and anally. Curiously, Ayurvedic internal purification is far less popular with tourists than the oil massage component! Ayurvedic massages are available all over Goa and involve a massage with warm medicated oil, followed by a steam bath. This is a relaxing way to pass an hour, but gaining any long-term benefits may require rather more dedication – usually a 15-day or longer commitment, which will generally involve an Ayurvedic diet, exercises and a range of treatments as well as regular massages. If you want to learn more, pick up a copy of *Ayurveda: Life, Health & Longevity* by Dr Robert E Svoboda, or check out www.ayur.com.

packages. Its excellent, individually styled rooms are set around its secluded pool.

As with other beach towns in Goa, many places offer yoga courses, reiki, massage and Ayurvedic treatments; ask around or look for signs. The ever crowded **Infantaria Pastry Shop** (☎ 2277421; Unta Wado, Calangute) has a notice board out the front where you might stumble across something. Alternatively, head for Johnny's Hotel (p131), which has yoga on the rooftop and runs reiki courses.

MARKETS
There are two Saturday night markets in the Baga area that make a pleasant change from the hype of the Anjuna flea market. They're much smaller, there's not as much hard sell and they're held in the cool of the evening. The emphasis is as much on food stalls and entertainment as it is on the usual collection of handicraft, jewellery and clothing stalls.

Ingo's Saturday Nite Bazaar (☼ 6pm-midnight Sat Nov-Mar) at Arpora, halfway between Baga and Anjuna, is spacious and very well organised, with live music and fire-twirling at the heart of things. Food stalls are set up by restaurants around the area, so come with an empty stomach and sample lots. There are outdoor bars, and you can find an enormous amount of clothes, handicrafts, jewellery and other miscellany. Ingo's is immensely popular with visitors, but is a source of contention among many locals who are concerned about the cultural threat it poses to the youth of the area and the traffic congestion it causes.

Mackie's Saturday Nite Bazaar (☼ 6pm-midnight Sat Nov-Mar), in the original location of the Saturday night market (before the two organisers parted company), is a smaller Goan-run affair. The entertainment here is not as edgy as Ingo's. It's within walking distance from Baga.

WALKING
If you're feeling energetic, a good walk is to cross the Baga River, either via the covered bridge or along the beach at low tide, and keep going for about 30 minutes around the headland to Anjuna Beach.

Sleeping
SOUTH CALANGUTE
Kerkar Retreat (☎ 2276017; www.subodhkerkar.com; r Rs 2000) Attached to the Kerkar Art Complex and Waves Restaurant, the retreat is an

afterthought to the art – and the richer for it. There is a kitchenette on every floor of the three-storey guesthouse, with a fridge, a stove and basic cooking facilities. Rooms all have bathroom facilities.

Jay's Place (☎ 2277074, 9890539130; jaysplacegoa@ hotmail.co.uk; r Rs 2000) One of the newest (and already one of the nicest) on this strip of Holiday St, Jay's Place stands out because both the building and grounds are immaculate. The five rooms are spacious and airy, with shiny immaculate floors. Some rooms have adjoining bathrooms, others have en suites. The beach is a four-minute walk away. The owners of Jay's have arranged for their guests to have access to the pool across the road.

Arabian Retreat (☎ 2279053; arabianretreat@yahoo .com; d with/without AC Rs 900/800, both incl breakfast; ✷) Rooms at this great-value gem are unusually large, with two separate sitting areas and two entrances. Every room has a TV and fridge.

Gabriel Guest House (☎ 2279486; fax 2276509; r Rs 800) The main feature of low-key, lovely Gabriel is its garden restaurant, which dishes out very nice Goan cuisine. It has 12 rooms with private facilities. You'll find it tucked down a lane with busy streets on either side.

Other smart choices that are particularly good for beach access:

Hotel Goan Heritage (☎ 2276761-4, 2276253; www .goanheritage.com; Gaura Vaddo; d standard/deluxe Rs 2450/2875; ✷ ✷) A family-friendly resort with a fenced-off pool and play equipment.

White House (☎ 2277938; fax 2277356; r Rs 1200) Justifiably popular with well-maintained grounds, comfortable rooms and a busy little restaurant.

Hotel Golden Eye (☎ 2277308, 2277309; info@hotel goldeneye.com; d with/without AC Rs 750/1000, r deluxe Rs 2000-2500; ✷) Prime choice for beach proximity; you actually have to walk on sand to get here.

CENTRAL CALANGUTE

Coco Banana (☎ 2276478, 2279068; www.cocobanana goa.com; d Rs 500-1500) This is a favourite among those fortunate enough to have stayed there. Run by a charismatic Swiss-Goan couple, Marina and Walter Lobo, Coco Banana is in some ways a slice of Goa the way it was 10 years ago. Rooms are cottage style and set in friendly gardens decorated with statues, mosaic tiles and even the tombstone of Lulu the cat.

Casa Leyla (☎ 2276478, 2279068; www.cocobanan agoa.com; ste Rs 1500) Another great choice if you're looking to enjoy the beach and your own company. These two self-contained apartments are hidden among other houses a short walk from the beach. Its owner's frustrations at the demise of his town are emblazoned on the wall with a mural reading 'Tourists please shut up! Quiet go to sleep or beach after 10pm'. Units have a separate bathroom, bedroom and lounge area, and the top-storey unit has a balcony.

Almeida Villa (☎ 279358; zaccaall@hotmail.com; r Rs 350) A good option for long-term stayers, Almeida has three rooms above the family home. The spacious, secure rooms are good value given they have hot water. Discounts are available for longer stays. The rooms open up onto a communal balcony, which is the perfect place to be lazy.

Varma Beach Resort (☎ 2276077; www.calan gutebeach.com; d from Rs 800; ✷ ✷) Along the road parallel to the main road in Calangute, Varma Beach Resort is a nice place away from the hullabaloo. It has a nicely maintained pool and gardens. Rooms with balconies overlooking the pool are the best. Travellers with children may appreciate the secluded grounds, which are a safe distance from main roads and busy beaches.

O'Camarao Beach Resort (☎ 2276229; camarao@ rediffmail.com; r Rs 800-1000) Of the accommodation in the warren of lanes just off the beach, the best of the bunch is this comfortable resort with low-key rooms around a relaxed quiet garden. It's only 100m or so from the beach.

The cheaper options in the same spot are **Angelo's Inn** (☎ 2282505; r Rs 300-600) and **Hotel Clisher** (☎ 2276873; r Rs 700), which has a few rooms and great food.

Other options worth giving a go:

Ale Pa's (☎ 2276701, 2277479; r Rs 600) The 12 well-maintained rooms, each with a bathroom and hot water, are perfectly located a short walk to the beach.

Hotel Conria (☎ 2497261, 98050761480; r Rs 350) A friendly budget option, if there's a room available.

International Guesthouse (☎ 9822689484; r Rs 250-350). Good price and good beach view. Rooms in this big white building have a bathroom. There's also a low-key beach-shack restaurant attached.

Garden Court Resort (☎ 2276054; mata_goa@ sancharnet.in; Umta Vaddo; r standard Rs 300-350, larger Rs 800) A pleasant old place run by a very pleasant family. It's at the busy roundabout.

CALANGUTE TO BAGA

Budget

Hallmark Guesthouse (☎ 2275030; r Rs 500) Hallmark is a great-value choice that has managed to create a quiet place in an otherwise loud area. The building is shaded by trees, and rooms are enormously spacious for their price. All rooms have access to the balcony that surrounds the building, beds have mosquito nets and there is a general airy feel to the place. The grounds and the room are kept proudly tidy by the friendly staff.

Johnny's Hotel (☎ 2277458, 2094795; johnnys _hotel@yahoo.com; 1st-/2nd-/3rd-fl r Rs 400/500/600) Johnny's is a sociable and genuine place to stay that's popular with backpackers. There is no hot water but Johnny and co will bring you buckets on request. There are also yoga classes on the rooftop in the evening. It's a good base for getting yourself initiated into the world of yoga and reiki.

Joanita Guest House (☎ 2277166; r Rs 300-350) Here's an opportunity to experience the hospitality of a real Goan family in an area otherwise censored to tourists. Down a small laneway off the main road, Joanita Mendonca has four basic rooms out the back and some marginally larger ones out the front. Each room has a small veranda and bathroom.

Other basic places to hang your hat:

Stay Longer Guest House (☎ 2276969; r Rs 600) Has 17 clean but overpriced budget rooms. Good location if you're a Tito's junkie.

Angela Guest House (Rs 200-400) A true backpackers' establishment with six basic rooms.

Ancora Beach Resort (☎ 2276096, 2279787; ancora@ goatelcom.com; r Rs 650)

Midrange

Hotel Riverside (☎ 22773377, 2276186; www.hotelriversidebaga.com; r Rs 1300;) Nicely located on the river, Hotel Riverside has rooms with balconies overlooking north Baga. The Hibiscus restaurant isn't a bad feature either. At night, a balcony room is perfectly delightful.

Hotel Hacienda (☎ 2277348, 2276511; r with/without AC Rs 1500/800;) The slightly interesting design of the building, with wandering Escheresque stairs, makes it a warm place for a large building. There is a pleasant eating area in the courtyard. Rooms themselves are basic, but clean and spacious. Most have a balcony.

GTDC Residency (☎ 2276109; d with/without AC Rs 800/500;) It's getting as tired as the rest of them, but the GTDC Residency is well placed if you want to be in the heart of action with easy beach access.

If you can't find a place to stay, the following should do the trick:

Casa Esmeralda (☎ 2277194; san_enterprise@yahoo .com.co.in; r with/without AC Rs 950/750;) Well-priced rooms. The Indian Impact restaurant is attached.

Bernard's Place (☎ 2276712; bernardsplace@hotmail .com; d Rs 1500) Good midrange option with a popular restaurant-pub that serves sugary sherbet drinks.

Angelina Beach Resort (☎ 2279145, 2279268; angelinabeachresort@rediffmail.com; r Rs 600-900) Not everyone's favourite place, but great if you want to be in the party zone. Rooms fill up with Indian party seekers over Christmas.

Top End

Casa Baga (☎ 2276957, 22892903/31; casabaga@sanch arnet.in; 40/7 Saunto Vaddo, Baga; d incl breakfast Rs 6000;) A brand-new world-class hotel with loads of charm. The 11 rooms in the main building have four-poster beds and decorative mosquito nets, and face the Arabian Sea. The white porcelain bathrooms are elegant affairs, though not nearly as thrilling as those in the four rooms around the pool, where open-air bathrooms allow you to bathe under the sun and stars. Furniture and fittings have been imported from Bali, and the stone floors add class.

Colonia Santa Maria (☎ 2276107; www.csmgoa .com; Cobra Vaddo, Baga Beach; d Rs 2750;) This is an upmarket establishment that manages to maintain an unpretentious air. There is no ocean view from the pool, but the eating area near it is lovely. The whitewashed buildings and the neat and comfortable rooms give Colonia Santa Maria a fresh feeling.

Villa Bomfim (☎ 2279384, 2281069; www.villabomfim.com; r Rs 1950-2450;) This pleasant place, with a trippy mosaic pool, has rooms in four fresh buildings. The interesting colour scheme makes the place look like confectionary. There is a nice restaurant specialising in seafood. You'd have to be committed to pay Rs 4500 to 5500 over Christmas.

Vila Goesa (☎ 2277535, 2281120; www.vilagoesa .com; r Rs 1670-2700) Vila Goesa is set in a quiet area 200m or so back from the beach, with it's own garden path leading to it. Vila Goesa has pleasant rooms scattered through gardens and a restaurant on site.

Hotel Linda Goa (☎ 2276066; www.hotellindagoa .com; r Rs 2500; ⊠) Fairly characterless rooms in a fairly characterless building, but pleasant enough if you can get one overlooking the pool.

BAGA

Cavala Seaside Resort (☎ 2276090, 2277587; www .cavala.com; s without AC Rs 600, d Rs 850-2000; ⊠ ⊠) This is a prime choice, and repeat visitors rave about it. The outside of the resort is English manor–style brick, with greenery growing over everything but the windows. Long high corridors have black-and-white tiles, and there are pool and suite rooms across the road at Cavala's Banana Republic, which has a laid-back party vibe. As the rooms were built at different times they vary in style and character. The atmosphere down at the restaurant is one reason people keep coming back.

Alidia Beach Cottages (☎ 2276835; alidia@rediff mail.com; r/ste Rs 800/2500) Alidia is a pleasant place that's in the heart of Baga but feels pleasantly far away from everything. To get to it, you have to walk through the manager's back yard. There are several areas amid the rooms for enjoying a drink, including the pleasant open-air restaurant. The suite has an ocean view and, at the top of a cast-iron spiral staircase, a rooftop balcony that could comfortably host 40 of your closest friends.

Villa Fatima Beach Resort (☎ 2277418, 2497103; www.villafatima.com; Baga Rd, Calangute Baga, Saunta Vaddo; r with AC Rs 1500, without AC Rs 800-1000; ⊠ ⊠) An unabashedly quiet place to stay, with statues of crocodiles and turtles in the garden. There is a basic bar and pool table in the courtyard, and a small clean pool out the back – the sort of pool you used to swim in at your friends' house in the suburbs. This is a popular backpacker choice, though it has some midrange rooms with a budget vibe.

Hotel Baia Do Sol (☎ 2276084, restaurant 3375482; baiadosol@ndnaik.com; r Rs 2500) This place's rooms are overpriced, but they have a pleasant view over the Baga River. There's also a restaurant, Aquamarine, on the premises. It's nicely located close to the action at Britto's.

NORTH OF BAGA RIVER

Divine Guest House (☎ 5623550; divinehome@satyam .net.in; s/d Rs 700/1200) This righteously named guesthouse is very proper; everywhere you turn is another passage from the bible advising good behaviour. Despite its uprightness, there's a homely air and a nice courtyard eating area.

Nani & Rani's (Nani's Bar & Rani's Restaurant; ☎ 2276313, 2277014; r Rs 450) At the end of the river, this is a soulful place run by a friendly family. The high ceilings lend character to the house, and guests enjoy lingering on the balcony for long breakfasts. There are 16 rooms and a self-contained cottage that is a bargain if you can get it for a long-term stay (it's the same price as the rooms).

Melissa Guest House (☎ 2279583; r Rs 800) If you can't get in to Nani & Rani's, plan B would be to head to this nearby guesthouse, which has some basic rooms.

Sun Village (☎ 52279409; www.desouzahotels.com; r Rs 8000) A tasteful top-end choice away from the hustle and bustle of Baga. Rooms have divine balconies overlooking a lovely patch of Goan landscape.

Maizons Lakeview (☎ 2279389; www.maizons .com; r Rs 1500; ⊠) Near Sun Village but without the same polish, Maizons is a nicely situated resort of 140 rooms in a few well-kept buildings. There's a pleasant pool near the river.

Eating
SOUTH CALANGUTE

Waves Restaurant (☎ 2276017; Kerkar Art Complex; mains Rs 160-220) The brainchild of resident artist Subodh Kerkar, Waves is a celebration of creativity with artistic attention to detail: the coasters are ceramic paint palettes and in the glass holding the serviettes are a few paintbrushes. The spinach and mushroom crepe (Rs 180) and the Goan prawn curry (Rs 150) both exemplify why the restaurant describes itself as serving 'art cuisine'; dishes are creative interpretations of traditional fare.

Coffee Garden (☎ 9890200840; mains Rs 90-180; ◷ 9am-midnight) An Italian cafeteria that takes ingredients seriously, Coffee Garden offers real espresso (Rs 30) and genuine gelato (Rs 110 to 170). Fresh pastas (around Rs 170) are made with imported cheeses, olive oils and salamis, and showcase the authenticity on offer here. This adaptable Italian establishment even offers a full English breakfast (Rs 130), which goes down best with the morning paper. The atmosphere is well thought out: you can play chess on the balcony or simmer in the garden. Dinner is served upstairs in La Fenice by the same attentive people.

Emma's Kitchen (☎ 9890392073; emmajgoa@yahoo .com; mains Rs 150-250) The latest on the list of English establishments geared towards English patrons, Emma's is a minimalist but elegant affair on a terrace. Tablecloths, full English breakfasts and traditional mains (including beef-and-red-wine casserole served with garlic potatoes and vegetables for Rs 250) suggest that Emma caters for the more discerning English traveller – as opposed to the Englishman who discusses cultural difference in terms of beer.

Nirvana (mains Rs 40-150) This is a nice place to eat near the beach. It's open for breakfast, lunch and dinner, and serves beach-shack food to foreign and domestic tourists. It's opposite Hotel Golden Eye.

Midaas Touch (☎ 2282808/9; www.midaastouch .com; mains around Rs 150; ⏰ 11.30am-midnight) Worth mentioning if only to explain the mystery of the advertisements all over the Goa, this mother ship of primary colours is here, in all its oversized glory.

Two Italian restaurants with bona fide Italian chefs are vying for your patronage:

Little Italy (☎ 3953597; www.littleitaly-india.com; 136/1 Guaravaddo, South Calangute; mains Rs 150-350) A grand, if slightly tacky, building just off Holiday St. The entirely vegetarian food gets mixed reviews. At the time of research a swimming pool was under construction here.

Roma Restaurant (☎ 9822950869, 9226415992; mains Rs 90-340; ⏰ 8.30am-3pm, 6.30-11pm) More low-key and just around the corner from Little Italy, this place is basked in orange candlelight and classical music.

CENTRAL CALANGUTE

Casandre (Golden Beach Rd; mains Rs 100-150) This elegant restaurant, set on the veranda of a colonial Portuguese building, seems unperturbed by the urban busyness around. It is an oddly placed Goan oasis on an otherwise rough-and-ready strip of road.

Souza Lobo (☎ 2766463, 281234; www.souzalobo .com; mains Rs 80-250) Souza Lobo is something of a leader on the beach and gets good reports. It pleasantly faces the sea, and you even have the option of dining on the beach. Its increasing popularity has made it increasingly classy – and pricey.

Rock Café (Steak House; mains Rs 80-250) A meaty place popular with meaty English tourists.

It's in an odd location, heavily doused in traffic fumes. There is a selection of hearty food such as jacket potatoes (Rs 130 to 160) and pepper steak with jacket potatoes and salad (Rs 220). If you really want to pack an artery, get the surf and turf (Rs 250).

Tibetan Kitchen (☎ 2275744, 9326137750; chung dhak@yahoo.co.uk; mains Rs 80-150; ⏰ 9am-1pm & 5-10.30pm) Run by a funky bunch of guys who take a great deal of pride in the food and atmosphere on offer, this place has a menu that's eclectic and reasonably priced; the avocado-stuffed prawns (Rs 140) are as earthy and zesty as the atmosphere and the people who create it. Salads are washed in fresh water.

Royal Foods (mains Rs 30-100; ⏰ 7.30am-10pm) This popular place is a food court that has the efficiency and cleanliness of a fast-food joint, but a more interesting atmosphere and far more interesting food. There is a bakery, a Lebanese barbecue, a juice bar, and a selection of sandwiches and various chicken dishes. The fresh juices (Rs 30) are blended before your eyes, and the other food has an impressively high turnover: the tasty chicken biryani (Rs 35) is churned out at an amazing speed. In fact almost anything with chicken in it could be considered a Royal Foods speciality. The outdoor eating area comes to life on balmy nights when the chefs cook up a storm in the great outdoors.

If you want some respite from the crowds, try the following:

Café Anand (☎ 2279616; mains Rs 15-40) Behind the barbershop at the roundabout, this is a popular local choice that is always brimming with patrons.

Anand (mains Rs 15-35; ⏰ 6am-11pm) Good food and good prices at the roundabout. This local favourite churns out authentic Indian staples; drop in for a dosa (paper-thin lentil-flour pancake) and some chai.

BAGA

Lila Café (☎ 2279843; www.lilacafegoa.com; mains Rs 60-150; ⏰ 9am-6pm) Sitting on the banks of the Baga River, this is one of the most pleasant places to while away time. Local hippies and foreign tourists rub shoulders here; the white curtains and purple cushions are inviting to them all. Delicious pastries are baked in the on-site German bakery. If you're wanting something lighter than the freshly made sweet pastry temptations, try the wholesome muesli with yoghurt and nuts (Rs 60).

Electric Cats (☎ 3958156; Santa Vada Baga Beach Rd; mains r Rs 40-120) A good choice for a range of budgets and tastes. Any selection on the multicuisine menu is extremely well prepared and the atmosphere is lovely without being uppity. The bar chairs on the street facing down into the restaurant are a nice touch. The sizzlers are recommended, and whatever else you have, make sure you try the cheese naan. There's another branch in Calangute.

Sublime (☎ 3953610; mains Rs 200-295) On the Baga side of the bridge, Sublime lives up to its name. Run by a creative Indian-English team, Sublime fuses European and more exotic cuisines; its Indian chef has worked in the USA and Germany, and brings his various influences to the menu. Pickings are slim for vegetarians, but the few choices there are won't disappoint. The candlelit laterite atmosphere is also, well, sublime.

Britto's (☎ 2277331; Baga Beach; mains Rs 50-200) A Baga institution that's open from the crack of dawn right through to 3am during peak season, and busy right the way through the day. Britto's popularity is partly due to its lively reputation and partly due to the fact that its menu covers the whole spectrum of options, from Goan curries and pasta to freshly baked pastries and cakes. Cravings at odd hours will be satisfied by alpine chocolate mousse (Rs 60) or perhaps baked beans on toast (Rs 60). Bottles of wine on the extensive wine list go right up Rs 750.

Drop Anchor (☎ 9371005456) This is one of the more permanent shack-style restaurants. It's a pleasant place for some authentic food, and is decorated in the style of an Arabian harem. On its roof – and sometimes all around – is Club Goa.

Other options worth trying in the area:

J&A's (☎ 9823139488; H No 560; Baga River; mains Rs 265-895) On the north side of the Baga River, elegant and upmarket J&A's gets mixed reviews. The seafood platter costs Rs 895; entertainment nights are hit and miss.

Kamasutra (☎ 9890517969, 980517565, 980141879; mains Rs 60-200; ☺ from 6pm) As the name implies, Kamasutra is trying to make itself a sexy place to be; it has dishes like lusty lobster and tantric tikka in a dimly lit lounge. It sometimes turns into more of a party after 9pm.

Casa Portuguesa (☎ 2277024; mains Rs 60-200; ☺ 7-11pm Tue-Sun) The food gets mixed reviews but the pleasant garden alongside an old colonial villa couldn't be a better place to try *bebinca* (richly layered pancake-like Goan dessert made from egg yolk and coconut).

39 Steps (mains Rs 50-180) Recommended for its laid-back atmosphere and good selection of Indian food. The tandoori chicken (Rs 130) is packed with all the flavour you expect from this old favourite, and the steaks have been recommended. At entrance to Colonia Santa Maria.

Italic (☎ 2277672; mains Rs 80-240) A recently opened chain Italian restaurant. Clean and classy, but not cheap. The classic spaghetti bolognaise (which is, admittedly, classic), will set you back Rs 195.

Drinking

Indian Impact (☎ 2277194) If you're looking for somewhere that's less like a nightclub and more like a lounge bar, this is a pleasant place for a drink.

OPM Lounge Bar and Restaurant (beers Rs 60, spirits Rs 40; ☺ till late) Has set up the perfect atmosphere for a night out; whether it happens or not can be hit and miss.

Kamasutra (cocktails Rs 80-140) This place is sometimes successful in its bid to change from a family restaurant to a lounge bar after 9pm or so.

Entertainment

The Calangute-Baga area is something of a base for clubbers these days. Around the festive season, young people from Mumbai and Delhi pour into Calangute to chase the parties. At night, trucks trawl the streets advertising the parties, and the competition passes by playing music even more loudly. The scene changes quickly though: clubs fall in and out of favour, with the newer kids on the block either rising to acclaim or falling by the wayside. And a good party night is hit and miss. It's easy to find out what's happening though; during season you'll barely be able to move for all the leaflets thrust at you as the scene chops, changes, bumps and grinds its way along. The clubs that have proven that they are there to stay are Tito's and Club Cubana.

Tito's (☎ 2279895, 2275028; www.titosgoa.com; woman/man/couple Rs free/300/500) This is the epicentre of nightlife in Calangute. For Indian tourists, Tito's is synonymous with 'party in Goa'. Tito's gets going at dinner time and really cranks up after that, sometimes until around 2am. In addition to its food, it boasts an 'Ibiza-style discotheque'. During the party season entry price skyrockets; single women still pay nothing, but single men pay up to Rs 800 to gain access to them.

Mambo's (☎ 2279895; admission from Rs 200; ⏰ 10pm-4am) Closer towards the beach and attached to Tito's, Mambo's has a less thumping vibe. Over the festive season, the party gets going at 8pm and keeps going in a carnival of international DJs, dancers and holiday giveaways.

Congo Lounge (☎ 2276957, 40/7 Saunto Vaddo) A strong rival to Tito's, Congo Lounge has made a clear effort to maintain a degree of class often missing from the Tito's craziness.

Utopia (☎ 2282904; www.utopia.goa.com; Holiday St; ⏰ from 9pm) In south Calangute, this place is almost at the end of imaginatively named Holiday St. One suspects that its designer has been to Bali a few times; wooden lounge chairs are scattered all the way down to the beach. The whole place is presided over by a golden Buddha, seemingly impervious to the noise going on below. At peak season, the cover change can be around Rs 1500.

On the Rocks (☎ 3954400, 3954411, 2277878) At the time of research, On the Rocks was working hard to get itself off the ground. This is a restaurant-nightclub with a lounge area at the front and a fully fledged restaurant set back from the road. Time will tell whether it can withstand the competition of its already established neighbour, Tito's.

Club Cubana (☎ 9823232910, 9823539000; www.clubcubana.net; woman/man Rs 500/650; ⏰ 9.30pm-5am) This is the most happening place in the area, if not all of Goa. Club Cubana is an open-air multilevel nightclub at the top of Apora Hill, and hence is referred to as the 'nightclub in the sky'. The layout is quite decadent, with tiered balconies, lounge chairs and a swimming pool. Every night has a different theme. Wednesday night is popular because women enter free. The entry fees include unlimited drinks.

Matrix (☎ 9890291417, 9850963929; Maizons Lake View Resort) Not nearly as popular as Club Cubana but closer to Baga and Calangute is Matrix, which advertises itself as an 'underwater' nightclub. It's opposite Sun Village.

Club Westend (Eiverra; ☎ 5629141; ⏰ from 9.30pm) Further out of town and somewhat bumped off the radar by the likes of Club Cubana, this club uses its remote destination as its gimmick, referring to itself as a jungle party. Westend can organise pick-up (it can be tricky to find, particularly at night).

Shopping

In line with its status as the tourist capital of Goa, Calangute has grown to become the shopping capital. Flashy Western-brand shops such as Lacoste, Levi's, Benetton, Gucci and Nike have sprouted up along the road to Candolim, just south of Calangute's market. Also here are upmarket gold and jewellery shops, boutique fashion stores and arts-and-craft emporiums.

However, it's probably the small-time stalls that will catch the eye of most foreign visitors. Calangute and Baga have been swamped by Kashmiri traders eager to cash in on the tourist boom. There is a fantastic range of things to buy – Kashmiri carpets, embroideries and papier-mâché boxes, as well as genuine and reproduction Tibetan and Rajasthani crafts, bronzes, carvings and miniature paintings. This is all the same sort of stuff you'll see at the Anjuna flea market, so it's worth comparing prices.

There are two permanent but rather makeshift markets along Calangute–Baga road, mostly with wares laid out on blankets. There's a Tibetan handicrafts market between the church and the roundabout in central Calangute, and another handicrafts market in Baga. These markets can be surprisingly hassle-free places to visit, and you can peruse at relative leisure.

Magic Shop (Baga Rd) For kids (and the young at heart) this is an absorbing place. It sells all sorts of tricks, props and illusions, and the owner promises to teach you magic in three minutes.

Sangolda (☎ 2409310; sangolda@sancharnet.in; Sangolda-Saligao; ⏰ 10.15am-7pm Mon-Sat) One of the greatest shopping excursions you can make is a trip out to Sangolda. Set in an old colonial building, this is worth the trip not only for the resplendent items on sale, but also for the architecture and the drive inland to the town of Sangolda. Everything you see is for sale, and there couldn't be a more picturesque and inspiring place to enjoy a cup of coffee. It's opposite Mae de Deus Chapel in the town of Sangolda.

Saudades (Sangolda-Saligao) Sangolda's neighbour specialises in 'colonial furniture and ethnic artefacts' and is also worth a visit.

Getting There & Away

Most buses start or end at the market in Calangute, although a few go on to Baga.

Buses leave for Calangute from the Kadamba bus station in Panaji when they're full (Rs 10, 40 minutes, every 10 to 15 minutes). An autorickshaw from Panaji to Calangute will cost around Rs 150, and a taxi costs Rs 150 to 200 and takes about 30 minutes. There are frequent buses to Mapusa (Rs 7); a motorcycle taxi to Mapusa costs Rs 50, a taxi Rs 100.

A taxi to Anjuna will cost around Rs 200. Taxis charge around Rs 200 to go to Ingo's Saturday Nite Bazaar or Club Cubana.

Paulo Tours & Travels (☎ 2281274; Golden Beach Rd) has a small office near the beach. It is the main operator for private buses to Hampi, Mumbai and Bangalore; pick-up is available in Calangute.

Getting Around

Motorcycle and moped hire is easy to arrange in Calangute, and if you're here outside the peak season, you should be able to bargain a reasonable price. Try to pay around Rs 100 a day for a Honda Kinetic if you hire it for a week or more, though you're doing well if you manage to get one for Rs 150. Expect to pay Rs 250 a day around Christmas. Ask around near the steps to the beach in central Calangute, near the roundabout or at the market area where taxis hang out. Up in Baga, taxis congregate towards the end of the road near Britto's.

Take particular care riding on the Calangute–Baga road and near the market area, which gets congested with buses and taxis. The sandy area leading to the covered bridge at Baga is another place where many inexperienced riders come to grief.

Bicycles can also be hired (around Rs 40 per day) in the market area – there are no shops as such, just ask around and look for signs.

MAPUSA
☎ 0832 / pop 40,100

Mapusa (*map*-sa) is the largest town in north Goa. There's not much to see or do, but it's a nice bustling break from the beaches and a good base for supplies and errands. It's also small enough for you to jump off the bus and get pretty much anywhere you need to go on foot. If you're driving in, be attentive to one-way streets.

Information

Phone calls can be made and faxes can be sent from any of the numerous private phone offices around town.

Bank of India ATM (☒ 24hr) At the north end of the Municipal Gardens.

Corporate Bank ATM (☒ 24hr) Immediately next door to Pink Pantha.

Directorate of Tourism (☎ 2262390) For a slightly more technical slant than the GTDC; immediately next door to Mapusa Residency.

ICICI Bank ATM (☒ 24hr) Down the lane opposite the police station off the Mapusa–Anjuna road.

Mapusa Clinic (☎ 2263343, 2263346; Mapusa Clinic Rd; ☒ 24hr) A well-run medical facility with a small fleet of ambulances.

Mapusa Residency (☎ 2262794, 2262694) Head to this GTDC-run hotel (opposite) for tourist information.

GETTING INVOLVED: GOA'S SERIOUS SIDE

Mapusa is a good base if you're after information about the wider issues of Goa; there are several NGOs based here that are chipping away at the economic, social and environmental issues that affect the state.

The **Goa Desc Resource Centre** (☎ 0832-2252660; www.goadesc.org; 11 Liberty Apt, Feira Alta) is a local lobby group that works on human-rights issues including women's rights and tourism development. Their latest project is Goa Can, a consumer-rights initiative for which they are requesting that travellers provide feedback on consumer issues that affect them. The Goa Desc Resource Centre has an interesting collection of resources that you can ask to access.

Goa's leading conservation and environment group, the prolific **Goa Foundation** (☎ 0832-2256479; www.goacom.com/goafoundation; G/8 St Britto's Apt, Feira Alta), is accessed from Mapusa Clinic Rd. This is the place to go if you're wanting to find out more about Goa's environmental problems, how you can minimise your contribution to them or how to become a volunteer. You can also make enquiries at the **Other India Bookstore** (☎ 2263306; www.otherindiabookstore.com; Mapusa Clinic Rd), which stocks many Goa Foundation publications.

For more information about the work of El Shaddai in helping Goa's children, see p138.

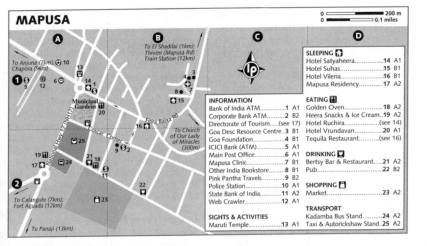

MAPUSA

INFORMATION
Bank of India ATM	1 A1
Corporate Bank ATM	2 B2
Directorate of Tourism	(see 17)
Goa Desc Resource Centre	3 B1
Goa Foundation	4 B1
ICICI Bank (ATM)	5 A1
Main Post Office	6 A1
Mapusa Clinic	7 B1
Other India Bookstore	8 B1
Pink Pantha Travels	9 B2
Police Station	10 A1
State Bank of India	11 A2
Web Crawler	12 A1

SIGHTS & ACTIVITIES
Maruti Temple	13 A1

SLEEPING
Hotel Satyaheera	14 A1
Hotel Suhas	15 B1
Hotel Vilena	16 B1
Mapusa Residency	17 A2

EATING
Golden Oven	18 A2
Heera Snacks & Ice Cream	19 A2
Hotel Ruchira	(see 14)
Hotel Vrundavan	20 A1
Tequila Restaurant	(see 16)

DRINKING
Bertsy Bar & Restaurant	21 A2
Pub	22 B2

SHOPPING
Market	23 A2

TRANSPORT
Kadamba Bus Stand	24 A2
Taxi & Autorickshaw Stand	25 A2

Other India Bookstore (☎ 2263306; www.otherin diabookstore.com; Mapusa Clinic Rd) Hailed as the best bookshop in Mapusa, it has a solid collection of nonfiction, including many publications of the Goa Foundation. The collection is well-organised and there is a strong focus on social and environmental issues in Goa.

Pink Pantha Travels (☎ 250352, 252816; fax 263180) This busy agent is reliable for currency exchange and credit-card cash advances.

State Bank of India Will exchange cash and travellers cheques.

Web Crawler (per hr Rs 20) One of several cheap Internet cafés; down a lane opposite the police station.

Sights & Activities

Founded in 1594 and rebuilt several times since, **Church of Our Lady of Miracles** (St Jerome's) is famous more for its annual festival than for its architecture. It was built by the Portuguese on the site of an old Hindu temple, which the Hindu community still holds sacred. Thus on the 16th day after Easter, the church's annual feast day is celebrated here by both Hindus and Christians – one of the best examples of the way in which Hinduism and Christianity coexist in Goa.

The small but attractive **Maruti temple** was built in the 1840s at a site where the monkey god Hanuman was covertly worshipped. After temples had been destroyed by the Portuguese, Rama devotees placed a picture of Hanuman at the fireworks shop that once stood here. In April 1843, the picture was replaced by a silver idol and an increasing number of worshippers began to gather here. Eventually, the business community of Mapusa gathered enough funds to acquire the shop, and the temple was built in its place. The intricate carvings at the doorway of the temple are the work of local artisans.

The **Mapusa market** (☽ 8am-6.30pm) really gets going on Friday. It's a raucous affair that attracts vendors and shoppers from all over Goa (and interstate) with an entirely different vibe to the Anjuna market; here you'll find locals haggling for clothing and produce, and you can also find antiques, souvenirs and textiles.

Sleeping

There are several places to stay in Mapusa, though none are particularly special. Given the better choices on offer at nearby beach towns there's little reason to stay, but if you are in transit or need respite from the coast, the following options should do the trick.

Hotel Satyaheera (☎ 2262849, 2262949, 2263379; satya_goa@sancharnet.in; d with/without AC Rs 850/590; ❄) Hotel Satyaheera has the range of facilities befitting a midrange hotel, but with the quaint attitude of a place that prides itself on being the best hotel in town. It certainly lives up to that title as far as its location goes.

Mapusa Residency (☎ 2262794, 2262694; d with/without AC Rs 750/540, ste Rs 1050; ❄) Service is indifferent and rooms are in the bland but functional mould you expect from GTDC accommodation. Over the peak season, this is a good option.

Hotel Vilena (☎ 2263115, 2256649; vito@sancharnet .in; Feira Baixa Rd; d with/without bathroom Rs 500/400, tr Rs 650) A good budget option run by an endearing married couple who are very traveller friendly.

Hotel Suhas (☎ 2263115; dm Rs 70, s/d with bathroom Rs 99/150) A bit grimy and disorganised, but it's as budget as they come. It's off Feira Baixa Rd.

Eating & Drinking

For cheap street eats and rich street atmosphere, head for the area around the private bus stands. Things get going at around dusk.

Hotel Vrundavan (☎ 2253879; mains Rs 10-30) A great place with authentically local food and authentically local people. You just might be the only non-Indian in the restaurant, which makes for a pleasant change if you're in town for a break from the beaches. It's near the Municipal Gardens.

Heera Snacks & Ice Cream (☒ 8am-noon & 4pm-midnight) A decent place for a quick drink or ice cream in a pleasant sort of garden. Located at the roundabout, it's a stone's throw from the station but a world away in atmosphere.

Pub (☎ 2262657; mains Rs 30-130; ☒ 10am-9pm Mon-Sat) This is a small Austrian-run place with a balcony where you can enjoy a beer or a pasta and watch the busy street below.

Bertsy Bar & Restaurant (☒ 9am-11pm) Perfect for a quiet drink and some privacy while you're waiting for a bus. Bertsy's is a relatively spacious hole in the wall that offers a chance to get away from the city fumes. Its tinted door doesn't look too inviting but it's surprisingly wholesome on the inside. Look for the red-brick entrance.

Tequila Restaurant (☎ 2263115, 2256649; Hotel Vilena) This is a low-key rooftop restaurant serving Goan and other Indian dishes.

Hotel Ruchira (☎ 2263869; 5th fl, Hotel Satyaheera) For a classier feed go to Ruchira, which Mapusa locals (but few others) consider fine dining.

Golden Oven (☒ 9am-6.30pm) For some clean and shiny comfort, duck into this bakery, which is a civilised respite from the chaos of the bus stand.

Getting There & Away

Mapusa is the jumping-off point for the northern beaches of Goa. There are private operators selling tickets near the Kadamba bus station for buses to Mumbai (normal/air-conditioned Rs 300/700, 14 hours) and Bangalore (normal/air-conditioned Rs 500/700, 12 hours). There are also state-run buses to Pune (Rs 54, 15 hours) and Belgaum (Rs 57, five hours).

Every 20 to 30 minutes local express buses leave for Panaji (Rs 7, 25 minutes), Calangute (Rs 7, 20 minutes) and Anjuna (Rs 7, 20 minutes). Other buses go to Chapora, Candolim and Arambol (Rs 12, 20 minutes).

A motorcycle taxi to Anjuna or Calangute should cost around Rs 50, an autorickshaw Rs 70 and a taxi around Rs 100.

HOMES FOR KIDS

While you're lounging around on Goa's beaches, it's easy to forget that the state shares most of India's social problems.

El Shaddai (☎ 0832-2266520, 5613286/7; www.childrescue.net; El Shaddai House, Duler, Mapusa) works to get Goa's homeless children off the streets and into schools, and has made an enormous contribution to that end.

El Shaddai was founded by Anita Edgar and Matthew Kurian. Anita is an Englishwoman who was shocked by the child poverty during a trip to Goa in 1996. With local community help and the support of visitors to Goa, it has established five children's homes, three night shelters and day care units and a nonformal school and vocational training college. The Vidya Niketan Vocational Training College was opened in November 2005. El Shaddai also has feeding programmes in Mapusa, Margao and Vasco da Gama.

You can visit the homes and meet the children. Shekinah House and Victory House are boys' homes in Assagao and Saligao. Rainbow House is a home for girls. Asha Deep and Stepping Stones are night shelters in Panaji and Margao. There is also a house in Calangute called Little Acorns.

If you are interested in volunteering your time to meet the kids, or would like offer sponsorship support, contact El Shaddai's head office in Mapusa, opposite the football grounds.

Thivim, about 12km northeast of town, is the nearest train station on the Konkan Railway. Local buses for Mapusa (Rs 5, 25 minutes) meet the trains; an autorickshaw costs around Rs 80.

ANJUNA
☎ 0832

Famous throughout Goa for its Wednesday flea market, Anjuna has long held the mantle of Goa's favourite 'hippy beach'. Unlike Calangute, Anjuna has retained some of its charm.

There's a weird and wonderful collection of defiant ex-hippies, overlanders, monks, gentle lunatics, artists, artisans, seers, searchers and itinerant expatriates who have wandered far from the organic confines of health-food emporia in San Francisco and London. They've been joined by hard-core partygoers, who are a mix of macho Israelis just released from military service and European ravers on charter flights, all drawn by the area's reputation for trance parties.

The beach itself – at the southern end at least is one of the most alluring in north Goa, and since it's not easily accessible from the village, it's rarely crowded.

Orientation
Anjuna is quite spread out and much of the land behind the beach is still farmland. There are three distinct areas: the main crossroads and bus stand where paths lead down to the beach; the back part of the village, where you'll find the post office, convenience stores and some travel agents; and the flea market area, a couple of kilometres to the south, which also marks the southern end of the beach.

Information
BOOKSHOPS
There are various second-hand bookshops scattered around; most are attached to restaurants or hotels.
Manali Guest House (☎ 2274421, 2273477) There's a small second-hand bookshop downstairs, and upstairs a collection of new books next to the Internet café.

INTERNET ACCESS
Most Internet cafés charge between Rs 40 to Rs 50 for an hour. If you need to use the Internet for an extended period, it may be worth going to a smaller town where they

charge half the price. Apart from the following, try the area at the coast where the road ends.
Connexions Travel (☎ 2274347, 2274439; fax 2274347, connexion23@rediffmail.com; Internet access per hr Rs 50) Next to Paradise Guest House.
German Bakery (☺ 8.30am-11pm) Has now set up a wireless Internet facility for laptop users.
Manali Guest House (☎ 2274421, 2273477; per hr Rs 40) The most pristine Internet café, and the one with the most computers.
Nehal Travels (☎ 2273288, 2273309, 2273475; nehaltravels@rediffmail.com) A couple of computers with good Internet speed (per hr Rs 40). Also a decent place to recharge your phone card.
Nikhil Travels (☎ 2274508; Internet access per hr Rs 40; ☺ 9am-9pm) Internet access.

MONEY
Travel agencies will change cash and travellers cheques, and give cash advances on Visa and MasterCard. Most are also open longer than banks.

There are no ATMs in Anjuna; the closest are in Mapusa or Calangute.
Bank of Baroda (Anjuna Beach Rd; ☺ 9.30am-2.30pm Mon-Wed & Fri, 9.30am-noon Sat) Gives cash advances on Visa and MasterCard. There's also a 'safe custody' facility for your valuables, but the safe at your hotel will be cheaper. Here, you have to pay Rs 170 any time you want to access your property.
Villa Anjuna (☎ 2273443, www.anjunavilla.com; Anjuna Beach Rd) If you need to get cash out of a machine, this hotel has facilities but will charge for the service.

POST
You can have your mail sent poste restante to the Anjuna post office.

TRAVEL AGENCIES
There are numerous travel agencies that can make onward travel bookings, get flights confirmed and change foreign currency, including the following:
Connexions Travels (☎ 2274437, 2274439; connexion23@rediffmail.com) Next to Paradise Guest House.
Kwick Travels (☎ 2273477) At the Manali Guest House.
MGM Travels (☎ 2274317) On the main road.
Speedy Travels (☎ 2273208; Mazal Vaddo) Next to the post office.

Dangers & Annoyances
Anjuna is well known as a place to procure drugs (although it doesn't have a monopoly

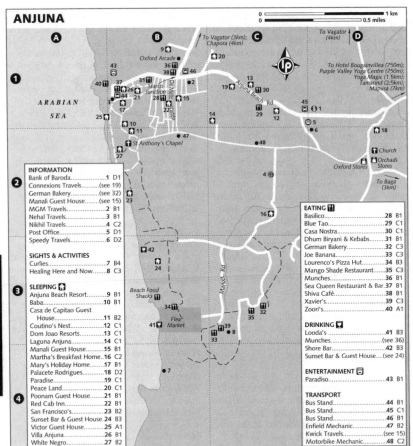

ANJUNA

INFORMATION
Bank of Baroda....................1 D1
Connexions Travels..........(see 19)
German Bakery................(see 32)
Manali Guest House........(see 15)
MGM Travels......................2 B1
Nehal Travels.....................3 B1
Nikhil Travels.....................4 C2
Post Office..........................5 D1
Speedy Travels...................6 D2

SIGHTS & ACTIVITIES
Curlies..............................7 B4
Healing Here and Now......8 C3

SLEEPING
Anjuna Beach Resort..........9 B1
Baba................................10 B1
Casa de Capitao Guest
House.............................11 B2
Coutino's Nest.................12 C1
Dom Joao Resorts.............13 C1
Laguna Anjuna.................14 C1
Manali Guest House..........15 B1
Martha's Breakfast Home...16 C2
Mary's Holiday Home........17 B1
Palacete Rodrigues............18 D2
Paradise...........................19 C1
Peace Land.......................20 C1
Poonam Guest House........21 B1
Red Cab Inn.....................22 B1
San Francisco's.................23 B2
Sunset Bar & Guest House..24 B3
Victor Guest House...........25 A1
Villa Anjuna.....................26 B1
White Negro.....................27 B2

EATING
Basilico............................28 B1
Blue Tao...........................29 C1
Casa Nostra......................30 C1
Dhum Biryani & Kebabs....31 B1
German Bakery..................32 C3
Joe Banana.......................33 C3
Lourenco's Pizza Hut.........34 B3
Mango Shade Restaurant....35 C3
Munches...........................36 B1
Sea Queen Restaurant & Bar..37 B1
Shiva Café........................38 B1
Xavier's............................39 C3
Zoori's..............................40 A1

DRINKING
Looda's.............................41 B3
Munches.......................(see 36)
Shore Bar.........................42 B3
Sunset Bar & Guest House....(see 24)

ENTERTAINMENT
Paradiso...........................43 B1

TRANSPORT
Bus Stand.........................44 B1
Bus Stand.........................45 C1
Bus Stand.........................46 B1
Enfield Mechanic..............47 B2
Kwick Travels.................(see 15)
Motorbike Mechanic.........48 C2

on them). Illicit substances, though not so freely available these days, can still be found here, but participate at your peril – the police Anti-Narcotics Cell has been known to carry out checks on foreigners.

Take great care of your possessions in Anjuna; theft can be a problem, especially on market day and party nights.

Activities

Anjuna is a place to hang out, meet people over a few drinks, watch the sunset and go to the occasional party – if the police don't beat you there. Apart from market day there's no real reason to day trip here since there's nothing to see except the 'scene' itself.

The extremely popular **Purple Valley Yoga Centre** (☎ 9370568639; www.yogagoa.com) is a great place to attend regular sessions. The centre offers classes in the full range of yoga styles and attracts teachers from around the world. There are 8am classes, suitable for all levels, on every day except Sunday. At 9.30am on Mondays, Wednesdays and Fridays there are special classes for beginners. It costs around Rs 400 for a single class, or Rs 3000 for 10. Check the website for the latest information. If you really want to immerse yourself in the yoga culture, you can stay on site at Hotel Bougainvillea (p142). Upmarket accommodation option Yoga Magic (p142) offers yoga and massage.

Healing Here & Now (☎ 32273487; www.healing hereandnow.com; St Michael's Vaddo), tucked behind Xavier's restaurant, is a peaceful place with lots of different yoga classes (including classes for children and pregnant women). It also offers several other healing treatments, such as colonic cleansing, naturopathy and foot reflexology.

If you are interested in paragliding, go to Curlies (p144) on southern Anjuna Beach (behind the flea market), where a colourful collection of adrenaline junkies congregate to escape their European winters. The jumps usually start from the top of the hill just behind Curlies or sometimes further north in Vagator, depending on the wind. Either way, Curlies is the place to start. Tandem glides cost Rs 1300.

Even if you're not planning on gliding, the view of the coast from the cross at the top of this hill is spectacular, and well worth the very easy walk up there from the beach.

Sleeping

BUDGET

Manali Guest House (☎ 2274421, 2273477; d without bathroom Rs 100-200) This guesthouse is everything a budget hotel should be; rooms are

basic no-fuss budget jobs, there are motorcycles to rent, a money exchange service, backpackers hanging around the small restaurant, an Internet café and bookshop upstairs – clean, basic, home.

Red Cab Inn (☎ 274427; redcabinn@rediffmail.com; H No 893/1 De Mello Vaddo; r/ste Rs 500/600) This is efficiently run by a delightful couple. The one and only honeymoon suite is a bargain, and it has studded blue lights on the ceiling in an attempt to create a starry night sky. The atmosphere is charming, peaceful and red, and its location just back from the road gives it a secluded though central feel.

Peace Land (☎ 2273700, 9822685255; s/d Rs 300/ 500) This is a real find: a chilled-out place away from the main road. Rooms are immaculate, and open out onto a nice common space with well-placed hammocks. There's also a tiny restaurant.

Paradise (☎ 2274347, 2274439; janet965@hotmail .com; St Michael's Vaddo; r Rs 350-400) This quirky house full of cats is kept neat and orderly by the lovely Janet. Rooms have hot water and a bathroom; some have a fridge.

Other homely and economic places:
Martha's Breakfast Home (☎ 2273365, 2274194; mpd8650@hotmail.com; H No 907, Monteiro Vaddo) As homely as the name implies.

THE ANJUNA MARKET EXPERIENCE

'Anjuna Beach in Goa is an anthropologist's dream,' said Gita Mehta in the book *Karma Cola*, and that's as true today as when she wrote it back in the still psychedelic 1970s.

The Wednesday flea market is a major attraction for everyone visiting Goa. Tibetan and Kashmiri traders, colourful Gujarati tribal women, blissed-out 21st-century hippies, Indian tourists, businesspeople, Western package tourists and travellers from around the world pour into Anjuna on motorcycles, buses and boats.

The market had humble beginnings, and was originally started by long-term Western residents who needed to sell a few belongings so they could afford some more time at this seaside paradise. From time to time the authorities closed the market down, mostly when the number of bottles of Scotch, Marlboro cigarettes or electronic devices indicated that this was becoming less of a flea market and more of a black market.

Western residents would make cakes and cookies to sell here (they still do today, and chocolate chips are not the only ingredients) and it soon became the highlight of the week, the place to catch up on the gossip, make a little money or just hang out. Westerners still trade goods and services (piercing, tattoos and haircuts), but the market has now developed into a souvenir bazaar.

Whatever you need, from a paperback to a second-hand Enfield motorcycle, rave clothing, hammocks, henna or spices; it's all here. This is the best place to browse for souvenirs or, if you're not interested in shopping, get comfortable under a tree with a beer or cappuccino and enjoy the show.

The best time to visit is early morning (it starts around 8am) or late afternoon (from about 4pm); the latter is good if you plan to stay on for the sunset and party at the Shore Bar (p144) or some live music at Looda's (p144).

NORTH GOA

Coutinho's Nest (☎ 2274386, 2273389; www.travelin goa.com/Coutinhosnest; r Rs 150-400) Rooms with a range of facilities in a family home.

Sunset Bar & Guest House (☎ 2273917; r with/ without bathroom Rs 500/250) Down on the beach, Sunset Bar has basic rooms in a good location for both market and beach access. It's well placed to keep you in the know if beach parties happen.

Baba (☎ 2273847; r small Rs 350-400, larger Rs 700-800) Only the larger rooms have hot water.

MIDRANGE

Palacete Rodrigues (☎ 273358, 250291; www.palacete rodrigues.com; Mazal Vaddo; s/d without AC Rs 850/950, d with AC Rs 1050; 🖳) Somewhere between a heritage museum and a bric-a-brac store, Palacete Rodrigues and the friendly family who runs it extend a warm welcome and are sure to secure a place in your memory. There are 15 rooms in this 200-year-old Portuguese mansion, each with its own individual style and elements of quirkiness. It is close to the everything that makes Anjuna famous, but worlds away in atmosphere.

Hotel Bougainvillea (Grandpa's Inn; ☎ 2273270; fax 2274370; Gaunwadi; r Rs 1200-2700; 🖳) This pleasant colonial building, which is more than 200 years old, has a lovely restaurant on its veranda. There's a pool table and the place is full of character and characters. It shares a garden with the Purple Valley Yoga Centre.

Casa De Capitao Guest House (☎ 2273832; apt Rs 700) Long-term stayers should consider Casa De Capitao Guest House, located just behind the church, which has very nicely furnished apartments with small and inviting balconies.

Villa Anjuna (☎ 2273443, www.anjunavilla.com; Anjuna Beach Rd; d Rs 750-1000; 🖳 🖳) Villa Anjuna is well located and well endowed with facilities such as a 24-hour café and a small but clean pool. There are also good facilities with regard to Internet, safe lockers etc. Rooms around the pool have far more of villa feel than the ones out the back, which seem overpriced.

Anjuna Beach Resort (☎ 2274499, 227443; fabjoe@ sancharnet.in; r Rs 600-800) Rooms that have hot water and private balconies are lovely; those that don't are devoid of character. On the whole, this is a safe and friendly place to stay, and it can be sociable.

Victor Guest House (☎ 9822176982; r Rs 1000) Perched on top of the cliff, Victor has the best views around. Rooms 1 and 2 are the ones to go for; they preside over an endless view south down the coast.

Other popular options:

White Negro (☎ 2273326; r basic/standard Rs 300/500) Standard rooms with TV and hot water are neat, tidy and good value. The garden restaurant gets good reviews.

Poonam Guesthouse (☎ 2274394, 2273194; poon amghr@yahoo.co.in; d from Rs 600) A good central budget option with several rooms for a range of prices. Those with their own veranda are the best.

Dom Joao Resorts (☎ 2274325; donjoaoanjuna@ yahoo.co.in; d Rs 600-1200; 🖳) The only place in Anjuna built higher than two storeys. Apartment-style rooms have a fridge, a lounge area and a balcony. There is also a small pool.

TOP END

Yoga Magic (☎ 5623796; www.yogamagic.net; tent/ lodge/ste £179/199/219) A truly special experience is on offer at Yoga Magic, located in the middle of the sprawling Goan countryside. Accommodation is in spacious Rajasthani style tents with private open-air hot-water showers and ecotoilets. Guests do yoga in the morning on their verandas, then head to the laid-back restaurant for a healthy meal. Everyone is waiting to see how the pool pans out.

Laguna Anjuna (☎ 2274305, 2273248, 227413, 274132; www.lagunaanjuna.com; 1-/2-bedroom ste Rs 3600/ 5500; 🖳) Laguna Anjuna has a nice set up; the dense green gardens are scattered with beach lounges and hammocks, and there's a reasonably sized pool. There is a shady restaurant in the dim main building, which is classic colonial and a fitting place for a game of pool. The rooms all vary, but some really hit the mark for boutique style.

Tamarind (☎ 2274319; www.thetamarind.com; r Rs 1400-2200; 🖳) A couple of kilometres out of Anjuna on the Mapusa–Anjuna Rd, the Tamarind has 22 rooms in a lovely setting. The restaurant is set on the veranda of an old colonial building, but the building containing the rooms are of Tuscan-style stone overlooking the pool. There's also minigolf. Rooms have no TV, but there is a communal TV room. Children aged under 12 are not permitted to stay here.

Eating

There is a handful of beach shacks concentrated along the strip near the flea market. There are also a few restaurants overlooking the beach and some lining the main road. The more interesting places to eat are hidden in the village. The local foreigners shop for groceries at Oxford Stores and Orchard Stores, opposite each other in the village, and at Oxford Arcade, near the junction. The latter has everything from fresh bread to international imports like Heinz baked beans, Colgate toothpaste and Vegemite for homesick Aussies.

German Bakery (mains Rs 40-130; 8.30am-11pm) Recollections of the German Bakery will stir in your memory long after you've left Goa. Tripped-out trees form the walls and ambient music fills the air. Local expats pick a cushion and spend hours catching up with friends. The menu is consistently good, and you can justify indulging in the decadent fried apple pancake (Rs 45) on the basis that it's fruit based. The spaghetti Napolitana (Rs 90) is a wholesome indulgence too. Whatever you order has to be washed down with a concoction from the juice bar – try the fresh and minty sea breeze (Rs 30). And there's real coffee. Restaurants all over Goa incorporate 'German Bakery' into their names, trying to ride the coat-tails of this one. This is *the* German Bakery.

Zoori's (2273476; hornykarma@hotmail.com; H No 652, St Anthony Praise; mains Rs 40-160) A must-do in Anjuna. There are multiple levels of seating at this cliffside eatery, with cushions and lounge chairs overlooking the ocean. There's an eclectic mix of food, from pastas and Mexican fare to chicken schnitzel (Rs 165), as well as good vegetarian (Rs 130) and nonvegetarian breakfasts (Rs 140) and a range of coffee – but really the food isn't so important when there's a view like this.

Mango Shade Restaurant (mains Rs 15-50; 8am-4pm) This is a laid-back and extremely cheap place to eat, with as much character as value. There's real expertise in breakfast foods, though people hang out here all day. The Israeli salad (Rs 25) is a quick and fresh tomato-and-cucumber combination catering to the clientele. Unfortunately the size of the apple-cinnamon pancake (Rs 30) is not in proportion to its flavour; order a second one and wash it down with a thick Turkish coffee or cappuccino (Rs 25). If you're indecisive, go old school and get a burger (Rs 40).

Blue Tao (2273977, 9850419782; martaceriani@ yahoo.com; mains Rs 80-130; 8.30am-11pm) One of the leaders in the healthy-lifestyle culture of Anjuna, Blue Tao sells a range of natural products and has a lovely courtyard. The menu is a creative collection of Indian and Italian dishes, all of which are organic and vegetarian. Rare treats such as pesto-embellished pasta are available here, along with exotic juice drinks with a healthy twist.

Joe Banana (dishes Rs 10-80; 8am-6pm) This spot is a favourite among local foreigners for its clean fresh food and low prices. The vegetable thali (traditional all-you-can-eat meal; Rs 50); pumpkin *bhajia* (pumpkin fritter; Rs 10) and blueberry juice (Rs 50) are all good. It's diagonally behind Xavier's restaurant. Ask for directions.

Sea Queen Restaurant & Bar (Anjuna Beach Rd; mains Rs 25-110) There is a range of Italian, Indian and Israeli food here, none of which is spectacular, but the restaurant plays two movies every night. Sea Queen is next to Villa Anjuna.

Xavier's (mains Rs 80-350; from 7pm) This place comfortably has the status of best seafood restaurant in town. It prepares prawns, lobster and whatever fish is available in creative though distinctly Goan style. It is nicely located behind the flea market area.

Other established eateries in the area:

Casa Nostra (mains Rs 80-150; 7-11pm) Diagonally opposite Blue Tao, this Italian restaurant serves pizza and pasta.

Munches (mains Rs 25-80; 24hr) Popular for juice or snacks, or when the munchies hit.

Lourenco's Pizza Hut (pizza Rs 100-140) A popular lunch venue, particularly on market days given its location. It serves wood-fire pizzas.

Basilico (2273721; mains Rs 80-130) An Italian restaurant with a nicely enclosed eating area.

San Francisco's (5611264; pasta Rs 80) A friendly place to watch the sea and have Indian or Italian food.

Shiva Café (2270586; mains Rs 60-100) At the intersection on the 1st floor, the mostly Indian menu is a bit light on the spice but offers a good range.

Dhum Biryani & Kebabs (9326124699; Biryani Palace, Anjuna Beach Rd; mains Rs 50-150) Loved by visitors and locals alike. Turns out fantastically tasty kebabs.

Drinking & Entertainment

The Starco Junction also manages to keep a flicker of a pulse going when everything else is dead; if you're intent on keeping on at it, you'll be able to procure a beer somewhere at this corner; try Munches (above).

Anjuna Beach Rd hits the coast and peters down into a series of stall-lined dirt paths. You'll be approached here by hangers around offering ganja and pills; they're a good source of information as to when and where the next party will be. On market days, party invites are handed out. The nearby restaurants do good business on Wednesday nights as weary shoppers wander towards the beach for a drink.

Looda's (Anjuna flea market; mains Rs 40-100) At the time of research this was the place to go on Wednesday; when the market winds down, live bands play against the spectacular backdrop of the ocean. A good night at Looda's can be one of your most memorable nights in Goa.

Shore Bar (Anjuna Beach; ☉ till late on market days) This used to be the centre of action, but now is just one of many beachside restaurants that compete for the crowds with music, atmosphere and seafood menus.

Sunset Bar (☎ 2273917) It's difficult to distinguish or single out options along the dense strip of restaurants and watering holes along the beach. Sunset Bar does a good enough job to be an example of the kinds of places you'll find: somewhere you can spend a day making orders from the varied menu, and then switch drinks' list after sunset.

Curlies (South Anjuna Beach; mains Rs 40-100; ☉ till late) Curlies is one of those special places where no-one fits but everyone does, and where something always seems to be going on even though nothing much is actually happening. One suspects that the rocks between Curlies and the rest of Anjuna are actually the dividing line between Curlies and the rest of the world. The collection of people who are magnetically drawn back each season from lives one can only speculate about are an earthy blend of folk; their chilling out is an experience to take part in or just observe.

Paradiso (☎ 9326100013) The party scene in Anjuna is a transient one but Paradiso is always on, though it doesn't really get started until midnight. In the wee hours of the morning you will see people stumbling home legless – and sometimes shoeless. Paradiso boasts clay sculptures, a surreally displaced chai market, and even a Coffee Day Express.

Getting There & Away

There are buses every hour or so from Mapusa to Anjuna (Rs 7). They park at the end of the road to the beach and continue on to Vagator and Chapora; some go up to Arambol. You can also hail down a Mapusa-bound bus at the Starco Junction, or further east along the road just before the Bank of Baroda.

Plenty of motorcycle taxis gather at the Starco Junction, and you can also hire scooters and motorcycles easily at this intersection. There's an Enfield mechanic and a normal motorcycle mechanic, the latter tending to the scooters often used by the Anjuna crowd.

VAGATOR & CHAPORA

☎ 0832

This is one of the most rugged and interesting parts of north Goa's coastline and it's the place to be if you're seeking Goa's infamous party scene. Much of the inhabited area nestles under a canopy of dense coconut palms, and the little fishing village of Chapora is dominated by a rocky hill topped by an old Portuguese fort. The views from the ramparts of the fort are superb.

Rather than the long, open stretch of sand found on most of Goa's developed coastline, secluded coves dominate the northern side of this rocky outcrop. Although Vagator is not a particularly crowded beach, it's popular with day-trippers from Calangute and is a major stop on the bus tours of north Goa, so for a few hours each day the parts of the beach closest to the bus stop are flooded with interlopers. There are three main beaches: Vagator (the largest), Little Vagator and Ozran. There is a Shiva face carved into the rocks at Little Vagator Beach, which features in posters and postcards.

Many Westerners stay here on a long-term basis during the winter season, but it's not a tourist ghetto. The local people remain amenable and it's much more laid-back than even Anjuna – particularly Chapora, which is little more than a narrow main street and a string of village homes between the harbour and Siolim. Vagator is where the night-time action happens; there are some regular party venues here.

Information

The nearest banks are in Anjuna or Mapusa, but many shops and travel agencies offer money exchange. On Chapora's narrow

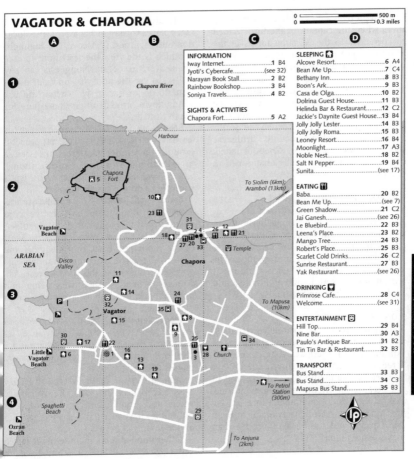

VAGATOR & CHAPORA

NORTH GOA

main street there are several STD/ISD booths, as well as two small bookstalls and a store for provisions.

Bethany Inn (Vagator; per hr Rs 40)

Iway Internet (per hr Rs 40) Tucked in the tightly backed bend in the road.

Jyoti's Cybercafe (per hr Rs 50) Formerly Eddie's.

Narayan Book Stall (☎ 9326137063) Small stall for book purchase and exchange.

Noble Nest Travels (☎ 2274335) Plane, bus, boat and train ticketing, and has an Internet café. It's near the chapel.

Rainbow Bookshop (☎ 273715) Bookshop and exchange, plus Internet and phone calls; opposite Primrose Cafe.

Soniya Travels (☎ 2273344) Transport bookings, foreign exchange and Internet access.

Sights & Activities
CHAPORA FORT

Though Bardez taluka (district) ceded to the Portuguese in 1543, the security of the territory continued to be a major headache for many years. The lands were threatened by several enemies – the Muslims from the north, Maratha horsemen from the east and the local chieftains in the area itself.

As a result, the Portuguese set about building a series of fortifications between the mid-16th and early 17th centuries. Chapora fort, on the very northern edge of the new territory, was constructed in about 1617 – only five years after work began on Fort Aguada. Whereas Aguada was never taken by force, Chapora fell twice. The first time, it was reportedly taken without a shot being fired, when the captain of the fort decided to surrender to the Maratha forces of the Hindu leader Sambhaji in 1684.

The Portuguese rebuilt the fort in 1717, adding features such as tunnels that led from the bastion down to the seashore and the river bank to enable resupply or escape in times of trouble. The fort fell again to the Marathas in 1739. But when the northern taluka of Pernem came into Portuguese hands the significance of Chapora faded, and the fort was eventually abandoned in the 1890s.

CHAPORA HARBOUR

Taking the road to the northwest of the village brings you to the small harbour, an area of pungent smells where colourful fishing boats bob idly and the day's catch is hauled in each morning and evening. The mouth of the Chapora River is a good spot for photographs and you can buy fish and seafood directly from the boats.

YOGA & AYURVEDA

Keep your eye out for various yoga classes. In addition to the very popular courses in Anjuna (p140), there are yoga courses offered at Bean Me Up (below).

There are so many Ayurvedic centres in the area, it is difficult to recommend one. Ask around for recommendations, or try the Ayurvedic treatments available at Bean Me Up and out the back of the German Bakery in Anjuna.

Sleeping
VAGATOR

Bean Me Up (☎ 2273479; beanmeup@usa.net; H No 1639/2 Deul Vaddo; d with/without bathroom Rs 550/350) This is a very special place of extraordinary good value. Rooms are set around the courtyard restaurant, with a toy-filled kid's corner and an adult-oriented chill-out corner. Every room is immaculate, and those with tiled hot-water bathrooms have small elements of style (like coordinated wallhangings and decorative mosquito nets over big beds) to give them a slightly indulgent feeling. All of them are winners. The restaurant here is very popular and hosts the occasional live music event.

Alcove Resort (☎ 2274491, 2273349; alcove2002@ rediffmail.com; r with/without AC Rs 2000/2500; 🔀 🔊)

For location and facilities, this is one of the nicer places to stay in Vagator, for its location and facilities, is Alcove, the highlight of which is the view the restaurant terrace offers over the ocean. Nonguests can pay Rs 100 to use the pool. It won't suit if you want to go to bed early; when Nine Bar winds down, crowds often come here for the live music.

Boon's Ark (☎ 2274045; www.goasearch.com /boonsark.html; r Rs 1000) This place has peaceful grounds on a quiet backstreet but is close to everything. The design of the rooms, which have nonperpendicular walls, lends warmth, as do the small verandas.

Bethany Inn (☎ 2273731; www.bethanyinn.com; d from Rs 450) Room rates can change from day to day at this well-kitted-out establishment next to China Town restaurant. Most of the rooms are basic but adequate, and there is a travel agency and Internet café on the premises. At the time of research, cottages (around Rs 1800) were being built out the back; they'll have everything short of a kitchen.

Leoney Resort (☎ 2273634, 2274914; www.leoney resort.com; d/ste Rs 1500/2900; 🔊) Very nice, secure small hotel; rooms are set around a clear swimming pool, which outsiders can pay Rs 200 per day to use.

Sterling Vagator Beach Resort (☎ 2273276, 2274470, 2274471; d Rs 2500; 🔊) The overpriced rooms and grounds here are looking stale, but it does have nice palm-shaded grounds and a pool.

Other good choices include the **Jolly Jolly Lester** (☎ 2273620, 2274897; www.hoteljollygoa.com; r with/without AC Rs 1000/1500; 🔀) and **Jolly Jolly Romma** (d Rs 800), both of which are clean and well run.

Places that are popular in the Vagator area:

Dolrina Guest House (☎ 2274896, 2958170; dolrina@ hotmail.com, dolrinagoa@yahoo.com; H No 536/1, PO Vagator, Bardez; Rs 270/500) Simple rooms with a garden and café out the back.

Garden Villa (☎ 5629454; Vagator Beach St; r standard Rs 600, deluxe Rs 1000-1500; 🔀) Very private in a spaced-out complex with restaurant. More expensive deluxe rooms have air-con.

Salt N Pepper (☎ 2273596; www.saltnpeppervagator .com; r Rs 500) Rooms are good value with hot water and TV. There's also a restaurant here.

Jackie's Daynite Guest House (☎ 2274320, 2273018; melforddsouza@hotmail.com; d Rs 300-600) Staff are sometimes apathetic, but it's a nice quiet place. There is also a small restaurant and shop for basic provisions.

Sunita (☎ 2273690; sunitagoa@rediffmail.com; d Rs 300) Quintessentially Vagator. Rooms are no frills, there's a garden area to chill out in and it's near the action.

Moonlight (☎ 2273690; sunitagoa@rediffmail.com; d Rs 300) No-frills rooms near the action in Vagator.

Siddeshwar Rest House (☎ 2273963; d Rs 300) Basic doubles.

CHAPORA

There's not much variety in the accommodation at Chapora; most of it is budget and most guests are long-term stayers.

Casa de Olga (☎ 2274355; Chapora; d without bathroom Rs 150, d with bathroom Rs 300-700) Casa de Olga, near Chapora Jetty and next to Custom House, is a lovely choice run by the very cordial Olga and her husband. The rooms are all extremely clean; even the shared bathrooms are spotless. Some rooms have their own balcony, hot-water showers and kitchenette facilities. Prices depend on facilities and duration of stay.

Helinda Bar & Restaurant (☎ 2274345; r with/ without bathroom Rs 400/150) In 2004, Helinda built lovely new rooms that still have a fresh feel. Ask for one of these newer rooms, which have clean tiled bathrooms, though the older ones are cheaper. There's also an attached restaurant.

Other basic options include **Noble's Nest** (r without bathroom Rs 150), which is primarily a quiet place for a drink but has some basic rooms, and **Baba** (☎ 2273213; d without bathroom Rs 150), which also has basic rooms.

Eating & Drinking
VAGATOR

Bean Me Up (☎ 2273479; beanmeup@usa.net; H No 1639/2 Deulvaddo; mains Rs 100-200; ❤ noon-4pm & 7-11pm Sun-Fri) This popular vegetarian courtyard restaurant offers healthy and hearty wraps, pizzas, pastas, juice concoctions and miscellaneous fare under heaving parachutes and leaf-filled nets. Bean Me Up also organises various cultural musical nights and hosts the occasional spontaneous party.

Mango Tree (☎ 3094464; mains Rs 50-150; ❤ from 9am) The big drawcard here is the movie screened at 7.30pm every night. The wooden bar facing into the restaurant is an aesthetic positive, and the roof, furnished to look like something to do with mangos, looks more

like an egg sac. The Indian, Thai, Chinese, Italian and Mexican food is overpriced given the serving size, and it can sometimes take an unforgivably long time to arrive.

Le Bluebird (☎ 2273695; mains Rs 100-300; ❤ 9.30am-2pm & 7-11pm) This is an oddly situated and unusually classy French restaurant that does fine dining in a great outdoor area. Francophiles can enjoy imported wine here, and there's a good selection of vegetarian dishes on offer.

Robert's Place (☎ 2274392; ❤ 8.30am-4.30am) Trying to cater for and cash in on the Primrose Cafe crowd, Roberts serves a bit of everything and is open for insane hours.

CHAPORA

Given that the restaurants and bars of Chapora are so tightly packed in together it's difficult for anything to stand out; in fact it's sometimes difficult to tell where one establishment stops and another starts.

Sunrise Restaurant (mains Rs 30-100; ❤ from 7am) This is a nice place to sit in the shade for a drink and chat. It has a good-value veg English breakfast (Rs 80).

Welcome (mains Rs 25-100) Another good option, with generous servings and reasonable prices. It's location on the corner affords it a great view of the passing parade of people.

Leena's Place (mains Rs 40-120) Leena's is a popular restaurant with Thai, Chinese, Indian and Western offerings, plus an obligatory 'German Bakery'. This is one of the more polished places to eat in Chapora; being set back off the main drag helps it keep its class.

Green Shadow (mains Rs 30-80) Just off the main street, Green Shadow is a quiet place that serves Indian, Chinese, Mexican and Italian.

Yak Restaurant (☎ 2274170; mains Rs 30-90) On the small intersection marked by a banyan tree and a distinctive temple, Yak has Israeli food in among the usual Indian and Chinese suspects. The food is fine but the staff are sometimes indifferent.

Jai Ganesh (juices Rs 15-30) Right next door to Yak, this fruit juice centre is a popular place to smoke and drink while you watch (and are watched by) passers-by.

Scarlet Cold Drinks (drinks & desserts Rs 15-25) Popular for cold beverages and enormous fruit salads with big blocks of ice cream (Rs 15).

PARTY'S A GOA?

Goa has a long and vibrant history of hosting parties. When the Portuguese were here, the colony became notorious as an immoral outpost where drinking and dancing lasted till dawn. The tradition continued when the 'Goa Freaks' arrived on the northern beaches in the 1960s. But the beach parties and full-moon raves of the 1970s and '80s seem like innocent affairs compared with the trance parties that replaced them in the '90s. This era also hailed the arrival of synthetic substances, so that ecstasy seemed the drug of choice over ganja.

Changing Times

The late '90s and early 2000s heralded a big change; controversy over drugs and the state government's acknowledgment of the economic potential in appropriating the scene have threatened the future of party life in Goa. Today you'll hear the party veterans complaining about the increasing commercialisation of the scene, and general consensus seems to be that parties nowadays are not a patch on what they were. The synthetic drugs are still here (ecstasy, acid, speed, ketamine) but the hard hand of the law has meant that these have been pushed further behind the scenes (see p220). On top of this is the sudden diligence of the police in enforcing the ban on loud music after 10pm. The better organised (and more publicised) a party is, the more likely it is to be shut down before it even begins. But baksheesh still talks, and the random and remote locations of the raves still manages to sometimes foil law enforcers.

But parties are here to stay, albeit as altered incarnations of their more soulful ancestors. Visitors who have heard the notorious stories of wild nights in Goa are generally disappointed these days, but on the other hand the locals who once had to put up with what they perceived as self-indulgent Westerners gyrating in a drugged stupor to an incomprehensible beat have enjoyed the restoration of the quieter days of old. For the more hard-core partiers though, their party culture is not noise pollution, but a cosmic experience that, according to DJ Goa Gil, is there '…to uplift people's consciousness through the trance-dance experience'.

Where to Party

Open-air rave parties have generally taken place around Anjuna and Vagator, at places such as Bamboo Forest (behind the market site in Anjuna), and Disco Valley and Spaghetti Beach (in Vagator). However, given that the police are party savvy, these often don't get up and running. The scene seems to have moved to Arambol, often at the lake, and people are ferried to parties by in-the-know taxi drivers. Locals in this area are increasingly agitated about having acquired the problems that were quashed further south. Groups of ravers heading off on their bikes is a sign that a party is on – or that someone *thinks* they know where a party is on. Often, false alarms or last-minute cancellations will result in a lot of aimless searching. The Christmas and New Year period is particularly hit and miss; local authorities either turn a blind eye or up their law-enforcement efforts.

Parties that do get the green light are an odd mix of ravers in psychedelic club wear swaying to the beat and glowing like radioactive waste, tourists joining in the Goa experience and locals angling for business – 'taxi?', 'chai?', 'cigarettes?' It's a heady mix that continues on well past dawn.

The gap left by the receding 'true' trance parties has been filled by the more aboveboard mainstream operators. Paradiso (p144) in Anjuna tries to recreate the scene with psychedelic paint and a chai market next to a Coffee Day Express – starkly symbolic of the way the scene is being commercialised. Growing frustration at fruitless searches for parties has also done wonders for Vagator's Nine Bar (opposite), which is allowed to have parties every night on the condition that it comes to a dead stop at 10pm. Another popular venue is Hill Top (opposite). The fact that Hill Top hasn't yet managed to get too cosy with the law means that its plans are frequently foiled, but when they get off the ground the result can be a night to reminisce about.

The difficulties faced by the Goa trance scene have worked to the advantage of mainstream club operators further south. The growing popularity of the big commercial operators like Club Cubana in Arpora have lead to more and more venues of this ilk popping up along the coast.

Paulo's Antique Bar (drinks Rs 20-40) A tiny patch of socialness that has pride of place on this fascinating street.

Entertainment

Chapora village doesn't have much in the way of nightlife, but it's a fascinating place to drink beer and watch people parade past.

Vagator is the centre of north Goa's party scene – along with several established bars, impromptu rave parties are occasionally organised at places like Disco Valley and Spaghetti Beach. Disco Valley is an open area of beach at the southern end of Vagator Beach, while Spaghetti Beach (also called Ozram Beach) is a flat area overlooking the ocean in a deserted area south of Little Vagator Beach.

However, given that the police are on a diligent quest to shut this sort of activity down these days, parties are being pushed further and further into the jungle. For this reason, they are rarely overtly advertised. Though parties are sometimes shut down before they begin, others get the green light and up, up and away they go. Find out what's going on by talking to local motorcycle taxi drivers or ask at places like Primrose Cafe and Hill Top.

Nine Bar (Sunset Point, Little Vagator Beach) A standard night out in Vagator usually starts at this open-air place overlooking Little Vagator Beach. It is still the central point of partying where trance and house music plays to a packed floor. Crowds start to gather at around 5pm and it's all over at 10pm when people wander about like lemmings, hoping someone else knows where the next party is.

Primrose Cafe (☎ 2273210) Towards the back of Vagator village, this is often where the next party is at. At Primrose the music usually continues till 2am or 3am (depending on restrictions) under a canopy of psychedelically painted trees.

Alcove (Little Vagator Beach; drinks Rs 20-80; ☺ till midnight) Some Nine Bar patrons overflow here for a quieter drink and occasional live music.

Hill Top (☎ 2273025, 2273665; hilltop104@hotmail .com) By day this is a peaceful place on the edge of the action, but by night it flouts the 10pm music restrictions to create action of its own. Hill Top throws parties on spe-

cial occasions and occasionally hosts fully fledged concerts of local and visiting musicians. There is the distinct smell of ganja in the air.

Tin Tin Bar & Restaurant (mains Rs 40-110; ☺ till late) On the main road down to Vagator Beach, Tin Tin occasionally has live music and is a relaxed place to play pool.

Getting There & Around

Fairly frequent buses run to both Chapora and Vagator from Mapusa (Rs 10) throughout the day, some via Anjuna. The bus stop is close to the road junction near Soniya Travels in Chapora village. Buses to Mapusa also leave from the intersection near Mango Tree. Buses also continue up to Arambol via Siolim.

Vagator and Chapora villages are quite spread out and most people staying here rent a motorcycle or scooter – the Vagator hills are constantly alive with the buzz of these machines, and the number of bikes outside Nine Bar or Primrose Cafe during the evening is phenomenal (if you plan to leave early don't park too close or you might get blocked in). You can ask about motorcycle hire down near the beach at Vagator (try the car park) or anywhere along the main street in Chapora. Bicycle hire is more difficult and the steep hills around here make cycling a relative pain.

CHAPORA TO ARAMBOL

The further you get from Panaji the quieter and less touristy the countryside becomes, although development and people are finding their way to the once deserted beaches north of the Chapora River. Where there once was a ferry crossing, now stands an enormous Siolim–Chopdem bridge. Drive carefully, but pause for a moment, if you can, to admire the view on either side. At present, the area between Chapora and Arambol is blooming; some beaches have a small and exclusive scene, while others are just peaceful pockets of coastline.

Heading north from Anjuna, Chapora or Mapusa, make for Siolim, the village on the south bank of the Chapora River. The main road through the village leads to the bridge that takes you across to Chopdem. From there, take the first left at the signpost to Morjim. This is the coast road, which takes you the slow way up to Arambol.

Siolim

☎ 0832

Siolim is overlooked by travellers, who use it as a mere fulcrum between Anjuna and Arambol, but it is actually a particularly pleasant place in its own right. If you're looking to rent a house for an extended period in Goa, this might be a sensible place to do it. Almost any side street leads you through authentic slices of village living, where signs offer houses for rent.

There's an atmospheric **market** along the Chapora River, where you can watch women open the shells of mussels at a speed that will impress. On Wednesday mornings there is another small **market** (⏱ 7.30-10am), which is full of home-grown produce; it's near St Anthony Church.

Computer Shop (☎ 9822485672; nrohan@sanch arnet.in; Shop EW6, St Anthony Community Centre; per hr Rs 20) is a good Internet café near St Anthony Church.

A finalist in 2001 for the Unesco World Heritage Asia Pacific Award, **Siolim House** (☎ 2272138; www.siolimhouse.com; Wadi; d standard/ superior Rs 3000/3750; 🗷) is exclusive without the artificiality that often comes with exclusivity. The seven rooms have elegant and individual class, and the simple but prominent pool next to the house can be admired from the breezy open-air sitting area. The restaurant is set among proud white pillars around the central courtyard and is only open to guests and their friends. If you can't afford to stay, try bidding in the online silent auction.

Morjim

☎ 0832

Welcome to Russia Town. For some inexplicable reason, Morjim is the destination of choice for Russians on holiday, and only receives a trickle of day-trippers from other beaches.

Morjim is a tiny village at the mouth of the Chapora River, 4.5km southwest of Chopdem. The clean, quiet beach is an exposed strip of sand heading north from the river mouth and backed as much by pine trees as by palms. There are good views south to the headland and Chapora Fort. The southern end of Morjim Beach is a protected area for rare olive ridley turtles (opposite).

Accommodation options have increased over the last few years as the beach has grown in popularity. Rooms can be rented in village homes for around Rs 150 per night, but the best option is the handful of guesthouses and huts at the northern end of the beach; there are also beach shacks here. To get here you can either walk a couple of kilometres along the beach or drive back through the village, turning north on the road to Asvem and Mandrem Beach (passing Milagres Church), then left at the signposted turn-off to the beach. At the junction here, Amigos is a small shop offering Internet access and currency exchange.

Shanti (☎ 9881289334; webb.elena@gmail.com; huts Rs 300-500) is a charming Russian-run choice for beach-hut life. The huts are across the road from the beach, but there's a lovely beachside restaurant and services such as massage.

As well as its standard rooms, **Julian's Guest House** (☎ 2244632; r Rs 500) has more-basic rooms in a more basic building out the back for Rs 250.

Camp 69 (☎ 2244458; huts Rs 250) is not as picturesque as beachside living should be: it sits near a rather filthy patch of beach. Having said that the facilities are adequate and there's no shortage of people (mostly Russian) wanting to stay here.

Goan Café (Lobos; ☎ 2244394; www.goaplaces .com; huts/rooms incl breakfast Rs 450/600) has a lovely restaurant.

For those that prefer actual rooms to huts, **Britto's Guesthouse** (☎ 2244245; r Rs 250) is a very hospitable option run by a family who will also provide breakfast upon request.

Asvem Beach

☎ 0832

Asvem Beach is a long, flat and hassle-free stretch of beach that attracts only the most determined idlers. Although virtually unheard of by travellers until recently, groups of palm-thatch and bamboo huts have sprung up here, attracting visitors looking to do nothing more than relax. It's said that one of Goa's first bamboo beach huts was built here by a British carpenter in 1996 – now they're all over the place!

The beach is small and picturesque, backed by sparse stands of palm trees. It's easily accessible since the road is only about 100m back.

The rooms at brand-new **White Feather Guest House** (☎ 985024201; whitefeather_gh@yahoo.co.in;

TURTLE BEACHES

Goan beaches have provided nesting places for olive ridley turtles for many years. These giant turtles have a remarkable in-built homing device that enables them to return to nest at the beach where they first hatched – even after 15 years out at sea. One of those beaches is Morjim, but the turtle numbers began to dwindle dangerously because of poaching – locals were digging up the eggs and selling them in the markets for a couple of rupees each. If a turtle was found out of the water it was usually killed for its meat and shell. Increased tourism in the area also posed a threat; eggs were trampled at rave parties and pollution threatened the survival of those that managed to hatch.

In 1996 the Goa Foundation, on the urging of a local resident, stepped in and enlisted the help of the Forest Department to patrol the beach and start a turtle conservation programme. Locals who once profited from selling the eggs are now paid to protect them at the Turtle Sanctuary (at the south end of Morjim Beach), which has been established for this very purpose.

The practice of picking up recently hatched turtles and putting them in buckets to show tourists should be discouraged, since environmentalists believe these baby turtles may not survive, even if they're released into the sea.

The turtle nesting season is from October to March, and the turtles usually come ashore only between full moon and new moon nights.

---

r Rs 2000) are overpriced, but this will perhaps change. Superbly arranged with a separate sleeping and sitting area, rooms have a fridge and some basic kitchenware. There's a balcony around the entire building, and a rooftop area from where you can enjoy the view of the coast. The family who runs it are justifiably proud of the effort they have put into small details; for example, towels are folded into animals – though we'd rather drip-dry than unravel a crocodile!

Gopal (☎ 2244431; gopal@ingoa.com; huts/r/beach-front huts Rs 300/500/1000) has a range of rooms and a good restaurant selling set breakfasts (Rs 75).

Nearby **Change Your Mind** (☎ 5613716; huts Rs 150), which obviously hasn't been told what the going rate for beach huts is, practically gives its huts away.

The nicest place to eat along the beach (and to stay for that matter) is **Le Restaurant Francais** (☎ 9822121712; mains Rs 40-160), next to Gopal. With flowing white décor, this is a perfect place to while away an hour or two, though it's not the cheap affair that its neighbours are.

Further down the beach and heading towards Mandrem are another couple of good options with a nice piece of beach. **Arabian Sea** (☎ 9850686134; huts Rs 300) has a pleasant restaurant that's conducive to settling in for the day. **Paradise** (☎ 2247832; r Rs 350) is a similar affair but has rooms in a building across the road from the beach. Further down the

beach, heading towards the town of Asvem, is **Antonio's Paradise** (☎ 9822100964; huts Rs 500), which has standard beach huts.

Mandrem

Continuing north, turn left at the T-junction for Mandrem Beach, or right for Mandrem village. The beach and the majority of the accommodation is a kilometre or so past the village. Mandrem is another peaceful area with a broad beach and some good accommodation among the coconut groves. There are several groups of bamboo huts along the beach, all with semi-open-air restaurants facing the Arabian Sea. Mandrem beach has a series of typical beach huts and restaurants. The other accommodation option is to head towards the beach in the Junasawaddo area of Mandrem and find something there.

Salvador Dali would highly approve of **River Cat Villa** (☎ 2247928; www.villarivercat.com; d €15-33), with its hammocks hanging from the roof and palm trees growing through its balconies, shading mattresses in the open air. You could stay for a month and every day discover a new nook or cranny to read in. Rooms open up onto the enormous circular balconies, and the entire property backs onto the river.

Little Nest (☎ 2247413, 9422394809; d/apt Rs 250/400) is an absolute bargain. Brand-new rooms all have bathrooms and balconies. For those looking to stay longer, the facilities in the

NORTH GOA

apartments will enable self-sufficiency. While there's no beach view to speak of, the short walk is worth the fantastic value.

D'Souza Residency (☎ 2247483; albert_d16@ rediffmail.com; r Rs 400) has a nice sunken restaurant situated in a pleasant bend in the road. The D'Souza family are hospitable, and at the time of research were building more rooms to accommodate guests.

Among the cluster of beach huts in Mandrem is the very prominent **Dunes** (☎ 2247219, 2247071; www.dunesgoa.com; huts & cottages Rs 600). The thatched huts and stone cottages are all reasonably kept, and there is a laid-back vibe. There is also a Ayurvedic massage centre.

Near Dunes, **Riva** (☎ 2247088; enquiry@rivaresorts .com; huts from Rs 1000) is trying for a more upmarket feel – and it's doing a good job. Some bamboo huts face the sea and are fitted out with TV and hot water. There's also a decent restaurant, and a party atmosphere is sometimes mustered on the dance floor.

Before the road narrows to the path that leads to River Cat Villa, you'll find **Sing A-Long Resort** (☎ 2247931; ambrose_pinto@rediffmail .com; d Rs 800) in a brand-new white building. Rooms are unimaginative but are clean and happily situated in a quiet area with a pleasant stroll to the beach.

ARAMBOL
☎ 0832

Although it is one of Goa's more far-flung beaches, Arambol (Harmal) has well and truly been discovered.

Travellers have been drifting up here for years, attracted by the remote location and the prominent headland with beautiful, rocky bays. A mushrooming industry of facilities and accommodation has appeared to service them, and in the high season the beach and the road leading down to it can be crowded. Arambol is still a lot quieter than anything south of Vagator though, and it generally attracts travellers looking to chill out for a while. There are burgeoning adventure-sports and music scenes here. Women should be cautious; we have had reports of attacks on quiet areas of the beach.

Orientation
Buses from Mapusa stop on the main road at the back part of Arambol village, where there's a church, school and a few shops,

but no bank. From here, a side road leads 1.5km down to the village, and the beach is about 500m further on. There are a few stores, travel agencies and Internet places on the road running parallel to the beach, but most services can be found on the busy, narrow road leading down to the beach. It's easy finding a seaside restaurant or hotel that suits in Arambol. Just continue to follow the path along the coast and you will be lead through the options.

Information
Internet access is widely available, often in travel agents.

Arambol Police Outpost (☎ 2242914) The police are based here.

Blue Fin Communications (per hr Rs 40)

Cyberzone (per hr Rs 40)

Delight Cyber Café (per hr Rs 40)

Divya Travels (☎ 2242297; per hr Rs 40)

Ganga Travels (569B Khalchawada)

JBL Enterprises (☎ 3953640) A well-dressed (in hard-to-miss purple) new kid on the block, where you can surf the Net in air-conditioned comfort.

St Anthony Cybercafé (Playlist; per hr Rs 40) An inland option where you can also stock up on music.

Sanket Travels (663/3 Khalchawada)

Tara Travels (☎ 2417617)

Activities
The main beach is good for swimming, but over the headland are several more attractive bays. At low tide, if you continue past the headland and keep walking for about 45 minutes you'll come to the near-deserted Querim Beach. You can also walk south along the beach to Mandrem (about one hour).

Behind the second bay is a small **freshwater pool** that's pleasant to splash about in, although it's fast being swallowed up by the encroaching sea and, away from the source of the spring, the water is quite brackish. This is where rave parties sometimes happen.

There's a healthy adventure-sports scene in Arambol. Much to the enormous delight of locals, there are no jet skis or other such noise polluters, but there are enthusiastic paragliders and kite-surfers around. To find them, head to the Surf Shack in front of the **Surf Club** (☎ 2292484, 9850554006; flyinfishbarbados@ hotmail.com; Dando Wada) at South Arambol Beach, close to Mandrem, which also

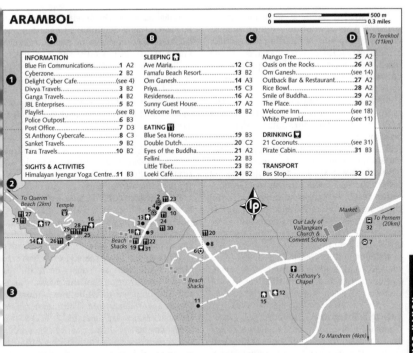

ARAMBOL

INFORMATION	
Blue Fin Communications	1 A2
Cyberzone	2 B2
Delight Cyber Cafe	(see 4)
Divya Travels	3 B2
Ganga Travels	4 B2
JBL Enterprises	5 B2
Playlist	(see 8)
Police Outpost	6 B3
Post Office	7 D3
St Anthony Cybercafe	8 C3
Sanket Travels	9 B2
Tara Travels	10 B2

SIGHTS & ACTIVITIES	
Himalayan Iyengar Yoga Centre	11 B3

SLEEPING	
Ave Maria	12 C3
Famafu Beach Resort	13 B2
Om Ganesh	14 A3
Priya	15 C3
Residensea	16 A2
Sunny Guest House	17 A2
Welcome Inn	18 B2

EATING	
Blue Sea Horse	19 B3
Double Dutch	20 C2
Eyes of the Buddha	21 A2
Fellini	22 B3
Little Tibet	23 B2
Loeki Café	24 B2

Mango Tree	25 A2
Oasis on the Rocks	26 A3
Om Ganesh	(see 14)
Outback Bar & Restaurant	27 A2
Rice Bowl	28 A2
Smile of Buddha	29 A2
The Place	30 B2
Welcome Inn	(see 18)
White Pyramid	(see 11)

DRINKING	
21 Coconuts	(see 31)
Pirate Cabin	31 B3

TRANSPORT	
Bus Stop	32 D2

has surfboards and boogie boards for hire. **Kite Surf Goa** (☎ 9822867570, 9850475241; airambol2000@yahoo.de; equipment hire per day Rs 800) is a registered business run by Uwe and Stefan from Germany. You can usually hunt them down in person through the Surf Shack. As well as renting equipment, Kite Surf Goa runs 10-hour kite-surfing courses (Rs 9500).

On the sand dunes of Arambol Beach is **Himalayan Iyengar Yoga Centre** (www.hiyoga centre.com; Arambol Beach), which runs five-day courses in hatha yoga from mid-November to mid-March. This is the winter centre of the iyengar yoga school in Dharamsala, and is run by the same teacher, Sharat Arora. Five-day courses for new and more-experienced students cost Rs 1800, but the more days you do the less you pay. Booking and registration must be done in person at the centre on Tuesday at 2pm. Courses start on Friday. There are also intensive two- to three-week courses for more experienced hatha yoga devotees and special short courses combining yoga with Ayurvedic treatment.

Sleeping

Accommodation in Arambol is mostly in the form of cliffside rooms or huts at the north end of the main beach. Given the extraordinary location perched on the rocks overlooking this pleasant stretch of beach, it's surprising that the accommodation has managed to avoid big development and is still exclusively focused on budget and mid-range travellers.

Sunny Guest House (☎ 2297675; r Rs 400-600) This is a good example of the classic Arambol accommodation: no unnecessary frills but the necessary cliffside location.

Om Ganesh (☎ 2297675; r Rs 400-600) In a similar vein to Sunny, Om Ganesh is another popular choice. It has options on either side of the path, but the more happily situated corner rooms are as close to the beach as you can be without getting wet. They fill up fast.

Residensea (huts Rs 350) At the north end of the beach, Residensea is a collection of simple, lockable bamboo huts that are representative of the type of accommodation you'll find in these parts.

Ave Maria (☎ 2242974; d with/without bathroom Rs 350/250) This comfortable option is hard to miss; it's in a large building painted like a child-care centre. Ave Maria is off the beach but is nicely situated in a quiet area of coconut palms. There's also a very pleasant rooftop restaurant.

Priya (☎ 2292661; d with/without Rs 200/150) The premises and rooms here are smaller than what's on offer at its more outlandish neighbour, but its size just adds to the cosy family feel. It can be an intimately sociable place depending on who else has checked in.

Famafu Beach Resort (☎ 2242516; H No 470 Arambol Beach Rd; r Rs 400) On the road leading to the beach, Famafu is an uncharacteristic three-storey concrete-block hotel, but it gets good reviews. Rooms have hot water and are clean and good value, and the staff are always smiling.

Welcome Inn (☎ 2242510; d Rs 350-400) Also on the road leading towards the beach, Welcome Inn has seven small but clean doubles.

Eating & Drinking

There's a nice assortment of eateries in Arambol. So far, there's nothing too shiny and flash in the area; restaurants remain thick on atmosphere and high on quality. There is a seemingly endless selection of eating places that wrap around the rocks at the north end of the beach.

Double Dutch (mains Rs 30-120; ☽ breakfast, lunch & dinner) This is a great place that doesn't try too hard; its sign reads 'Nothing allowed, lousy service, good food'. There's a very useful notice board at the entrance, with information about various courses and treatments.

Fellini (mains Rs 60-150) Serving fantastic Italian food, this is Arambol's top restaurant. There is a good range of pizzas, calzones and pasta, as well as satisfying focaccias.

Place (mains Rs 60-160) This is an interesting option that sets up in the middle of a residential area during season. The Bulgarian restaurant with orange cushions and candlelight under the trees has a lovely atmosphere. Veal with vegetables and rosemary (Rs 155) is about as far away from Goa and into the heart of Bulgaria as it sounds, and the fruit punch (Rs 40) is the best in the world, seriously. Follow the red-and-white arrows through the warren of pathways to find it.

Om Ganesh (☎ 2297657; mains Rs 40-100) This is a pleasant but small eating area perched out on the rocks with very cheap food, that is very, very tasty. The veg hakka noodles (Rs 40) are a real winner.

White Pyramid (mains Rs 40-130; ☽ from 9am) Next to the Iyengar Yoga Centre on the sand dunes overlooking the beach, this is the perfect place to while away hours on a cushion under a tree. The menu ranges from sushi to roast vegetables.

Welcome Inn (☎ 2242510; mains Rs 20-80) A dimly lit German bakery and hotel with a curiously conspiratorial air in among the pastries. It's a popular hang-out for Israelis.

Loeki Café (mains Rs 25-100) This is a very unassuming place with a laid-back vibe. It serves Goan, Chinese and European dishes and is a good spot for a drink. Jam sessions are held on Sunday and Thursday.

Blue Sea Horse (☎ 9823883510; mains Rs 40-300) Located where the road meets the beach, Blue Sea Horse has a predominantly seafood menu and arranges the occasional party during season.

THE AUTHOR'S CHOICE

Fort Tiracol Heritage Hotel (☎ 0832-227631, 9226360618; nilaya@sancharnet.in; r/ste incl breakfast & dinner Rs 5500/12,000) If a historical monument like a fort has to be converted into a hotel then you couldn't possibly ask for a more tasteful effort than the Fort Tiracol Heritage Hotel. It is, in fact, one of the nicest places to stay in the entire state; at least that's what you'll be thinking as you're sitting at the rooftop restaurant at the northernmost point of Goa, looking south over what feels like the entire state. The seven rooms (named for the days of the week) preside over the meeting point of the Arabian Sea and the Terekhol River, where an occasional dolphin can be spotted. There is an intentionally Mediterranean feel to the décor, complete with white umbrellas, rounded stone walls, airy bathrooms with open showers and wood-framed windows that swing out to the ocean. If you can, stay in Wednesday. Querim Beach across the river is yours and, sometimes, yours alone.

Among the endless choice of restaurants dotted along the cliffside or overlooking the sea are the following:

Mango Tree (mains Rs 40-90) Self-proclaimed chill-out place, where cushions and Chinese lanterns set the mood.

Rice Bowl (☎ 982248032; mains Rs 40-90) Chinese, Japanese and Tibetan menu with a view stretching for miles down the beach.

Little Tibet (mains Rs 40-80) A low-key place that meets Arambol's *momo* needs.

Smile of Buddha (mains Rs 30-140) Israeli, Indian, Chinese and Goan cuisine.

Eyes of the Buddha (mains Rs 30-120) Standard extensive menu. Popular spot for breakfast.

Outback Bar & Restaurant (mains Rs 30-80) Boasts seafood specialities.

Oasis on the Rocks (mains Rs 60-250) Well located and low key. Candles create romance at night.

Entertainment

In addition to the parties during peak season, there is a healthy music scene in Arambol, which attracts musicians from far and wide. It's hard to generalise about any music 'scene' but, depending on the line-up, the crowd and your perspective, a night of live music in these parts can either keep the Goan spirit alive or shoot it in the foot. Keep an eye on posters advertising live music.

Surf Club (☎ 2292484, 9850554006; flyinfishbarbados@hotmail.com; Dando Wada) On Tuesdays and Fridays this place has film nights and live music, with the line-up of talent depending largely on who's floating through town.

Loeki Café (Arambol Beach Rd; ☙ 8am till late) Has jam sessions on Sunday and Thursday.

Parties are sometimes organised where the road meets the beach, and where **Pirate Cabin** (mains Rs 40-250) meets **21 Coconuts** (mains Rs 40-200, local beer Rs 20). Pamphlets will flutter down the coast of north Goa inviting the masses, sometimes to such good effect that it's difficult to give credit to any one establishment. On other nights, the drinking just spontaneously turns to partying. And on other nights still (there really is no rhyme or reason) you can catch a quiet flick at 21 Coconuts.

Getting There & Away

There are buses from Mapusa to Arambol (Rs 12, 1½ hours), via Siolim and Chopdem, every couple of hours. Buses also head north to Terekhol and Pernem, and a few buses take the back road past Mandrem and Morjim.

You could get a group together and hire a taxi to travel here (around Rs 350 from Mapusa or Anjuna). From Dabolim Airport, prepaid taxis cost Rs 682 for the 65km journey.

If you're coming by bus from Mumbai, you can ask to be let off at Pernem and take a local bus, taxi or autorickshaw from there. The nearest train station on the Konkan Railway is Pernem, about 2km from the town itself. Again you can get off here and catch a taxi to Arambol.

Motorcycles can be hired from touts at the main northern entrance to the beach. In the high season a Honda Kinetic costs around Rs 200 a day.

There are boats every Wednesday to the Anjuna flea market (one way Rs 75).

NORTH OF ARAMBOL
Querim Beach

North of Arambol and south of the Terekhol River lies the almost untouched sand of Querim Beach, plus a couple of beach shacks. Querim is accessible from Arambol via a narrow path that leads around the headland from the second bay, or by road through the exceptionally pretty countryside along the south bank of the Terekhol River. There are some very basic rooms available behind the beach shacks but visitors are better off staying in Arambol or Terekhol, and walking, cycling or motoring here for the day.

Terekhol Fort

At the northernmost point of Goa is Terekhol (Tiracol), on the north bank of the river of the same name. Its key feature is a small Portuguese fort (☙ 11am-5pm), which has a tiny whitewashed chapel within its walls and is now an upmarket hotel, the Fort Tiracol Heritage Hotel (opposite).

Originally built by the rajas of Sawantwadi, the fort was finally captured by the viceroy, Dom Pedro de Almeida, in 1746. The fort was rebuilt and the church, which takes up almost all of the available space within the fort, was added.

The fact that the fort was on the wrong side of the natural border (the river) led it to be involved in considerable controversy. In the early 19th century the British demanded that it be handed over, and later, when the first Goan-born governor,

Bernado Peres da Silva, was ousted, his supporters took over the fort. Finally, in the years before Independence, the whole of the northern border was at the centre of anti-Portuguese demonstrations, and several demonstrators were killed here.

The fort makes a good outing on a motorcycle. The winding 11km road from Arambol passes through villages and rice paddies and rises up to provide sensational views over the countryside.

Amid the few budget options in Terekhol is the prudently named **Hygienic Restaurant** (☎ 0832-227670; r Rs 300), which has a couple of rooms just below the fort. It's run by a friendly family.

Ferries from Querim to Terekhol leave every 30 minutes or so between 6.15am and 10pm. As usual people can cross for free but bikes sometimes cost Rs 4 and cars Rs 10.

INLAND BARDEZ

Away from the coast, north Goa has less to offer the tourist than the central or south parts of the state, and consequently receives fewer visitors. However, Bardez taluka has several sights east of National Highway (NH) 17, between Panaji and Mapusa. This is a peaceful area of rural villages, farmland, churches and temples, and makes a pleasant day trip if you have your own transport. The best way to explore this area is by hired motorcycle, or with a car and driver from Panaji, Mapusa or any of the beach resorts.

The most convenient and scenic route is to follow the back roads from Panaji along the north bank of the Mapusa River, then turn west towards Mapusa itself. Heading northeast from the Mandovi Bridge, the first village you come to is Britona. Following the road north to Aldona, visit Corjuem Fort before turning west to Mapusa and either heading back to Panaji or continuing to the coast.

Britona & Pomburpao
☎ 0832

The parish church at Britona, **Nossa Senhora de Penha de Franca** (Our Lady of the Rock of France), occupies a fine location on the junction of the Mandovi and Mapusa Rivers, looking straight across to Chorao Island on one side and the Ribandar Causeway on the other.

Nossa Senhora de Penha de France was a Spanish saint. After one hair-raising voyage

---

DETOUR: ALDONA & CORJUEM FORT

Another 4km north of Pomburpao you reach the large village of **Aldona**. The **Church of St Thomas** on the banks of the Mapusa River is a grand sight, particularly when viewed from the now defunct ferry crossing. The church was built in 1596 and has been renovated in recent years. There is a legend about the treasure that once adorned the church's statues. On one occasion, as a group of thieves crossed the river into Aldona, they were met by a young boy who warned them not to carry out their crime. As they were attempting to remove valuables, the church bells started to ring. Fleeing in a panic, some of the thieves drowned, while others were captured. As the leader was led out, he recognised the statue of St Thomas as the boy who had cautioned him against his mischief.

From Aldona you can cross the disturbingly modern new bridge across the river to visit the abandoned **Corjuem Fort** on the other side of Corjuem Island. Until the early 18th century, the Mapusa River formed the boundary of Portuguese influence, and the dark red laterite wall above the ferry point in Aldona betrays the ancient lines of the fortress that used to stand here. Around 1705, however, the Portuguese influence extended eastwards, and the small fort on Corjuem Island was built.

Squat and thick walled, standing alone on a small hillock, the fort has an ironic element of *beau geste* about it. Although there's not a whole lot to see here, it's easy to imagine this place as a solitary outpost in the jungle nearly three centuries ago, filled with homesick Portuguese soldiers half expecting to be overrun at any moment. One of the defenders of the fort is said to have been Ursula e Lancastre, a Portuguese woman who travelled the world disguised as a man, eventually finding herself here as a soldier. It was not until she was captured and stripped that her secret was discovered. This did not put an end to her military career, however – she married the captain of the guard.

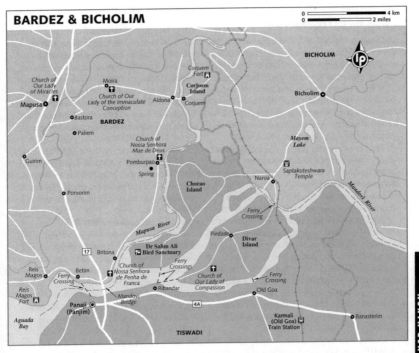

BARDEZ & BICHOLIM

in which the sailors saved themselves from certain death by appealing to Nossa Senhora, she came to be associated with seafarers, and thus she was favoured by many of those who had survived the voyage to India.

The interior of the church is beautifully decorated, with a high vaulted ceiling and a simple reredos (ornamented screen behind the altar in Goan churches) with painted scenes on it. The church is best visited in the morning and holds one service (in Konkani) on most days.

About 5km north of Britona is the village of Pomburpao, where the church of **Nossa Senhora Mae de Deus** (Our Lady Mother of God) is also notable for its beautiful interior and reredos.

Porvorim
☎ 0832

Porvorim is an easy trip from either Mapusa or Panaji. It can also be an add-on to a trip through the rest of inland Bardez, but given that it's on the NH17, a trip from a main town in a taxi is probably the most

sensible way of getting here. The reason to visit Porvorim is the museum **Houses of Goa** (☎ 2410711; Torda, Salvador do Mundo; admission Rs 25; ☼ 10am-8pm). This unmistakable triangular building, the work of renowned architect Gerard da Cunha, shows the Goan fusion of Indian and Portuguese architecture. To find it, take the Britona Rd from O'Coqueiro junction and turn left at the fork. You can't miss it.

BICHOLIM
To the east of Bardez, Bicholim taluka is good place to head on a hired motorcycle if you want to explore the Goan countryside.

With your own transport you can combine Bardez and Bicholim with a scenic loop by riding from Panaji to Old Goa, crossing by ferry to Divar Island, continuing to the north of the island and crossing by ferry again to Naroa. From here head east to Mayem Lake, then north to Bicholim.

Another option is to take the ferry from the small island of Pomburpao to Chorao Island, then head to the bridge on the east

---

CRIME PAYS AT O'COQUEIRO

O'Coqueiro (☎ 2417806), a well-known Goan restaurant in Alto Porvorim, boasts more than just a decent pomfret *recheiado* (fish stuffed with red masala filling). It was the scene of one of India's most famous captures (or at least recaptures), and after a Rs 5 million renovation in 2005 the restaurant reopened to unveil a life-sized statute of Charles Sobhraj to commemorate the event.

Sobhraj (also known as 'the Serpent') was a notorious con man, thief, murderer and suspected serial killer. In the mid-1970s, this Vietnamese-Indian-French man was Asia's most wanted man, facing arrest for murdering travellers in Thailand, Nepal, Afghanistan and India. Sobhraj would charm foreign tourists with his charisma, but one by one they would disappear, and their bodies would be found drugged and disfigured.

After being briefly jailed in Bombay in 1973 over a bungled jewellery theft, Sobhraj flitted around Asia pulling off various scams, establishing a cultlike family of followers and travelling under enough disguises and stolen passports to elude police and the International Criminal Police Organization (Interpol) for years. He finally came unstuck after attempting to drug a group of French tourists in Delhi in 1977. Amazingly, he was charged just with that offence and one count of manslaughter, and was jailed for only 12 years.

With a 20-year warrant for his arrest outstanding in Thailand (and a certain death penalty), he bided his time in Delhi's gruelling Tihar Prison, where he lead a relatively comfortable life by befriending and manipulating prison guards and fellow prisoners. In 1986 he threw a party, drugged the prison guards and walked out.

Not long after, Sobhraj was spotted by a policeman in Goa, where authorities swooped on him in O'Coqueiro and sent him back to Tihar Prison for another 10 years. Sobhraj later claimed he had allowed himself to be caught to escape extradition to Thailand.

In 1997 he was freed from prison and fled to France, a free man at the age of 52. But in August 2004, Sobhraj was arrested again in a Nepalese casino for the 1975 murder of an American tourist.

During his time in France, Sobhraj made a fortune living off his notoriety; he was reportedly paid US$15 million for a book and movie deal. And now the proprietors of O'Coquiero are cashing in on his crimes.

Australian writer Richard Neville wrote *The Life and Crimes of Charles Sobhraj*. A film about his life, *Bottom Line*, was released in 2002.

---

of the island, which will take you to the Bicholim area. You may need to ask for directions occasionally, but there are some signs to both Mayem Lake (Mayem Lake GTDC Resort) and Saptakoteshwara Temple.

Saptakoteshwara Temple

Among the most famous sights in the area is the Saptakoteshwara Temple, near the village of Naroa. The temple itself is tiny and is beautifully complemented by its natural surroundings. Tucked away in a narrow emerald green valley, the little hamlet is undisturbed by anything apart from a few mopeds and the occasional tour bus.

The deity worshipped here is an incarnation of Shiva. According to Hindu legend, the Saptarishis (Seven Great Sages), performed penance for seven million years, a feat that pleased Shiva so much that he came to earth personally to bless them. The incarnation that he appeared in at the time was Saptakoteshwara, which was to become the favoured deity of the great Kadamba dynasty.

The lingam (phallic symbol of Shiva) that now resides in this temple underwent considerable adventures before arriving here. Having been buried to avoid the ravages of the Muslims, it was recovered and placed in a great temple on Divar Island, but when the Portuguese desecrated the spot it was smuggled away and subsequently lost. Miraculously discovered again, it was placed in a simple temple on this new site. It is said that the great Hindu leader Shivaji used to come here to worship, and personally saw to it that the temple was reconstructed, leading to the small but solid structure that stands today.

If you've got your own transport, finding the temple may require some asking around. From the ferry point at Naroa (from Divar

Island), follow the road for approximately 2km before forking right down a small tarmac lane. The temple is on your left, 1.5km down this lane. Follow the red and green archaeology arrows until you arrive at the temple, and don't get distracted by decoys – you'll know the temple when you see it.

Mayem Lake

East of Naroa and about 35km from Panaji, Mayem Lake is a pleasant sort of place that's popular among Indian families as a picnic spot; tours run by the GTDC also stop for lunch here. The key reason to go to Mayem Lake is to escape beaches and tourists; it really is a quiet retreat.

Mayem Lake View (☎ 0832-2362144; d with/without AC Rs 700/550; ✸) is probably the nicest GTDC establishment in the state. Its rooms are extremely good value, particularly those perched at the river's edge. If you want to be on your own, this is really the place to come to.

There's also a restaurant run by the GTDC on the other side of the river, and an area where you can hire paddleboats for Rs 80/120 per 30 minutes/one hour.

You can get here from Mapusa via Thivim and Bicholim, The road crosses some desolate and sunbaked countryside, after which the small valley and lake come as a relief. Coming from Panaji, the quickest and most scenic route is to take the ferry to either Chorao or Divar Island, then another ferry across to the mainland, and then head east about 3km to the lake. This is a good outing on a motorcycle, but a bit of a long haul for little reward if you're on a bicycle.

South Goa

Separated from central Goa by the Zuari River, the southern part of the state has a remarkably different character to the north. If anything, the coastline of south Goa is more varied and picturesque, the beaches longer and straighter, the sand more squeaky underfoot, and the villages – even those close to the beaches – retain a very rural feeling. For the moment, fewer visitors head south, which is generally reflected in the level and type of development.

However, big-money developers have punctuated the coast with big-scale developments, and more and more holidaymakers are tiring of the concrete jungles of Calangute and looking for the Goan dream down south. One of Goa's most beautiful beaches is Palolem, which has been well and truly 'discovered' in the last decade by a steady stream of backpackers who are moving camp. But on either side of this are unspoilt patches of sand with much to offer travellers. In short, south Goa is a great place to come to if you want to escape the worst of the holiday crowds. Even if you just want to escape the beaches, there are a number of interesting villages and sights within easy reach of Margao (the administrative centre and transport hub of the region), as well as Cotigao Wildlife Sanctuary in the far south.

HIGHLIGHTS

- Spend a couple of days or weeks on postcard-perfect **Palolem Beach** (p191)
- Hire a motorcycle and drive along the picturesque rural coastline from **Benaulim** (p185) to **Bogmalo** (p178)
- Explore the colonial mansions of **Chandor** (p167) and **Loutolim** (p166)
- Travel from Palolem to Rajbag by **bike** (p195), taking some time (say half a day) at Patnem Beach on the way.
- Hire a motorcycle and ride from **Cavelossim** (p187) via the untouched inland to the fortress of **Cabo da Rama** (p189).

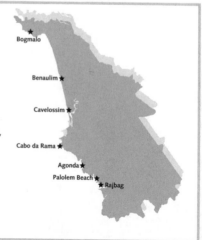

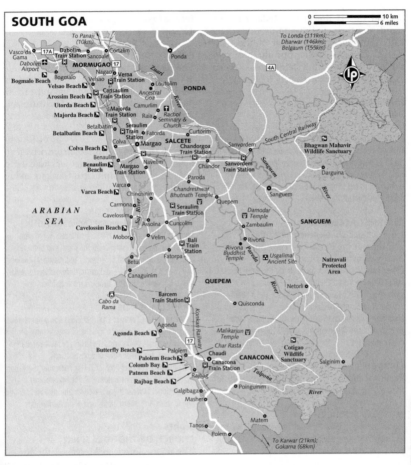

SOUTH GOA

(map labels)

To Panaji (10km)
To Londa (111km); Dharwar (146km); Belgaum (155km)
Vasco da Gama
Dabolim Train Station
Dabolim Airport
Sancoale
Cortalim
Ponda
MORMUGAO
Nagao
Verna
Velso
Train Station
Loutolim
Bogmalo
Bogmalo Beach
Velsao Beach
Cansaulim
Train Station
Ancestral Goa
PONDA
Arossim Beach
Utorda Beach
Majorda
Train Station
Camurlim
Raia
Rachol Seminary & Church
Majorda Beach
Betalbatim
Seraulim
Train Station
Fatorda
Curtorim
South Central Railway
Betalbatim Beach
Colva
Margao
SALCETE
Chandorgoa Train Station
Sanvordem
Bhagwan Mahavir Wildlife Sanctuary
Colva Beach
Benaulim
Chandor
Sanvordem Train Station
Darguina
Benaulim Beach
Margao Train Station
Navelim
Paroda
Varca
Varca Beach
Chinchinim
Chandreshwar Bhutnath Temple
Quepem
Sanguem
River
ARABIAN SEA
Carmona
Cavelossim
Seraulim Train Station
Damodar Temple
SANGUEM
Cavelossim Beach
Assolna
Cuncolim
Zambaulim
Mobor
Velim
Bali Train Station
Rivona
Natravali Protected Area
Fatorpa
Rivona Buddhist Temple
Usgalimal Ancient Site
Betul
Canaguinim
QUEPEM
River
Netorli
Cabo da Rama
Barcem Train Station
Quisconda
Agonda
Agonda Beach
Malikarjun Temple
Butterfly Beach
Palolem
Char Rasta
Cotigao Wildlife Sanctuary
Palolem Beach
Chaudi
CANACONA
Salginim
Colomb Bay
Canacona Train Station
Patnem Beach
Rajbag
Talpona
Rajbag Beach
Galgibaga
River
Mashem
Poinguinim
Tanos
Matem
Polem
To Karwar (21km); Gokarna (68km)

0   10 km
0   6 miles

MARGAO

☎ 0832 / pop 94,392

Margao (Madgaon) is the capital of Salcete taluka (district) and Goa's busiest city. As a hub of economic activity things are quick to develop; the latest feather in its progressive cap is the 8m-high skybus test-track, which was set up here, albeit problematically. For travellers, Margao's attraction lies in its position as the service and transportation hub for south Goa – this is the junction for the South Central Railway and the Konkan Railway. But beyond its logistical value, Margao is a good reminder that there's more to Goa than beaches. The covered market provides a definitive slice of traditional India, and there are Portuguese houses down elegant avenues in varying states of alluring decay.

Margao holds a large fair to celebrate the Feast of Our Lady of the Immaculate Conception around 8 December.

Orientation

In the centre of Margao, the Municipal Gardens consist of a small, shady and rather unkempt patch of grass and trees, around which the life of Margao churns at breakneck speed. Most of the facilities of interest to visitors are around or near this square, and the red-coloured Secretariat Building at the south end of the park is a useful landmark.

Around 1.5km to the north of the park is the Church of the Holy Spirit, and 1km beyond this is the main (Kadamba) bus stand, and the new fish-and-produce market. About 1.5km southeast of the Municipal Gardens and beyond the old train station is the new train station (also known as Madgaon Train Station).

Information
BOOKSHOPS
Golden Heart Emporium (☎ 2732450; fax 2736339; Confidant House, Abade Faria Rd; ☺ 9am-9pm Mon-Sat) The best bookshop in south Goa. It's about 100m north of the main post office and down a small laneway off Abade Faria Rd. It has a large selection of novels and a whole section dedicated to books about Goa and India. There is also Internet access here.

INTERNET ACCESS
Internet access is much cheaper in Margao than at the beach resorts, and there are plenty of cybercafés to be found.
Cyber Inn (Valaulikar Rd; per hr Rs 25; ☺ 9am-11pm Mon-Fri) In the Kalika Chambers.
Cyberlink (Abade Faria Rd; per hr Rs 20; ☺ 8.30am-7.30pm Mon-Sat) In the Caro Centre.
Netzone (Valaulikar Rd; per hr Rs 20; ☺ 8am-11pm) Directly opposite Cyber Inn; has around 10 computers with fast connections.

LIBRARIES
Municipal library (☺ 9am-1pm & 3-6pm Mon-Fri) On the west side of the Secretariat Building.

MEDICAL SERVICES
Hospital (Hospicio; ☎ 2705664; Padre Miranda Rd) Has a casualty department and a 24-hour pharmacy. It's about 500m northeast of the Municipal Gardens.

MONEY
There are several ATMs in Margao, including a Centurion Bank ATM located just off Luis Miranda Rd, and a Citibank ATM a few minutes' walk south of the bus stand. UTI Bank has an ATM just south of the roundabout, near the Kadamba bus stand, as well as an ATM on the northeastern corner of the Municipal Gardens.
Bank of Baroda (Isodora Batisata Rd; ☺ 10am-2pm Mon-Fri, 10am-noon Sat) To the east of the Municipal Gardens; gives cash advances on credit cards.
HDFC Bank ATM (Ground fl, Caro Centre; ☺ 24hr) Accepts international cards; opposite the Municipal Gardens.
State Bank of India (Abade Faria Rd; ☺ 10am-3.30pm Mon-Fri, 10am-1pm Sat, 10am-2pm Sun) On the west side of the Municipal Gardens; changes travellers cheques and cash.

Thomas Cook (☎ 2714768) A reliable place to change money, on the east side of the Municipal Gardens.

POST
The main post office is on the north side of the Municipal Gardens. Poste restante is held in the adjoining building and can be picked up between 8am and 10.30am, and 3pm and 4.30pm Monday to Friday.

TELEPHONE
There are plenty of places from which to make international phone calls and send faxes around the Municipal Gardens and in the streets just behind.

TOURIST INFORMATION
Goa Tourism Development Corporation (GTDC) Tourist Office (☎ 2712790; ☺ 10am-5.30pm Mon-Sat) In the Margao Residency, at the south end of the Municipal Gardens. Staff are friendly and reasonably helpful, and there's an interactive audiovisual information terminal, which is mainly useful for amusing small children.

TRAVEL AGENCIES
International Travels (☎ 3955533) A few doors from Longuinhos, this is one of a handful of private bus agencies in this area that books and sells tickets to Mumbai, Bangalore, Hampi and other interstate destinations.
Paramount Travels (☎ 2731150; paramount5@yahoo .com; Shop 5, Commerce House) Right next door to International Travels, this is a well-established and reliable agency handling international and domestic flights.

Sights
CHURCH OF THE HOLY SPIRIT
The main church in Margao is the town's most interesting attraction. The first church was built here in 1565, on the site of an important Hindu temple. Before the demolition started on the temple, local Hindus managed to rescue the statue of the god Damodara, to whom the building was dedicated. It was secretly moved to a new site in the village of Zambaulim, where there is still a large temple today.

The new church didn't last long – it was burned to the ground by Muslim raiders in the same year it was built. It was soon replaced and a seminary was established, but both were subsequently destroyed, after which the seminary was moved to Rachol.

The present church was built in 1675, and is notable not only for its size and

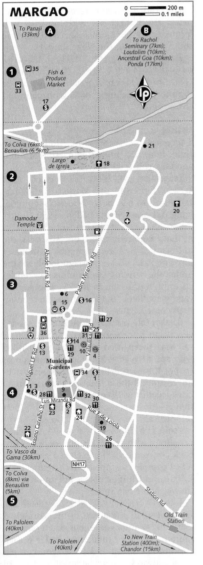

it. The ancient pipe organ gives the church a suitably aged feel. Access is via the side entrance.

LARGO DE IGREJA
Largo de Igreja, the area around the Church of the Holy Spirit, features a number of traditional old Goan houses. The most famous is the **Sat Burnzam Ghor** (Seven Towered House). Originally, as its name suggests, there were seven of the distinctive high-peaked gables, of which only three remain, and the house looks imposing rather than attractive. Inside, it's reputed to be

the fine decoration inside the building, but also for the fact that it is still an active parish church. The reredos (ornamented screen behind the altar in Goan churches) is extremely impressive, rising from ground level to the high ceiling, but is made more distinguished by the gilded and carved archway that stands in front of

MOUNT CHURCH

Located about 500m southeast of Sat Burn-zam Ghor and a fair climb up Monte Hill, Margao's only hill, Mount Church is a simple whitewashed building, faced by a similarly diminutive piazza cross. A detour up here is worth it for the view: from the shade of a grove of palm trees in front of the church, it's possible to see straight across the coastal plain to the beaches of Colva and Benaulim.

COVERED MARKET

Margao is the market centre of south Goa. You can easily get lost in the covered market, also called New Market, just north of Station Rd. This crowded canopy of colourful stalls is a fun place to wander around, but it's not really a place to hunt for souvenirs. Much of the merchandise here is household items, second-hand junk and cheap Indian clothing, so you'll see lots of local women poking around looking for bargains, and there are tailors' shops and fabric merchants where you can have clothing made or mended.

Sleeping

Margao doesn't have the range of accommodation that you'd expect in a town of this size, and with the beaches of Colva and Benaulim only 6km away, there's no pressing reason to stay here. Some travellers, however, do spend a night or two here when arriving or departing by train, and it makes a reasonable base if you're planning a tour of the attractions east of here. Most of the cheap places are strung out along Station Rd between the Municipal Gardens and the site of the old train station.

Hotel La Flor (☎ 2731402; laflor@goatelecom.com; Erasmo Carvalho St; s/d from Rs 450/550, with AC Rs 580/650; 🔀) By far Margao's best choice, La Flor is clean and efficiently run, away from the hustle and bustle in a quiet corner of town. The 36 rooms come with TV and bathroom, and are great value. There's also a restaurant on site.

Rukrish Hotel (☎ 2715046; s/d without bathroom Rs 125/175, d with bathroom Rs 300) Probably the best of a relatively unappealing lot in this price category. Rooms don't score too high, but overall it doesn't have the dingy feel that many budget hotels do and it's well located near the town's activity (near the south entrance of the New Market).

Margao Residency (☎ 2715528; Luis Miranda Rd; s/d Rs 425/500, d with AC Rs 650; 🔀) This is the GTDC hotel. Recent renovations have made it a more appealing choice, with plain but clean rooms.

Eating

There are plenty of gems hidden down small laneways in Margao. Hunt around and take your pick.

Longuinhos (☎ 2739908; Luis Miranda Rd; mains Rs 40-90) Opposite the Margao Residency, Longuinhos has been Margao's colonial hang-out since it opened in 1950. Longuinhos has retained some of the charm of that by-gone era and, one suspects, the uniforms. There are an equal number of foreigners, locals and foreign locals sitting under the fans of Longuinhos. A 'tender coconut soufflé' costs Rs 25. The service can be apathetic, but the atmosphere more than compensates.

Bombay Cafe (Station Rd; snacks Rs 10-20) A busy vegetarian place with cheap snacks such as samosas (deep-fried pastry triangles filled with spiced vegetables or meat) and dosas (paper-thin lentil-flour pancakes); prices hover around the Rs 10 mark. It's often so crowded that getting a seat is a challenge, though it's sometimes randomly closed at impractical hours – like lunchtime.

Venice (☎ 2710505; mains Rs 40-150) A garden restaurant with upmarket service but a laid-back atmosphere. The enclosed garden offers a complete escape from the city. Goan, Indian and Chinese dishes are on offer; try the vegetable biryani.

Tato (☎ 2736014; thalis Rs 25; 🕙 closed Sun) Down a small street east of the Municipal Gardens is another excellent vegetarian restaurant. If you're indecisive, order a thali (traditional South Indian all-you-can-eat meal), always a magical mystery tour of flavour, and here they're particularly representative of the classic Indian meal.

Banjara (☎ 2714837; D'Souza Chambers, Valaulikar Rd; mains Rs 60-125; 🕙 noon-3pm & 7-11pm; 🔀) Margao's best Indian restaurant, specialising in North Indian dishes (around Rs 95) and seafood. The subterranean air-con dining room is intimate and the service is good.

beautifully preserved and furnished, but unfortunately it is not open to visitors.

Gaylin (☎ 2733348; Valaulikar Rd; mains Rs 50-95; ⊗ 11am-3pm & 6.30-11pm) This popular Chinese restaurant is 100m north of Banjara. The dining room is intimate and the menu has a big range of soups, noodles and Cantonese dishes.

Marliz Cafeteria (Padre Miranda Rd) This is a modern, open-fronted café with a wacky design. It looks out at the busy town centre and Municipal Gardens, and is a great spot for coffee and cake while watching the traffic whizz by.

Dalima Fast Food Centre (Erasmo Carvalho St) This tiny place serves up a decent fish curry rice for only Rs 20.

Royal Foods (Rua F de Loiola) Sells the usual bakery items, fresh meat, ice creams, drinks and predominantly chicken-based dishes. It's always immaculate.

Getting There & Away

BUS

All local buses operate from the busy Kadamba bus stand about 2km north of town, but many also stop at the old bus stand in the centre of town. Catch buses to Palolem, Colva and Benaulim from the Kadamba bus stand or from the bus stop on the east side of the Municipal Gardens. All buses coming to Margao from Benaulim and Colva stop by the old bus stand in the centre of town and continue to the Kadamba bus stand.

There is a daily public bus from the Kadamba bus stand to Mumbai (Rs 700, 16 hours), Bangalore (Rs 300, 14 hours) and Pune (Rs 450, 10 hours).

There are also buses to Hubli (Rs 65, six hours), Belgaum (Rs 60, five hours) and Mangalore (Rs 146, 10 hours). A better option for most interstate trips is the long-distance private buses; they are more comfortable, there are more of them and they're no more expensive. Private booking offices are clustered around the Margao Residency along Luis Miranda Rd. Private buses to Mumbai (AC/non-AC Rs 600/350, 12 hours), Pune (Rs 500/300, 11 hours), Bangalore (Rs 700/350, 12 hours) and Hampi (sleeper Rs 550, eight hours) depart from the bus stand opposite the Kadamba bus stand.

Buses to Vasco leave every 10 minutes or so (ordinary/direct Rs 12/15).

Margao has good local bus connections with beaches and other towns in Goa:

Colva Beach There are hourly buses to Colva from the Kadamba bus stand and from the Municipal Gardens (east side), from 7am to 7pm (Rs 7, 20 minutes). Some services go via Benaulim (Rs 4 to Benaulim).

Palolem & Chaudi There are around eight buses a day direct to Palolem from Kadamba bus stand (Rs 18, one hour) and many others heading south to Karwar (Rs 30) that stop in nearby Chaudi, an easy autorickshaw or taxi ride to Palolem, Patnem or even Agonda beaches.

Panaji Buses depart from the Kadamba bus stand approximately every 15 minutes from 6am to 9.15pm (public bus/ direct Rs 12/17, about one hour). The alternative route taken by some buses is via Ponda (Rs 9, at least two hours).

You can find buses to most other destinations in Goa from the Kadamba bus stand. There are buses to Mangalore (7.15am and 2.30pm), Bangalore (6pm), Mysore (4.15pm) and Gokarna (1pm). Timetables are approximate; buses leave when full. There are reasonably frequent local buses to Vasco da Gama (for the airport), Ponda, Chandor and Rachol. To the smaller villages, such as Betul (Rs 10), Mobor and Agonda, they're much less frequent, so it's best to make inquiries at the bus stand in advance.

TAXI

Both Colva and Benaulim are close enough to take a taxi without breaking the bank – about Rs 80 from the Municipal Gardens or Kadamba bus stand. If you're solo, a motorcycle taxi to either of the villages costs about Rs 40, and there are no problems taking backpacks. Autorickshaws charge around Rs 60. Prepaid taxis will cost around Rs 180 to Colva and Benaulim.

If you're going further afield, prepaid taxis go from Margao train station to Panaji (Rs 550), Palolem (Rs 550), Calangute (Rs 670), Anjuna (Rs 780) and Arambol (Rs 980). You can bargain cheaper rates from taxis in the town centre and meet with less cut-throat people than those to be found at the prepaid taxi stand.

TRAIN

Margao's new train station, which serves both the Konkan and South Central Railways, is about 1.5km southeast of the town centre; vehicle access is via the road south of the train line. It's a fairly chaos-free train station (and clean thanks in part to signs warning of Rs 100 fines for spitting and littering). If you're walking there, however, you can cross the tracks at the footbridge past the old station. There's a **reservation hall** (☎ 2712790; ☽ 8am-2pm & 2.15-8pm Mon-Sat, 8am-2pm Sun) on the 2nd floor of the main building, as well as a **tourist information counter** (☎ 2712790) and retiring rooms. See p234 for train information.

A taxi between the train and bus stations costs about Rs 40 and a motorcycle taxi around Rs 25.

The Konkan Railway provides an alternative to using the buses, but since there are only a handful of services a day, and since buses to Chaudi and Palolem are easy to catch from the main bus stand, the train is only likely to be useful for getting to the far north of the state (eg Arambol). There are half-a-dozen trains a day north via Thivim (Mapusa Rd) Station (2nd class Rs 27, one hour), at least two of which stop at Pernem Station (for Arambol), and three trains south to Canacona (Rs 23, 35 minutes).

AROUND MARGAO

As tempting as it is to head west to the beach, the area to the east and northeast of Margao is a rich patchwork of rice paddy fields, lush countryside, somnolent rural villages, superb colonial houses and a smattering of historical and religious sites. With a day to spare and a hired motorcycle or taxi, you can cover most of the sights listed here, assuming you don't get hopelessly lost, which is easy to do in the tangle of unsigned back roads!

With a bicycle you can do a loop out to Chandor, up to Loutolim via Rachol Seminary and back to Margao (about 45km) in a long day. Finding a detailed map of this area is virtually impossible, and since you'll come to many multidirectional crossroads, the best advice is to keep stopping to ask directions.

Rachol Seminary & Church

The Rachol Seminary and Church is seven kilometres from Margao, near the village of Raia. Although not technically open to visitors, you might be able to find someone to show you around. After some very lean years when the religious orders were banned in Goa, the seminary is now full of life again; men study for seven years here to become priests.

As you enter through the huge front door into a hall with a single central pillar, the two murals are striking – on the left wall is an image of hell, and on the right is an image of heaven.

The Portuguese first came into possession of the fortress that once stood on this site in 1520, when Krishnadevaraya, the Hindu Raja of Vijayanagar, captured it from the Muslim Sultan of Bijapur, Ismail Adil Shah, and voluntarily ceded it to the Portuguese.

The seminary, established under the sponsorship of King Sebastian of Portugal, was built by the Jesuits between 1606 and 1610. It became a noted centre of learning, a position that was enhanced by setting up the third printing press in the Portuguese eastern empire. Among the seminary's most famous members were Father Thomas Stevens, who by 1616 had translated the Bible into Konkani and Marathi, and Father Ribeiro, who produced the first Portuguese-Konkani dictionary in 1626.

In 1762 Rachol was raised to the status of diocesan seminary and in 1833, when other religious institutions in Goa were being forcibly closed, it was saved by its rector, Monsignor Rebello. The buildings you see today were mostly built from the early 17th century, and are contemporaries of Se Cathedral in Old Goa.

The seminary church, dedicated to St Ignatius Loyola, the founder of the Jesuits, has been maintained in excellent condition. The reredos fills the whole wall above the altar with its carved and gilded yet simple design. The most striking features are the carved and painted wooden panels that cover the sides of the chancel – a mass of colour and detail. One of the side altars also displays the Menino Jesus, which was originally installed in the Colva church but was taken back to the seminary amid much controversy.

Loutolim
☎ 0832
Ten kilometres from Margao and about 6km north of Rachol is the tiny, peaceful village of Loutolim. If you have your own wheels, the countryside here is a pleasure just to ride through.

Set up purely for tourists, **Ancestral Goa** (☎ 2777034; admission Rs 20, camera Rs 10; ☽ 9am-6.30pm) is a mildly diverting attraction. You will be shunted from guide to guide, who explain the self-explanatory mock-up scenarios depicting daily life in Goa under the Portuguese. The Portuguese lady being fanned by her Goan servant hardly represents the 'harmony' that it intends to. Another claim to fame at Ancestral Goa (in addition to India's longest laterite sculpture) is a rock known as 'big foot', where you can place your own foot and make a wish. There are unintentionally comical elements to this quirky attraction, like the 'Hidden Turtle' enclosure, which may or may not in fact contain a turtle.

Much more interesting, though not really tourist attractions, are a couple of grand old houses in the village. The largest of these, which visitors are occasionally permitted to view inside, is the **Miranda House** (☎ 2777022), a three-minute walk southwest from the church, down an unsurfaced access road. The two-storey whitewashed house has re-mained in the hands of the same family through the years. The current owner is well-known artist and illustrator Mario Miranda. The Miranda coat of arms presented by the King of Portugal in 1871 still adorns the front door. This is one of the best existing examples of Goan country-house architecture. Call in advance if you want to visit. **Casa Arajao Alvarez** (☒ 9am-6.30pm; admission Rs 100) is also open to the public.

Chandor

About 15km east of Margao, on the border between Salcete and Quepem talukas, is the small village of Chandor, once the site of the most spectacular city on the Konkan coast, Chandrapur. Capital of the ancient state of Govarashtra, Chandrapur was situated within the loop of the river, which, unbelievable as it may seem today, was large enough to make the city a viable port.

CHANDOR'S COLONIAL MANSIONS

Visiting the superb colonial mansions in Chandor gives you a peek at the opulent lifestyle of the Goan landowners during the height of their fortunes in the Portuguese era. Best known is **Braganza House**, which takes up one complete side of Chandor's village square and dates back to the 17th century. It's now divided into east and west wings – two separate houses – which stretch outwards from a common front entrance. The exterior façade of the mansion, with 24 windows, is the longest in Goa.

Ongoing restoration is gradually returning the house to its former glory, but wandering through the ballrooms with their Italian marble floors, Belgian glass chandeliers and carved rosewood furniture, it's not hard to imagine the sort of parties that were thrown here. The east wing is owned by the Braganza Pereira family, and includes a small family chapel containing a carefully hidden relic of St Francis Xavier – a fingernail. The clutter of bric-a-brac collected by the family over the years gives the house an air of faded magnificence. The original owner of the house, Braganza Pereira, was knighted by the King of Portugal and given this land in the 17th century. Generations later, the mansion was divided into two halves: Menezes Braganza (west wing) and Braganza Pereira (east wing).

The west wing is crammed with beautiful furniture and Chinese porcelain from Macau. The two large rooms behind the entrance halls contain Dr Menezes Braganza's extensive library – Luís de Menezes Braganza was a journalist and a leader in the Goan Independence movement.

Both houses are open daily from 10am to 5pm, but you may want to call ahead to ensure the **owners** (Braganza Pereira ☎ 2784227, Menezes Braganza ☎ 2784201) will be there, or else you will be lead around by staff who can do little more than point at furniture and name it. There is a box where you can leave a donation towards the upkeep of the mansion, though a minimum of Rs 100 is sometimes insisted on. The front door of the house is usually left open; head up the stairs and ring the small doorbell you will find on the wall.

Nearby, **Fernandes House** (☎ 2784245) is not as grand, but it has a longer history and the enthusiastic family who live here have put in effort to make your visit interesting. The original Hindu house here dates back more than 500 years, while the Portuguese section was built by the Fernandes family in 1821. One feature is the secret basement hideaway with an escape tunnel to the river, which the Hindu occupants used to flee attackers. A donation is also be appreciated here; given the extensive maintenance that is required, Rs 50 to 100 is reasonable.

Although there was a town here during the time of the Mauryan empire (321–184 BC), Chandrapur's promotion to capital city came later. After centuries of infighting following the demise of the Mauryans, the Bhojas eventually gained control of the area, and ruled almost undisturbed from AD 375 to 525, promoting trade with other areas along the Indian coast and further afield. In 979 the Kadamba dynasty came to power, ruling from Chandrapur until 1052.

Ironically, the Kadambas' success signalled the end of Chandrapur's pre-eminence; as the empire expanded, the Kadambas captured the port of Govepuri on the Zuari River. Within a short time more trade was flowing through Govepuri than Chandrapur, and the capital was shifted in 1053. When Govepuri was levelled by the Muslims in 1312, the Kadambas moved the seat of power back to Chandrapur, though it was not long before Chandrapur itself was sacked in 1327. There's now an archaeological site in the village, where the foundations of an 11th-century Hindu temple and stone Nandi (the bull, vehicle of Shiva) have been unearthed.

Chandor's premier attraction today is its beautifully preserved colonial mansions (see p167); two of the grandest, **Braganza House** and **Fernandes House**, are open to the public.

On 6 January Chandor is one of three Goan villages that host the **Feast of the Three Kings** (the others are Reis Magos and Cansaulim), a colourful festival in which local boys re-enact the arrival of the three kings bearing gifts for Christ.

Damodar Temple

Approximately 12km southeast of Chandor and 22km from Margao on the border of Quepem and Sanguem talukas is the small village of **Zambaulim**, home to the Damodar Temple. The deity in the sanctum was rescued in 1565 from the main temple in Margao, which was destroyed by the Portuguese to allow the Church of the Holy Spirit to be raised symbolically on the site.

The temple is fairly modern in appearance but the ancient ablutions area, built 200m back from the main buildings on the banks of the Kushavati River, is attractive and the water is said to have medicinal properties. The celebration of Shigmotsav (Shigmo) here is spread over several days, and is particularly colourful (see p218).

Rivona Buddhist Caves

Continuing south from Zambaulim for about 3km, the road passes through **Rivona**, which consists of little more than a few houses spread out along the highway. As the road leaves the village, curling first to the left and then right, there is a small sign on the left, pointing to Shri Santhsa Gokarn. A short way up the dirt track, which comes to an end at a tiny temple, the **Rivona caves** (also called Pandava caves) are on the left. You need your own transport to get here.

It's thought that the caves were occupied by Buddhist monks, who settled here some time in the 6th or 7th century AD. There's little to see, but the tiny compartments are an interesting reminder that religions other than Hinduism, Islam and Christianity also made it to Goa. There's a small staircase cut through the rock between the upper and lower levels of the caves; if you plan to look inside you'll need a torch.

On the other side of the road, some way down the slope and off to the left, is another larger cave that is also believed to have been used by the monks.

Usgalimal Rock Carvings

Carved into laterite stone on the banks of the Kushavati River in Sanguem taluka, these prehistoric **petroglyphs** (rock art) show various scenes, including a dancer, wild animals, a pregnant women and a man with a harpoon. They are thought to be the work of one of Goa's earliest tribes, the Kush. The carvings are underfoot, rather than on a wall and, depending on the light, it can be difficult to make out the shapes.

To get here, continue past Rivona for about 6km and look out for the green-and-red Forest Department 'protected area' signs. An unsealed road off to the right of the main road leads 1.5km down to the river bank and carvings.

Chandreshwar Bhutnath Temple

Approximately 14km southeast of Margao near the village of Paroda, a number of hills rise out of the plain, the highest of which is Chandranath Hill (350m). At the top in a small clearing stands the Chandreshwar Bhutnath Temple, a small but attractive building in a lovely setting.

(Continued on page 177)

Bebinca (traditional Goan dessert made from egg yolk and coconut milk; p53)

GREG ELMS

Spices are an integral part of Goan cooking (p51)

PAUL HARDING

A selection of *feni* (Goan alcoholic drink; p54)

GREG ELMS

Kingfish, a common Goan food (p52)

GREG ELMS

Mandovi River, near Panaji (p82)

Cliffside guesthouses, Arambol (p152)

Dudhsagar Falls (p116)

Motorcycles are a common form of transport (p237)

Beach volleyball, Palolem Beach (p191)

PAUL HARDING

Rice paddies, Ponda taluka (p110)

GREG ELMS

GREG ELMS

Fishing boat, Benaulim Beach
(p185)

JOHN PENNOCK

Shantadurga Temple, Ponda taluka (p113)

Fort Aguada (p120)

ALAIN EVRARD

Typical street scene, Calangute (p126)

Portuguese architecture, Fontainhas (p86), Panaji

Ruins of the Church of St Augustine (p106), Old Goa

View over Querim Beach from Terekhol Fort (p155)

Soapstone carver, Anjuna flea market (p141)

PETER PTSCHELINZEW

Left: Handicraft stall, Anjuna flea market (p141)
CHRISTINE OSBORNE

Fish market, Margao (p161)

RICHARD I'ANSON

Vendor, Mapusa market (p137)
PAUL BEINSSEN

Kudle Beach (p200), Gokarna

Crocodile, near Jog Falls (p202)

Virupaksha Temple (p204), Hampi

Vittala Temple (p204), Hampi

(Continued from page 168)

Although the present buildings date from the 17th century, there has been a temple here for more than 1500 years. The site is dedicated to Chandreshwar, an incarnation of Shiva who is worshipped as Lord of the Moon. Consequently it is laid out so the light of the full moon shines into the sanctum and illuminates the deity, which is carved from the natural rock. It is said that when the moonlight falls on it, the lingam (phallic symbol of Shiva) oozes water.

Leaving through the side entrance there is another small shrine standing separately that is dedicated to the god Bhutnath, who is worshipped in the form of a simple stone pinnacle that sticks out of the ground.

To get to the temple you will need your own transport as it's a fair way off the beaten track. Head to Paroda, and ask there for the turn-off that takes you up the narrow winding hillside road. There's a small parking area near the top, from which the approach to the temple is via a steep flight of steps.

VASCO DA GAMA
☎ 0832 / pop 97,000

Vasco da Gama is a busy port and was once a major transport hub for travellers. These days it's a noisy, industrial town with a seedy feel on its outskirts. It's only 4km from Dabolim Airport, so if you fly into Goa it's possible you may want to spend a night in Vasco, but there's little need.

Situated at the base of the isthmus leading to Mormugao Harbour, Vasco sports an oil refinery and Goa's biggest red-light district at Baina, where there's also a small (filthy) beach and a steady influx of sailors and truck drivers. The city has a reputation for being the crime centre of Goa – you're safe enough in the town centre, but it is probably unwise to go wandering by yourself much further than the main part of town at night.

Information
Centurion Bank ATM (Pe José Vaz Rd; 24hr) Near the Vasco Residency.
GTDC Tourist Information (☎ 2512673; 9.30am-5pm Mon-Sat) In the foyer of the Vasco Residency.
HFDC Bank ATM (24hr) Opposite the bus station, and also just west of the train station along Swatantra Path.
Internet Cafés (Pe José Vaz Rd; per hr Rs 25) There are a handful of Internet cafés in the Apna Bazar Building.

Kamaxi Book House (GTDC Residency) The only bookshop in town is in the lobby of the GTDC Residency.
Mubeen Travels (☎ 2512345; fax 2513106; www.mubeen.com) A professional travel agent for booking flights.
State Bank of India (FL Gomes Rd) Will exchange both travellers cheques and cash.

Sleeping
Twiga Lodge (☎ 2512682; d Rs 200) Near the main bus stand, Twiga Lodge is the best rock-bottom budget option in town. The old Portuguese house looks odd amongst all the nondescript blocks of Vasco. There are just five basic rooms with bathrooms. It's often full so call ahead.

Maharaja (☎ 2514076; mahahotl@sancharnet.in; d Rs 500) Maharaja is a bit further away from the centre than the Vasco Residency, but has more character. Standard rooms are quite spacious, and have hot water and TV. You can pay more (Rs 700 to 1300) and get a bit more class but not much more quality.

Vasco Residency (☎ 2513119; s/d Rs 275/350, d with AC Rs 600;) This hotel is secure and central. Like most GTDC hotels it's a bit run-down, but it's the best budget place in the city centre.

Hotel Karma Plaza (☎ 2518928; karmas@rediffmail.com; Rajendra Prasad Ave; r standard with/without AC Rs 999/899, deluxe Rs 1299/1199;) This is the pick of the midrange places. It's clean and the hotel is part of a modern shopping complex with restaurants. Rooms attract a 10% tax.

Hotel La Paz Gardens (☎ 2512121; www.hotellapazgardens.com; Swatantra Path; s/d standard Rs 1200/1500, premium Rs 1700/2000, executive ste Rs 2200/2500, deluxe ste Rs 3000/3500;) This is the top place in town. It's a typical business hotel with 72 rooms with air-con, satellite TV, a gym, a sauna and three restaurants.

Eating & Drinking
There are plenty of cheap thali places around the centre. Karma Plaza shopping centre has clean, modern restaurants, including Ginza for Chinese and Japanese and Temptations for burgers or ice cream.

Hotel Annapurna (mains Rs 20-50) Hotel Annapurna, near the market, is clean and the best budget option in town; vegetarian thalis cost Rs 20.

Goodyland (mains Rs 20-50) This is a family-friendly fast-food place serving good pizzas,

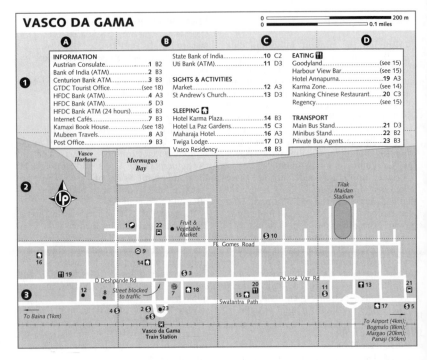

VASCO DA GAMA

INFORMATION				SLEEPING 🛏		
Austrian Consulate	1	B2		Hotel Karma Plaza	14	B3
Bank of India (ATM)	2	B3		Hotel La Paz Gardens	15	C3
Centurion Bank ATM	3	B3		Maharaja Hotel	16	A3
GTDC Tourist Office	(see 18)			Twiga Lodge	17	D3
HDFC Bank (ATM)	4	A3		Vasco Residency	18	B3
HDFC Bank (ATM)	5	D3				
HDFC Bank ATM (24 hours)	6	B3		EATING 🍴		
Internet Cafés	7	B3		Goodyland	(see 15)	
Kamaxi Book House	(see 18)			Harbour View Bar	(see 15)	
Mubeen Travels	8	A3		Hotel Annapurna	19	A3
Post Office	9	B3		Karma Zone	(see 14)	
				Nanking Chinese Restaurant	20	C3
State Bank of India	10	C2		Regency	(see 15)	
Uti Bank (ATM)	11	D3				
				TRANSPORT		
SIGHTS & ACTIVITIES				Main Bus Stand	21	D3
Market	12	A3		Minibus Stand	22	B2
St Andrew's Church	13	D3		Private Bus Agents	23	B3

vegetarian patties, sausage rolls and refreshing ice cream.

Nanking Chinese Restaurant (mains Rs 40-120) Around the corner from Goodyland, it has reasonably good Cantonese food, but is a dark place.

Regency (Swatantra Path; mains Rs 80-150) At Hotel La Paz Gardens, the Regency is one of the better restaurants in Vasco da Gama, specialising in Goan and Indian food. Also here at the La Paz is the top-floor Harbour View Bar.

Karma Zone (☎ 2511028; mains 45-90) A predominantly Chinese and Indian restaurant with a couple of Japanese options thrown in. A clean air-conditioned affair.

Getting There & Away

Express minibuses run nonstop from the city bus stand north of the train station to Margao (Rs 15, 45 minutes) and Panaji (Rs 17, 45 minutes). There are also regular buses from here to the airport (Rs 5) and Bogmalo (Rs 6). For long-distance state buses you have to go to Margao or Panaji, but private buses to Mumbai (Rs 300)

and Bangalore (Rs 500) depart daily from outside the train station, where there are booking agents. Heading from the main bus stand near the fruit and vegetable market east towards the airport, there is another bus stand where you can flag down eastbound buses.

A taxi from the airport costs around Rs 60 and an autorickshaw Rs 50.

BOGMALO
☎ 0832

Eight kilometres southeast of Vasco, and only 4km from the airport, Bogmalo Beach is a small, sandy cove dominated by the huge, five-star Bogmalo Beach Resort, which somehow evaded the restriction requiring all hotels to be built at least 500m from the high-tide line. Somewhat surprisingly, given it's proximity to Vasco da Gama, the beach is quite pleasant despite (or perhaps because of) the air of exclusivity. Having said that, there's nothing overly special about it compared to the vast expanses of beach you'll find further south, and it's not as economical.

Sights & Activities

Bogmalo is a bit of water-sports centre – you can hire windsurfers, jet skis and boats. **Goa Diving** (☎ 2555117, 2538204; www.goadiving.com) is behind Joets Guest House and offers a full range of courses, including introductory dives (Rs 2200), four-day PADI openwater courses (Rs 15,000), advanced courses (Rs 10,000), rescue diver courses (Rs 15,000) and dive master courses (Rs 20000). Guided dives cost Rs 1430 (one tank) or Rs 2200 (two tanks), including equipment. Goa Diving uses Grande Island (off Bogmalo Beach) and Pigeon Island (off the coast from Murudeshwar, 85km south).

At the naval base, on the road above Bogmalo Beach, is the **Naval Aviation Museum** (☎ 5995525; adult/child Rs 15/5, camera/video Rs 10/25; ☽ 10am-5pm). It's easy to spot by its inhospitable fence, and the preserved military planes sitting just behind it. There are displays on the history of India's navy along with uniforms, model naval ships and photographs. There are also some very blokey rooms containing heavy-duty weaponry and an evocatively damaged eject seat. This is the man's revenge for all the shopping excursions he's had to endure.

Sleeping & Eating

In keeping with its exclusivity, there are only a handful of sleeping places in Bogmalo. Apart from hotel restaurants, there are a few beach shacks serving the usual fare of seafood, continental dishes and breakfasts but they're more expensive than you'll find elsewhere in Goa – some even quote menu prices in pounds sterling!

Coconut Creek (☎ 2538090; fax 2538880; cottages from Rs 2950; ☒ ☒) Stylish cottages are set up around a pool in a coconut grove, with laidback but attentively choreographed ambience permeating every detail of every room. The self-contained experience of Coconut Creek, is one that may be a highlight of your time in Goa. This is an entirely quiet Goan getaway, and it's only a two-minute walk to the beach.

Joets Guest House (☎ 2538036; joets@sancharnet .in; d Rs 2500) Joets is a lively upmarket place, with refurbished suites. The bar and restaurant in this clean blue-and-white building is consistently popular, and staff are often in a tizz trying to keep up with it all. It's often full from mid-December.

Sarita's Guest House (☎ 2538965; saritasguest house@rediffmail.com; d with/without AC Rs 1100/750; ☒) Sarita's has clean but unremarkable rooms. There is an understated common balcony with an unimpeded view of the beach. Prices fluctuate depending on the time of year.

Bogmalo Beach Resort (☎ 2538222; bbrtshl@ sancharnet.in; s/d standard US$80/90, deluxe US$140/150; ☒ ☒) This formidable high-rise presides over the southern end of Bogmalo Beach, and affords a lovely view of the beach. All rooms face the ocean. There's a pool, restaurant, casino and large breezy foyer that extends from reception to the rear of the building and is a nice place to sit. Buffet meals are reasonable value for this type of establishment (breakfast/lunch/dinner Rs 175/275/350).

Getting There & Away

An irregular bus service runs between Bogmalo and Vasco da Gama (Rs 6, 25 minutes). Buses depart from the car park in front of the entrance to the Bogmalo Beach Resort. Taxis wait in the same area; a return trip costs around Rs 150.

VELSAO & MAJORDA

This 6km-long stretch of beaches (Velsao, Arossim, Utorda and Majorda) is an undeveloped patch of Goa, dotted with just a few beach shacks at entry points from the road, and the occasional hotel. Almost immediately upon leaving Colva and entering this region, the pace notably slows down. Time spent meandering through coconut groves and villages is a respite from tourism and an insight into rural Goa.

Sleeping

Though the area primarily caters for the more upmarket traveller, there are a handful of small guesthouses along Majorda Beach Rd, which still have a freshness that many of those in the more popular areas have long lost.

BUDGET

Dom Pedro's House (☎ 713251; r with/without AC Rs 600/500; ☒) A two-storey house set in a perfect patch of Goa, replete with smiling people milling about in the countryside. Rooms are ideal if you're looking to immerse yourself in the quiet life for a while.

Rainbow's End (☎ 9822586596; shalome81@satyam
.net.in; r Rs 600) An ideal place for those looking to stay for a while. These self-contained
units are on the corner of the Beach and
Majorda Beach Rds, and comfortably accommodate three people.

MIDRANGE

Casa Ligorio (☎ 2755405; www.casaligorio.com; Utorda
Beach, Utorda-Majorda, Salcete; d with AC Rs 2000; 🞨) A
proud modern building down a quiet private
street with nine impeccably kept rooms, all
with fridge and private balcony overlooking rice fields and palm trees. Rooms are
not cheap, but you'll feel like you're getting a good deal compared to your neighbours at the overpriced Hotel Keniworth,
who are paying hundreds (of US dollars,
not rupees). Breakfast is included in the
price. The beach is a nice walk down a quiet
rural street.

Palm View Guest House (☎ 2881591; palmview4@
hotmail.com; Rs 1000) A very pleasant place with
private rooms built around a blue pool.
Rooms are slightly small, the bathrooms
especially so, but otherwise are good value.
At the time of research the owners were in
the throes of building more rooms, which
will be needed when it becomes as popular
as it should be.

Hotel Shangrila (☎ 2881542; www.shangrilagoa
.com; r with/without AC Rs 900/700; 🞨) This long-
running hotel hasn't yet grown tired. There
is nothing fancy about the rooms, but nor is
there anything lacking – all have hot water
and TVs. There's also a very pleasant restaurant attached.

TOP END

Horizons Beach Resort (☎ 8322754923; www.hori
zonbeachresortgoa.com; Velsao Beach; r/ste Rs 2375/2850;
🞲) A series of yellow Mediterranean-style
buildings and a simple bright-blue pool.
The resort is set back away from the beach,
but within walking distance. Rooms are not
as elegant as the building exteriors would
lead you to believe, but are certainly up to
scratch for this pricey category.

Majorda Beach Resort (☎ 2754871; www.majorda
beachresort.com; s/d Rs 6750/7500; 🞲) A five-star
resort with everything necessary to befit
the name. If you are accustomed to this
level of luxury, there is nothing that particularly distinguishes this resort from any
other.

Eating

Surprisingly for so quiet an area, there is an
impressive collection of restaurants in this
area, hidden away in coconut groves and
small streets off the road. There are some
absolute dining treats here, if you know
where to find them.

Skie Grille (☎ 3953053; www.skiegrille.com; mains
Rs 100-200; 🕑 6.30-11.30pm) The recently established Skie Grille offers you the chance to
'dine with history'. The dining area is set
up outside a spectacularly lit 450-year-old
palatial home and whitewashed chapel. The
affable husband-and-wife team behind this
project plan to open an indoor dining area
soon. Imaginatively created grilled dishes
include chicken citrus kebab with orange
sauce, and prawn with rosemary and wine.
There are some exquisite desserts; try the
grilled cinnamon apple. The Skie Grille is
near Piedade chapel, between the Kenil-
worth and Majorda hotels in Utorda.

Martin's Corner (☎ 2880061, 2880413; www.mar
tinscornergoa.com; Betalbatim, Salcette; mains Rs 50-
350) A must-do if you're in the area. It's
enormously popular due to its great menu,
often charismatic staff and finely tuned
atmosphere. Mains are surprisingly still
cheap, when they could arguably justify
charging more as rent for the detail-laden
atmosphere that is oddly reminiscent of a
German-style restaurant. They have some
kind of live entertainment every night.

Pentagon (☎ 2881402; mains Rs 90-300) Near
the entrance to the Majorda Beach Resort
is a partly undercover and partly open-air
restaurant catering to resident tourists.
There are retro and jazz nights.

COLVA

☎ 0832 / pop 10,200
Colva has changed a lot since its days as
a sleepy fishing village. It's now the main
package-holiday resort of south Goa, but
you can easily find quiet stretches of beautiful beach to the north and south of the
main village.

This peaceful yet bustling atmosphere
has made Colva popular with an older
crowd of British, European and domestic
holidaymakers, and with weekending Indian families avoiding the hype of Calangute. The market area and road leading to
the main beach is lined with souvenir stalls,
restaurants and midrange hotels, but walk

or cycle a kilometre or two in either direction and you'll find parched farmland, coconut groves and fish drying in the sun.

Orientation

The centre of action in Colva is the roundabout area at the end of the road to the beach. This is where the taxis wait, the fruit vendors ply their trade, and a dozen or so small restaurants and shops are to be found. Colva village, where you'll find the church, post office and other facilities, is strung out a long way back along the road to Margao.

Information
BOOKSHOPS

Damondar Bookshop (Colva Beach Rd) In the huddle of shops near the end of the beach road. There isn't an enormous choice, but you'll find some beach reading.

INTERNET ACCESS

Hello Mae Communications (Colva Beach Rd; per hr Rs 40) Close to the beach.
IDA Online (Beach Rd; per hr Rs 25; 10am-1am) The cheapest Internet café in town. Also has a photocopy machine (Rs 1 per page).

MONEY

Near the seafront are several travel agencies that keep longer hours than banks, and can efficiently change money and give credit-card cash advances.

Bank of Baroda (9am-1pm Mon, Tue, Thu & Fri, 9am-11am Sat) Near the church; will change cash and travellers cheques, and give cash advances on MasterCard and Visa.
CICI Bank ATM (Colva Beach Rd) At Vincy's Beach Resort.
Meeting Point Travel (2788003, 2788005; fax 278804; 9am-6pm) Has a money exchange service.

UTI Bank ATM (Colva Beach Rd; 24hr) Near Gatsby's nightclub.

POST

Post office (poste restante 9am-1pm, 2-4pm) On the lane that runs past the eastern end of the church.

TELEPHONE

World Linkers (2788064; world_linkers@hotmail .com; H No 405, 4th Ward) A reliable place to recharge phone cards and make international calls.

TOURIST INFORMATION

There's no official tourist office in town, and staff at the **GTDC Colva Residency** (2788047, 2788048) can't do much more than herd you onto GTDC tours.

TRAVEL AGENCIES

Meeting Point Travel (2788003, 2788005, fax 278804; 9am-6pm) The most professional travel agent in town can help with money exchange and travel arrangements.

Sights & Activities

Founded in 1630 and rebuilt in the 18th century, the **Church of Our Lady of Mercy** contains the statue of the Menino (Baby) Jesus, famous throughout Goa for its miracle-working abilities (see below).

Water sports are prevalent in Colva. You won't have trouble finding operators hanging around; it's more difficult to avoid them. Parasailing costs around Rs 800 per two people (Rs 500 per single). Stand there long enough looking curious (or feigning indifference) and you'll be approached by operators like Chris Watersports or Ruena.

THE MIRACLES OF MENINO JESUS

The original carving of the Menino Jesus was found in 1640 by a Jesuit missionary, Father Bento Ferreira, after he had been shipwrecked off the coast of Mozambique. In 1648 when Father Ferreira became the first vicar at the Church of Our Lady of Mercy in Colva, he brought the statue with him and soon noticed a strange light emanating from it. Within a short space of time it had become known for granting favours.

When the Jesuits were forced to leave Goa in 1834, they insisted that the statue should go with them, although one ring that had been on the finger of the carving was left behind in the church. This was placed on the finger of a replacement statue. Immediately the miracles started again, while the original statue, which now resides in the chapel of Rachol Seminary, is said never to have granted another request.

On the feast day, on the second Monday in October, the Menino is brought out, and there's a fair. Among those who make a special effort to appeal to the statue are young men and women in search of a partner, to whom the infant is said to be especially favourable.

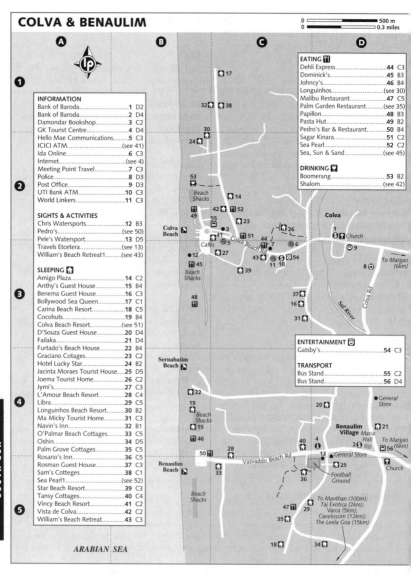

COLVA & BENAULIM

INFORMATION
Bank of Baroda.................................**1** D2	
Bank of Baroda.................................**2** D4	
Damondar Bookshop.......................**3** C2	
GK Tourist Centre............................**4** D4	
Hello Mae Communications..........**5** C3	
ICICI ATM...............................(see 41)	
Ida Online...**6** C3	
Internet................................(see 4)	
Meeting Point Travel.......................**7** C3	
Police...**8** D3	
Post Office...**9** D3	
UTI Bank ATM................................**10** D3	
World Linkers.................................**11** C3	

SIGHTS & ACTIVITIES
Chris Watersports..........................**12** B3	
Pedro's.....................................(see 50)	
Pele's Watersport...........................**13** D5	
Travels Etcetera.......................(see 13)	
William's Beach Retreat1.........(see 43)	

SLEEPING
Amigo Plaza....................................**14** C2	
Anthy's Guest House......................**15** B4	
Benema Guest House.....................**16** C3	
Bollywood Sea Queen....................**17** C1	
Carina Beach Resort.......................**18** C5	
Cocohuts...**19** B4	
Colva Beach Resort..................(see 51)	
D'Souza Guest House.....................**20** D4	
Failaka..**21** D4	
Furtado's Beach House...................**22** B4	
Graciano Cotages...........................**23** C2	
Hotel Lucky Star.............................**24** B2	
Jacinta Moraes Tourist House.......**25** D5	
Joema Tourist Home.......................**26** C2	
Jymi's...**27** C3	
L'Amour Beach Resort....................**28** C4	
Libra...**29** C5	
Longuinhos Beach Resort..............**30** B2	
Ma Micky Tourist Home.................**31** C3	
Navin's Inn......................................**32** B1	
O'Palmar Beach Cottages.............**33** C5	
Oshin...**34** D5	
Palm Grove Cottages.....................**35** C5	
Rosario's Inn...................................**36** C5	
Rosman Guest House......................**37** C3	
Sam's Cotteges...............................**38** C1	
Sea Pearl1...............................(see 52)	
Star Beach Resort...........................**39** C3	
Tansy Cottages...............................**40** C4	
Vincy Beach Resort........................**41** C2	
Vista de Colva.................................**42** C2	
William's Beach Retreat.................**43** C3	

EATING
Dehli Express................................**44** C3	
Dominick's....................................**45** B3	
Johncy's...**46** B4	
Longuinhos...........................(see 30)	
Malibu Restaurant........................**47** C5	
Palm Garden Restaurant.......(see 35)	
Papillon...**48** B3	
Pasta Hut.......................................**49** B2	
Pedro's Bar & Restaurant.............**50** B4	
Sagar Kinara..................................**51** C2	
Sea Pearl.......................................**52** C2	
Sea, Sun & Sand...................(see 45)	

DRINKING
Boomerang....................................**53** B2	
Shalom..................................(see 42)	

ENTERTAINMENT
Gatsby's...**54** C3	

TRANSPORT
Bus Stand.......................................**55** C2	
Bus Stand.......................................**56** D4	

ARABIAN SEA

Head to **Williams Beach Retreat** to relax by the pool. For Rs 50 you can spend half a day eating by the pool or drinking a beer at its swim-up bar.

Tours

The same people who organise water sports often arrange dolphin trips too. If you don't feel comfortable dealing with a tout, ask at Domnick's (p184), which runs 45-minute trips for Rs 300 per head.

Hello Mae Communications (☎ 2780108) arranges bus rides to the Anjuna flea market on Wednesday (Rs 150). It sometimes promotes the tour in beach shacks. This is a good option if you're not travelling up north but want to see the market, given that getting there independently requires three bus changes (Margao–Panjim–Mapusa) or an expensive taxi ride.

Sleeping
BUDGET

There is a good range of budget accommodation in Colva, ranging from well-run hotels with restaurants, to rooms in family houses.

Navin's Inn (☎ 2788550, 2732575, 2737509; carvin@ satyam.net.in; H No 290/3, 3rd Ward; s without bathroom Rs 200, d with bathroom Rs 300-400) A pleasant place to stay at the quiet north end of town. Rooms are clean and private; doubles have bathrooms and vary slightly in price depending on size. The one and only single room is smaller and doesn't have a bathroom. Navin's Inn is unobtrusively well run, and attracts Europeans who stay for months on end. Book ahead.

Sam's Cottages (☎ 2788753; r Rs 300) Across the road from Navin's Inn, Sam's Cottages has recently expanded and has a range of rooms around a courtyard. There's also a restaurant on site. Call ahead; it's often full.

Hotel Lucky Star (☎ 2788071; pradorbarad@hotmail .com; r Rs 450-500) An overpriced but popular choice, near Longuinhos Beach Resort. Rooms are quite large with cold-water bathrooms and safes. Ask for a newer room; they're less dingy and stuffy than the old rooms behind the restaurant (Rs 450). It has a popular restaurant and small, sociable bar.

Sea Pearl (☎ 2780176; downstairs/upstairs r Rs 370/ 450) A great budget option, if you're lucky enough to get a room. Downstairs rooms are small and entirely comfortable, but upstairs rooms with private balconies are the real winners. Clean bathrooms, TV, plenty of space to do whatever requires space and lots of natural light. Good value.

Jymi's (☎ 2788016; r Rs 400) Jymi's is well located just behind the heart of town. Rooms are spacious and all have bathrooms.

At the budget end of the budget range, are some respectable choices. One of the best is **Ma Mickey Tourist Home** (☎ 2788190; r Rs 200), which has four spacious, immaculate and airy rooms, all adjoining a common area with a TV. The bathroom is clean and the atmosphere is homely but private. **Benema Guest House** (☎ 2788698; r Rs 200) is run by a very pleasant family and has rooms of a decent size. If they're all full, try nearby **Rosman Guest House** (☎ 2489341; Novovaddo; r Rs 150), which has a few dingy rooms behind a very nice house.

Hidden in the cluster of coconut trees behind the main road are a few options. Check them all out before you commit to one:

Garden Cottages (☎ 2780776; d Rs 250) A nice and peaceful choice with well-maintained rooms that have their own veranda; it doesn't feel like a hotel.

Joema Tourist Home (☎ 2888782; 395, 4th Ward) Next door to Garden Cottages with a 'candlelight café' in a comfortably secluded garden setting.

Casa Roiz (☎ 2788767; www.casaroiz.com; 393 Four Crossroads, 4th Ward, Colva Beach; r Rs 500) A bizarre out-of-place building that feels like it has been deserted by all but the cleaners and the quirky woman who ages behind the tinted glass, waiting to 'interview' potential guests. But rooms are spacious and clean with hot-water bathrooms and small balconies.

MIDRANGE

William's Beach Retreat (☎ 2788153, 2780303, 2788056; www.goagateway.com; r with/without AC Rs 1500/1200; 🖫 🖳) William's has really got its act together. Rooms are pricey but bright and happy, and the hotel is well run, with an airy restaurant that is out the front but off the street.

Amigo Plaza (☎ 2789285, 2789384; www.amigo plaza.com; r with/without AC Rs 1500/1000; 🖫) A good midrange choice with absolutely immaculate rooms that have hot water and TV. Angled rooms remove the box feel of many hotels, and there are balconies that sit around the simple but pleasant garden. Discounts can be arranged for long-stayers and good bargainers.

THE MORNING CATCH

Colva's days as a sleepy fishing village are long past but the activities of the local fisherman in their motorised outrigger boats are still one of the highlights of the day. Rise early (around 7am) and head down to the beach north of the main access road (in front of the Lucky Star restaurant) to see locals carrying baskets of fish – mostly small-fry mackerel caught in nets – ashore and dumping them in drying pens. It's a great photo opportunity.

Graciano Cottages (☎ 2788787, 2789022, 3955700; gracianogoa@sify.com; r with/without AC Rs 800/700, all incl breakfast; 🕲) Graciano is a pleasant mid-range choice. Rooms all have satellite TV.

In the category of 'beach resorts' that sound better than they are:

Star Beach Resort (☎ 2788166; fax 2788020; d Rs 1000-2500) Has a pool, Ayurvedic massage and a travel counter. Rooms all have cable TV.

Longuinhos Beach Resort (☎ 2788068; www.longuinhos.net; s with/without AC Rs 1500/1300, d Rs 1700/1400; 🕲) Staff sometimes seem to have got out of the wrong side of bed, and the noise can get downright irritating at the open-air restaurant; it's popular nonetheless.

Colva Beach Resort (☎ 2788053, 2788043, 2788135; fax 2788134; r standard/superior Rs 600/1500; 🖭) The pool is uninviting, given its green colour and the people hanging around to watch swimmers. Saved by its proximity to the beach and the couple of good restaurants. The manager is keen to use his power to discount so it's a good fall-back when pickings are slim elsewhere.

TOP END

Vista de Colva (☎ 2788144; www.vistadecolva.com; r Rs 3000; 🖭) A crisp, fresh and classy hotel in a sometimes unkempt, stale and tacky town, Vista de Colva stands out. Rooms are pleasant and staggered casually around the pool. There's nothing oppressively opulent about Vista de Colva, it's just a well-tended and confidently stylish place to stay. Lavish breakfasts cost extra (Rs 500).

Bollywood Sea Queen (☎ 2789040; www.bollywoodhotel.com; r Rs 3000-4000; 🖭) The most top-end place in town, but with little else to strongly recommend it other than a groovy name. Bollywood Sea Queen feels over-priced given that many of the balconies have no discernable view, but its secluded location does give it a 'world of its own' feel.

Vincy Beach Resort (☎ 2788087; r Rs 2000; 🖭) This place is at the cheaper end of top-end accommodation, with a swimming pool, a popular restaurant and everything that a place in this price range should have. However, it's looking a bit tired.

Eating

The speciality in town is of course seafood, and there are many choices as to where to eat it.

Sea Pearl (mains Rs 60-220; ⏰ 8.30am-2pm & 6-11pm) Comes to life at night with a stream of customers, and fairy lights that make the seafood meals all the more appealing.

If you can't choose from among the range of seafood dishes, you can never go wrong with cultural staples such as fish curry with Goan rice (Rs 35), or a beef steak with chips and vegetables (Rs 75). The latter makes a fair stab at satiating cravings for food from home. Vegetarians are better off heading elsewhere.

Sagar Kinara (☎ 2780479; mains Rs 20-60) A real gem that has resisted the urge to adapt its menu and prices to tourists, this is a pure vegetarian restaurant with a fantastic array of North and South Indian delights.

Delhi Express (Colva Beach Rd; mains Rs 25-80) A good choice for some proactively tasty food. It's a low-key but well-run place with authentic food and a great range of sweets. You are unlikely to try a spicier or more tasty *dal tarka* (lentils flavoured with garlic, chillies, onions, cumin seeds, mustard seeds, ginger and tomatoes) anywhere else; the menu warns of the extra hot selections.

There are some well-established beach shacks within easy distance of the end of the road. The menu and service at all of them is relatively high given their enthusiasm to win your loyalty:

Domnick's (Colva Beach; mains Rs 40-180) Has a strong menu; the set Indian breakfast is good value at Rs 50.

Sea, Sun & Sand (Colva Beach; mains Rs 40-180) Next to Domnick's, this place has an equally eclectic menu and very friendly staff. A cup of coffee and a chocolate pancake goes down a treat.

Papillon (☎ 2789257; mains Rs 40-200) Further south, this is a fairly popular beach shack, perhaps because it isn't surrounded by a fleet of others. An appropriate meal for the Indian seaside is the seafood biryani (Rs 75). A vegetable stuffed naan (Rs 25) is an excellent postswim snack. And for dessert, or perhaps breakfast, if you're really in holiday mode, a rum pancake (Rs 30).

Drinking & Entertainment

In short, entertainment in Colva demands a do-it-yourself approach.

Gatsby's (☎ 2789745; man/woman Rs 250/free) If you need more action than the beach affords, head to this 24-hour coffee shop, pub and disco. The action usually lasts between 9pm and 3am. The majority of its clientele are men.

Boomerang (Downunder; ⏰ till late) This social bar has a fully-fledged circular bar and chairs spilling onto the sand towards the volleyball net. There's also a pool table that is perpetually monopolised by European men in Speedos. It's a nice place to laze about and meet a few people (not all of whom, thankfully, wear Speedos).

Shalom (Vista de Colva; ⊙ till late) If you're in a sophisticated mood, head for Shalom, which makes a concerted effort to resist the laissez-fare approach of its neighbouring watering holes and maintains a lounge-bar feel; a far cry from the tragically Western-themed 'stud bar' it used to be.

Longuinos Beach Resort (☎ 2788068) The restaurant here has live music (and dancing when it can extract the requisite enthusiasm from its audience) from around 6pm. Head here if you're up for an engaging evening of rock renditions of the hokey-pokey.

Getting There & Away

Buses run from Colva to Margao about every half-hour (Rs 7, 20 minutes), departing from the roundabout in front of the GTDC Colva Residency. The first bus from Colva departs around 7.30am and the last returns from Margao about 7pm.

Taxis, share taxis, autorickshaws and motorcycles can also be picked up here. A taxi from Colva to Margao costs from Rs 80 to 100, and a motorcycle about Rs 40.

Getting Around

Motorcycles and mopeds are available for hire from Rs 100 to 350 a day. The best place to ask initially is your hotel, but also try the market area near the beach. A small stall opposite Colva Beach Resort rents bicycles for Rs 40 to 80 a day.

BENAULIM
☎ 0832

Only 2km south of Colva, Benaulim seems a world away – though development is beginning to make a faint imprint, it's much more peaceful and rural, the beach is cleaner and tourist facilities are few and far between. It's this rustic atmosphere that makes Benaulim a popular place for long-term visitors.

Benaulim has a special place in Goan tradition, for it is said to have been here that Parasurama's arrow landed when he fired it into the sea and created Goa.

Orientation & Information

There are a couple of reliable travel agents in Benaulim that can arrange air, bus and train tickets, and change money.

Bank of Baroda ATM (Vasvaddo Beach Rd) Near Maria Hall.

GK Tourist Centre (☎ 2770476, 2771221, 2770471; gktouristcentre@hotmail.com; H No 1592/2 Vasvaddo Beach Rd) Recommended.

Travels Etcetera (New Horizons; ☎ 2770635, 2771218; newhorizonsgoa@sancharnet.in; No 1595 Beach Rd) Very professionally run.

Sights & Activities

On the main road through the village, about 600m south of Maria Hall, **Manthan** (☎ 2271659) is a beautifully restored century-old Portuguese-era home that has converted into a heritage gallery stuffed with art, sculptures, antiques and designer clothes. Almost everything is for sale, but even if you don't want to buy pricey contemporary Goan art, Manthan is a labour of love worth visiting.

Yoga classes (Rs 100) are held every Tuesday at 5pm at Pedro's Bar & Restaurant (p186) near the beach.

Water sports in Benaulim are not as prevalent as they are at more crowded Colva, though some operators hang around the beach shacks. One of the most prolific is **Lucky Remy's Watersports** (☎ 9850458489). Another is **Pele's Water Sport** (☎ 9822080045); jet skis cost Rs 500, and speed boats Rs 500.

Pedro's is a good place to ask about dolphin trips (Rs 250) and excursions to Anjuna (Rs 250), though the latter is cheaper to arrange from Colva.

Sleeping
BUDGET

Oshin (☎ 2770069; inaciooshin@rediffmail.com; r Rs 475) An impressive budget choice, Oshin is quite a pleasant building that looks slightly out of place in a pleasant green part of Benaulim. Rooms all have bathroom and balconies.

Cocohuts (☎ 9372170572; huts with/without bathroom Rs 500/300) Budget accommodation at a top-end location; the huts here are more solid than many with concrete floors and proper beds. The grounds could certainly be cleaner and tidier, but Wilma, its manager, couldn't be any friendlier.

Simon Cottages (☎ 2770581; r Rs 200-300) Simon Cottages (where cottage actually means room in a building) is not near the beach but creates a very distinct atmosphere. Rooms have bathrooms, some even have fridges.

The quirky management is harmlessly intrusive, but these economical rooms, with pleasant shared balconies and in Benaulim's leafy heart, are worth the occasional imposition.

O'Palmar Beach Cottages (☎ 2770631; opalmar@sancharnet.in; r Rs 350) Rooms are extremely large with a separate sitting room from the bedroom, which is a bit useless given how dark it is, but the space is a rarity. Despite the lack of natural light, the location is great for this price.

Hotel Failaka (☎ 771270; hotelfailaka@hotmail.com; Adsulim Nagar, Benaulim; r Rs 400) Failaka is fair walk from the beach (near Maria Hall), but great value if you have wheels. Rooms are nicely furnished and have hot water, TV and balconies. It's a chunky red-and-white concrete building brightened by its happy colours and balconies.

Rosario's Inn (☎ 2770636; Benaulim Beach Rd; r with/without bathroom Rs 300/150) Almost on the football pitch, Rosario's is a large establishment that's great value and has a committed traveller vibe. Rooms open onto a balcony.

Libra (☎ 2770598; r Rs 300) There are plenty of basic family-run places on the main roads such as this one, which has basic rooms in a family-run establishment. Keep an eye out for signs for similar options.

D'Souza's Guest House (☎ 2770583; r Rs 400) This place is popular (often full) for its clean rooms in a proud blue building.

There are a few no-fuss options around the main strip:

Jacinta Moraes Guest House (☎ 2770187; H No 1608, Benaulim Beach Rd; r Rs 200) Clean and basic rooms behind the main house of the friendly family.

Tansy Cottages (☎ 2770547; tansytouristcottages@yahoo.co.in; r Rs 300) Has nine rooms, all with bathroom.

MIDRANGE

Palm Grove Cottages (☎ 2770059, 2771170, 2770411; www.palmgrovegoa.com; r Rs 400-1150) A praiseworthy option that has a range of rooms throughout a dense green garden. Rooms range from simple but spacious accommodation behind the main house, to separately situated newer rooms. The place gets rave reviews, and people enjoy the quality restaurant. There's a security guard posted at the gate and the whole place is pleasantly secluded.

L'Amour Beach Resort (☎ 2770404, 2770562; www.lamourbeachresort.com; cottages Rs 600) A great location with well-kept grounds and smartly uniformed staff. The cottage-style rooms are a bit tired but there's nothing wrong with them. The resort is attached to the pleasant Sea Rose Restaurant.

Anthy's Guesthouse (☎ 2771680; anthysguesthouse@rediffmail.com; r Rs 1300) A fantastic choice, albeit slightly overpriced for rooms with no air-con or hot water, but it is well maintained and has real character. The staff are happy, the guests are happy, the food is great. Stay here if you can.

Furtado's (☎ 2770396; r with/without AC Rs 1200/800; ✕) The food gets quite good reviews and the location couldn't be better, but we have had some very serious complaints about management here and Furtado's right to a recommendation is in serious doubt.

TOP END

Carina Beach Resort (☎ 2770413, 2770414; bookings@carinabeachresort.com; s/d Rs 1300/1800, d with AC Rs 2000; ✕ ☰) About the closest thing to a top-end hotel in Benaulim. You could stay on the beach for the price you pay, but the resort has its own swimming pool and large grounds for lounging about in relative privacy.

Taj Exotica (☎ 2771234; www.tajhotels.com; Calwaddo, Benaulim; r Rs 28,600-45,500; ☰) A pleasant drive from Benaulim, the 140-room Taj Exotica is a famous place to stay in these parts. Prices here make other top-end hotels look like budget accommodation. Well done if you can afford to stay; you're in for sheer indulgence.

Eating

Johncy's (☎ 2771390; mains Rs 50-130) Johncy's has been a popular place to meet and socialise for the last couple of decades. There is a mixed menu of Indian, Chinese, and Goan.

Pedro's Bar & Restaurant (mains Rs 60-120; ⊙ 8am-midnight) This is a popular place to eat, largely because of its location. The extensive menu offers everything from traditional Goan dishes to sizzlers. There's also live music on Tuesday night.

Malibu Restaurant (Calvaddo, Benaulim; mains Rs 40-130) This very pleasant restaurant is a lovely place for al fresco dining in a very green eating area. It's a popular choice for breakfast.

Palm Garden Restaurant (☎ 2770059; mains Rs ▪-140) A spotlessly clean and sometimes leasantly sociable restaurant set in a azebo-shaped building in the secluded ardens of Palm Grove Cottages.

Taj Exotica (☎ 2771234; mains from Rs 300) If you re interested in some fine upmarket din-ng, the restaurants at Taj Exotica are the est in the area.

etting There & Away

uses to Margao from Benaulim (Rs 4) are equent, and leave from the bus stand at 1aria Hall. Buses heading south to Varca nd Cavelossim can be picked up at the rossroads. Minibus taxis tend to hang round opposite the Royal Goan Beach Club, while motorcycle taxis and autorick-haws hang around the crossroads.

etting Around

enaulim village is quite spread out and a ot of accommodation is well back from the each, so it pays to have some form of trans-ort. There are plenty of places in Benaulim hat rent motorcycles – ask at guesthouses r at the car park on the beach.

Bicycles are available for rent in front f Pedro's or outside Furtado's on Serna-atim Beach for around Rs 40 to 80 a day. At low tide you can ride 15km along the each to Mobor, at the southern end, then ack along the road through Cavelossim nd Varca.

VARCA, CAVELOSSIM & MOBOR
☎ 0832

he 10km strip of pristine beach south of ▪enaulim has become Goa's most upmar-ket resort frontage. The five-star resorts are xclusive, luxurious self-contained bubbles vith pools, extensive private grounds (some ave golf courses) and cavernous marble obbies.

Thankfully, it's still possible to enjoy this elatively deserted stretch of coastline with-out spending a small fortune on accom-modation. With your own transport you an find one of several beach access points n between the big hotels; there's generally a few beach shacks and sun beds at the end of these lanes catering to the few independ-nt tourists who come here. Public buses un from Margao and Colva to Varca and Cavelossim villages, but you can't get right

to the beach by public transport. A good spot to access the beach in Varca is just south of the Goa Renaissance Resort in a small area called Zalor. From here you can wander north or south and find a deserted bit of sand.

Cavelossim, 7km south of Varca, is an incongruous strip of shops and hotels. Both Varca and Cavelossim villages have impres-sive whitewashed **churches** that are worth a stop if you're exploring this region under your own steam. The ride along the back roads from Benaulim to Cavelossim takes you through coconut groves, farmland, paddy fields and small settlements.

Continuing on through Cavelossim brings you to Mobor on the tip of the peninsula, where the Sal River meets the Arabian Sea. **Boat trips** on the Sal River can be organised here.

Tours

There are numerous tour operators now advertising along the main road, which are healthily competitive. Ask around for something that suits. Alternatively, **Bet-ty's Place** (☎ 2871456) runs leisurely cruises and activities such as river bird-watching (Rs 250), one-hour dolphin-spotting cruises (Rs 300) and fishing trips (Rs 500, extra if you want your catch to be cooked and served to you) and two-hour evening bird-watching trips (Rs 250). Betty's Place also arranges a variety of water sports.

Sleeping & Eating
VARCA
Radisson White Sands Resort (☎ 2727272; www .radisson.com; Pedda, Varca-Salcete; d Rs 9000-28,000; 🏊) On the beach about 2km west of Varca village, Radisson is a five-star resort hotel with all the trimmings. The cavernous pool with an artificial waterfall is a particularly decadent feature.

Club Mahindra (☎ 2744555; www.clubmahindra .com; Survery No 176/1, Varca Village, Salcete; d Rs 5000, studios Rs 6000, ste Rs 7000; 🏊) Also facing Varca Beach, this is a reasonable choice, outside the peak season, for affordable luxury. It's a family-friendly place with plenty to keep kids occupied, a terraced pool, three res-taurants and 135 rooms. It's also a favour-ite among Russian package tourists. There are packages available, which include meals and some sightseeing trips.

Ramada (☎ 2745200; www.ramadahotels.com; d Rs 6600; 🏊) The enormous lobby of this 202-room resort, formerly Goa Renaissance Resort, is adorned with towering archways beyond which manicured gardens stretch to the beach, a big pool, tennis courts, a golf course, nightclubs and a casino designed by the same people that created Caesar's Palace in Las Vegas. All rooms have a balcony facing the gardens or the sea.

Michette's (☎ 2745732; michetteholidaycare@red iffmail.com; d & apt Rs 500) A family-run place just south of the crossroads to the beach. It has a good-value two-bedroom apartment with two balconies and a sitting room that would be ideal for a family or group, and some smaller doubles nearby. The inexpensive restaurant turns out authentic food.

Dona Sa Maria Holiday Home (☎ 2745290; www .donasamaria.com; d Rs 1000; 🖥) Further south on the same road is this pleasant midrange hotel with a small pool, bar and restaurant. The family that runs it are very friendly, and the rooms are all well decked out with very pleasant balconies. A good place, if you want peace and quiet.

CAVELOSSIM & MOBOR

As well as the restaurants and bars at the flash hotels there are several good eating and drinking places in this area, though menu prices generally reflect the upmarket nature of the tourism.

Leela (☎ 2871234; www.ghmhotels.com; pavilion r US$320, ste US$495-2200; 🏊) With 152 rooms on 75 acres of luxury, this enormous expanse of manicured Goan perfection has its own riverside Italian restaurant, a 12-hole golf course, and various rooms of varying degrees of decadence. The villas are particularly pleasant, overhanging the artificial lagoon and complete with their own plunge pool (one of which is left vacant for a chairman, but still cleaned daily even in his absence). Leisure facilities include tennis and squash courts, a gym, a pool and health spa, a casino, plus a full range of water sports. The expanse of beach exclusively available to guests is particularly good, with palm trees providing much-needed shade, and the elegant road built for buggies to transport guests even extends to this private beach.

Gaffino's Beach Resort (☎ 2871441; briangaffino@ gmail.com; d with/without AC 1500/1200; 🏊) This popular, though slightly overpriced, guesthouse has an excellent restaurant, which caters to a variety of tastes and makes a genuine stab at the authenticity of its Western dishes.

Dona Sylvia (☎ 2871321; www.donasylvia.com; d with AC Rs 8500; 🏊 🏊) Dona Sylvia operates 'all-inclusive' package deals (including three meals a day and booze between 11am and 11pm), or slightly cheaper accommodation-and-meals packages. If all you want to do is laze around the pool, eat, drink and party, it may be for you.

Sao Domingo's Holiday Home (☎ 2871461; www .saodomingosgoa.com; d with/without AC Rs 1600/1200; 🏊) Down a laneway opposite Goan Village, this midrange hotel is in a pleasant area of coconut palms just a few minutes' walk from the River Sal. Tidy rooms have balconies and hot water, and some have air-con.

Holiday Inn Resort (☎ 2871303; www.holidayinn goa.com; s US$140-165, d US$140-225; 🏊) Smaller than some of the resorts in this part of Goa but still impressive with rooms arranged around a pool just back from the beach. It has a few distinct restaurants and facilities catering for young kids.

Goan Village (☎ 2871629; saodomingos@rediffmail .com; mains Rs 60-200) Opposite Sao Domingo's, Goan Village is a garden restaurant with live music on Saturday and Tuesday, and beach parties on Wednesday. It has a menu of Goan cuisine backed by Indian and continental staples. Recommended is pomfret *recheiado* (stuffed with red masala filling, Rs 180).

Mike's Place (☎ 2871248; www.mikesplacegoa.com) A popular place for evening meals and drinks, Mike's Place arranges live-music nights in its polished outdoor setting and beach parties every Wednesday. There are also some rooms here.

Entertainment

Goan Village (☎ 2871629; saodomingos@rediffmail .com) Goan Village has live music on Saturday and Tuesday. It also arranges beach parties on Wednesday nights, where customers all move to the beach and can be served their food there.

Jazz Inn (jazzinn_2000@yahoo.com) Near Gaffino's on the main road to Mobor is this popular night-time spot with live music, which is sometimes not so much jazz as reggae.

BETUL TO AGONDA

To the south of Mobor is the mouth of the Sal River. To continue down the coast you either need to backtrack and head inland via Chinchinim for the National Highway (NH) 17 or take the small road leading east from Cavelossim, cross by ferry to Assolna, and then continue down the coast road.

This coast road is the most interesting way to explore southern Goa, if you have your own transport – preferably a motorcycle. The area south of Betul is one of the few parts of the Goan coast where the Western Ghats project westwards far enough to form imposing headlands. The coastal road is hilly, winding and in many places poorly surfaced, but it's quiet, scenic and good for a spot of motorcycle touring. Another reason to take the coast road is that you can detour to the old fort, or what remains of it, at Cabo da Rama.

The ferry from Cavelossim to Assolna theoretically runs every half-hour between 6.15am and 8.30pm, and between 6.30am and 8.45pm coming back the other way. In practice though it continually goes back and forth so there's very little waiting time. The journey takes four minutes. To get to the ferry crossing, turn left at the timetable just near the church, and continue for 2km to the river. On the other side, turn left towards Assolna then take a right in the village to head south to Betul, passing through the town of Velim.

Betul

☎ 0832

Following the coast southwards from the Sal River, opposite the narrow peninsula occupied by the Leela Palace resort is the ramshackle fishing village of Betul. Few foreign tourists stay here and, apart from getting local boatmen to take you out on the river or watching the fishermen unload their catch at the harbour, there's not much to do, but it's very peaceful and a good taste of rural Goa.

Off the main road on the banks of the estuary, **Betul Beach Resort** (☎ 2774923; betulbeachresort@yahoo.co.in; Plot No 1, Rangali, Velim, Salcete; betulbeachresort@sancharnet.in; d with AC Rs 1000-1600; ❄ ⊠) is a reasonable, albeit overpriced, choice if you're staying in the area. There are 32 plain rooms and cottages in a garden setting, a decent sort of pool

and a very basic restaurant. At high tide you can take boat trips on the river from here and cross to the adjacent beach.

Cabo da Rama

The laterite spurs along the coastline of Goa, providing both high ground and ready-made supplies of building stone, were also natural sites for fortresses. These were used along the length of Goa's coastline – Mormugao, Aguada, Chapora and Terekhol. The headland of Cabo da Rama is no exception and there was a fortress here long before the Portuguese ever reached Goa.

The **fortress** on this site, named after Rama of the Hindu Ramayana epic who was said to have spent time in exile here with his wife Sita, was held by various rulers for many years. It was not until 1763 that it was gained by the Portuguese from the Raja of Sonda and was subsequently rebuilt; what remains today, including the rusty cannons, is entirely Portuguese.

Although the fort saw no real action after the rebuild, it was briefly occupied by British troops between 1797 and 1802 and again between 1803 and 1813, before being allowed to fall into ruin. It was used as a prison for a period until 1955.

There is little to see of the old structure beyond the front wall with its dry moat and unimposing main gate, and the small church that stands just inside the walls, but the views north and south are worth coming for. Services are still held in the chapel every Sunday.

To get to the fort from the coast road between Betul and Agonda, turn west at the signposted turn-off about 10km south of Betul. The road dips into a lush valley then winds steeply up to a barren plateau punctuated by farmhouses and wandering stock. The fort is at the end of this road, about 3km from the turn-off.

There are local buses direct from Margao or Betul several times daily but since there's nothing to do once you've explored the fort you should check on times for returning buses. There are a couple of simple cafés and drink stalls outside the fort entrance to while away some time while waiting for a bus, but nowhere to stay the night.

A return taxi to Cabo da Rama costs around Rs 300 from Betul and Rs 500 from Palolem, including waiting time.

Agonda

☎ 0832

Twelve kilometres south of the turn-off to Cabo da Rama (and 8km north of Palolem), the coast road passes the small village of Agonda. Following the small road 2km to the coast you eventually come to a T-junction just behind the beach itself. There are a few places to stay along the road in either direction, though turning right at the junction takes you to the most beautiful (and unspoilt) part of Agonda Beach.

Agonda Beach is an almost completely untouched 2km stretch of white sand. It's a great place to chill out if you're feeling mellow and have a stack of good books, but don't come here if you like to spend your afternoons playing beach volleyball and boozing in the beach shacks – with the exception of a couple of restaurants attached to guesthouses, there are none. Almost every guesthouse can arrange a taxi or a dolphin trip and can help you source a bicycle.

On the road between Agonda and Palolem, near a small drink stall, look for a sign pointing to **Butterfly Beach**. A narrow path leads over a headland to this tiny secluded beach, accessible only by boat or this path. It's a stiff one-hour walk with a steep ascent then descent to the beach, so allow plenty of time to get there and back. Boat trips from Palolem also go out to Butterfly Beach so you may not be entirely alone.

SLEEPING & EATING

There are several guesthouses in Agonda, and, much to the displeasure of many, there are more on the way.

Forget Me Not (☎ 2647611; mahahotl@goatelecom .com; huts Rs 400-1000, r from Rs 700) Forget Me Not espouses the laid-back Goan *susegad* philosophy, with a side order of serious beach appreciation. Amid the cocohuts and mud-brick rooms are chill-out areas, hanging chairs and a manager who makes a concerted effort to ensure that guests respect his right to enjoy his patch of paradise. Forget Me Not is at the north end of Agonda, at one of those special beaches that precariously endures the challenge of remaining unspoilt.

Palm Beach Lifestyle Resort (☎ 2647783; www .palmbeachgoa.com; d Rs 900) The most upmarket in appearance, Palm Beach Lifestyle Resort

is a collection of rooms that are built up a hill – the one at the very back is the highest, and nice if you can get it. The manager prides himself on not having moved a tree or stone in the construction of the resort, and indeed some balconies have been built around palm trees and the rooms are scattered almost haphazardly around the area. The buildings are mixed mud and concrete of a pleasant red earthy colour.

Dunhill Resort (☎ 2647328; d Rs 400) This place was one of the first to cotton on to the tourist potential of Agonda with its 13 well-maintained cottage-style rooms, all with bathroom and a restaurant with an amicable air. The friendly family that runs this place is giving in to the trend with plans to build cocohuts at the beach in the near future.

Abba's Glory Land (☎ 2647822; Dovel Kazan, Agonda Beach; huts & r Rs 400) On the main road behind the beach, Abba's is relatively new and very good value. There are clean but adequately sized huts with bathrooms. Even better are the four rooms that have sensible wardrobes, which you can secure with your own padlock.

Maria Paulo (☎ 2647606; d with/without balcony Rs 500/400) Just left of the church at the T-junction is a very pleasant guesthouse at a friendly family home. Rooms are exceptionally clean and airy with unusually large windows. There is also a nice common balcony that guests can enjoy. Look for the small painted sign that reads 'well furnished guest house'.

Mahnamahnas (☎ 2647846; the.mahnamahnas@ gmail.com) At the time of research, these hard to miss blue-and-white wooden-board cottages were in the process of being completed (much to the chagrin of locals). They're different from the competition in that there is a bathroom downstairs and a bedroom upstairs, with an enormous balcony with hammock. The space would suit a family.

Sunset Bar (☎ 2647381) Perched up on a hill at the southern end of the beach, it has a great outlook and a small open-air restaurant – a great place to watch the sun sink into the Arabian Sea. There are also some rooms here.

Turtle Lounge (☎ 9423813150; mains Rs 75-325; ☼ 8am-late) A great place for a drink at any time, the recently opened Turtle Lounge has a boutique charisma that doesn't seem to quite fit Agonda. The wooden four-poster canopied beds on the sand make the perfect base for a day at the beach, particularly given luxurious private open-air showers. The shaded tables are resplendently candlelit at night.

Other good choices off the beach:

Denyson's (☎ 2647242; r Rs 250) Respectable rooms at a family house on the road as it starts to climb.

Defny's (r Rs 300) Two simple but adequate rooms managed by the same people who run Denyson's, but on the road across from the beach.

Dersy Beach Resort (☎ 2647503; huts Rs 200, r with bathroom Rs 500) Five spotless doubles across the road from the beach and 11 simple palm-thatch huts on the beach side. There is also a pleasant shaded restaurant.

GETTING THERE & AWAY

As with any out-of-the-way place, reaching Agonda is best with your own transport – you can cycle here from Palolem in about an hour. A taxi from Palolem or Chaudi costs about Rs 150 and an autorickshaw Rs 90. Local buses run to Agonda from Chaudi sporadically throughout the day (Rs 5), stopping at the T-junction near the church. If you're coming from Palolem you can wait at the junction of the main highway (NH17) and the Agonda road and flag down a passing bus. Coming from Margao, there are a few direct buses, or you can go to Chaudi and get another bus from there.

PALOLEM
☎ 0832

Opinions flow fast and firm when it comes to Palolem. The older fraternity of the travel community has tied itself into tantric knots over 'the way it has changed'. They lament its metamorphosis from deserted paradise into a 'bamboo Calangute', while others (who obviously aren't familiar with 'the way it was', say the cynics) think it's the best beach in Goa.

Whatever Palolem was a decade ago, it's best appreciated as it is – a postcard-perfect crescent of white sand fringed by a shady rim of coconut palms and coco-huts. Palolem's mix of lazy beach life, large nomadic population, and down-to-earth nightlife is an affably hospitable mix. And it's hard to criticise the influx of backpackers to Palolem when you're sharing a beer or game of volleyball with them.

Information

The lane leading from the end of the road (where buses stop) to the main beach entrance is lined with stalls selling all the usual handicrafts, souvenirs and clothing.

There are plenty of places to access the Internet in Palolem, including a 24-hour Internet café right on the beach next to Cuba. International phone calls can be made at most Internet places.

Bliss Travels (☎ 2643456; blisstravels@rediffmail .com) Near the main entrance to the beach. Bus and flight bookings, currency exchange and Internet access (Rs 50 per hour).

Post office In Chaudi, 4km to the east of Palolem.

Rainbow Travel (☎ 2643912; sitaben@hotmail.com) Reliable travel agent on the main road in the village.

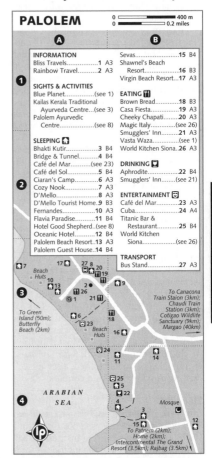

PALOLEM
0 — 400 m
0 — 0.2 miles

INFORMATION
Bliss Travels.................1 A3
Rainbow Travel...........2 A3

SIGHTS & ACTIVITIES
Blue Planet..............(see 1)
Kailas Kerala Traditional
  Ayurveda Centre...(see 3)
Palolem Ayurvedic
  Centre.................(see 8)

SLEEPING
Bhakti Kutir.................3 B4
Bridge & Tunnel...........4 B4
Café del Mar..........(see 23)
Café del Sol..............5 B4
Ciaran's Camp.............6 A3
Cozy Nook..................7 A3
D'Mello.......................8 A3
D'Mello Tourist Home.9 B3
Fernandes..................10 A3
Flavia Paradise...........11 B4
Hotel Good Shepherd..(see 8)
Oceanic Hotel.............12 B4
Palolem Beach Resort.13 A3
Palolem Guest House..14 B4

Sevas........................15 B4
Shawnel's Beach
  Resort..................16 B3
Virgin Beach Resort...17 A3

EATING
Brown Bread.............18 B3
Casa Fiesta................19 A3
Cheeky Chapati.........20 A3
Magic Italy............(see 26)
Smugglers' Inn...........21 A3
Vasta Waza.............(see 1)
World Kitchen Siona..26 A3

DRINKING
Aphrodite..................22 B4
Smugglers' Inn........(see 21)

ENTERTAINMENT
Café del Mar............23 A3
Cuba........................24 A4
Titanic Bar &
  Restaurant............25 B4
World Kitchen
  Siona..................(see 26)

TRANSPORT
Bus Stand.................27 A3

To Canacona
Train Staion (3km);
Chaudi Train
Station (3km);
Cotigao Wildlife
Sanctuary (9km);
Margao (40km)

To Green
Island (50m);
Butterfly
Beach (2km)

Beach
Huts

ARABIAN
SEA

Mosque

To Patnem (2km);
Home (2km);
Intercontinental The Grand
Resort (3.5km); Rajbag (3.5km)

SOUTH GOA

Activities

Travellers coming to Palolem are generally looking to relax on the beach, but there's plenty to do. The sea is excellent for swimming and you can rent boogie boards and even surfboards from stalls near the main entrance to the beach.

There is also an adventure-sport base; local operators are starting to dabble in canyoning trips and trekking. Ask around and keep an eye peeled for signs.

There are various Ayurvedic treatments available. The **Palolem Ayurvedic Centre** (☎ 226 40193; palolemayurvediccentre@yahoo.co.in), behind Hotel Good Shepherd, has been recommended. A general massage (from a male or female masseur) will cost Rs 500 (one hour), and there are various other treatments on offer.

Yoga, massage and meditation courses are advertised at restaurants. Check the notice board outside Brown Bread café, which has information on meditation, astrology, holistic healing, tarot and various courses. Bhakti Kutir (opposite), near Colomb Bay, runs workshops in yoga, meditation and natural healing; it also has the **Kailas Kerala Traditional Ayurveda Centre** (☎ 264372; www.bhak tikutir.com; 296 Palolem, Patnem).

Blue Planet (☎ 9850456228; www.doctor-of-the -future.com; ☷ 9am-5pm) is an internationally run natural-healing centre that prides itself on being able to offer almost any type of massage you can think of for Rs 500 per hour. Booking ahead is advised. There are also morning yoga classes.

Tours

Boat tours to see dolphins or to visit tiny Butterfly Beach are easy to arrange – it seems just about everyone in Palolem owns a fishing boat or knows someone who does. A one-hour trip costs around Rs 150 per person and you can organise this through your accommodation or just wander along the beach and ask around. Most trips leave in the morning (around 8am) or early evening. Every now and then, after an accident, trips will cease for a couple of days.

Sleeping

Cozy Nook (☎ 2643550; small huts without bathroom Rs 500, large cottages with bathroom Rs 1500) Cozy Nook is a hippy nouveau Palolem institution. Balconies, eating areas and the interior of some

huts have been created using concrete shapes and rocks to remove dull corners and straight walls, and add colour and shape. Walls that aren't already vibrantly tiled are covered with interesting wall hangings. Other assets of Cozy Nook are its restaurant and its location between a lake and an ocean.

Sevas (☎ 2639194; www.sevasgoa.com) Sevas is a good runner-up to its neighbour, Bhakti Kutir. Gardens here have not grown to the same extent as Bhakti's and rooms are less memorable, but the grounds are very well kept, the rooms are more economical, and the staff aren't as apathetic. There is also a holistic healing ethos at work here; yoga and massage are available.

Oceanic Hotel (☎ 2643059; www.hotel-oceanic .com; Tembiwaddo; r Rs 1500-2500; ☷) This delightful white building is set off the beach on the road between Palolem and Patnem. It is a lovely space that has a more private feel than many other options in Palolem, and boasts the only swimming pool around (which outsiders can use for Rs 200).

Ciaran's Camp (☎ 2643477; johnciaran@hotmail .com; r Rs 1000-2000) Ciaran's has worked hard to keep its distinction over the years. Rooms aren't cheap but they are lovely, set around a pretty garden, and all with their own veranda area. There is lovely attention to detail here; guests can enjoy chai at 4.30pm every day. There is also an inviting restaurant that churns out barbecued seafood at candlelit tables under white umbrellas.

Palolem Guest House (☎ 2644880; palolemgues thouse@hotmail.com; r Rs 1400-2000, huts Rs 400; ☷) Popular with the slightly older crowd who aren't into late-night music and have done their fair share of budget hotels, Palolem Guest House offers spacious rooms that are well-equipped with everything that you could need (including TV, air-con and hot water) and a cosy restaurant. There are two cheap and basic huts on the premises.

Bridge & Tunnel (☎ 9326100699; shoumirsh@ rediffmail.com; huts Rs 900-2500) Some of the huts here are not the best value in town, but Bridge & Tunnel is beyond reproach in light of its location right on the headland of rocks. Climb up one side of the rocks and down the other to get to your hut and your own private little stretch of sand. The huts are pleasantly spaced away from each other.

Shawnel's Beach Resort (☎ 2643912, 2644745; sitaben@hotmail.com; huts Rs 500-1200) Shawnel's is

---

THE AUTHOR'S CHOICE

Bhakti Kutir (☎ 2643472; www.bhaktikutir.com; 296 Palolem, Patnem; r Rs 1500) A commendable project of a Goan and his German wife, Bhakti Kutir is an ecologically sensitive and atmospherically sublime place to stay.

The 22 cottage-style rooms are all unique and boast extraordinary attention to detail: Goan style red-tiled roofs, lampshades made of coconuts and luxuriant mosquito nets set the tone. Sometimes there are curtains where walls should be, and many bathrooms are open air, allowing you to bathe between bamboo trees under the sun or stars. Cushions and hammocks are strung up inside and outside the cottages, some of which have private curtained-off areas in the coconut grove, others have sofas or rocking chairs on the balcony.

Rooms are connected by stone pathways, above which nets are strung like spider webs to catch lazy leaves that gather like great pastel-coloured clouds. As well as yoga, an Ayurveda centre, and a school for guests' children, Bhakti Kutir has an outdoor organic restaurant, where the parachute roofs heave in the wind like deep-breathing lungs.

---

not so much a 'beach resort' as six huts that are sort of near the beach. They are enormously good value if you're not fussed about the two-minute walk. Huts are solidly built with wooden walls, and have concrete floors and proper beds, as well as tiled bathrooms. They are commendably spacious and aren't within conversational distance of your neighbour. Contact Rainbow Travel (p191) for more information.

Palolem Beach Resort (☎ 2643054; www.goainns .com/palolembeachresort; tents with/without bathroom Rs 450/350, r with/without AC Rs 700/1200; ⌨) Surprisingly well-priced for so professionally run an establishment, Palolem Beach Resort has tents and rooms set around a pleasant grassed area. Basic tents are set up on solid concrete grounds, and have twin beds and a fan; the shared bathroom is clean. There are also rooms that are good value for their location and compared to their neighbours. It's a pleasant place for families to stay with the small playground in the middle of the well-kept and friendly grounds.

Hotel Good Shepherd (☎ 2643814; s with/without bathroom Rs 200/150, d with bathroom Rs 350) Hotel Good Shepherd is a central but well-priced budget hotel. There is a common balcony area, and the restaurant downstairs is a good night-time hangout. This is an economic option for solo travellers who don't want to pay for a whole cocohut; there are a couple of clean single rooms with a bed, desk and shared or private bathroom.

D'Mello (☎ 643057, 643439; r Rs 800) A good budget choice away from the beach, this a well-priced hotel on the main road. If you're after a clean and basic hotel, this is

it. Rooms have a balcony, some even with a vaguely interesting view (of the street, not the beach). The floors are clean white tile.

D'Mello Tourist Home (d Rs 300-400, without bathroom Rs 250) The same pleasant couple who have recently built D'Mello also run this more budget place at their family home; rooms here are not as new but are clean and comfortable, some with balconies.

Virgin Beach Resort (☎ 2643451; d from Rs 600) Another good choice if you want a hotel as opposed to a hut. It's nothing flash at all, but rooms are a comfortable size and we've had good reports about it.

Café del Sol (☎ 9823313981; kennedys@sancharnet .in; huts up to 6 people Rs 1000-3400) and **Café del Mar** (huts Rs 950-1400) are built and managed by the same people, and have similarly distinctive huts. The difference between them is that Café del Sol is a lot quieter, whereas Café del Mar has a 24-hour bar; the music is turned down at midnight but never actually stops. Other than the noise, it's a lovely sociable and comfortable place to stay, with stylish and well-facilitated huts.

Among the myriad cocohut choices along the beach:

Fernandes (☎ 2643743; huts Rs 1000-1400) Pleasant though somewhat overpriced spacious wooden huts with raised balconies. The restaurant also gets good reviews.

Flavia Paradise (☎ 2643676; r without bathroom Rs 200, beachfront r Rs 500) Good value considering its location; the pleasant verandas and balconies are quite close together. It can be a sociable place.

Eating

It's worth leaving the beach to go and explore the restaurant range in Palolem.

World Kitchen Siona (mains Rs 60-180; ☺ 8.30am-late) World Kitchen Siona is a multicuisine restaurant, which has an impressive range of Italian, Chinese, Indian and Israeli food. The atmosphere is comfortable and some of its pasta dishes could rival its Italian competition (try the Spicy Bella). World Kitchen Siona often wins the closing time standoff with its neighbours, and manages to stay open the longest. Staff are unfailingly friendly and there's occasionally live music.

Cheeky Chapati (mains Rs 40-150) This endearingly named English-run establishment is recommended. The atmosphere is laid back but proud, and a lot of effort goes into the vegetarian and seafood menu. The sandwiches and wraps are chunky and its pastas are popular. If you're feeling like a hearty Italian meal that pays homage to the beach, try the mixed seafood penne (Rs 150), which varies depending on the seafood that's floating around on any given day but is always delicious. The blue-cheese and spinach pizza (Rs 130) is fresh and zesty.

Magic Italy (mains Rs 160-200; ☺ 6.30-11pm) A place popular for its splendid atmosphere and fresh Italian food. Ingredients are imported from Italy, and pizzas and pastas are made fresh.

Vasta Waza (☎ 9850925668; mains Rs 40-130) Something new and a little bit different, this tiny Kashmiri restaurant, next to Bliss Travel, serves Middle Eastern fare in an overtly Middle Eastern environment. There's even free delivery...within a 1km radius.

Brown Bread (☎ 2643604; Palolem Rd; mains Rs 40-120) The ideal breakfast venue with a healthy menu of fresh breads from the bakery, fruit shakes and real coffee.

Smuggler's Inn (☎ 9822381303; smugglers_goa@yahoo.co.in) A recommended English pub-restaurant, the Smuggler's Inn has a pool table, good atmosphere and, out the back, a surprisingly authentic bar, which may even remind you of your own local. There's traditional English fare and a breakfast buffet (hot/cold Rs 250/150).

Casa Fiesta (mains Rs 50-140) Mexican food and miscellaneous other dishes (like pasta and seafood options) in a pleasantly lit garden. The Latin tunes add to the commendable attempt at making authentic Mexican burritos in a Goan beach town. The consistent crowds testify to Casa Fiesta's popularity.

Drinking & Entertainment

Titanic Bar & Restaurant (☺ till late) A leader on the beach in terms of entertainment. Sometimes the crowd just sits around and relaxes, but other times a live musician or band will turn the place into an unpretentious party.

Cuba (☺ 8.30am-2am) Also has organised drinks nights, with singles night on Tuesday and gay night on Wednesday.

Café del Mar (☺ 24hr) The music at this bar is loud until around midnight.

Smuggler's Inn (☎ 9822381303; smugglers_goa@yahoo.co.in) A popular place for a drink by the bar with whoever else is hanging around to enjoy the surprisingly successful effort of English authenticity in India.

Aphrodite (cocktails Rs 80-240) For more sophistication and beachside sipping, head here to one of the most classy beach shacks, with an extensive cocktail list.

Some of the restaurants along the roads, such as World Kitchen Siona (left), have live music nights and some restaurants cater for the quieter crowd by occasionally playing DVDs.

Getting There & Away

BUS
Ordinary buses leave from the Kadamba bus stand in Margao and drop you off in the very heart of Palolem (Rs 18, one hour).

Alternatively, if the bus stops at Chaudi, Palolem is only 3km away. An autorickshaw from here should cost around Rs 40. All Karwar-bound buses stop at Chaudi.

Private buses to Mumbai, Hampi, Bangalore and Mangalore can be booked at travel agents in Palolem and some will pick you up in the village (check with the agent).

TRAIN
Between the Char Rasta crossroads and Chaudi is Canacona train station, from where there are services north to Margao (Rs 10, 35 minutes) and other stations in Goa. The 5am *Netravati Express* goes direct to Mumbai's Lokmanya Tilak station, but it's more convenient to take a bus or train to Margao and an express train from there. Heading south the same train stops at Canacona at 11.06pm and goes to Kankanadi (for Mangalore) and Ernakulam (for Kochi).

Private booking agents in Palolem can organise train tickets for you. A train to Mumbai costs around Rs 1500.

SOUTH OF PALOLEM

With beach huts and shacks spreading unstoppably across the sands of Palolem Beach, it's hardly surprising that travellers are drifting south in search of peace and space. There is also an eclectic array of long-term visitors in this area, who have found themselves village houses to rent.

Colomb
☎ 0832

Around the headland from Palolem is a small, rocky bay called Colomb, where rustic restaurants and family guesthouses shelter in a peaceful clump of coconut trees. The rocky bay here is better suited to paddling than swimming, but the short walk to Palolem to the north and Patnem to the south makes this a good low-key choice.

The most predominant place to stay in Colomb, **Laguna Vista Resort** (☎ 2644457; lagoonview5@yahoo.com; huts at front/rear Rs 1000/800, huts without bathroom Rs 500) has overpriced huts with bathrooms, and only a handful of standard cocohuts without bathrooms, but the area is secluded and the sunrise and sunset views over the bay are lovely.

Boom Shankar Restaurant (☎ 2644035; mains Rs 50-130; ⏰ 8am-11pm) is as popular for its view over the bay as for its cuisine. The Indian, Goan, Chinese, Thai and Western food here is good value compared to that found in Palolem. There are also some rooms.

Patnem
☎ 0832

A couple of kilometres south of Palolem is beautiful Patnem Beach, a small peaceful bay that runs into Kindlebag and Rajbag further south. Patnem has a strip of laid-back beach shacks; it's smaller than Palolem, but in recent years has begun to absorb some of its overflow. For the time being, though, this is a good place to escape the crowds – the sand is perfect and Patnem gets a bit of swell, which is ideal for boogie-boarding or windsurfing (you can rent boards in Palolem). It's also just small enough to have the more friendly feel of a place where nomads can meet. To find out what's going on in the way of yoga and massage, and other such essential Goan beach things, see the notice boards at the staircase leading from the main road onto the beach.

SLEEPING & EATING

Most of the beach shacks have basic accommodation in palm-thatch or bamboo huts for around Rs 200 to 600 a night. There are also a couple on the roads away from the beach that are worth considering.

Hotel Sea View (☎ 2643110; d Rs 250-800) A great-value guesthouse, about 200m back from the beach. The cheaper basic rooms in the old building have their own bathroom, though the newer building has cleaner, bigger doubles, with prices varying according

---

DETOUR: CYCLING AROUND PALOLEM

If you tire of the beach scene, there are some interesting cycling routes through the countryside around Palolem. The most obvious is down to the Talpona River mouth at **Rajbag Beach**, with a stop at **Patnem Beach** along the way.

Riding out of Palolem village (towards the highway), take the right turn at the small general store and head south, roughly parallel with the coast. The first right turn along here leads down to Colomb Bay. If you keep going straight for about 2km, you come to the turn-off to Patnem Beach. Back on the coast road, continue riding through paddy fields and the village of Kindlebag before reaching Rajbag and the Talpona River at the road's end. There are a couple of shacks here where you can get a drink and something to eat – and you can marvel at (or pour scorn on) the multi-million-dollar resort that's been built at this humble village.

Another possibility is to ride to **Agonda Beach**, around 8km from Palolem. Just before you reach the highway there's a sharp left-hand turn (signposted) for the winding and hilly road to Agonda (and on to Cabo da Rama and Betul). The left-hand turn off this road to Agonda Beach is not well marked but it comes before you start the steep hill climb – if your legs are getting tired you've probably gone too far. Agonda is a good antidote to Palolem and a relaxing place to spend the afternoon before riding back.

Gearless Indian bicycles can be hired in the market area at Palolem for around Rs 40 a day (Rs 80 in peak season).

to size. Some rooms have fantastic balconies and windows. There is also an Internet café downstairs (Rs 40 per hour).

Home (☎ 2643916; homeispatnem@yahoo.com; d Rs 500-800) A popular choice run by an English-Swiss team, with eight spotless and stylish rooms of varying sizes but all with bathrooms. If these are full (which they probably will be) the staff may be able to direct you to other choices. The Euro-style restaurant gets rave reviews and serves up superb pasta, fresh salads, pastries and real coffee from an espresso machine. It's not cheap (an Austrian apple strudel costs Rs 70) but the atmosphere is perfect and the quality of food is unquestionable.

Parvati Huts (☎ 9822189913; www.parvatihuts.in; huts Rs 1200, without bathroom Rs 400-600) A good choice that stands out from the flimsier huts around it; Parvati's huts are built of solid varnished bamboo, and mosquito nets and wall hangings add character to the round huts. There are also small but serviceable verandas attached to each.

Goyam (☎ 9890457375; www.goyam.net; huts at the beach Rs 3000, back from the beach Rs 1500, large family huts back from the beach Rs 2500) Classier (and pricier) than most, Goyam has wooden huts that it has jazzed up with details in a bid to justify the high price tag, such as a coat of bright paint, and balconies that are piled high with cushions and shaded with breezy curtains.

Nature's Green (☎ 09822185553; huts with/without fan Rs 250/200) If even Patnem Beach is too crowded for you, and you're in search of a quirky hideaway, head to the banks of the river. There are a handful of small cocohuts with shared bathroom, and an equally compact restaurant on the banks of the river. One of the real highlights of staying at this little ghetto of character is the fabulously juxtaposed view of the Goa Grand Intercontinental Resort.

Oasis (☎ yoga 9822969910; ☒ 8am-late) A popular place to eat for its Russian and Japanese cuisine and social atmosphere. Movies are played every night (often in Russian) and yoga classes are held four times a week (admission by donation, 8am to 9.30am).

Tantra (mains Rs 30-120) Has an undeniably effective gimmick to distinguish itself from other beach shack restaurants: there is a small elevated eating area built into the roof which is a perfect place at sunset if you can get to it first.

Namaste (beach huts Rs 600, huts back from beach Rs 250, cottages Rs 1000) This is a sociable place to eat (mains Rs 30 to 100) with friendly staff. There are also huts available and one quaint cottage.

GETTING THERE & AWAY
Patnem Beach is reached from the back road running south from Palolem (past the Oceanic Hotel), then turning right at the Hotel Sea View. Alternatively, walk about 20 minutes along the path from Palolem via Colomb Bay or catch a bus heading in the right direction (Rs 4).

Rajbag
☎ 0832
Beyond Patnem is Rajbag Beach, an exposed but isolated stretch of sand that ends at the mouth of the Talpona River. It's an easy walk along the beach between Patnem and Rajbag, but this once-deserted beach is now dominated by the massive five-star **Goa Grand Intercontinental Resort** (☎ 2667777; www .intercontinental.com; Raj Baga, Canacona; ste garden-view/ sea-view/luxury/presidential ste US$275/325/650/1500; ☒). Despite the somewhat formidable appearance, the space is enormously well-used.

DETOUR: AROUND RAJBAG

Although there are other beaches to the south of Rajbag, they are inaccessible by road, apart from **Polem Beach**, which is at the very southern tip of Goa, only a couple of kilometres from the state border and 26km from Palolem.

The beach is indeed deserted, but this may largely be because of the slightly seedy feel of the town behind it, apparently something of a port for smugglers of goods from neighbouring Karnataka state. If you have some reason for wanting to go here (perhaps you're hiding from the law?) you will find a room at the small building at the beach; it serves a few drinks and has a couple of less-than-basic rooms (that may not even have a bed) for Rs 100. There's one cocohut on the beach (Rs 200).

To find Polem Beach head down the NH17 towards Karwar. A couple of kilometres before the border of Karnataka you will see a yellow bus stand, opposite which is a very poorly signed turn-off to Polem Beach.

The hotel was a source of controversy when it was built partly on ground held sacred by local people. A small Hindu temple stood at the proposed entrance to the resort. Finding they were unable to demolish the temple, the developers built a fence – and the entire resort – around it and now market it as part of the attraction! You can visit the temple without entering the resort.

A narrow road runs behind the beach from Patnem, via the tiny village of Kindlebag, to the Talpona River and there's a sandy path from there to the beach. Local boatmen can ferry you across the river if you want to explore further south to **Galgibaga**, a small beach and protected area visited by rare olive ridley turtles. There are a couple of rustic restaurant-shacks on the banks of the Talpona where the road ends.

At Kindlebag, **Molyma Resorts** (☎ 2643028; molyma2001@yahoo.co.in; d Rs 430-540), a fair way back from the beach, is the only budget place to stay in this area but it has a rather deserted, forlorn feel. You would do better even at overpriced Palolem Beach nearby.

COTIGAO WILDLIFE SANCTUARY

Proclaimed as a conservation area in 1962, **Cotigao Wildlife Sanctuary** (adult/child Rs 5/2, camera/video Rs 25/100, motorcycle/car Rs 10/50; ☷ 7am-5.30pm) is the second-largest sanctuary in Goa with an area of 86 sq km. As with the other sanctuaries, most of the animals prefer to remain hidden, so you may have to stay overnight to see much more than a monkey. Your chances are best if you spend either a late evening or early morning in the tree-top watchtower.

For those who have the time and patience there is the chance to see, among other species, Indian bison or gaur, barking deer, sambar and jackals. If you come here on a day trip, there are pleasant walks through the forest and the area contains some unspoilt ghat scenery.

There's a small **Nature Interpretation Centre** and reception about 1.5km in from the main road, where there is some basic information and even samples of various animal faeces, which you can peruse while your tickets are painstakingly written up. Also here is the 'Animal Rescue Centre'; perhaps it could be more appropriately named 'Animal Detention Centre' given that the rescuee was not the animal, but rather the person the animal

bit. Whether their rescue has been a raging success is at issue given that a panther once managed to get into the enclosure.

The park boundary is a further 1.5km in from the reception centre, and the two observation towers are 6km and 9km from the park entrance, so it makes sense to have your own transport or be prepared to put in a lot of walking. Ideally, make an early start from Palolem.

SLEEPING

There is actually some Forest Department accommodation available. There is the small **Bulbul Cottage** (d without bathroom Rs 250) just behind the Nature Interpretation Centre. There are more cottages being built in its image. The far better option if you can get it is the stunningly good value **Peacock Cottage** (cottages Rs 500), which is the size of a small house. It has a well-kept garden, enormous bedroom and a separate but private bathroom and toilet. To book either of these cottages, call the **Cotigao Wildlife Sanctuary office** (☎ 0832-2639265).

An interesting place to stay is **Pepper Valley** (☎ 0832-2633370; www.peppervalley.com; Cotigao Wildlife Sanctuary, Dabemola, Partagal, Canacona; huts Rs 350, r Rs 700), which consists of six well-made cocohuts with mosquito nets, fans and pleasant curtained walls built alongside a picturesque river, and four plain but private rooms. There is also yoga on site, and a pleasant chill-out area built alongside the lake, where there is sometimes a bonfire at night. The small restaurant in the pepper plantation is comprised of a few tables placed under the trees – a rather pleasant place to eat a meal. Staff also arrange trekking and river tours throughout the area. There is a large sign heading to Pepper Valley at the entrance to the sanctuary, or you can turn left at the nature interpretation centre and follow the smaller signs.

GETTING THERE & AWAY

The entrance to the park is 7km southeast of Chaudi on the NH17. As you head south from Chaudi, the first entrance you come to (signposted 'Govt of Goa Forest Check Post') allows general access to the area. The second, some 2km further on, is the entrance to the wildlife sanctuary. Any bus heading south to Karwar can drop you on the main road, 2km from the park entrance.

Around Goa

It's easy to forget that Goa is part of a bigger country, but it's just as easy to get out there and explore it. There are several interesting excursions that are no more than a day's journey over the border in Karnataka, one of India's most interesting states.

Gokarna is situated about 60km south of the southern border of Goa in northern Karnataka. The village itself is one of the most holy Hindu sites in South India, but it's the beautiful near-deserted beaches that have drawn travellers over the years – many of them ex-Goa hippies escaping the hype, or new adventurers who've heard the rumours. It will indeed be interesting to see how Gokarna evolves (or devolves) over the years.

About 50km southeast of Gokarna are Jog Falls, the highest in India. The flow of the falls is not as grand as it once was, but an exploration of the surrounding countryside still makes for a worthy excursion. The ultimate journey (albeit an easy bus ride) from Goa is to Hampi, the magnificent ruined city of the Vijayanagar Empire and a renowned travellers' centre. The Virupaksha Temple stands proudly at almost 50m, and is one of the earliest structure in this evocatively historical area. Hampi's Vittala Temple, with its magnanimous sculpture and alluring 'musical' pillars, is unlike anything you'll see in Goa, and one of the most distinct memories you'll hold long after you've left.

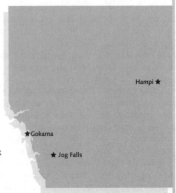

HIGHLIGHTS

- Do some easy trekking through the spectacular countryside around **Jog Falls** (p202)
- Float with pilgrims through the sleepy town of **Gokarna** (opposite)
- Immerse yourself in the thick of the colourful chaos of **Hampi Bazaar** (p204)
- Explore the maze of stone walls of Hampi's **Royal Centre** (p204)
- Take in the World Heritage–listed **Vittala Temple** (p204) and bask in the regality of its sculptural work

Hampi ★

★Gokarna

★ Jog Falls

AROUND GOA

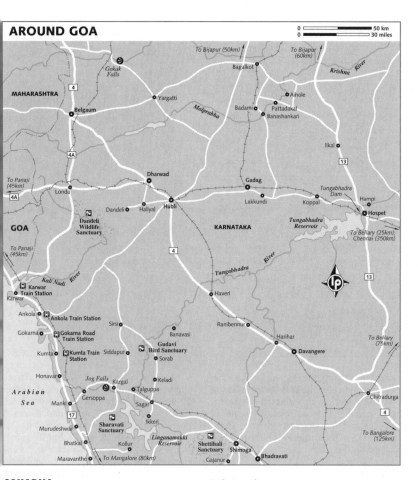

AROUND GOA

GOKARNA
☎ 08386

Gokarna (Cow's Ear), 50km south of Karwar, attracts a potpourri of Hindu pilgrims, Sanskrit scholars, hippies and beach-lovers. For Hindus, Gokarna is one of the most sacred sites in South India, and the atmosphere is colourful and devout. It's a sleepy, charming town with wooden houses on the main street and attractive traditional houses in nearby alleys. Some locals feel the foreign influx has tarnished the holy atmosphere, while others are happy with the extra income it has generated. Modesty is probably your best policy here: keep shoulders and knees covered and take your parties to the beach.

Information
Pai STD Shop (Main St; ☯ 9am-9pm) Changes cash and travellers cheques and gives advances on Visa.
Shema Internet (Car Rd; per hr Rs 40; ☯ 7.30am-midnight)
Sub post office (1st fl, cnr Car & Main Sts)
Swastik Laundry (☯ 8.30am-1pm & 4-9pm)

Sights
TEMPLES
Foreigners are not allowed inside Gokarna's temples, but you'll certainly bear witness to religious rituals around town. At the western end of Car St is the **Mahabaleshwara Temple**, home to a revered lingam (phallic symbol of Shiva). Nearby is the **Ganapati Temple**, which honours the role Ganesh

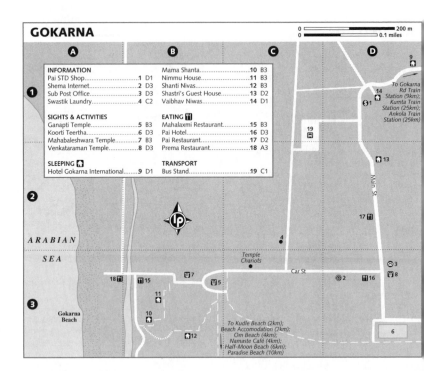

GOKARNA

INFORMATION
Pai STD Shop...........................**1** D1
Shema Internet.......................**2** D3
Sub Post Office.......................**3** D3
Swastik Laundry.....................**4** C2

SIGHTS & ACTIVITIES
Ganapti Temple......................**5** B3
Koorti Teertha........................**6** D3
Mahabaleshwara Temple.........**7** B3
Venkataraman Temple............**8** D3

SLEEPING
Hotel Gokarna International.......**9** D1

Mama Shanta........................**10** B3
Nimmu House........................**11** B3
Shanti Nivas.........................**12** B3
Shastri's Guest House............**13** D2
Vaibhav Niwas......................**14** D1

EATING
Mahalaxmi Restaurant............**15** B3
Pai Hotel..............................**16** D3
Pai Restaurant.......................**17** D2
Prema Restaurant..................**18** A3

TRANSPORT
Bus Stand.............................**19** C1

To Gokarna
Rd Train
Station (9km);
Kumta Train
Station (25km);
Ankola Train
Station (25km)

Main St

ARABIAN

SEA

Temple
Chariots

Car St

Gokarna
Beach

To Kudle Beach (2km);
Beach Accomodation (2km);
Om Beach (4km);
Namaste Café (4km);
Half-Moon Beach (6km);
Paradise Beach (10km)

played in rescuing the lingam. At the other end of the street is the **Venkataraman Temple**, and 100m south of this is **Koorti Teertha**, the large temple tank (reservoir), where locals, pilgrims and immaculately dressed Brahmins perform their ablutions next to dhobi-wallahs on the ghats.

BEACHES

Travellers have been drifting into Gokarna for some time now, lured by stories of beaches that rival anything Goa has to offer. Gokarna village has its own beach, but the best sands are via a footpath that begins on the southern side of the Ganapati Temple and heads southward (if you reach the bathing tank – or find yourself clawing up rocks – you're on the wrong path).

Twenty minutes on the path will bring you to the top of a barren headland with expansive sea views. On the southern side is **Kudle Beach** (kood-lee), the first in a series of four perfect beaches, backed by the foothills of the Western Ghats. Several shops on Kudle Beach sell basic snacks and drinks and offer basic accommodation.

At the southern end of Kudle a track climbs over the next headland, and a further 20-minute walk brings you to **Om Beach**, with a handful of chai shops and shacks. A dusty road provides vehicle access to Om (Rs 200 in an autorickshaw), but it's generally deserted except on holidays and some weekends, when day-trippers come by the car load. By the time you arrive, however, the new mega resort may have disrupted Om's *shanti* (inner peace and tranquillity). To the south, the more isolated **Half-Moon Beach** and **Paradise Beach** are a 30-minute and one-hour walk, respectively.

Depending on the crowds, boats run from Gokarna Beach (look for the fishermen) to Kudle (Rs 100) and Om (Rs 200).

Don't walk between the beaches and Gokarna after dark, and don't walk alone at any time – it's easy to get lost and muggings have occurred. For a wee fee, most lodges will safely stow valuables and baggage.

Sleeping

The choice here is generally between a rudimentary shack on the beach or a basic but more comfortable room in town. The advantages of being on the beach are obvious and, since it's a fair hike from town, you're pretty much left to your own devices.

BEACHES
December to January is high season on the beaches. Most places provide at least a bedroll, but you'll want to bring your own sleeping sheet or sleeping bag. Padlocks are provided and huts are secure. Communal washing and toilet facilities are simple.

Spanish Place (☎ 257311; huts Rs 70, d Rs 350; 🖳) This chilled spot in the middle stretch of Kudle Beach has palm-thatch huts, and two lovely garden rooms with private shower but common 'toilet' (ie the bushes).

Namaste (☎ 257141; huts Rs 125, s with shared bathroom Rs 150, deluxe hut with private bathroom Rs 300; 🖳) Namaste, on Om, is where the action's at during the high season. It's spotless and has a spacious restaurant/hangout that some travellers can muster no reason to leave.

Om Beach Resort (www.ombeachresort.com; s/d from US$55/80; ✺) Many Om Beach regulars aren't happy about this new resort, which will likely have opened by the time you arrive. As resorts go, though, you couldn't find a better location. Accommodation is in cottages set back from the beach, and the focus is on Ayurvedic treatments.

Both Kudle and Om Beaches have several other options in the form of huts and rooms – shop around. Huts and basic restaurants open up on Half-Moon and Paradise Beaches in the high season.

GOKARNA
Most guesthouses in town offer discounts in the low season.

Shastri's Guest House (☎ 256220; dr_murti@ rediffmail.com; Main St; r Rs 150) Shastri's has claustrophobic singles, but the doubles out back are big and sunny; some have balconies and palm-tree views, and all have a comforting 1950s-hospital vibe.

Vaibhav Nivas (☎ 256714; s/d/tr Rs 100/120/300, r without bathroom Rs 100) This cosy, recently renovated place, off Main St, is bustling in the high season and placid in the off months. It has snug rooms and a Western restaurant.

Nimmu House (☎ 256730; nimmuhouse@sanchar net.in; r with/without bathroom from Rs 200/90, r with balcony Rs 700; 🖳) Simple rooms set in relaxed green grounds near the beach.

Hotel Gokarna International (☎ 256622; fax 256848; Main St; s/d/tr from Rs 200/230/300; ✺) It has more class than character, but it's well organised and modern and all rooms have balcony and TV.

Several kind-hearted families around town have begun to rent out rooms. Our favourites:

Mama Shanta (☎ 256213; r with/without bathroom Rs 150/100; ✹ Oct-May) Tender loving care, just past Nimmu House.

Shanti Nivas (☎ 256983; s/d without bathroom Rs 100/ 150) Cosy, colourful rooms tucked away in the woods near the beach; bear right off the Kudle Beach path.

Eating
The chai shops on all of the beaches rustle up basic snacks and meals.

Prema Restaurant (meals Rs 20-60; ✹ 8am-9pm) Beachfront Prema has excellent masala dosas (paper-thin lentil-flour pancakes stuffed with spiced vegetables; Rs 10) and thalis (traditional all-you-can-eat meals; Rs 30) along with traveller treats: coffee milkshakes, and yogurt with muesli and honey.

Mahalaxmi Restaurant (meals Rs 30-70; ✹ 8am-10pm) Its menu was heavily inspired by Prema, but the spaghetti and tomato sauce – and the location, near the beach – are quite good.

Pai Restaurant (Main St; mains Rs 20-40; ✹ 6.30am-9.30pm) Halfway along Main St, Pai is a friendly place with inspired vegetarian 'meals'.

Pai Hotel (Car St; mains Rs 15-30; ✹ 6am-9.30pm) Around the corner on Car St, Pai Hotel is unrelated to the other Pai but also happens to churn out tasty thalis (Rs 15).

Namaste Café (meals Rs 30-80; ✹ 7am-11pm) Om Beach's 'It' café serves OK Western standbys – pizzas and burgers – and some Israeli specials.

Getting There & Away
BUS
From Gokarna's **bus stand** (☎ 256233), one bus daily heads to Margao (Rs 50, four hours) or you can go to Karwar (Rs 22, 1½ hours, three daily), which has connections to Goa. Direct buses run to Hubli (Rs 56, four hours, five daily), and a daily 6.45am bus goes direct to Mangalore (Rs 95, six hours), continuing on to Mysore (Rs 120, 14 hours). If you miss this, get an hourly local

bus to Kumta, 25km south, then one of the frequent Mangalore buses from there. Daily deluxe buses set off to Hospet for Hampi (Rs 120, 10 hours) at 7am and 2.30pm, and to Bangalore (Rs 298, 12 hours) at 7pm.

TRAIN

The Konkan Railway is the best way to reach Goa and Mangalore, among other destinations, though only two slow passenger trains stop at **Gokarna Rd train station** (☎ 279487), 9km from town. A 10.45am train heads to Margao (Rs 24, two hours); another leaves at 6.30pm (Rs 55, 1½ hours). For Mangalore (Rs 45, five hours), trains depart from Gokarna Rd at 4pm and 1.45am. Trains head to Kochi (sleeper Rs 281, 15 hours) on Saturday, Sunday and Tuesday; you must buy a sleeper ticket and upgrade, if you like, upon boarding. Many of the hotels and small travel agencies on Main St can book tickets.

Autorickshaws charge Rs 100 to take you out to the station, but buses go hourly (Rs 6) and to meet arriving passenger trains.

Several express trains stop at Ankola and Kumta stations, both about 25km from Gokarna and accessible by local bus.

JOG FALLS

☎ 08186 / pop 12,570

Jog Falls are the highest waterfalls in India, though the excitement of them is not in proportion to their height; the Linganamakki Dam further up the Sharavati River limits the water flow. The longest of the four falls is the Raja, which drops 293m.

The lush, spectacular countryside here, though, is perfect for gentle hiking. The bottom of the falls is accessible via the 1200-plus steps that start close to the bus stand; beware of leeches during the wet season.

Jog Falls' friendly **tourist office** (☎ 244747; 10am-5pm Mon-Sat) is located close to the bus stand.

Jog Falls has two inspection bungalows, usually reserved for VIPs. The **British Bungalow** (r Rs 60) sits atop the falls about 3km from the bus stand. Reserve with the **Siddapur Public Works Department** (☎ 08389-322103). The **PW Guesthouse** (per person Rs 250), across from the Karnataka State Tourism Development Corporation (KSTDC) hotel, is pretty fancy.

The **KSTDC Hotel Mayura Gerusoppa** (☎ 244747; s/d Rs 200/300), about 150m from the car park, has enormous, musty rooms.

Stalls near the bus stand serve omelettes, thalis, noodles and rice dishes, plus hot and cold drinks. KSTDC's mediocre **restaurant** (meals Rs 20-40) is just next door.

Jog Falls has buses roughly every hour to Shimoga (Rs 45, three hours) and to Sagar (Rs 12, one hour), two a day to Siddapur (Rs 10, one hour) and three daily to Karwar via Kumta (Rs 38, three hours), where you can change for Gokarna (Rs 12, 45 minutes). There are two painfully slow daily buses to/from Mangalore (Rs 112, ten hours); you may be better off going via Shimoga.

The nearest train station is at Talguppa, between Sagar and Jog Falls. There's only one train daily, at 6pm, to Shimoga (Rs 28, three hours), on a romantically slow and scenic narrow-gauge line.

HAMPI

☎ 08394

The fascinating ruins of Vijayanagar, near Hampi, are set in a sublime boulder-strewn landscape that resonates with a magical air. Once the capital of one of the largest Hindu empires, Vijayanagar was founded by Telugu princes in 1336 and hit the peak of its power in the 16th century. With a population of about 500,000, the empire controlled the regional spice trade and cotton industry, and the city, surrounded by seven lines of fortification, covered 43 sq km. The bazaars were centres of commerce brimming with precious stones and merchants from far away. The empire came to an end in 1565 when the city was ransacked by a confederacy of Deccan sultanates.

The region is much less dramatic these days – in fact, time seems to stand still in the bubble of Hampi, and you can spend a surprisingly large amount of time just boulder-watching. It's a thriving centre for travellers, the kind of place to connect and reconnect with people, and visitors tend to stay a while. It is, however, possible to see the main sites in a day or two – by bicycle, moped or, if you start early, on foot – but this goes against the laid-back grain of Hampi. Signposting in some parts of the site is inadequate, but you can't really get lost.

Orientation

Hampi Bazaar and the village of Kamalapuram to the south are the two main points of entry to the ruins. The KSTDC hotel and

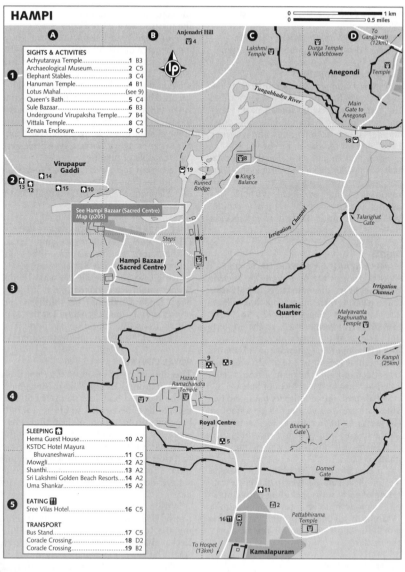

HAMPI

SIGHTS & ACTIVITIES	
Achyutaraya Temple	1 B3
Archaeological Museum	2 C5
Elephant Stables	3 C4
Hanuman Temple	4 B1
Lotus Mahal	(see 9)
Queen's Bath	5 C4
Sule Bazaar	6 B3
Underground Virupaksha Temple	7 B4
Vittala Temple	8 C2
Zenana Enclosure	9 C4

SLEEPING	
Hema Guest House	10 A2
KSTDC Hotel Mayura Bhuvaneshwari	11 C5
Mowgli	12 A2
Shanthi	13 A2
Sri Lakshmi Golden Beach Resorts	14 A2
Uma Shankar	15 A2

EATING	
Sree Vilas Hotel	16 C5

TRANSPORT	
Bus Stand	17 C5
Coracle Crossing	18 D2
Coracle Crossing	19 B2

the museum are in Kamalapuram. The main travellers' scene is Hampi Bazaar, a village crammed with budget lodges, shops and restaurants, dominated by the Virupaksha Temple. The ruins themselves can be divided into two main areas: the Sacred Centre, around Hampi Bazaar; and the Royal Centre, to the south around Kamalapuram.

Information

Aspiration Stores (Map p205; ⏰ 10am-1pm & 4-8pm) For books on the area, including *Hampi*, by John M Fritz and George Michell, which is a good architectural study.

Canara Bank (Map p205; ☎ 241243; ⏰ 11am-2pm Mon, Tue & Thu-Sat) Changes travellers cheques and gives cash advances on credit cards. The numerous authorised moneychangers around offer slightly worse rates.

Sree Rama Cyber Cafe (Map p205; per hr Rs 60; ☽7am-11pm)
Tourist Office (Map p205; ☎ 241339; ☽ 10am-5.30pm Sat-Thu) Can arrange guides for Rs 500 per day.

Dangers & Annoyances

Hampi is a safe place, generally free of any aggression. That said, don't wander around the ruins at sunrise or sunset, particularly on the climb up Matanga Hill, and don't wander alone, as muggings and violence have been on the rise in recent years.

Foreigners should register at the **police station** (Map p205) inside the Virupaksha Temple upon arrival. This is a simple process, involving logging your details in a book – it's as routine as a hotel check-in. The station, which is just inside the temple entrance on the right, has a photo gallery of crooks.

Sights
HAMPI BAZAAR & VIRUPAKSHA TEMPLE
Now that locals are occupying the ancient buildings lining the main street, **Hampi Bazaar** (Map p205) is once more a bustling village. The **Virupaksha Temple** (Map p205; ☎ 2441241; admission Rs 2; ☽ sunrise-sunset), at the western end, is one of the city's oldest structures. The main *gopuram* (gateway tower), almost 50m high, was built in 1442, with a smaller one added in 1510. The main shrine is dedicated to Virupaksha, a form of Shiva.

If Lakshmi, the temple elephant, and her attendant are around, you can get a smooch (blessing) from her for a Rs 1 coin. The adorable Lakshmi gets her morning bath at 7.30am, just down the way by the river ghats.

To the south, overlooking Virupaksha Temple, **Hemakuta Hill** (Map p205) has a scattering of early ruins including Jain temples and a monolithic sculpture of Narasimha (Vishnu in his man-lion incarnation). It's worth the short walk up for the view over the bazaar.

VITTALA TEMPLE
From the eastern end of Hampi Bazaar a track, navigable only on foot, leads left to the **Vittala Temple** (Map p203; admission US$5; ☽ 8am-6pm), about 2km away. The undisputed highlight of the Hampi ruins, the 16th-century Vittala Temple is a Unesco World Heritage site. It's in a good state of preservation, though purists may gasp at

the cement-block columns erected to keep the main structure from collapsing.

Work likely started on the temple during the reign of Krishnadevaraya (1509–29) and, despite the fact that it was never finished or consecrated, the temple's incredible sculptural work is the pinnacle of Vijayanagar art. The outer 'musical' pillars reverberate when tapped, although this is discouraged to avoid further damage. There's an ornate stone chariot in the temple courtyard containing an image of Garuda. Its wheels were once capable of turning.

Keep your temple entry ticket for same-day admission into the Zenana Enclosure and Elephant Stables in the Royal Centre (below).

SULE BAZAAR & ACHYUTARAYA TEMPLE
Halfway along the path from Hampi Bazaar to the Vittala Temple, a track to the right leads to deserted **Sule Bazaar** (Map p203), which gives you some idea of what Hampi Bazaar might have looked like if it hadn't been repopulated. At the southern end of this area is the **Achyutaraya Temple** (Map p203). Its isolated location at the foot of Matanga Hill makes it quietly atmospheric.

ROYAL CENTRE
This area of Hampi is quite different from the area around Hampi Bazaar, since most of the rounded boulders that once littered the site have been used to create a mind-boggling proliferation of beautiful stone walls. It's a 2km walk on a track from the Achyutaraya Temple, but most people get to it from the Hampi Bazaar–Kamalapuram road. This area is easily explored by bicycle since a decent dirt road runs through its heart.

Within various enclosures here are the rest of Hampi's major attractions, including the **Lotus Mahal** (Map p203) and the **Elephant Stables** (Map p203; admission US$5; ☽ 8am-6pm). The former is a delicately designed pavilion in a walled compound known as the **Zenana Enclosure**. It's an amazing synthesis of Hindu and Islamic styles and gets its name from the lotus bud carved in the centre of the domed and vaulted ceiling. The Elephant Stables is a grand building with domed chambers, where the state elephants once resided. Your entry ticket to the Zenana Enclosure and stables is valid for same-day admission to the Vittala Temple.

Further south, you'll find various temples and elaborate waterworks, including the **Underground Virupaksha Temple** (Map p203) and the impressive **Queen's Bath** (Map p203), which is deceptively plain on the outside.

ARCHAEOLOGICAL MUSEUM
The **archaeological museum** (Map p203; ☎ 241561; Kamalapuram; admission Rs 5; ⏰ 10am-5pm Sat-Thu) has well-displayed collections of sculptures from local ruins, Neolithic tools, 16th-century weaponry and a large floor model of the Vijayanagar ruins.

ANEGONDI
North of the river is the ruined fortified stronghold of **Anegondi** (Map p203); much of the old defensive wall is intact. The unruffled area, amid paddy fields, makes for a good afternoon's ambling. There are numerous small temples worth a visit, including the whitewashed **Hanuman Temple** (Map p203; ⏰ sunrise-sunset), which is perched on top of a rocky hill. The climb is a fine undertaking, but not in the heat of the day. Fittingly, lots of cheeky monkeys roam about, so don't walk up wearing bananas.

To get to Anegondi take a coracle (small boat made of waterproof hides) across the river (Rs 20) and follow the dusty road north.

Sleeping
Listed rates are for the high season, but prices shoot up by 50% or more during the manic fortnight around New Year's Day, and drop just as dramatically in the low season (from April to September). Checkout is usually around 10am. Aside from the KSTDC hotel, rooms are quaint but basic; if you want a cushy abode, stay in Hospet.

HAMPI BAZAAR
Dozens of cute, basic lodges freckle the alleys leading off the main road.

Rama Guest House (Map p205; ☎ 241962; s Rs 250, d Rs 300-350) The kind owners here are very proud of their four rooms, recently redone with cheerful, garish floor tiles and new

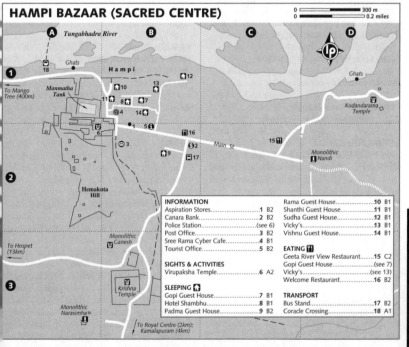

HAMPI BAZAAR (SACRED CENTRE)

bathrooms. Its rooftop restaurant does excellent food and is a nice place for a drink.

Shanthi Guest House (Map p205; ☎ 241568; s/d without bathroom Rs 180/250) The Shanthi is a Hampi tradition, with a peaceful courtyard, bike rental (Rs 30), morning bakery delivery and a small shop that runs on the honour system.

Vicky's (Map p205; ☎ 241694; vikkyhampi@yahoo .co.in; r Rs 400; 🖳) The swing chair on the front porch is as comfy as Vicky's seven brightly painted rooms. The rooftop restaurant (opposite) has better views than most.

Hotel Shambhu (Map p205; ☎ 241383; angadi paramesh1@hotmail.com; r Rs 300) The rooms at this little guesthouse are small but sweet. Plus, they have lavender walls and are named after deities. The hallway has plants and an opalescent chandelier, and the rooftop restaurant isn't bad.

Gopi Guest House (Map p205; ☎ 241695; gopi guesthouse93@yahoo.co.in; s/d Rs 300/400) Shiny new tiles and fresh paint make the rooms at Gopi sparkle. Comes with requisite roof garden and restaurant (opposite).

Padma Guest House (Map p205; ☎ 241331; hampi padma2002@yahoo.co.in; d Rs 600-800, s/d without bathroom Rs 200/350) Padma's rooms are clean and cosy and feel like part of the family home. There's also a rooftop restaurant.

Other decent options:

Sudha Guest House (Map p205; ☎ 441451; s without bathroom Rs 150, d with bathroom Rs 250) Could be a lot cleaner, but there's a good family vibe and some doubles fit three.

Vishnu Guest House (Map p205; ☎ 441415; r from Rs 250) A family place exuding friendliness.

VIRUPAPUR GADDI

The most laid-back scene is just north of the river in tranquil Virupapur Gaddi, and during the high season this is the place to be for parties after hours. Many travellers, though, find the isolation a little unnerving, and you should keep your wits about you after dark. To reach Virupapur Gaddi, take a coracle (Rs 5) from the ghats north of Virupaksha Temple. We've received complaints from readers about the coracle guys: be sure to return by nightfall or you may find yourself feeling uncomfortable and/or paying 20 times the standard fare. In the monsoon season, when the river is running high, boats may not be able to cross.

Shanthi (Map p203; ☎ 08533-287038; r without bathroom Rs 150, bungalows Rs 300) Shanthi's bungalows have paddy-field, river and sunset views and front porches with couch swings, while the restaurant, which does exceptional thalis (Rs 30) and pizzas (Rs 70 to 85), is in a quasi-treehouse.

Mowgli (Map p203; ☎ 08533-287033; mowgli96@ hotmail.com; r without bathroom Rs 100, bungalows with bathroom Rs 350) Lush, shady gardens shelter hammocks and thatch-roof bungalows, some with sunset views.

Hema Guest House (Map p203; chemahome@yahoo .com; dm/bungalows Rs 50/300) This compound is highly advanced. Its little houses are shiny and new, with maximum-security screening, and the restaurant is in a lovely wooden belvedere with the best views in town.

Uma Shankar (Map p203; ☎ 08533-287067; r Rs d 200-450) This place is a little jewel run by a friendly, hard-working woman. The rooms, set amid pretty gardens, were recently renovated.

Sri Lakshmi Golden Beach Resorts (Map p203; ☎ 08533-287008; d Rs 150-350; 🏊) The important thing here is the pool – a big one – that non-guests can use for Rs 50 per hour. Rooms are quite nice, as well, especially the Rs 200 circular cottages, which have circular beds.

KAMALAPURAM

KSTDC Hotel Mayura Bhuvaneshwari (Map p203; ☎ 241574; s with/without AC Rs 400/250, d Rs 450/300; ❄) On very quiet grounds, this place is modern and well maintained, and all rooms have solar-heated shower. There's a massage and yoga centre, and a bar-restaurant.

Eating

Most restaurants here serve vegetarian Indian and Western food catering to the traveller palate, but Hampi is not renowned for its cuisine. Due to Hampi's religious significance, alcohol is not permitted – though travellers have been known to (discreetly) bend the rules. For a respectable, legal drink, head for the bar at Hotel Mayura Bhuvaneshwari (above) in Kamalapuram.

Mango Tree (mains Rs 25-60; 🕑 7am-10pm) Even the walk out here is delicious: 400m west of the ghats down a path through a banana plantation. The thalis (Rs 30) are a treat, and the straw mats outside are ideal spots to laze with a book, while a swing hangs contentedly from the eponymous mango tree.

Geeta River View Restaurant (Map p205; mains Rs 25-45; ⏰ 7am-10pm) This quiet outdoor spot on the river has great food; try the *pakodas* (rice-flour fritters, Rs 20) or the subtle cashew veg curry (Rs 35). The restaurant's at the start of the path leading to Vittala Temple.

Welcome Restaurant (Map p205; mains Rs 20-45; ⏰ 7am-11pm) Along with offering all the usual suspects, the humble little Welcome makes a worthy attempt at *kim chi* (Korean relish, Rs 10)! The woman who runs the place is an old soul.

Kamalapuram has a few simple eateries, such as **Sree Vilas Hotel** (Map p203; meals Rs 16; ⏰ 5am-8.30pm), opposite the bus stand.

Several of Hampi's lodges have good rooftop joints:

Gopi Guest House (Map p205; mains Rs 25-40; ⏰ 6.30am-11pm) Serving espresso with milk (Rs 50) and 'Japanese' food – tomato don (Rs 30), for example – among lots of plants.

Vicky's (Map p205; mains Rs 20-45; ⏰ 6.30am-10.30pm) Really good food, amazing views, purple tables and a family atmosphere.

Getting There & Away

While some buses from Goa and Bangalore will drop you in Hampi Bazaar, you have to go to Hospet to catch most buses out. The first bus from Hospet (Rs 5, 30 minutes, half-hourly) is at 6.30am; the last one back leaves Hampi Bazaar at 8.30pm. An autorickshaw costs Rs 80.

Karnataka State Road Transport Corporation (KSRTC) has a daily Rajahamsa bus service between Hampi and Bangalore (Rs 204, nine hours) leaving Hampi at 8pm. The overnight sleeper bus to/from Goa (Rs 400), which runs during the high season, is a popular option – but don't expect a deep sleep. Solo travellers have to share a bunk. Numerous travel agents in Hampi Bazaar are eager to book onward bus, train and plane tickets or arrange a car and driver. See p208 for bus and train information for Hospet.

Getting Around

Once you've seen the Vittala and Achyutaraya Temples and Sule Bazaar, exploring the rest of the ruins by bicycle is the thing to do. There are key monuments haphazardly signposted along the road from Hampi Bazaar to Kamalapuram. Bicycles cost Rs 30 to 40 per day in Hampi Bazaar. Mopeds can be

hired for around Rs 200 plus petrol. You can take your bicycle (extra Rs 5), or motorcycle (extra Rs 10), across the river on a coracle.

Walking is the only way to see all the nooks and crannies, but expect to cover at least 7km just to see the major ruins. Autorickshaws and taxis are available for sightseeing, and will drop you as close to each of the major ruins as they can. A five-hour autorickshaw tour costs Rs 250.

Organised tours depart from Hospet; see below for details.

HOSPET
☎ 08394 / pop 163,284

Hospet is an active regional centre with none of Hampi's atmosphere, but you'll certainly swing through here to make transport connections. It has some good hotels, but otherwise there's no reason to linger. You might want to check out Tungabhadra Dam; it's 590m long and 49m high.

Information

College Rd has a few Internet joints with sluggish connections for Rs 40 per hour. The cloakroom at Hospet's bus stand holds bags for Rs 10 per day.

Andhra Bank (☎ 228249; ⏰ 10.30am-4.30pm Mon-Fri, 10.30am-1.30pm Sat) Cash advances on Visa and MasterCard with a 1% commission. It's next to Hanuman Temple, off College Rd.

Hotel Malligi (☎ 228101; Jabunatha Rd) Changes travellers cheques.

KSTDC tourist office (☎ 228537; Shanbhag Circle; ⏰ 7.30am-8.30pm)

State Bank of India (☎ 228576; Station Rd; ⏰ 10.30am-4pm Mon-Fri) Changes currency; the ATM here sometimes accepts MasterCard.

Tours

KSTDC's Hampi tour (Rs 110) runs daily in the high season and on demand the rest of the year; it departs from the tourist office at 9.30am and returns at 5.30pm. It's in the lap of the gods whether you get an informative guide or one who rushes through the ruins. Book ahead in high season, but just show up other times as the tours won't run with fewer than 10 people.

Sleeping & Eating

Hotel Priyadarshini (☎ 228838; priyainnhampi@india .com; Station Rd; standard s/d without AC Rs 400/600, deluxe d without AC Rs 400/950, s/d with AC Rs 1300/1350; 🅿)

Between the bus and train stations is this classy place with fresh, tidy rooms, all with balcony. Its nonveg restaurant (mains Rs 35 to 70), among trees and with sugarcane views, is worth a visit.

Hotel Malligi (☎ 228101; malligihome@hotmail .com; Jabunatha Rd; r Rs 300-2000; 🍴 🖳 🔊) Rooms vary widely in the Malligi compound, from OK cheaper old-wing rooms to stylish modern rooms in the new wing. It has Internet facilities, various restaurants and a pool (Rs 25 for nonguests).

Waves (mains Rs 45-80; 🕑 6am-11pm) The delicious veg and nonveg offerings at Hotel Malligi's multicuisine restaurant make it a great place to feast.

Udupi Sri Krishna Bhavan (meals Rs 15-40; 🕑 6am-11pm) Opposite the bus stand, this clean, no-nonsense spot dishes out North and South Indian fare.

Getting There & Away

BUS

Hospet's **bus stand** (☎ 228802) is unusually chaotic. Buses to Hampi depart from bay No 10 every half-hour from around 6.30am (Rs 5, 30 minutes), with the last bus returning to Hospet at 8.30pm. Several express buses run to Bangalore (ordinary/deluxe Rs 123/197, nine hours) in morning and evening batches, and three overnight buses head to Panaji via Margao in Goa (Rs 150, 11 hours). Two buses a day go to Badami (Rs 75, six hours), or catch one of the many buses to Gadag (Rs 42, 2½ hours) and transfer. There are frequent buses to Hubli (Rs 58, 4½ hours) and Bijapur (Rs 90, six hours), four overnight services to Hyderabad (ordinary/deluxe

---

HOSPET ON FIRE

Hospet comes alive during the Shiite Muslim festival Muharram (February or March), which commemorates the martyrdom of Mohammed's grandson, Imam Hussain. Fire-walkers walk barefoot across the red-hot embers of a fire that's been burning all day and night. Virtually the whole town turns out to watch or take part and the excitement reaches fever pitch around midnight. The daytime preliminaries appear to be a bewildering hybrid of Muslim and Hindu ritual, and those who are scheduled to do the fire-walking must be physically restrained from losing control just before the event.

Rs 160/229, 10 hours) and one direct bus, at 9am, to Gokarna (Rs 150, 10 hours). For Mangalore or Hassan, take one of the many morning buses to Shimoga and change there.

TRAIN

Hospet's **train station** (☎ 228360) is a 20-minute walk or Rs 10 autorickshaw ride from the centre of town. The daily *Hampi Express* heads to Hubli at 7.45am (2nd class Rs 47, 3½ hours) and Bangalore at 8pm (sleeper/two-tier AC Rs 212/881, 10 hours), or go to Guntakal (Rs 42, 2½ hours) and catch a Bangalore-bound express there. Every Tuesday, Friday and Saturday, an 8.45am express heads to Vasco da Gama in Goa (sleeper/two-tier AC Rs 169/690, 9½ hours).

To get to Badami, catch a Hubli train to Gadag and change there.

Directory

CONTENTS

ACCOMMODATION

Most hotel prices are based on high, middle and low seasons. The high season covers the period from mid-December to late January (with the exception of the peak period between 22 December and 5 January), the middle seasons are from October to mid-December and February to June, and the low season is from July to September. Unless otherwise stated, prices in this book are for the high season. Outside of this period, count on discounts of 25% in the middle season and up to 60% in the low season.

If you turn up at a popular beach during peak season you may end up homeless or paying more than you want to; conversely, in low season not all of the options reviewed in this book will be open. If you arrive early in the season there should be a healthy range of available rooms, giving you scope to shop around and bargain. The rule of thumb is that the longer you stay the cheaper it gets. As peak season draws near, discuss the issue of pricing. Don't assume it will remain the same; some prices suddenly skyrocket over Christmas, even if you've booked ahead. Try not to feel too hard done by during this period; remember that not all hoteliers are greedy, and for many the money they make in this period is what their families must live off when there is not tourism at all.

Accommodation in this book is categorised as budget (Rs 100 to 500), midrange (Rs 500 to 1500) and top end (Rs 1500 or more), though the lines are sometimes blurred by places that offer the whole range or arbitrarily swing between categories. Prices vary according to demand, location (ie beachfront or out the back), duration of stay and the whims of management.

Bear in mind there's a luxury tax of 8% on rooms over Rs 500 and 12% for those over around Rs 800. For most of the budget places, the prices quoted include this tax, but at midrange and top-end hotels you can expect tax to be added to the bill. Some hotels add a further 10% 'service tax'. When you're negotiating prices, clarify whether tax is included or not.

Budget accommodation can be anything from a basic room with a shared cold-water bathroom to a bamboo hut right on the beach.

Midrange accommodation varies enormously. Basically you can expect a hotel with a fan, perhaps a TV and sometimes even a swimming pool.

Top-end hotels vary from modern boutique affairs to classic heritage hotels or gen-eric beachside resorts replete with casinos, shopping arcades and swimming pools that rival the size of the Arabian Sea.

Accommodation is cheaper in towns like Panaji, Mapusa and Margao, which see fewer tourists. Unless stated otherwise, rooms reviewed have a bathroom.

PRACTICALITIES

- The electric current in Goa is 230V to 240V AC, 50 cycles. Sockets are of a three round-pin variety, similar (but not identical) to European sockets. There are two sizes; one large, one small (the latter is more common). European round-pin plugs will go into the smaller sockets, but the fit can be loose. Universal adaptors are widely available at electrical shops in Goa for around Rs 20. Electricity in Goa can be unpredictable – save your work regularly if you're using a computer, and use a voltage regulator for sensitive electrical equipment.

- Although India is officially metricated, imperial weights and measures are still sometimes used. You may hear the term lakh (one lakh equals 100,000) and crore (one crore equals 10 million) referring to rupees, cars, apples or whatever.

- Goa has three English-language dailies: the *Herald,* the *Navhind Times* and the *Gomantak Times*. Also check out the interesting monthly magazine *Goa Today*. Many foreign newspapers and magazines are available in large hotels and some newsagencies, though they're expensive.

- The government TV broadcaster is Doordarshan. Satellite TV, which has BBC, CNN, Star Movies, MTV and HBO, is more widely watched.

- All India Radio (AIR) transmits local and international news. There are private broadcasters In addition to this government-controlled station.

One final warning must be issued with respect to checkout times. Checkout time can vary enormously throughout Goa; some can be as early as 8am and others can be as casual as whenever. Make sure you know what time you're expected to leave – some hotels will demand an extra 50% if you're late.

Bamboo Huts

The quintessential Goan experience is the bamboo hut, known locally as cocohuts. These were originally constructed on stilts, using surrounding coconut trees as support, but nowadays bamboo huts have moved far beyond their primitive genesis. It's not hard to tell a budget hut from a more expensive one; the better it looks, the more it costs. Palolem is a good example of the range of huts available; the coast is still predominantly lined with flimsy huts on stilts, but between them are an increasing number of larger and more stylish versions; some huts are even double-storey affairs with spacious hot-water bathrooms. There are also more-linear but often roughly slapped together wooden huts constructed of plywood. The décor in these kit-home jobs often accounts for price variations – a coat of paint and a few decorative cushions on a makeshift balcony can mean a difference of a few hundred rupees. A real downside to the cocohut experience can be one's proximity to the neighbours, whose nocturnal noises are often no more than a foot of air and flimsy sheet of bamboo away.

Camping

Given the range of budget accommodation, few people travel with their own tent. An increasing phenomenon though (and a far cry from the triangular tents of yesteryear) is the organised camp of tepee-style tents, such as Bai Tereza Beach Camp (p120) at Coco Beach, where the guests gather around a bonfire at night. Places such as Yoga Magic (p142) in Anjuna also have Rajasthani-style tents that have a strong eco-friendly ethos, while other hotels, such as Palolem Beach Resort (p193), set up the occasional tent around their premises to squeeze a few more people in.

Guesthouses

The most common form of budget accommodation is the guesthouse. These can be a dedicated building, a building out the back of a family home, or even rooms in the family home. The general rule is that the closer your sleeping quarters are to the host family, the cheaper the room. The diversity of choices and experiences is enormous. Staying in a family-run guesthouse can be a wonderful way to get an insight into Goa, and can sometimes be more comfortable and economical than staying in a cocohut.

Hotels

There is a range of hotels in Goa; some are soulless buildings with a host of amenities but all the character of a shopping mall, while others dub themselves resorts in light of their proximity to the ocean and their pool. Either way, a hotel in Goa is much the same as a hotel anywhere else in the world: an organised establishment with a reception, room service, TVs, private bathrooms and sometimes minibars.

Rental Accommodation

Renting houses by the month or longer is not an uncommon thing to do in Goa, particularly given the increasing number of Westerners who live in Goa for six or so months of every year. There are real-estate agents who can help, but it's easy enough to find your own home without them. Ask around, check out notice boards at foreigner hot spots, or simply select the area you would like to live and take note of phone numbers on the many 'For Rent' signs, some of which even specify 'Foreigners Only'. Obviously, the closer you are to the coast, the more you will pay. There are a couple of websites worth checking out:

Goa Heritage Action Group (www.goaheritage.org) As part of its work to protect Goa's heritage homes, the Goa Heritage Action group facilitates their sale and purchase. Click on the Heritage Mall link.

Goa Holiday Homes (www.goaholidayhomes.com) A good general website to start looking for places in a range of prices.

Resorts

There is no shortage of resorts in Goa. Some are more like miniresorts, with facilities are spread over a smaller area than the larger resorts. These are often oriented towards the domestic market, and can be good value; a day bed by the swimming pool by the ocean is indulgent even if you're paying rupees rather than US dollars. At the other end of the spectrum are the mass-scale resort complexes that have their own golf course and casino, and are too big to cover on foot.

H IS FOR HOUSE

Throughout this book and Goa, the abbreviation 'H' is used to denote a house or small building in addresses.

BOOK ACCOMMODATION ONLINE

For more accommodation reviews and recommendations by Lonely Planet authors, check out the online booking service at www.lonelyplanet.com. You'll find the true insider lowdown on the best places to stay. Reviews are thorough and independent. Best of all, you can book online.

ACTIVITIES

The number of activities on offer in Goa has steadily increased over the years. Some of the busier beach towns are flooded with courses and treatments in everything from art appreciation and Ayurveda to shiatsu and sitar playing. Keep your eyes on cluttered notice boards to see what's going on.

Ayurveda

Ayurveda is an ancient method of holistic healing deriving from Kerala. The most popular Ayurvedic treatment among tourists is the ubiquitous oil massage. See p129 for more about Ayurveda.

Your Ayurvedic experience in Goa can be a hit and miss affair. There are some extremely established operators giving very professional treatments, whereas other operators have set up shop with no more than a vague idea and a vat of oil.

Some of the options in Goa:

Ayurvedic Natural Health Centre (ANHC; ☎ 0832-2409275, 0832-2409036; www.healthandayurveda.com) An accredited centre in Baga (p128) with lots of information. Some massages can be better than others here.

Kailas Kerala Traditional Ayurveda Centre (☎ 0832-2643472; www.bhaktikutir.com; 296 Palolem, Patnem) Based in Bhakti Kutir at Patnem Beach (p192).

Palolem Ayurvedic Centre (☎ 0832-22640193; palolemayurvediccentre@yahoo.co.in) This Ayurvedic centre in Palolem (p192) is recommended.

Pousada Tauma (☎ 2279061; www.pousada-tauma .com) An upmarket option in Calangute (p128).

Bird-Watching

It seems that the beach distracts people from the birds; it's a little known fact that Goa is actually a prime bird-watching area. One of the best places to do it is Dr Salim Ali Bird Sanctuary (p100).

Southern Birdwing (☎ 0832-2402957; www.southernbirdwing.com) is a reputable organisation that organises bird-watching excursions.

Diving

Although Goa is not internationally renowned as a diving destination, its waters are regarded as the third-best spot for diving in India (after the Andaman and Lakshadweep Islands). You can also make dive excursions to sites off the Karnataka coast.

The shallow waters off the coast are ideal for less experienced divers; typical dives are at depths of 10m to 12m, with abundant marine life to be seen. The only problem is that visibility is unpredictable; on some days it's 30m, on others it's closer to 2m. The dive season is from November to April.

Marine life you are likely to encounter include tropical fish such as angelfish, parrotfish, wrasses, lionfish, sharks (reef tip and shovel-nosed among others), stingrays, gropers, snapper, damselfish, barracuda, sea cucumbers and turtles. The highlights of diving in Goa are the wreck dives – there are literally hundreds of wrecks along Goa's coastline, including Portuguese and Spanish galleons and more recent wrecks of merchant and naval ships.

Popular dive sites include Grande Island and St George's Island. South of Goa, off the Karnataka coast, Devbagh Island (near Karwar) and Pigeon Island are popular.

The following dive schools are all affiliated with the Professional Association of Dive Instructors (PADI):

Barracuda Diving (☎ 0832-2437001; www.barracudadiving.com) This place is based in Panaji; see p89 for more information.

Goa Dive Center (☎ 9822157094; www.goadivecenter.com) Operates out of Sinquerim and Baga, with its main office on Tito's Rd. See p128 for more information. **Goa Diving** (☎ 2555117; 2538204; www.goadiving.com; goadivin@sancharnet.in; House No 145P, Chapel Bhat, Chicalim 403711) This Bogmalo-based company runs trips and courses; see p179 for details.

Motorcycling & Cycling

Most tourists hire a moped or motorcycle at some time during their stay in Goa, but few venture further than the next beach or the nearest town. There are some worthwhile longer rides:

- From Benaulim or Cavelossim, ride down the coast road via Betul, Cabo da Rama and Agonda to Palolem.
- From Calangute, Anjuna or Vagator, head up the coast via Morjim and Mandrem to Arambol.
- From Arambol, ride up to Terekhol Fort.
- From Panaji, ride out to Old Goa and across to Divar Island, or continue to Ponda to explore the Hindu temples and spice plantations.
- From Margao, explore Salcete taluka (district) around Chandor and Loutolim.

Shorter rides (such as Panaji to Old Goa or Palolem to Rajbag) can also be done by bicycle. For information about hiring motorcycles and bicycles, see p237 and p235 respectively.

Paragliding & Kite-Surfing

Paragliding is common thing to do in season, when many instructors (mostly Europeans) set up in beach towns. Kite-surfing is also on the rise, and Goa is attracting more and more kite-surfing junkies. Often operators are working illegally and don't advertise; ask around or approach people who are engaged in the act – chances are they'll take you along for a fee.

The scene changes from season to season; at the time of research, there was a lively paragliding scene in Anjuna and Vagator Beaches in North Goa, and Arambol Beach was the place where the kite-surfers congregated.

Rafting & Kayaking

Although not in Goa itself, Dandeli Wildlife Sanctuary is only a couple of hours drive across the border in Karnataka, and here you can try white-water rafting, kayaking and caving. **Kali Rafting** (☎ 08284-234380; www.kalirafting.com) is a good place to start your Internet-based research. Also contact **Day Tripper Tours & Travel** (☎ 2276726; www.daytrippergoa.com; Calangute-Candolim Rd, Calangute) in Calangute. In south Goa, Pepper Valley (p197), in the Cotigao Wildlife Sanctuary, arranges tours that include rafting.

Yoga

For information about yoga courses, see p214.

BUSINESS HOURS

Just about the only rule about business hours in Goa is that many Goan shops and offices knock off for a siesta anywhere between 12.30pm and 3pm. Apart from this government offices are open from 10am to 5pm Monday to Saturday, and are closed every second Saturday. Sunday is a day of rest, and the business districts of towns like Panaji and Margao are ghost towns.

Banks are generally open from 10am to 2pm Monday to Friday, and 10am to noon on Saturday. To compete with moneychangers, which keep normal (and sometimes extended) business hours, some banks now have extended hours and even open on Sunday. Tourist-oriented businesses such as travel agencies, Internet cafés and souvenir shops stay open on Sundays and well into the evening.

CHILDREN

Goa is probably the most family-friendly state in India – almost everywhere you go you'll find enthusiastic baby-sitters and a whole community of travellers with children waiting to share their war stories. There are scores of young parents with young children who are keen on broadening their children's horizons from as early an age as possible, and you will find that your kids will benefit enormously from the range of activities and ideas on offer.

For more information on travelling with kids, get hold of a copy of Lonely Planet's *Travel with Children*.

Practicalities

Things like disposable nappies are available, but come at a cost and with the additional dilemma of how to dispose of them. The enormous environmental damage caused by such waste leads many parents to do what the locals do: use washable nappies. Formula milk is available in Goa, but not as widely as it is at home; you may have to shop around in chemists in larger cities like Panaji, Mapusa and Margao.

Be wary of hygiene; get into a regular routine of sterilising bottles with boiled bottled water and be sure that all food is cleaned and cooked properly.

With regard to breast-feeding in public, the general rule is avoid it or, if you must breast-feed, do it with discretion. Given that Indian mothers often tend to young babies in the privacy of home, babies who are dining alfresco are an unusual sight.

Also be wary of the heat, which is taxing enough for grown-ups, let alone little ones.

Sights & Activities

Apart from the beach – which is enough to keep most kids happy for weeks on end – there are water sports, a science park in Miramar (p98) and hotels that are used to accommodating children and often go to extra effort to keep them entertained with play equipment and facilities. This is particularly true of top-end hotels (though some bat for the other team and have no-child policies), but also of some of the smaller, more soulful places. A good example of this is the home school offered by Bhakti Kutir (p193) in Patnem. Keep an eye out for child-oriented courses in some of the beach towns.

CLIMATE CHARTS

The climate in Goa is not just an academic point; it affects the character, customs and culture. The main feature of the Goan climate is the monsoon between June and the end of September, which sees 250cm to 300cm of rain. During the two months preceding the onset of the monsoon, the humidity increases and the normally clear skies become hazy. High winds and lightning come just before the rain. Goans store enough firewood and food to last through the rains; fishing ceases almost entirely because of stormy conditions.

Surprisingly, the temperature throughout all of this drama remains fairly constant,

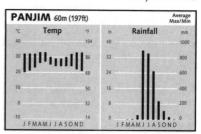

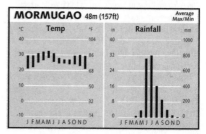

DIRECTORY

varying from a maximum of 28ºC or 29ºC in July to a maximum of 33ºC in May, and minimums for the same months of 24ºC and 26.5ºC.

For more information, see p12.

COURSES
Cooking

For information about Goan cooking courses, see p57.

Music & Dance

During season, there are many courses in traditional instruments such as tabla. To find these, check notice boards in popular foreigner hang-outs like Brown Bread in Palolem, the German Bakery in Anjuna and Double Dutch in Arambol.

For more dedicated musicians, the well-regarded Kala Academy (p95) in Panaji offers fully certified music and dance courses. The school of Indian music at the Kala Academy teaches classical singing, as well as the tabla, sitar and harmonium. The Kala Academy also has a school of Western music and a school of dance specialising in *kathak* and Bharat Natyam dance. The academy also hosts various performances and cultural festivals.

Yoga

Yoga courses are as common as cows in Goa, and many world-class teachers flock here over season. You could take your chances with a random flyer, but it may be better to contact an established organisation that runs yoga courses and classes. Some places run courses in conjunction with accommodation.

Popular places for yoga in Goa:

Ayurvedic Natural Health Centre (ANHC; ☎ 0832-2409275, 2409036; www.healthandayurveda.com) In Baga (p128).

Bhakti Kutir (☎ 0832-2643472; www.bhaktikutir.com; 296 Palolem, Patnem) Yoga is part of this holistic accommodation experience on Patnem Beach (p193).

Healing Here & Now (☎ 0832-32273487; www.healinghereandnow.com; St Michael's Vaddo) In Anjuna (p141).

Himalaya Iyengar Yoga Centre (www.hiyogacentre .com; Arambol Beach) In Arambol (p153).

Purple Valley Yoga Centre (☎ 9370568639; www .yogagoa.com) In Anjuna (p140).

Yoga Magic (☎ 0832-5623796; www.yogamagic.net) Stay in Rajasthani tents at this memorable place near Anjuna (p142).

CUSTOMS

The usual duty-free regulations for India apply in Goa: 1L of spirits and 200 cigarettes (or 50 cigars, or 250g of tobacco).

You're allowed to bring in all sorts of technological gadgets, but expensive items such as video cameras are likely to be entered on a Tourist Baggage Re-Export (TBRE) form to ensure you take them out when you leave. Failure to declare such items upon departure may mean a payable duty.

DANGERS & ANNOYANCES

Goa is essentially a safe destination for travellers, but this is India and the tourist industry carries with it a few inherent dangers that you should be aware of. Touts, pressure sales tactics and minor scams are annoying, but more serious are theft, harassment of women and the occasional mugging that occurs particularly over high season.

Crime

From time to time there are drugging episodes, usually on major tourist routes. Use your brain and your instincts before accepting food or drinks from strangers or even new friends.

There have also been incidents of attacks on women (see p228). Goans are understandably concerned by these incidents and blame them on criminals from neighbouring states. Some measures have been introduced, such as limited street lighting and security patrols on some beaches, but it's still not a good idea for women to wander alone in dark areas around beach shacks at night.

It pays for everyone, not just women, to be wary. Busy resorts are safe enough when there are people around, but late at night anyone can be vulnerable. Quiet resorts with poor street lighting have proven risky for travellers wandering alone. People visiting in the low season should avoid staying in isolated accommodation.

LIFE'S A BEACH

Try to be mindful of the fact that you're actually not invincible. Remember that foreigners die every year in Goa from road accidents, drowning and drug use. Don't let it ruin your holiday, but don't let your holiday ruin your life.

TIPS FOR SAFE TRAVEL

While the majority of travellers in Goa will have no serious or life-threatening problems, tourists have occasionally been the target of theft or assault. There are some common-sense steps you can take to minimise the risk:

- Don't open the door to someone you don't know.

- Leave windows and doors locked when you're sleeping and when you're out; things have been stolen using hooks through windows.

- Avoid quiet, poorly lit streets or lanes – take the longer way if it's brighter and more populated, and walk with confidence and purpose.

- If you are being sexually harassed or assaulted on public transport, embarrass the culprit by loudly complaining, and report them to the conductor or driver.

- As tempting as it is to stare someone down, women should just ignore stares. Dark or reflective glasses can help.

Scams

One scam involves groups of teenage pickpockets posing as students with sponsorship forms. One 'student' engages the victims in conversation while the others pick their pockets. The unfortunate part is that there are also a lot of genuine students who may stop you with a questionnaire or something similar; use your instincts.

Incredibly, the age-old export scam is still doing the rounds in India. Even more incredibly, people are still falling for it. The scam basically involves being befriended and eventually offered the opportunity to export products (jewellery, stones or carpets are common) to sell elsewhere at enormous profit. Or, after you've been plied with meals and entertainment, you'll be given a sob story about your new friend's inability to obtain an export licence. Don't be fooled; these guys are smooth operators and even worldly travellers have been successfully buttered up by the initial hospitality and generosity.

At airports, beware of scams to short-change you when you're exchanging money. Also (particularly if you're arriving on a charter flight) be prepared to be besieged by children and beggars asking for '£1 coins' or for some of your home-country currency for their 'coin collection'. Your contribution will likely be sold back to departing tourists.

Theft

Weigh up whether your passport and other valuables are safer at your hotel or on your person. If you are staying in a reasonable

hotel or family home where there is a safe or similar facility, leave them there, not just in your room. If you're more comfortable taking valuables with you, they should always be in a money belt under your clothing. There have been incidents of violent robberies of tourists in Goa so exercise great caution wherever you are. If you're travelling with expensive equipment like laptops, cameras or iPods, don't casually wave them around. It's also a good idea to padlock backpacks and lock them onto luggage racks or chairs on trains. Beware also of fellow travellers; some are set on defiling the spirit of the travel community by helping themselves to other peoples' things.

If you have something stolen in Goa, you must report it to the police if you want to make an insurance claim at home. According to the accounts of several travellers this is likely to be frustrating; policemen often attempt to dissuade you from filing a report. Being friendly, patient and persistent should get you your paperwork in the end. Reporting a theft does not mean that you will have to stay in Goa, despite what you may be told. Some policemen are friendly and helpful, but if you continually have trouble try enlisting the assistance of the Goa Tourism Development Corporation (GTDC) in Panaji.

Touts

When arriving by train or bus, visitors may be met by taxi drivers and autorickshaw drivers who want to take you to a 'nice' hotel – where nice usually means the one that pays the best commission. The hotels that simply refuse to pay touts risk stories that they are 'full', 'closed for repairs', 'no good any more' or even 'flooded'. It's almost always a lie. Be persistent and check it out for yourself.

Touts do have a use, though – not all of their recommendations are bad ones, and finding a place can be difficult if you arrive during the high season. Hop in an autorickshaw, tell the driver what price you will pay for a hotel, and off you go.

DISABLED TRAVELLERS

There are few provisions for disabled travellers in Goa outside of the most top-end hotels, and thus the mobility-impaired traveller will face a number of challenges. Few older buildings have wheelchair access; toilets have certainly not been designed to accommodate wheelchairs; and footpaths are generally riddled with potholes and crevices, littered with obstacles and packed with throngs of people. Nevertheless, the difficulties are far from insurmountable and if you want to visit Goa – do it! If your mobility is restricted you will need an able-bodied companion to accompany you, and you'd be well-advised to hire a private vehicle with a driver.

The **Royal Association for Disability and Rehabilitation** (RADAR; ☎ 020-72503222; www.radar.org.uk; 12 City Forum, 250 City Rd, London EC1V 8AF, UK) may be able to offer further information on the logistics of travelling in India. Also check out **Mobility International USA** (MIUSA; ☎ 541-3431284; www.miusa.org; PO Box 10767, Eugene, OR 97440, USA).

For specific information about disability issues in Goa, contact **Disability Goa** (www.disabilitygoa.com).

EMBASSIES & CONSULATES
Indian Embassies & Consulates

India's embassies, consulates and high commissions abroad:

Australia High Commission (☎ 02-6273 3999; www.hcindia-au.org; 3/5 Moonah Place, Yarralumla, ACT 2600); Consulate General (☎ 02-9223 9500; www.indianconsulatesydney.org; 27th fl, 25 Bligh St, Sydney, NSW 2000); Honorary Consulate (☎ 03-9384 0141; www.indianconsulate.org; 7 Munro St, Coburg, Melbourne, Vic 3058)
Austria Embassy (☎ 01-505 86 66-9; www.indianembassy.at; Kaerntnerring 2, 1010 Vienna)
Belgium & Luxembourg Embassy (☎ 02 64 091 40; www.indembassy.be; 217 Chaussee de Vleurgat, 1050 Brussels)

Brazil Embassy (☎ 061-3248 4006; www.indianembassy.org.br; SHIS QL 08 Coj 08, Casa 01, Lago Sul, Brasilia-DF 71 620285)
Canada High Commission (☎ 613-744 3751; www.hciottawa.ca; 10 Springfield Rd, Ottawa, Ontario K1M 1C9); Consulate General (☎ 416-960 0751; cgindia@cgitoronto.ca; 1835 Yonge St, Toronto, Ontario M4S 1X8); Consulate General (☎ 604-662 8811; www.cgivancouver.com; 325 Howe St, 2F, Vancouver, BC V6C 1Z7)
Denmark Embassy (☎ 045-39 18 28 88; www.indian-embassy.dk; Vangehusvej 15, 2100 Copenhagen)
France Embassy (☎ 01 40 50 70 70; www.amb-inde.fr; 15 Rue Alfred Dehodencq, 75016 Paris)
Germany Embassy (☎ 030-257950; www.indianembassy.de; Tiergartenstrasse 17, Berlin 10185); Consulate (☎ 069-15300518; www.cgifrankfurt.de; Friedrich Ebert Anlarge 26, Frankfurt 60325); Consulate (☎ 040-338036; Raboisen 6, 20095, Hamburg); Consulate (☎ 089-210 23 90; Widenmayer Strasse 15, Munich D-80538)
Ireland Embassy (☎ 01-497 0483; indembassy@eircom.net; 6 Leeson Park, Dublin 6)
Israel Embassy (☎ 03-510 1431; indembtel@indembassy.co.il; 4 Kaufman St, Sharbat House, Tel Aviv 68012)
Italy Embassy (☎ 064 88 46 42; www.indianembassy.il; Via XX Settembre 5, 00187 Rome)
Japan Embassy (☎ 0332-622 391; www.embassy-avenue.jp; 2-2-11 Kudan Minami, Chiyoda-ku, Tokyo 102)
Nepal Embassy (☎ 0144 10 900; www.south-asia.com/Embassy-India; 336 Kapurdhara Marg, Kathmandu 410900)
Netherlands Embassy (☎ 0703-46 97 71; www.indianembassy.nl; Buitenrustweg 2, 2517 KD, Den Hague)
New Zealand High Commission (☎ 04-473 6390; www.hicomind.org.nz/index.htm; 180 Molesworth St, Wellington)
Russia Embassy (☎ 7095-783 7535; www.indianembassy.ru; 6-8 Vorontsovo Polya, Moscow)
Sweden Embassy (☎ 08-107008; www.indianembassy.se; Adolf Fredriks Kyrkogata 12, Stockholm 11183)
UK High Commission (☎ 020-7839 6242; www.hcilondon.net; India House, Aldwych, London WC2B 4NA); Consulate General (☎ 013-1229 2144; indian@consulate.fsnet.co.uk; 17 Rutland Square EH1 2BB Edinburgh)
USA Embassy (☎ 202-939 7000; www.indianembassy.org; 2107 Massachusetts Ave NW, Washington, DC 20008); Consulate General (☎ 312-595 0405; www.chicago.indianconsulate.com; NBC Tower, 455 North Cityfront Plaza Drive, Suite 850, Chicago, IL 60611); Consulate General (☎ 713-626 2148; www.cgihouston.org; 3 Post Oak, Central Suite No 600, 1900 Post Oak Blvd, Houston, TX 77056); Consulate General (☎ 212-774 0600; www.indiacgny.org; 3 East 64th St, Manhattan, New York, NY 10021-7097); Consulate General (☎ 415-668 0662; www.indianconsulate-sf.org; 540 Arguello Blvd, San Francisco, CA 94118)

Embassies & Consulates in India

It's important to realise what your own embassy can and can't do to help you if you get into trouble. Generally it won't be much help if the trouble you're in is your own fault. Remember that you are bound by the laws of the country you are in; your embassy will not be sympathetic if you end up in jail after committing a crime locally, even if such actions are legal in your own country.

Most foreign diplomatic missions are in Delhi, but there are also a few consulates in the other major cities of Mumbai (Bombay), Kolkata (Calcutta) and Chennai (Madras). Austria, Germany, Italy, Portugal and the UK have honorary consuls in Goa.

The following is not an exhaustive list. If your country does not appear, it does not mean that it is not represented in India. Also, some of the listed countries have other consular offices; we've listed each country's embassy that is closest to Goa:

Australia Consulate General (Map pp62-3; ☎ 022-56692000; www.ausgovindia.com; 3rd fl, Makar Chambers VI, Jamnalal Bajaj Marg, Nariman Point, Mumbai)

Austria Consulate (Map p178; ☎ 0832-2513811; Salgaocar House, Dr F Luis Gomes Rd, Vasco da Gama)

Brazil Embassy (☎ 011-3017301; www.brazilembas syinindia.com; 8 Aurangzeb Rd, New Delhi)

Canada Consulate (Map pp62-3; ☎ 022-22876027; 41/42 Makar Chambers VI, Nariman Point, Mumbai)

Denmark Embassy (☎ 011-23010900; www.ambnew delhi.um.dk; 11 Aurangzeb Rd, Delhi) Consulate (☎ 044-28118140; 8 Cathedral Rd, Chennai)

France Consulate (Map p64; ☎ 022-5631400; 7th fl, Hoescht House, Vinayak K Shah Rd, Nariman Point, Mumbai)

Germany Consulate (Map p64; ☎ 022-22832422; www .germanconsulatemumbai.org; 10th fl, Hoescht House, Vinayak K Shah Rd, Nariman Point, Mumbai); Honorary Consulate (Map pp84-5; ☎ 0832-2235526; CMM House, Ourem Rd, Panaji)

Ireland (☎ 011-24626733; www.irelandinindia.com; 230 Jor Bagh, New Delhi, 110003)

Israel Embassy (☎ 011-3045400; www.delhi.mfa.gov.il; 3 Aurangzeb Rd, New Delhi)

Italy Consulate (Map pp62-3; ☎ 022-23804071; 72 Peddar Rd, Breach Candy, Mumbai); Honorary Consulate (☎ 0832-2438944; D1 Sesa Ghor, Patto Plaza, Dr Alvaro Costa Rd, Panaji)

Japan Embassy (☎ 011-26876564, www.in.emb-japan .go.jp; 4 & 5, 50G Shantipath, Chanakyapuri, New Delhi)

Nepal Embassy (☎ 011-23329969; Barakhamba Rd, New Delhi)

Netherlands Embassy (☎ 011-24197600; www.holland -in-india.org; 6/50F Shanti Path, Chanakyapuri, 110021, New Delhi)

New Zealand High Commission (☎ 011-26883170; 50N Nyaya Marg, Chanakyapuri, New Delhi)

Portugal Embassy (☎ 011-26142215; www.embport india.com; 8 Olof Palme Marg, Vasant Vihar, New Delhi) Honorary Consulate (Map pp84-5; ☎ 0832-438044; www .consuladoportugalgoa.com; LIC Bldg, Patto, Panaji)

Russia (☎ 011-26873799; www.india.mid.ru; Shantipath, Chanakyapuri, New Delhi)

South Africa Embassy (☎ 011-26149411; www.sahc -india.com/g_maite.html; B18 Vasant Marg, Vasant Vihar, New Delhi)

Spain Embassy (☎ 011-3792082; embespin@mail.mae .es; 12 Prithviraj Rd, New Delhi)

Sweden Embassy (☎ 011-2604961; embassy.new .delhi@sida.se; Nyaya Marg, Chanakyapuri, New Delhi)

Switzerland Embassy (☎ 011-26878372; www.edu .admin.ch/india_dlh; Nvaya Marg, Chanakyapuri, New Delhi)

UK Consulate (Map pp62-3; ☎ 022-56502222; 2nd fl, Maker IV Bldg, Jamnalal Bajaj Marg, Nariman Point, Mumbai); British High Commissioner Tourist Assistance Office (Map pp84-5; ☎ 0832-2438897; www.ukinindia.com; ground fl, S13/14 Dempo Towers, Patto Plaza, Panaji)

USA Embassy (Map pp62-3; ☎ 022-23633611; http:// mumbai.usconsulate.gov/; Lincoln House, 78 Bhulabai Desai Marg, Breach Candy, Mumbai)

FESTIVALS & EVENTS

Goa could easily be called India's festival state. At times it can seem as though there are as many holidays as working days. Along with Hindu festivals, Goans celebrate myriad Christian festivals – not only Christmas and Easter, but also many feast days specific to certain villages or parishes, as well as truly Goan events such as the Feast of St Francis Xavier. On top of this, more recent food and cultural festivals have been developed during the winter season to capitalise on Goa's tourist numbers. Whereas most Christian festivals occur on set dates, Hindu festivals follow the lunar calendar and change from year to year.

January

Feast of the Three Kings On 6 January at the villages of Reis Magos, Cansaulim and Chandor, local boys re-enact the arrival of the three kings with gifts for Christ. A church service is followed by food and entertainment.

Republic Day The anniversary of India's establishment as a republic in 1950 is on 26 January; though Goa was not involved it is celebrated anyway (Goans don't miss a chance to rejoice!).

DIRECTORY

Fontainhas Arts Festival Homes in the Fontainhas district are turned into galleries for this exhibition of Goan and Indian art. Held some time between January and March.

February/March

Pop, Beat & Jazz Music Festival Held over two days in February at the Kala Academy in Panaji.

Shigmotsav (Shigmo) Goa's version of Holi, this Hindu festival marks the end of winter. It normally takes place on the full-moon day of the month of Phalguna (February/March), and is widely celebrated by gangs of youths throwing coloured water and powder at one another. Don't wear your best clothes; tourists frequently become a target. Shigmo parades, with processions of colourful floats, are often held in Panaji, Margao, Mapusa and Vasco da Gama.

Carnival Originally a celebration of the arrival of spring, and a Catholic festival on the three days before Lent began, Carnival is now just one big party and one of Goa's maddest events. In Panaji festivities centre on a procession of colourful floats, which takes place on Sabado Gordo (Fat Saturday). The event is opened by the arrival of King Momo, who makes a traditional decree ordering his subjects to forget their worries and have a good time.

March/April

Ramanavami The birth of Rama, an incarnation of Vishnu, is celebrated at the temple in Partagal.

Procession of All Saints Held in Goa Velha on the fifth Monday in Lent, this is the only procession of its sort outside Rome. Thirty statues of the saints are paraded around neighbouring villages. The main road through Goa Velha becomes blocked with the traffic as people from all over Goa are drawn to the fair that takes place.

Good Friday & Easter Huge church services are held throughout Goa; the big congregations often overflow onto the street, or services are held outside to accommodate everyone. Christians mark the event with large family gatherings.

Feast of Jesus of Nazareth Held at Sindao on the first Sunday after Easter.

Feast of Our Lady of Miracles Held in Mapusa, 16 days after Easter; famous for its celebration by both Hindus and Christians.

Beach Bonanza On Sundays from mid-April onwards, this tourist-oriented festival of music, dancing and food stalls was originally held on the beach at Colva but has now been moved back to the football ground in the village.

Youth Fete Much the same as the Beach Bonanza, but on Calangute beach.

May/June

Igitun Chalne One of the most distinctive festivals in Goa, this is specific to the temple in Sirigao (near Corjurem Fort in Bicholim taluka), and is held in May. *Igitun chalne* literally means 'fire-walking', and the high point of the festival comes when devotees of the goddess Lairaya walk across a pit of burning coals to prove their devotion.

Feast of St Anthony St Anthony is Portugal's national saint, and the festival, held on 13 June, has taken on a particular significance in Goa. It is said that if the monsoon has not arrived by the time of the feast day, a statue of the saint should be lowered into the family well to hasten the arrival of the rain.

Feast of St John the Baptist (Sao Joao) Held on 24 June, this is a thanksgiving for the arrival of the monsoon. To mark the event the young men of the community jump into the water. Traditionally, each well owner must supply *feni* (alcoholic drink) to the swimmers.

Feast of St Peter & St Paul The fishing community, particularly in Bardez taluka, celebrates the monsoon on 29 June. Boats are tied together to form rafts, which serve as makeshift stages. After a morning church service and a large feast, the *sangodd* (bonding festival) is held, and *tiatrs* (local Konkani dramas), folk dances and music are performed before an audience that watches from the banks of the river.

August/September

Independence Day Anniversary of India's independence from the UK in 1947, held on 15 August.

Feast of St Lawrence Celebration of the end of the monsoon and the reopening of the Mandovi to river traffic.

Gokul Ashtami The celebration of Krishna's birthday; in some Krishna temples the deity is symbolically placed in a cradle.

Bonderam Celebrated on Divar Island on the fourth Saturday of August. Processions and mock battles commemorate the disputes that took place over property on the island.

Navidades An offering of the first sheaves of rice is made to the head of state on 24 August.

Ganesh Chaturthi An important Hindu festival celebrated throughout the state to commemorate the birth of Ganesh. The festival can last for 2 ½ days. Clay models of Ganesh are taken in procession around the areas of the temples, before being immersed in water. A period of fasting is observed.

September/October

Fama de Menino Jesus Celebrates the 'miraculous' favours granted by the 'Menino Jesus', which resides within the Church of Our Lady of Mercy; the festival occurs in Colva on the second Monday of October.

October/November

Diwali Hindu festival, also known as the Festival of Lights. Second in importance only to Ganesh Chaturthi, this marks the victory of good over evil. Symbolically, lamps are lit morning and evening within the homes of worshippers.

Govardhana Puja This Hindu festival is dedicated to that holiest of animals, the cow.

November/December

Liberation Day Held on 17 December, this day commemorates the end of Portuguese colonial rule.

Marathi Drama Festival Held from November to December at the Kala Academy in Panaji.

Food & Cultural Festival Five-day festival held on Miramar beach in November or December to highlight Goan cuisine and entertainment.

Konkani Drama Festival Held at Kala Academy in November and December.

Feast of Our Lady of the Rosary A feast held on the third Wednesday of November at Navelim, 5km south of Margao.

Tiatr Festival Held at the Kala Academy in November.

Goa Heritage Festival A two-day event of Goan food, folk music and dancing held in Panaji's Campal district in late November.

Feast of St Francis Xavier Celebrated in Old Goa with processions and services on 3 December.

Feast of Our Lady of Immaculate Conception On or around 8 December in Panaji and Margao, the feast is accompanied by a large fair.

Christmas Day On 24 December, Goa's Catholics flock to midnight mass services, traditionally called Missa de Galo or Cock Crow because they used to go on well into the early hours of the morning. Christmas Day is marked on 25 December with large family gatherings and feasting.

FOOD

Unless otherwise stated, eating establishments where mains are under Rs 50 are budget, between Rs 50 and 300 midrange, and Rs 300 or more top-end.

For more information about food in Goa, see p51.

GAY & LESBIAN TRAVELLERS

While overt displays of affection between members of the opposite sex, such as cuddling and hand holding, are frowned upon in India, it is not unusual to see Indian men holding hands with each other or engaged in other close affectionate behaviour. This does not mean they are gay.

Homosexual relations between men are illegal in India, although there is no legislation forbidding lesbian relations. The gay movement is confined almost exclusively to larger cities, and Mumbai is really the only place where there's a gay 'scene'. Since marriage is seen as important, being gay has a particular stigma – most stay in the closet or risk being disowned by their families.

However, Goa's liberal reputation draws a lot of gay men, and there's a discreet scene,

mainly around the Calangute-Baga area. A couple of the beach shacks are also becoming a bit braver with respect to gay events; on Palolem beach, Cuba (p194) hosts a gay night on Wednesday. As with relations between heterosexual Western couples travelling in India, gay and lesbian travellers should exercise discretion and refrain from displaying affection in public.

HOLIDAYS

The three official public holidays in India are Republic Day (January 26), Independence Day (August 15), and Mahatma Gandhi's Birthday (2 October). In addition to these, holidays are called during major festivals such as Diwali, Dussehra and Holi, Nanak Jayanti, Buddha Jayanti, and Easter and Christmas.

INSURANCE

A travel insurance policy to cover theft, loss and medical problems is a wise idea, if only because of the cosmic law that if you have it you won't need it. There is a wide variety of policies and your travel agent will have recommendations. Some policies specifically exclude 'dangerous activities', which can mean diving, motorcycling and even trekking. This is especially relevant in Goa, where most people hire a scooter or motorcycle at some time. Other increasingly popular activities in Goa are scuba diving and water sports such as water-skiing and paragliding, all of which may require special stipulations when you take out your travel insurance. For more information about health insurance see p241.

If your goods are stolen, you will also be required to file a police report (p214) to claim insurance.

Worldwide cover to travellers from over 44 countries is available online at www.lonelyplanet.com/travel_services.

INTERNET ACCESS

Internet and email services in Goa are plentiful, reliable and relatively cheap. In all major towns, beach resorts and even some small villages, you'll easily find somewhere to check email. The most common places offering Internet access are travel agencies and STD/ISD phone offices, but you'll also find many dedicated Internet cafés. Many hotels and guesthouses also offer Internet access for guests. Average charges are around Rs 40 per hour (though some places charge up to Rs 60), usually with a minimum of 15 minutes (Rs 10 to 15), but there are places in Margao, Vasco and Mapusa charging as little as Rs 20 per hour.

If you're travelling with a laptop remember that you'll need a universal adaptor. These are readily available in Goa, though finding a surge protector is more difficult. If you want to ensure that your computer's innards stay intact through power surges, it's worth investing in one at home.

In recent years, wireless Internet has began to sprout up in various places, though it still isn't common.

See p15 for some Internet resources.

LEGAL MATTERS
Drugs
For a long time Goa was a place where you could indulge in all sorts of illicit drugs with relative ease – they were cheap, good quality, readily available and the risks were minimal. Ecstasy and LSD (acid) are still the drug of choice for many ravers, and hashish (charas) is widely available – often brought down from Manali and the Kullu Valley in Himachal Pradesh, and peddled around the beach resorts.

Would-be users should not be lulled into a false sense of security in Goa; think extremely carefully about the risks before partaking. In addition to the fact that overdoses happen even in paradisal Goa, the drug laws in India are among the toughest in the world; possession of even a relatively small amount of hash (say 10g) can lead to 10 years in jail and a Rs 100,000 fine. Aguada Jail houses a number of prisoners, including Westerners, who are serving drug-related sentences.

Police
There was a period when police often conducted 'raids' of foreigners in Goa. These would take place at roadblocks or even at private homes or hotel rooms. Usually searches yielded nothing, but there were occasions where hapless searchees were planted with drugs and ended up in prison. Incidents of raids have decreased in recent years, perhaps in part due to increased efforts of the government to crack down on corruption in the public service. However, the fact remains that both drugs and corruption are still a problem in Goa, with rampant drug use giving poorly paid policemen opportunities for extortion.

Probably the best way to deal with police extortion should it happen to you is through polite (and though it might pain you), respectful persuasion. If that fails, attempt to bargain down the 'fine' before paying up, and try to establish the identity (or at least a good mental image) of the policeman.

In practical terms, the most contact the average traveller is likely to have with the law will be on the street; you may be unlucky enough to be flagged down for not wearing a helmet on certain parts of the NH17, or checked for papers by an opportunistic police officer who is hoping to extract a 'fine'. If this happens, keep your cool and you may be able to negotiate the fine down to Rs 0. For more information about such encounters, see p239.

The Directorate of Vigilance has been established by the government of Goa in a bid to stamp out corruption of public servants. You can file an anonymous complaint about police through http://vigilance.goa.gov.in.

Smoking & Spitting
On 1 January 2000 a law came into force in Goa banning smoking, spitting and the chewing of tobacco in all public places. It's a welcome move, but clearly impossible to enforce except in government buildings and places like train stations where transgressors face a Rs 1000 fine. Smoking is banned in many enclosed restaurants, especially if there is air-con, while other restaurants have nonsmoking areas. Both laws are implemented in Goa in a typically *susegad* (relaxed or laid-back) style; ashtrays are often provided in restaurants that bear 'no smoking signs' and a casual observer could assume that spitting is actually mandatory.

MAPS
There are plenty of maps available, but none are accurate enough to guide you around the back roads without having to stop and ask for directions.

A good map is *Goa and its Beaches*, published by Roger Lascelles in the UK. The TTK Discover India series has a Goa map for Rs 65. You can buy other maps in Goa for around Rs 20, but you often get more dvertisements than street directions. A ree map is also available from the GTDC, vhich is decent for general orientation. A good source of information on maps is vww.indiamapstore.com.

MONEY

The rupee (Rs) is divided into 100 paise p). There are coins of 5, 10, 20, 25 and 0 paise, and Rs 1, 2 and 5, as well as notes f Rs 10, 20, 50, 100, 500 and even 1000, vhich feel all the more valuable because hey're so hard to come by.

ATMs are so commonly available now hat you can rely on them as your primary ource of cash, though hard currency (or ravellers cheques) is recommended as ackup. You need to show your passport vhen you are changing money or cashing ravellers cheques.

See the inside front cover for exchange ates at the time of writing, and p13 for ypical costs.

ATMs

Several banks have introduced 24-hour ATMs into Goa, and more are constantly pening. These take international cards sing the Cirrus, Maestro, MasterCard and Visa networks. The main banks with ATMs re ICICI, Centurion, HDFC and UTI. Often ATMs are not actually attach-ed to a bank branch but are instead installed in hopping areas purely as cash-dispensing nachines. They are usually in an air-con-ditioned cubicle (which you may need your card to access) and are guarded by 24-hour rmed security. You can currently find ATMs in Panaji, Margao, Mapusa, Calan-gute, Candolim, Vasco da Gama, Ponda and Colva. Plan ahead when you're heading to he beaches away from these.

Cash

It pays to have some US dollars, pounds sterling or euros for times when you can't change travellers cheques or use a credit card. You won't have any problem chang-ing money in the tourist areas. The best rates are usually at Thomas Cook and the State Bank of India. Next best are private moneychangers. Hotels offer the least at-tractive rates. When changing money, don't accept notes that are damaged because you might be hard-pressed to pass them on.

Credit Cards

Credit cards are accepted in most major tourist centres, but don't expect to be able to use a card in budget hotels or restaurants. Upmarket hotels accept them, as do most travel agencies and practically all depart-ment stores. MasterCard and Visa are the most widely accepted cards. Cash advances on credit cards can be made at branches of Thomas Cook and Bank of Baroda, as well as at most moneychangers (which are often travel agencies) at the beach resorts.

Encashment Certificates

All money is meant to be changed at official banks or moneychangers, and you are sup-posed to be given an encashment certificate for each transaction. These can be useful if you want to re-exchange excess rupees for hard currency, buy a tourist-quota train ticket, or if you need to show a tax clear-ance certificate. ATM receipts serve the same purpose.

International Transfers

International money transfers can be ar-ranged through Thomas Cook or Western Union; both have branches in Panaji and some of the larger towns in Goa. Charges for this service are high – if you have a credit card it's cheaper to get someone to deposit money in your home account and draw a cash advance.

Moneychangers

Private moneychangers are everywhere in towns and beach resorts. They keep longer hours than banks, and are quick and ef-ficient. Many travel agencies double as ex-change offices and give cash advances on credit cards. Check rates at the banks first.

Tipping & Baksheesh

Although tipping is not necessary, particu-larly if you're hanging out on one of the more remote beaches, most people tip staff in their hotel and at restaurants. A waiter or a room boy gets paid about Rs 1000 to 2000 a month (US$25 to US$50), so they rely heavily on the tips they pick up in the tourist season.

There's no need to go overboard; Rs 10 to 20 is about right for members of the hotel staff who help you out, and the nor-mal 10% figure is adequate in restaurants.

Some hotels and restaurants prefer that you contribute to a general tips box so money can be distributed evenly among staff. It's not necessary to tip taxi drivers for short trips, but it's normal to tip the driver if you've hired a car for a day.

The term 'baksheesh' encompasses tipping and a lot more besides. In some situations it is an opportunity to respectfully give charity, in others it is a necessity to get things done. See p33 for more about baksheesh.

Travellers Cheques

All major brands of travellers cheques are accepted in India, with American Express (Amex) and Thomas Cook being the most widely traded. Pounds sterling, euros and US dollars are the safest bet. Charges for changing travellers cheques vary but hot competition among private moneychangers means you can usually change cheques without commission.

All travellers cheques are replaceable, but this does little good if you have to go home and apply for them at your bank. Keep an emergency stash of cash in a separate place from your cheques, along with a record of cheque serial numbers, proof of purchase slips and your passport number.

American Express and Thomas Cook travellers cheques are easiest to replace in Goa, provided you have the right documentation. If your travellers cheques are lost or stolen, contact the following offices in Panaji immediately:

American Express (☎ 0832-2432960; Menezes Air Travel, Ourem Rd)

Thomas Cook (☎ 0832-2221312; www.thomascook .co.in; 8 Alcon Chambers, Dayanand Bandodkar Marg; ☯ 9.30am-6pm Mon-Sat year round, 10am-5pm Sun Oct-Mar)

PHOTOGRAPHY

Goans are generally quite mellow about having their photograph taken, regarding it as the price one has to pay for encouraging the tourist industry. Do ask, however, before you poke your camera into someone's face – particularly before snapping women or older people. If anyone objects to having their photo taken, respect their wishes.

An easy way to make friends is to take their address and offer to send a copy of the photo when you get home (as long as you do

it, of course). It can also be tempting to take photos of some of the colourful scenes at the Anjuna flea market and the other big markets, but some of the vendors (both Western and Indian) strongly object to being photographed. Again, it is only polite to ask.

Do not take photos inside temples, and ask before you use a camera and flash in a church.

POST

The Indian postal and poste restante services are generally good. Letters almost always reach you, and letters you send almost invariably reach their destination, although they can take up to three weeks.

It costs Rs 8 to send a small postcard or aerogramme anywhere in the world from India, and Rs 15 for a large postcard or a standard letter (up to 20g).

Receiving Mail

Have letters addressed to you with your surname in capitals and underlined, followed by poste restante, GPO and the city or town in question. Many 'lost' letters are simply misfiled under given (Christian) names, so always check under both your given and last names. Letters sent via poste restante are generally held for one month only, after which they might be returned to the sender or just left in a box under the counter until they disintegrate.

Sending Mail

Sending parcels from Goa requires a little more than fronting up at the post office with your package, though it may take you a couple of trips before your parcel is on its merry way. First, take the parcel to a wrapping service (there's usually one very close to the post office – look for signs reading 'parcel post'), and get it stitched up. It can be quite an experience to watch your package get transformed with boxes, linen, calico and newspaper. You may even find that your possessions are sewn up with a needle and thread, and the stitching sealed with wax.

Book packages (up to 5kg) can be sent without a customs form and for considerably less money. They will need to be wrapped so that the contents of your parcel can be inspected on the way.

At the post office you'll get the necessary customs declaration forms, which will be attached to the parcel. To avoid excise duty at the delivery end, specify that the contents are a 'gift' with a value less than Rs 1000.

Express Mail Service (EMS) Speedpost is available at major post offices (such as Panaji and Margao), and charges to various destinations are as follows:

Australia Rs 700 for the first kilogram, plus Rs 300 for each additional kilogram.

Europe (including the UK) Rs 950 for the first kilogram, plus Rs 300 for each additional kilogram.

USA Rs 775 for the first kilogram, plus Rs 400 for each additional kilogram.

This is more expensive than ordinary post (which will cost Rs 570/645/500 for 1kg respectively), but is faster and much more reliable.

Sending parcels in the other direction (to India) is akin to gambling. Don't count on anything bigger than a letter getting to you. And don't count on a letter getting to you if there's anything of value inside it.

SHOPPING

Although Goa is not renowned for its handicrafts, a vibrant market culture lures traders from all over India. While this sadly means that you are unlikely to take home much that is genuinely Goan (apart from the odd decorative bottle of *feni*), it also means that you can find almost anything from Kashmiri carpets to fabrics from Rajasthan, carvings from Karnataka and paintings from Nepal.

The state's biggest market – and one of the state's key tourist attractions – is the Anjuna flea market held every Wednesday in season. Ingo's Saturday Nite Bazaar in

Arpora and Mackie's Saturday Nite Bazaar in Baga are both tourist-oriented affairs, and make for a great night out. The range of products on offer at these places is exceptional, but locals prefer to shop at local markets where things can cost less; Mapusa's Friday market is a popular one. Panaji and Margao also have busy municipal markets, though you may not find anything you're particularly interested in buying.

In Panaji the main shopping street is 18th June Rd, a long thoroughfare lined with craft and clothing shops, emporiums and shops selling cashews and spices; MG Rd has a collection of modern Western department stores, including Nike, Benetton and Levi's. Perhaps the greatest concentration of department stores, boutiques, jewellery and craft shops is in Calangute, on both the road that leads down to the main beach, and the Calangute–Candolim road. Prices are high here but so is the quality of the merchandise.

Be careful when buying items that include delivery to your home country. You may well be assured that the price includes home delivery and all customs and handling charges, but you may later find that you have to collect the item yourself from your country's main port or airport, and pay customs and handling charges.

Bargaining

While stores in the larger towns often have fixed prices, you are generally expected to bargain at markets, though some Western traders operate on a more efficient system of reasonable first quotes. But, mostly, bargaining is the name of the game. The trick with

---

THE ART OF HAGGLING

The friendly art of haggling is an absolute must in most parts of Goa, unless you don't mind paying above market value. Traders in towns and markets are accustomed to tourists who have lots of money and little time to spend it. This means that a shopkeeper's 'very good price' will be more often than not a very bad price.

If you have absolutely no idea what something should really cost, start by slashing the price by at least half. The vendor will probably look aghast and tell you that this is impossible, as it's the very price they had to pay for the item themselves. This is the usual story. This is when the battle for a bargain begins and it's up to you and the salesperson to negotiate a price. You'll find that many shopkeepers lower their so-called final price if you proceed to head out of the shop and tell them that you'll think about it.

Don't lose your sense of humour and sense of fairness while haggling – it's not a battle to squeeze every last rupee out of a poor trader, and not all vendors are out to rip you off. In truth, this can be a fun exchange.

DIRECTORY

bargaining is that you should have some idea of what you should be paying for any given article. You can find out by checking prices at fixed-price stores, asking other travellers what they paid and shopping around before settling on a vendor. If all else fails, a general rule of thumb is to offer half the original asking price and work up from there.

At the tourist markets, traders usually start very high with their prices.

What to Buy

ANTIQUES

Articles more than 100 years old are not allowed to be exported from India without an export clearance certificate. If you have doubts about any item and think it could be defined as an antique, check with the **Archaeological Survey of India** (http://asi.nic.in/) at the Archaeological Museum in Old Goa.

BRONZE FIGURES & WOODCARVING

Delightful small images of gods are made by the age-old lost-wax process. In this process, a wax figure is made, a mould is formed around it, then wax is melted and poured out. Molten metal is poured in and once it's solidified the mould is broken open. Figures of Ganesh, and of Shiva in his incarnation as dancing Nataraja, are among the most popular.

In South India, images of the gods are also carved out of sandalwood. Rosewood is used to carve animals, elephants in particular. Carved wooden furniture and other household items, either in natural finish or lacquered, are also made in various locations.

CARPETS

It may not surprise you that India produces and exports more handcrafted carpets than Iran, but it probably is more of a surprise that some of them are of virtually equal quality. India's best carpets come from Kashmir, and these can be found in traders' shops in Goa.

Carpets are either made of pure wool, wool with a small percentage of silk to give it a sheen (known as 'silk touch'), or pure silk. The latter are more for decoration than hard wear. Expect to pay from Rs 7000 for a good quality 1.2m by 1.8m carpet, but don't be surprised if the price is more than twice as high.

CLOTHING

Western-brand clothing stores are all the rage in Panaji and Calangute these days. Big names like Benetton, Levi's, Nike and Lacoste now make much of their produce in India, and these shops, which cater almost exclusively to tourists, sell their brand-name gear at prices lower than you'd find at home. Don't expect the cheap knock offs you might pick up in Bangkok – here, Levi jeans go for around Rs 2000 and Lacoste polo shirts retail at Rs 1000.

JEWELLERY

The heavy folk-art jewellery of Rajasthan has particular appeal for Western tastes. Tibetan jewellery is even chunkier and more folklike than the Rajasthani variety. If you're looking for fine jewellery, as opposed to folk jewellery, you may well find that much of what is produced in India is way over the top.

LEATHERWORK

Indian leatherwork is not made from cowhide but from buffalo, camel, goat or some other form of animal. *Chappals,* the basic sandals found all over India, are the most popular buy.

MUSICAL INSTRUMENTS

Indian musical instruments are an interesting buy in India, and you'll see new and second-hand guitars, sitars and tablas at the Anjuna flea market. There are also instrument shops in Panaji and Margao. Easier to carry and even easier to play are CDs and tapes. You can find Bollywood soundtracks, Goa trance and mainstream Western music at shops and stalls all over Goa for between Rs 100 and 600.

PAPIER-MÂCHÉ

This is probably the most characteristic Kashmiri craft. The basic papier-mâché article is made in a mould, then painted and polished in successive layers until the final intricate design is produced. Prices depend upon the complexity and quality of the painted design and the amount of gold leaf used. Items include bowls, cups, containers, jewellery boxes, letter holders, tables, lamps, coasters, trays and so on. A cheap bowl might cost only Rs 50, while a large, well-made item might approach Rs 1000.

ILKS & SARIS

ilk is cheap and the quality is often excellent. If you are buying a silk sari, it helps to now a bit about the silk and the sari. Saris re 5.5m long, unless they have fabric for a holi (sari blouse) attached, in which case hey are 6m. Sari silk is graded and sold by veight (grams per metre).

EXTILES

This is still India's major industry and 40% of the total production is at the village level, where it is known as *khadi* (homespun loth). Bedspreads, tablecloths, cushion covrs or fabric for clothing are popular *khadi* urchases. There is an amazing variety of loth styles, types and techniques around he country. In Gujarat and Rajasthan heavy naterial is embroidered with tiny mirrors nd beads to produce everything from dresses to stuffed toys to wall hangings. Tie-dye work is also popular in Rajasthan and Kerala. In Kashmir embroidered materials re made into shirts and dresses. Batik is a relatively recent introduction from Indonesia that has become widespread; *kalamkari* textile art that is hand painted or block printed) cloth from Andhra Pradesh and Gujarat is a similar but older craft.

SOLO TRAVELLERS

The general consensus is that travelling in Goa is markedly easier than travelling in the rest of the country, and many solo travellers wander down this way for some relaxation and respite from the challenge of travelling in the rest of India. It's a sociable place, so you only have to be as solo as you want to be. While most visitors to the Calangute-Baga beach resort areas travel in couples or groups, there are many solo travellers further north in the Anjuna-Vagator area and further south around Palolem. Meeting them at beach shacks, bars and parties is not difficult.

The downside to being a solo female is that often people will think that you obviously want company. Keep a book on hand to give off the appearance of busy contentedness so that unwanted company can be deterred. On the whole though, travelling as a solo female couldn't be easier. Attitudes to women are more liberal and accepting than in many other parts of India, and you can largely be yourself without running the risk of misinterpretation and mistreatment. Like anywhere though, there are serious risks to be aware of (see p228).

TELEPHONE & FAX

Even in the smallest town in Goa you'll find private STD/ISD call booths that have direct local, interstate and international dialling. Usually found in shops or other businesses, they are easy to spot because of the large STD/ISD/PCO signs advertising the service. Travel agencies and Internet places also generally offer a telephone service. Phone calls are digitally metered so you can keep an eye on the cost while you're talking and there are no nasty surprises at the end. Some booths offer a call-back service for a small per minute charge, but there's no such thing as a free reverse-charge call.

Direct international calls from these phones cost Rs 25 to 40 per minute, depending on the country you are calling. Internet cafés are starting to set up Internet phone facilities, by far the cheapest way of making an international call.

Fax

Many telephone offices have fax machine but are not cheap or consistent. Sending a fax internationally can cost between Rs 40 and 100 per page, plus line time. Faxes sent within India should only cost around Rs 10 per page. You can receive faxes for around Rs 10 per page. Private Internet cafés and telephone offices often offer this service, and many hotels have fax facilities.

Mobile Phones

These have been embraced with a passion in India, and if you intend to spend some time in Goa it may be worth getting hooked up to the local network. Call costs – even international calls – are relatively cheap in India.

You can bring your own handset and instantly get connected to a prepaid account on one of the local networks. The most popular companies are **Idea** (www.ideacellular .com), formerly AT&T, **Airtel** (www.airtelworld.com) and **BPL** (www.bplmobile.com). Your phone will only work in Goa and parts of Maharashtra, although most operators have a 'roaming' facility that allows you to receive calls and send SMS messages outside Goa. A SIM card

DIRECTORY

(from a PCO/STD/ISD booth, private office or Internet café) costs around Rs 100, plus an initial amount of call time. You may need a photograph of yourself and a copy of your passport when signing onto a network.

Top-up cards come in various denominations; the more credit on your phone, the cheaper the call rate. Call rates within India are around Rs 1 per minute and you can call internationally for less than Rs 30 per minute. SMS messaging is even cheaper at around Rs 5 per text message. Note that calls to your mobile phone are also charged to your account – check the network coverage and call costs for the specific places you'll before contacting before you commit to a service.

Cell Tone (☎ 2422888; 7 Kamat Nagar Apt) in Panaji (opposite Hotel Marva, off MG Rd), is a reliable place to get hooked up to the local mobile phone network.

Phone Codes

The area code for all places within the state of Goa is ☎ 0832, which you only need to dial when calling from outside the state or from a mobile phone.

To make an international call, you need to dial ☎ 00 (international access code from India), plus the country code (of the country you are calling), the area code and local number.

To make a call to Goa from outside the country, dial the international access code of the country you are in plus ☎ 91 (international country code for India), then ☎ 832 (Goa's area code omitting the initial 0) and then the local number.

TIME

India is 5½ hours ahead of GMT/UTC, 4½ hours behind Australia (EST) and 10½ hours ahead of America (EST). It is officially known as IST – Indian Standard Time, although many Indians prefer to think it stands for Indian Stretchable Time! When it's noon in London, it's 5.30pm in Goa.

TOURIST INFORMATION
Local Tourist Offices

Within Goa there are representatives of the national **Ministry of Tourism** (www.incredibleindia .org), and the state government's tourist efforts: **Goa Tourism** (www.goatourism.org) and **Goa Tourism Development Corporation** (GTDC; www.goa -tourism.com). From the tourist's perspective,

the latter are one and the same. The Government of India tourist office is next to the Municipal Gardens in Panaji, and there are GTDC tourist information counters in Panaji, Margao, Mapusa, Vasco da Gama and at Dabolim Airport.

Tourist Offices Abroad

The Government of India Ministry of Tourism maintains a string of tourist offices in other countries where you can get brochures, leaflets and some information about India.

Australia (☎ 02-9264 4855; indtour@ozemail.com.au; 2nd fl, Piccadilly, 210 Pitt St, Sydney NSW 2000)
Canada (☎ 416-962 3787; indiatourism@bellnet.ca; 60 Bloor St West, Ste No 1003, Toronto, Ontario M4W 3B8)
France (☎ 01 45 23 30 45; indtourparis@aol.com; 1-13 Bis Blvd Hausmann, 75008 Paris)
Germany (☎ 069-242 94 90; info@india-tourism.com; Baseler Strasse 46, 60329 Frankfurt-am-Main 1)
Italy (☎ 028 05 35 06; info@indiatourismmilan.com; Via Albricci 9, 20122 Milan)
Japan (☎ 0357-15 062; indtour@smile.ocn.ne.jp; Pearl Bldg, 7-9-18 Ginza Chou-Ku, Tokyo 104)
Netherlands (☎ 0206-20 89 91; info.nl@india-tourism .com; Rokin 9-15, 1012 KK Amsterdam)
Singapore (☎ 6235 8677; indtour.sing@pacific.net .sg; 20 Kramat Lane, £01-01A United House, 228773 Singapore)
South Africa (☎ 011-325 0880; goito@global.co.za; PO Box 412452, Craig Hall 2020, Johannesburg-2000)
Sweden (☎ 08-215081; info.se@india-tourism.com; Sveavagen 9-11, S-III 57, Stockholm 11157)
UK (☎ 020-7437 3677; info@indiatouristoffice.org; 7 Cork St, London W1X 2LN)
United Arab Emirates (☎ 04-227 4848; goirto@emirates.net.ae; Post Box 12856; NASA Bldg, Al Maktoum Rd, Dubai)
USA New York (☎ 212-586 4901; Suite 1808, 1270 Ave of the Americas, New York, NY 10020); Los Angeles (☎ 213-380 8855; indiatourismla@aol.com; Suite 204, 3550 Wilshire Blvd, Los Angeles, CA 90010)

TOURS

Tours of Goa are offered by private companies as well as by the GTDC. Book tours at the head office of the **GTDC** (☎ 0832-2224132 0832-2226728, 0832-2226515, 0832-243 6666; www.goa -tourism.com; Alvaro Costas Rd, Panaji), or at any of the GTDC hotels in Panaji, Margao, Calangute, Colva, Mapusa, Vasco da Gama, Mayem, Old Goa and Ponda.

GTDC's one-day tours are comprehensive and good value, though not ideal given the slapdash approach. If you're in a hurry and don't mind spending lots of time looking out a bus window, give them a go. Tours are dependent on numbers, and so don't necessary run when they're scheduled to.

The following is a summary of GTDC's tours from Panaji:

Backwater Thrills Cruise on the Mandovi River past Old Goa, Chorao and Divar Island to Savoi Plantation. It costs Rs 600, and runs from 9.30am to 4pm.

Dudhsagar Falls Dudhsagar, Tambdi Surla Mahadeva Temple. It costs Rs 600/700 for a normal/air-con bus, and runs from 9am to 6pm.

Goa by Night Dona Paula bay and sites around Panaji, and ends with a river cruise. It costs Rs 150, and runs from 6.30pm to 9.30pm.

North Goa Saptakoteshwara Temple, Mayem Lake, Mapusa, Vagator, Anjuna.

South Goa Covers Old Goa sites, ancestral Goa at Loutolim, Margao, Colva, Dona Paula and Miramar. It costs Rs 130/200 for a normal/air-con bus, and runs from 9.30am to 6pm.

One of the best of the private tour operators is **Day Tripper Tours & Travel** (☎ 2276726; www .daytrippergoa.com), based in Calangute. Within Goa it offers a range of overnights tours and day trips, including tours to Palolem (£5.50) and Dudhsagar Falls (£15), as well as longer interstate trips to places such as the Taj Mahal (£317/379/445 for economy/ midrange/top-end accommodation).

Southern Birdwing (☎ 2402957; www.southern birdwing.com) in Nerul runs wildlife tours and ecotours including crocodile-spotting on the Cumbrous Canal and bird-watching trips to Bondla and the Carambolim wetlands.

Ola Jeep Tours (☎ 2271249; www.olatoursgoa .com) has recommended trips in a 10-seater jeep to Dudhsagar Falls (Rs 1000) and Ponda's temples and spice plantations (Rs 900), as well as overnight cocohut stays at Morjim Beach and Palolem (both Rs 1300).

Peter & Friends Classic Bike Adventure (☎ 2254467; www.classic-bike-india.de; Casa Tres Amigos, Socol Vado No 425, Assagao) run good motorcycle tours (p240). There's also the cycling tour option; British-run **Cycle Goa** (☎ 0832-2871369; www.cyclegoa.com; Shop 7, Mobor Beach Resort, Cavelossim, Salcette) has been recommended. Its two-week tours cost £995.

For information on river cruises in Goa, see p91.

VISAS

Everyone except for Bhutanese and Nepalese needs to obtain a visa before entering India.

Six-month multiple-entry visas (valid from the date of issue) are issued to most nationalities regardless of whether you intend staying that long or are re-entering the country. Visa applications can be made at your nearest embassy or consulate in person or by post. You need to provide a completed visa application form, passport photographs, the visa fee and, in some cases, an itinerary and proof of onward travel (such as a flight ticket out of India). Check with your local Indian embassy (p216) for specific requirements. Many embassies have a website where you can download and print a visa application forms and get all the information you need. Visa fees vary from country to country: the cost is A$90 for Australians, UK£30 for Britons, and US$60 for US passport holders.

Tax Clearance Certificates

If you stay in India for more than 120 days, you officially need a 'tax clearance certificate' to leave the country, but we've never heard from anyone who has actually been asked for this document on departure. In Panaji, go to the foreign section of the **Income Tax Office** (Shanta Bldg, Emidio Gracia Rd) with your passport and a handful of bank exchange or ATM receipts (to show you have been changing foreign currency into rupees officially).

Visa Extensions

You can only get another six-month visa by leaving the country and coming back in on a new visa. Officially, visa extensions are only possible for certain types of visas, which does not include tourist and transit visas. The power to extend visas is vested in the Ministry of Home Affairs, but in certain situations Foreigners' Regional Registration Offices (FRRO) may be able to help you. They can either grant a short temporary extension and/or forward your passport and supporting documentation (extension form and photographs) on to the **Ministry of Home Affairs** (☎ 011-230932011; http://mha.nic.in/welcome .html; North Block, Central Secretariat, New Delhi) to be properly processed. But don't expect too much; general practice is to visit the ministry in person and hope for the best. Officially, visa extensions are only obtainable in Delhi and, even then, only in extenuating circumstances. In Panaji, visa extensions are not granted as a matter of course. If you're unsuccessful here, Mumbai and Bangalore are the nearest alternatives.

People travelling on tourist visas are not required to register with the FRRO; the form that you fill out each time you check into a hotel takes the place of this. Only foreigners with visas valid for longer than 180 days are required to register, as are nationals of Pakistan and Afghanistan. FRRO can be located in the following cities:

Mumbai (☎ 022-22621169, 022-22620721; 3rd fl, Special Branch Bldg, Badruddin Tayabji Lane) Behind St Xavier's College.

Panaji (Police Headquarters; ☎ 2224488; Malaca Rd; ⏲ 9.30am-1pm Mon-Fri) On the west side of Azad Maidan.

VOLUNTEER WORK

Numerous charities and international aid and development agencies have branches in India, where there are a few work opportunities for foreigners. Though it may be possible to find temporary volunteer work when you are in India, you'll probably be of more use to the charity concerned if you write in advance and, if they need you, stay long enough to be of help. A week on a hospital ward may go a little way towards salving your own conscience, but you actually may not do much more than get in the way of the people who work there long term. Many volunteer organisations arrange long-term placements (one to two years) for volunteers in India.

The following organisations may be able to help or offer advice and further contacts:

Action Without Borders (☎ 212-843 3973; www .idealist.org; Suite 1510, 360 West 31st St, New York, NY, USA)

Australian Volunteers International (☎ 03-9279 1788; www.ozvol.org.au; 71 Argyle St, PO Box 350, Fitzroy, Vic 3065, Australia)

Coordinating Committee for International Voluntary Service (☎ 01 45 68 49 36; www.unesco.org/cciv; Unesco House, 31 Rue Francois Bonvin, 7532 Paris Cedex 15, France)

Global Volunteers (☎ 800-487 1074; www.global volunteers.org; 375 East Little Canada Rd, St Paul, MN 55117-1628, USA)

Voluntary Service Overseas (VSO; ☎ 020-8780 7200; www.vso.org.uk; 317 Putney Bridge Rd, Putney, London SW15 2PN, UK)

Working Abroad (☎ in France 04 68 26 41 79; www.workingabroad.com; PO Box 454, Flat 1, Brighton, BN1 3Z5, East Sssex, UK)

One of the best places for foreigners to get involved in Goa is **El Shaddai** (☎ 0832-2266520; www.childrescue.net; El Shaddai House, Duler, Mapusa), which makes no bones about the fact that its work depends on the generosity of tourists. El Shaddai works hard to get children off the streets and into schools. For more information on the work of El Shaddai, see p138.

Other organisations that may be interested in your time and commitment:

Goa Foundation (☎ 0832-2256479; www.goacom .com/goafoundation; G/8 St Britto's Apt, Feira Alta, Mapusa, 403 508) A research-based environment and conservation organisation.

International Animal Rescue (Animal Tracks; ☎ 0832-2268328; www.iar.org.uk; Madungo Vaddo, Assagao, Bardez) Their animal sterilisation and vaccination programmes are making a noticeable impact on the street. Visitors are welcome to the centre; guided tours run at 11am and 3.30pm. For more information see p48.

WOMEN TRAVELLERS

Foreign women travelling in India have widely been viewed by Indian men as free and easy, based largely on what they see in cheap Western soaps. Fanning this flame is the fact that a sexual revolution has hit India, and marriage before or outside of marriage is less taboo than it once was. This new-found emancipation, combined with misconceptions about Western culture, mean that some men are wielding their sexuality like pubescent boys.

This issue in Goa is far from black and white. On one hand, Goa has a (sometimes justified) reputation of being a place where women let it all hang out at the beach and are sexually available. Thus for some Indian men, a perfect weekend away with their (male) friends is a trip to Goa, where booze and women are cheap. Generally it doesn't get beyond being extremely annoying – groups of men wander down the beach and either try to chat women up or just stare at them. It's not uncommon for hapless women to be surrounded by groups of Indian men wearing matching

It's better in Goa' singlets and forcefully requesting a photo, which will later be shown at home as proof that it is, in fact, better in Goa.

On the other hand, Goa is considered to be one of the most liberal states in the country. Women feel safe here and don't need to be as guarded over their behaviour as they do in many other parts of the country. Many years of many foreigners visiting this tiny state means that the local understanding of Western culture is nuanced enough that misinterpretations of women's behaviour are rarer here than in other parts of India.

But the sad fact remains – people have been raped in Goa. Foreign women have been attacked on secluded beaches at every hour of the day. Rapes have been reported even at busier beach towns during the day. Over Christmas, in particular, there are sometimes signs warning women to not wander off alone – even to go and relieve themselves in a nearby sand dune.

Though the biggest issue you're likely to face is the occasional lewd comment and being ogled at the beach by groups of Indian youths, the risks are real and mean that you should use your judgement. Check for peepholes in hotel rooms and protect your right to public space. Modest standards of dress will go some way towards minimising problems: topless bathing is illegal, and wearing bikinis and short skirts away from the beach is downright disrespectful. See p41 for more on this. It also pays to keep your wits about you and avoid situations that make you more vulnerable; diminished mental alertness through use of drugs and alcohol will make you far more of a target and far less able to defend yourself.

Transport

CONTENTS

THINGS CHANGE...

The information in this chapter is particularly vulnerable to change. Check directly with the airline or travel agent to make sure you understand how a fare (and the ticket you may buy) works for international travel. Shop carefully. The details given in this chapter should be regarded as pointers and not a substitute for your own careful, up-to-date research.

Flights, tours and rail tickets can be booked online at www.lonelyplanet.com/travel_services.

GETTING THERE & AWAY

ENTERING THE COUNTRY

Entering India is not particularly complicated; the standard immigration and customs procedures apply. For customs information, see p214.

Passports

You must have a valid passport, visa and onward/return ticket to enter India. Always carry copies of your visa or keep them in an online travel vault.

GETTING TO INDIA
Airports

On your way to Goa, you will most likely be flying into Mumbai or Chennai airports.

Chennai (MAA; Anna International Airport; ☎ 044-22560551; www.chennaiairport.com)

Mumbai (BOM; Chhatrapati Shivaji International Airport; ☎ 022-26829000; www.mumbaiairport.com)

Airlines

Aeroflot (SU; www.aeroflot.org) Sheremetyevo International Airport, Moscow (MUMBAI).

Air France (AF; www.airfrance.com) Charles de Gaulle, Paris.

Air India (AI; www.airindia.com) Indira Gandhi International Airport, Delhi.

Alitalia (AZ; www.alitalia.com) Fiumicino International Airport, Rome.

British Airways (BA; www.british-airways.com) Heathrow Airport, London.

Cathay Pacific Airways (CX; www.cathaypacific.com) Hong Kong International Airport.

Emirates (EK; www.emirates.com) Dubai International Airport.

Gulf Air (GF; www.gulfairco.com) Bahrain International Airport.

KLM – Royal Dutch Airlines (KL; www.klm.com) Schiphol Airport, Amsterdam.

Kuwait Airways (KU; www.kuwait-airways.com) Kuwait International Airport.

Lufthansa Airlines (LH; www.lufthansa.com) Frankfurt International Airport.

Malaysian Airlines (MH; www.malaysiaairlines.com) Kuala Lumpur International Airport.

Qantas Airways (QF; www.qantas.com.au) Kingsford Smith Airport, Sydney.

Royal Nepal Airlines Corporation (RA; www.royalnepal.com) Kathmandu Airport.

Singapore Airlines (SQ; www.singaporeair.com) Changi Airport, Singapore.

Sri Lankan Airlines (UL; www.srilankan.aero) Bandaranaike International Airport, Colombo.

DEPARTURE TAX

Departure tax to most countries is Rs 500, but in the vast majority of cases this is included in the cost of your ticket and is not payable at the airport – check with your travel agent.

TRANSPORT

Swiss International Airlines (LX; www.swiss.com) Zurich International Airport.

CHARTER FLIGHTS
The number of charter flights headed to Goa is increasing every year. The vast majority come from the UK, and Russians are heading over in steadily increasing numbers. There is talk of establishing such arrangements out of Israel and the US.

You can fly direct to Goa from the UK on a seat-only charter flight or on a package trip that includes accommodation. The latter can be great value but cuts back your flexibility to relocate to a different beach or hotel.

Be aware that it is illegal to enter on a scheduled flight and out on a charter flight, and vice versa: if you enter on a charter flight, you must also leave on one.

Reliable charter flight booking services:
Charter Flight Centre (☎ 08450-450153; www.charterflights.co.uk)
Flight Searchers (☎ 08000-935434; www.flightsearchers.co.uk)

Tickets
Stiff competition has resulted in widespread discounting. If you're buying your ticket online (which is smart given the excellent fares available), do it early; seats are usually sold in blocks with the cheapest economy fares going first.

Reputable international ticket sites:
Expedia (www.expedia.com)
Flight Centre International (www.flightcentre.com)
Flights.com (www.flights.com)
STA Travel (www.statravel.com)
Travelocity (www.travelocity.com)

Africa
Both **Rennies Travel** (www.renniestravel.com) and **STA Travel** (www.statravel.co.za) have offices throughout Southern Africa.

Asia
STA Travel (Bangkok ☎ 0 2236 0262; www.statravel.co.th; Hong Kong ☎ 852-27361618; www.statravel.com.hk; Japan ☎ 0353-912 922; www.statravel.co.jp; Singapore ☎ 6737 7188; www.statravel.com.sg) is found throughout Asia. Another resource in Japan is **No 1 Travel** (☎ 0332-056 073; www.no1-travel.com).

MALAYSIA
Malaysia Airlines (www.malaysiaairlines.com) flies to various cities in India.

NEPAL
Indian Airlines and Royal Nepal Airlines Corporation (RNAC) share routes between India and Kathmandu.

TRANSPORT

SINGAPORE
Return fares from Singapore to Mumbai or Chennai are available for about US$700 with Air India; you'll pay more with Singapore Airlines or Thai Airways International.

Flights direct to India can be purchased at www.singaporeair.com. **STA Travel** (☎ 6737 7188; www.statravel.com.sg/sta) has a strong presence in Singapore.

SRI LANKA
Tickets to Mumbai, Chennai, Delhi and Bangalore can be purchased at www.sri lankan.aero.

THAILAND
Bangkok is the most popular departure point from Southeast Asia into India. **STA Travel** (☎ 0662-2360262; www.statravel.co.th) has an office in Bangkok. Tickets to India from Thailand can be purchased at www.thaiair.com. Flight details and other information is available from within Thailand (☎ 02-15660).

Australia
Both **STA Travel** (☎ 1300 733 035; www.statravel.com.au) and **Flight Centre** (☎ 133133; www.flightcentre.com.au) have offices throughout Australia. For online bookings, visit **travel.com.au** (www3.travel.com.au).

Qantas is the only airline with direct, non-stop flights, flying to Mumbai from Sydney or Melbourne. Other airlines stop in a Southeast Asian city.

Canada
Fares from Canada are similar to fares from the US. **Travel Cuts** (☎ 1 866 246 9762; www.travelcuts.com) is Canada's national student travel agency. For online bookings try **Expedia.ca** (www.expedia.ca) and **Travelocity.ca** (www.travelocity.ca).

Most flights to India are via Europe, but there are options for travel via the US or Asia.

Continental Europe
For fares from Europe to Indian hubs, try the following agents.

FRANCE
Anyway (☎ 0892 893 892; www.anyway.fr in French)
Lastminute (☎ 0892 705 000; www.lastminute.fr)
Nouvelles Frontières (☎ 0825 000 747; www.nouvelles-frontieres.fr in French)

OTU Voyages (www.otu.fr)
Voyageurs du Monde (☎ 01 40 15 11 15; www.vdm.com in French)

GERMANY
Just Travel (☎ 089 7473330; www.justtravel.de)
Lastminute (☎ 01805 284366; www.lastminute.de)
STA Travel (☎ 069 74303292; www.statravel.de)
Usit Campus (☎ 030 2800 2800; www.usitcampus.de)

THE NETHERLANDS
Airfair (☎ 0900 7 717 717; www.airfair.nl)
NBBS Reizen (☎ 0900 10 20 300; www.nbbs.nl)

SPAIN
Barcelo Viajes (☎ 902 116 226; www.barceloviajes.com) is recommended.

New Zealand
Both **Flight Centre** (☎ 0800 243 544; www.flightcentre.co.nz) and **STA Travel** (☎ 0508 782 872; www.statravel.co.nz) have branches throughout the country.

There are no direct flights between India and New Zealand; airlines offer stopovers in Asia.

UK
Discount air travel is big business in London. Advertisements for many travel agencies appear in the travel pages of weekend broadsheet newspapers, *Time Out*, the *Evening Standard* and *TNT* magazine.

Good places to start hunting:
Flight Centre (☎ 0800 587 0078; flightcentre.co.uk)
Flightbookers (☎ 0800 082 3000; www.ebookers.com)
North-South Travel (☎ 01245 608 291; www.northsouthtravel.co.uk) Donates part of its profits to projects in the developing world.
Quest Travel (☎ 0870 442 3542; www.questtravel.com)
STA Travel (☎ 0870 163 0026; www.statravel.co.uk)
Trailfinders (☎ 0845 058 5858; www.trailfinders.co.uk)
Travel Bag (☎ 0800 082 5000; www.travelbag.co.uk)

USA
Discount travel agents in the US are known as consolidators. San Francisco is the consolidator capital of America, although some good deals can be found in other big cities.

For online bookings:
American Express Travel (☎ 1866 400 6736; www.itn.net)
CheapTickets (www.cheaptickets.com)
Expedia (☎ 1800 397 3342; www.expedia.com)

owestfare.com (www.lowestfare.com)

rbitz (☎ 1888 656 4546; www.orbitz.com)

TA Travel (☎ 800 781 4040; www.sta.com)

ravelocity (☎ 888 872 8356; www.travelocity.com)

GETTING TO GOA

.ir

abolim Airport (GOI; ☎ 540806; apdgoa_aai@satyam
et.in, apdgoa_aai@sify.net.in), Goa's only domes-
c and international airport, is in Dabolim,
ust outside Vasco da Gama. It's also known
s Goa Airport.

Recent years have seen an increase in
he number of new domestic airlines (such
s Kingfisher Airlines and SpiceJet), which
as upped competition. Online booking is
elatively simple and reliable, but flights
o/from Goa fill up fast between Decem-
er and February. The hour-long trip from
Mumbai costs around Rs 2000. Keep your
ye out for changes, but for the moment,
he following airlines offer domestic ser-
ices to Goa from various destinations.

ir Deccan (☎ 39 00 88 88; www.airdeccan.net)

ir India (☎ 1800 22 7722; www.airindia.com)

ir Sahara (☎ 1600 223 020; www.airsahara.net)

o Air (☎ 1600 222 111; www.goair.in)

ndian Airlines (☎ 1600 180 1407; www.indianairlines.in)

et Airways (☎ 1600 22 55 22; www.jetairways.com)

ingfisher Airlines (☎ 1600 1800 101; www.flyking
sher.com)

ahara Airlines (☎ 1600 22 3020; www.airsahara.net)

piceJet (☎ 1600 180 3333; www.spicejet.com)

or addresses of airlines in Goa, see p96.
ome only accept bookings online or online
ia agents, some only have counters at the
irport.

ar & Motorcycle

Renting a self-drive car in any of the main
ities in India and driving to Goa is pos-
ible, but given the danger and expense is
ot recommended.

Hertz (www.hertz.com) will charge around
s 1700 per day for a basic car. You'll be
equired to leave an insurance deposit of
round Rs 20,000 and hold an international
riving permit. There are also some private
perators that can hire cars for less than
s 1000 per day.

The other option is to make your way to
he nearest taxi rank and start bargaining.
The 600km trip from Mumbai to Goa takes
bout 14 hours; many drivers will happily

do this in one stretch. You'll have to pay for
the taxi's return trip, so the cost will be at
least Rs 7000 – it's cheaper to fly.

Motorcycles, on the other hand, are a
particularly popular way to get around
India. The **Royal Enfield** (www.royalenfield.com)
is synonymous with motorcycle travel in
India. Protective clothing and gear is best
brought from home. For more information
on motorcycle travel, see p237.

Bus

India has a comprehensive and extensive public bus system, but most state-run
vehicles are decrepit and overcrowded. From
neighbouring states you'll find frequent bus
services into Goa – it's just a matter of turning up at the bus station and checking timetables or jumping on the next available bus.

There are also plenty of private bus
companies running into Goa from Mumbai, Pune, Bangalore, Mangalore and other
interstate cities. These are more expensive,
but faster and more comfortable, with reclining seats and options of air-con or even
'sleeper' class.

KARNATAKA & CHENNAI

There are regular services into Goa from
the neighbouring state of Karnataka, including Bangalore (Rs 360, 14 hours), Mysore (Rs 225, 17 hours), Hampi (Rs 350, 10
hours) and Mangalore (Rs 180, 11 hours).
Private buses also have regular services on
these routes – see p97 and p165 for more
information.

Taking the bus to/from Chennai is not
really a viable option. There's one private
bus a week from Goa to Chennai (Rs 700,
22 hours). The easiest option is to take the
train or bus from Chennai to Bangalore and
then a bus from here. Private bus companies
in Chennai, with offices opposite Egmore
station, run super-deluxe video buses daily
to Bangalore (Rs 146, eight hours).

MUMBAI

Though the Konkan Railway is more comfortable and efficient than buses from
Mumbai, sleeper buses are popular. Erratic
driving means you might not sleep too well,
but for a long overnight trip it beats sitting
up all the way.

Private long-distance buses leave several
times daily for Goa from Dr Anadrao Nair

TRANSPORT

Rd, near Mumbai Central train station. Fares to Goa on non-air-con seater buses start at around Rs 350, and go up to Rs 750 for sleeper class. The Christmas–New Year period adds significantly to the fare. To check departure times and current prices, try **Paulo Travels** (www.paulotravels.com).

If you're staying in south Mumbai, a more convenient departure point for private buses to Goa is MG Rd, just north of Bombay Hospital (near Fashion St). It's best to purchase tickets directly from bus agents with pavement stalls clustered in either of these areas.

Train

Two railway systems cross the state. The South Central Railway has its terminus in Mormugao (past Vasco da Gama) and runs due east through Margao (Madgaon) and into Karnataka. The Konkan Railway, opened in 1998, runs from Mumbai to Mangalore through Goa, with some trains continuing south to Ernakulam and Trivandrum. The main stations in Goa include Pernem, for Arambol (Harmal); Thivim (Mapusa Rd) station, for Anjuna, Baga and Calangute; Karmali (Old Goa) station, for Old Goa and Panaji (Panjim); Margao, for Colva and Benaulim; and Canacona, for Palolem.

If coming from Mumbai or Mangalore you can book your ticket to these intermediate stations, but even if you book through to Margao you can get off at any station en route.

If you intend to do any serious train travel outside Goa, get hold of *Trains at a Glance* from book stalls in major train stations. It lists every major train service in India and includes distances.

Online sources:

Indian Railway Catering & Tourism Corporation (IRCTC; www.irctc.co.in) Tickets can be booked online here.
Indian Railways (www.indianrail.gov.in) The official Indian Railways website.
Train Travel in India (www.seat61.com/India.htm) An invaluable resource for train travel information in India.

TRAIN TYPES & CLASS

There are seven classes on mail and express trains, but not all trains have all classes. The most basic is 2nd-class seating, which has hard seats; five or six people will cram onto a bench made for three. Then comes

2nd-class sleeper (or sleeper class) which has open carriages where seats are padded and fold down to form three tiers of beds. Air-con sleepers are more comfortable and secure as each carriage has compartments. Bedding (sheets, blanket, pillow) is provided on some classes. The most common are three-tier (six beds in a compartment) and two-tier (four beds). Two-tier air-con is about twice the price of three-tier air-con and 1st class (two beds) is about double that again. Sleeping berths are only available between 9pm and 6am.

Finally there's chair car, which is individual reclining seats on certain air-con trains (such as the *Shatabdi Express*), and 1st class a more comfortable version of chair car.

With a couple of exceptions, fares are calculated by distance and are fixed regardless of which train you are on and where you are going.

Sample fares for a journey of 100km in the various classes:

Seat Type	Fare
2nd-class seat	Rs 57
2nd-class sleeper	Rs 91
Chair car	Rs 199
3-tier AC	Rs 256
2-tier AC	Rs 430
1st-class AC	Rs 794

RESERVATIONS & CANCELLATIONS

There are reservation charges for sleeper class (Rs 40) and anything above that, such as air-con multi-tiered or 1st class (Rs 60). The easiest way to reserve a ticket is to stay well away from the station and do it over the Internet through **IRCTC** (☎ 011-2334550; www.irctc.co.in). You first need to register on the site.

Tickets are refundable but cancellation fees apply: if you present the ticket more than one day in advance, a fee of Rs 20 to 5 applies, depending on the class; up to four hours before departure you lose 25% of the ticket value; and within four hours before and up to three to 12 hours after departure you lose 50%.

At most major stations there's a separate section in the booking hall dealing with the tourist quota. Only foreigners and nonresident Indians are allowed to use this facility. You must pay in foreign currency (cash or travellers cheques in US dollars or pounds sterling) or with rupees backed up by exchange certificates or ATM receipts. Only a limited number of seats are allocated to tourists, so if you can't get on it's worth trying for a normal reservation. When booking any ticket at a train station, you must fill out a reservation form *before* queuing.

If the train you want is fully booked, it's often possible to get a Reservation Against Cancellation (RAC) ticket. This entitles you to board the train and have seating. Once the train is moving, the Travelling Ticket Examiner (TTE) will find you a berth. This is different from a wait-listed ticket, which does not entitle you to board the train.

FROM CHENNAI
A direct Chennai–Vasco da Gama train, the 7311 *Chennai-Vasco Express,* runs on Friday, departing Chennai at 2pm and arriving in Vasco at 12.45pm the following day. Fares for sleeper/1st-class air-con are around Rs 350/960.

An alternative from Chennai is to catch the 7pm *Chennai-Mangalore Mail* to Mangalore (18 hours), then the 2.50pm *Matsyaghanda Express* (16 hours) to Margao.

In Chennai you can make train reservations on the 1st floor of the **Train Reservation Complex** (8am-2pm & 2.15-8pm Mon-Sat, 8am-2pm Sun), next to Central Station.

FROM MUMBAI
The journey to Goa (Margao) from Mumbai, takes 12 hours. From Mumbai's Victoria Terminus (Chhatrapati Shivaji Terminus; CST), there's an overnight 0111 *Konkan Kanya Express.* It leaves Mumbai at 11pm and arrives in Margao at 10.45am the following morning. Alternatively, the 0103 *Mandovi Express* leaves daily at 6.55am, reaching Margao at 6.40pm on the same day. Fares on both range from Rs 150 to Rs 345. Going to Mumbai, these trains leave at 6pm and 10.10am respectively.

The **reservation centre** (8am-8pm Mon-Sat, 8am-2pm Sun) is at the back of Victoria Terminus where the taxis gather. Tourist-quota tickets are available at **Counter 52** (1st fl; 8am-3pm Mon-Sat, 8am-2pm Sun) but can only be bought 24 hours before the date of travel. You can buy tickets (but not tourist-quota tickets) with a Visa or MasterCard up to 60 days in advance.

Another three day trains depart from Lokmanya Tilak station, 16km south of Mumbai's Victoria Terminus. The best option is the 2051 *Jan Shatabdi Express,* which departs Mumbai at 5.30am and gets in to Margao at 1.40pm. The 6345 *Netravati Express* departs at 11.40am and arrives at 10.30pm, and the 2619 *Matsyagandha Express* departs at 2.05pm, arriving at 12.10am.

GETTING AROUND

BICYCLE
Goa offers plenty of variety for cycling, with relatively smooth-surfaced highways, rocky dirt tracks, coastal routes through coconut palms and winding country roads through spice plantations, rural villages and ancient temples. A bicycle can also simply be a convenient way of getting around beach towns.

If you want a quality machine for serious touring, it's worth bringing your own. The downside is that your bike is likely to be a curiosity and more vulnerable to theft. Bring spare tyres, tubes, patch kits, chassis, cables, freewheels, a pump with the necessary connection and spokes, tools and a repair manual.

Hire
Hiring a bicycle is not difficult in Goa, but hiring a *good* bicycle is not so easy. Every beach in Goa has a multitude of people who are prepared to rent out bicycles – just ask around and someone will rent you *their* bicycle, more often than not an Indian-made single-gear rattler. Away from the main tourist areas, you won't find bicycle hire places.

Expect to pay around Rs 5 an hour or Rs 50 per day (less for rentals of a week or more). If you just want to hire a bike for a day in the high season, you may have to pay up to Rs 80.

Purchase
For a long stay of three months or more in Goa, it's worth considering buying a bicycle locally. Every town has at least a couple of shops selling various brands of basic Indian bikes including Hero, Atlas, BSA and Raleigh, almost always painted jet black. You should be able to pick up a second-hand bike for Rs 1000 to 1500.

TRANSPORT

BOAT

One of the joys of travelling around Goa is joining locals on flat-bottomed passenger-vehicle ferries that cross the state's many rivers. Ferries have been commuting people across waters for decades, but services are gradually being put out of business by massive bridge-building projects, the most recent being the ominous Aldona–Corjeum bridge.

Most of the remaining ferries operate a half-hourly service from early morning until late evening. Foot passengers ride for free, motorcycles sometimes cost Rs 4 and cars Rs 10. The main ferries of interest to travellers are: Panaji–Betim for the back road to Candolim and Calangute; Querim–Terekhol for Terekhol Fort; Old Goa–Divar Island; Ribandar–Chorao Island for Dr Salim Ali Bird Sanctuary and Chorao Island; and Cavelossim–Assolna for the coastal ride from Benaulim to Palolem.

BUS

The Kadamba Transport Corporation (KTC) is the state government bus service. It's overworked and underfunded, but it manages to provide cheap, regular services to most parts of the state. There are also a number of private operators that run parallel services.

Bus travel in Goa is cheap and enjoyable. Unless you're in a hurry or have a lot of luggage, the bus costs a fraction of a taxi fare, and you will probably meet a few friendly people along the way. If you're travelling between major centres, take an express (direct) service; for a few extra rupees, th express buses go directly to their final des tination without stopping to pick up mor commuters along the way.

For travel between the northern beache and southern beaches you'll generally hav to change buses at one or more of the majo centres – for instance, if you're going fror Anjuna to Palolem, you'll have to catch bus to Mapusa or Panaji, another to Marga and a third to Palolem.

At bus stands in Panaji, Margao, Mapus and Vasco da Gama, all destinations ar written in English, so there's little probler finding the bus you need. Bus-wallahs als shout destinations out in a bid to lure mor people aboard.

CAR

Few visitors to Goa bother to rent a self drive car. Given the crazy driving condi tions, and the fact that you're likely t spend a large amount of time on the beac anyway, it's easier to hire a car and drive when required. And it's cheaper.

Finding a car and driver is not a probler in the main towns – they will find yo If you'd prefer to rent through a busines head to any travel agency or ask your hote The typical cost for a day of sightseeing i a chauffeur-driven car, depending on dis tance and what sort of car it is, ranges fror Rs 600 to 1000.

If you do decide to choose the self-driv option, private agents generally charg

ROAD DISTANCE CHART (km)

	Bicholim	Calangute	Hampi	Mapusa	Margao	Molem	Old Goa	Palolem	Panaji	Pernem	Ponda	Vasco da Gama
Bicholim	---											
Calangute	35	---										
Hampi	390	396	---									
Mapusa	25	10	392	---								
Margao	53	50	370	46	---							
Molem	70	76	320	72	50	---						
Old Goa	23	26	370	22	37	50	---					
Palolem	93	90	403	86	40	83	75	---				
Panaji	19	16	380	12	34	60	10	74	---			
Pernem	43	28	410	18	64	90	40	104	30	---		
Ponda	38	43	350	39	25	30	19	53	29	47	---	
Vasco da Gama	49	46	390	42	30	70	35	70	30	60	34	---

around Rs 900 (for 24 hours) or around Rs 6300 per week for a basic car without air-con. The same car with a driver will cost around Rs 750 for an eight-hour day. See p238 for information about driving licences, road rules and hazards.

Another easy option is to approach a taxi driver; most will gladly set off anywhere in Goa.

HITCHING

Hitching is never entirely safe in any country in the world, and we don't recommend it. On the other hand, many travellers argue that it offers an interesting insight into a country. Ultimately it's up to you, but be mindful of the fact that people travelling in pairs will be safer than those going it alone. Solo women in particular are unwise to hitchhike.

The Goan caveat to the standard 'don't do it' is that sometimes (particularly at night when options are scare) it may be practical to hail down a passing motorcycle. Assuming the person can drive, you're probably safer on the back of a stranger's motorcycle than you are in a car.

LOCAL TRANSPORT
Autorickshaw

An autorickshaw is a yellow-and-black three-wheeled contraption powered by a noisy two-stroke motorcycle engine. It has a canopy, a driver up front and seats for two (or sometimes more) passengers behind. This typically Indian mode of transport is cheaper than a taxi and generally a better option for short trips – count on Rs 30 to 40 for a trip across Panaji. Even for a trip such as Anjuna flea market to Panaji (costing around Rs 100) it's a viable ride. Because of their size and manoeuvrability, they're quicker taxis for trips around town, though sometimes more hair-raising. At the time of research, fares had just been officially increased to Rs 10 for the first kilometre, and Rs 9 for subsequent kilometres, plus Rs 10 for each hour of waiting time. The practical affect of this will be negligible; pre trip negotiations will continue regardless of the official fares.

Motorcycle Taxi

Goa is the only state in India where motorcycles are a licensed form of taxi. You can tell the motorcycle taxis (or pilots as they are sometimes called) by the yellow front mudguard. They gather, along with taxis and autorickshaws, at strategic points in towns and beach resorts. They're fun and they're fast – no other form of transportation can so quickly and efficiently navigate through traffic. The downside is that there's an increased element of danger – motorcycle pilots may be experienced riders but that doesn't stop them coming off or colliding with other vehicles and you've got little or no protection in the event of a crash. The official rate is Rs 10 for the first kilometre and Rs 3 per kilometre thereafter. In practice, the minimum charge is around Rs 10 and a 10-minute journey will be about Rs 50.

Taxi

Though taxis are supposed to charge metered rates, the fact is that these days 'taxis' range from iconic yellow-and-black cabs, through to modern cars whose drivers are more fittingly described as chauffeurs and vans labelled 'tourist vehicle' regardless of who they're transporting. Other than the traditional taxi, none of these have meters. To avoid an argument at the other end, be clear on what you're agreeing to: does the final price include all passengers, luggage and waiting time?

A good rule of thumb is that a standard taxi should cost around Rs 10 per kilometre, a tourist van around Rs 12 and anything slightly more luxurious around Rs 20. Most taxi drivers in Goa are about as interested in fighting over rupees as you are, so finding a reasonable fare should be a fairly collaborative effort. If not, find another driver.

MOTORCYCLE

Getting around Goa by motorcycle is almost de rigueur, especially around the northern beaches; you only need to look at the sea of motorcycles parked at the Anjuna flea market or outside Vagator's Nine Bar to realise that it borders on a cliché. If you plan to spend most of your time lying on the beach, you may have little use for a motorcycle, but if you want to move around a bit, follow the parties, check out the scene and restaurants at different beaches or head inland for the day, you'll soon find it's a hassle without your own transport. The freedom that a motorcycle affords is hard to beat.

TRANSPORT

Driving Licence

An international driving permit is not technically mandatory, but it's wise to bring one. The first thing a policeman will want to see if he stops you is your licence, and an international permit is incontrovertible. Permits are available from your home automobile association.

Fuel & Spare Parts

Petrol is expensive compared to the cost of living in India. At the time of research it cost Rs 50 per litre (Rs 45 on lucky days). However, distances are short and the small bikes (such as the Honda Kinetic or Activa) are very economical, so you won't spend a lot of money on fuel and certainly less than you'd spend if you were catching a taxi around. There are petrol stations in all the main towns such as Panaji, Margao, Mapusa, Ponda and Vasco da Gama, including a 24-hour service station in Margao and another on the highway near Cuncolim. There's also a very busy pump in Vagator. Where there are no petrol pumps, general stores sell petrol by the litre; they don't advertise the fact, so you'll have to ask around. Sometimes petrol in plastic bottles has been diluted, so it may be wise to buy it from the same people you hired the bike from – someone who cares about its condition. A litre of petrol from a plastic bottle costs around Rs 55.

While it's usually possible to find someone selling petrol, if you're heading for a day ride inland or even along the coast, make sure you have adequate fuel to begin with; many rental motorcycles have broken gauges.

A Honda Kinetic holds 7L of fuel, and should go 40km on 1L. A 100cc Yamaha takes 10L to 11L and also does 40km per litre. Enfields hold about 18L; new models will do about 35km per litre, while older ones do considerably less.

Hire

Hiring a motorcycle in Goa is easier than you might think. Hirers will probably find you, and are more often than not decent guys who are just looking to make a bit of cash on the side. Private bike owners are not technically allowed to rent out a machine. This means that if you are stopped by the police for any reason, your hirer would prefer that you say you have borrowed it

from a 'friend'. Laws on this sort of thing are almost universally ignored in north Goa where anything goes, but police can be more opportunistic in the south. It's a good idea to keep registration papers in the bike – it gives the police one less argument against you, and if you don't have a valid licence, or you're not wearing a helmet on National Hwy (NH) 17, you'll need all the help you can get.

If you leave the state, you may need to produce original documents for the vehicle you are driving or riding. If you want to go further afield from Goa, you need to rent from a licensed agency to stay within the law.

WHICH BIKE?

At the bottom end of the scale are the most popular rental bikes – gearless scooters such as the 100cc Honda Kinetics or Bajaj scooters. They have *no* street cred whatsoever, but are extremely practical and easy to ride, which makes them the obvious choice if you don't have a lot of motorcycle-riding experience. You only need a car driving licence to ride these bikes.

Next up the scale are the 100cc and 135cc bikes – Yamaha being the most common. Fuel economy is good, they go faster than a Kinetic, and they tend to be a bit more comfortable over a long distance. Although they're easy to ride, you'll need to have had some experience on a motorcycle.

Finally, at the top of the pile are the real bikes – classic Enfield Bullets. Made in India since the 1950s, this old British-designed machine is real currency for image and status; the thumping sound of the engine reverberates around the hills of Anjuna and Vagator in the high season. They are far less fuel-friendly, require more maintenance than the others, and take a little getting used to. Most of the Enfields available for hire are 350cc, but there are also some 500cc models around.

COSTS & WHERE TO HIRE

Off season you can get a scooter for as little as Rs 100 per day. During high season (December to February) the standard rate is Rs 250 to 300. If you can get an old kinetic down to Rs 130 or so, you're doing very well. Expect to pay Rs 400 for a 100cc bike and up to Rs 600 for an Enfield. Obviously the longer you hire a bike (and the older it is), the cheaper it becomes.

Make absolutely sure that you agree with the owner about the price; clarify whether one day is 24 hours, and that you won't be asked to pay extra for keeping it overnight.

Queen Paulo Travels has been authorised by the government to hire motorbikes (an Activa or Kinetic costs Rs 250 and an Enfield Rs 400) and has offices in Panaji. However, simply renting a bike off the street at beach towns or through your hotel or a tout that approaches you is just as simple.

In Panaji, head to the cluster of bikes that hang around the post office. In Margao, you should have luck anywhere around the Municipal Gardens. In Colva, Arambol or Palolem and Calangute, head for the main entrance to the beach. In Anjuna, you'll find some decent guys hanging around the Starco Junction.

You'll probably be asked to pay cash upfront (which is fair enough too given that they're handing over their motorbike!), but get a written receipt and never leave your passport, licence or plane ticket as security. Try to get a phone number so you can call the owner if something goes wrong with the bike.

WHAT TO LOOK FOR

It makes sense to check the bike over before you hire it and make a note of any damage or broken parts, so that you're not blamed for it later. Make sure brakes, lights and the all-essential horn are working. You can manage without a petrol gauge but it's nice when it works. Mirrors are useful, but many older rental bikes are missing them. Take a look at the condition of the tyres to make sure that there's at least a skerrick of tread on them.

On the Road

GETTING STOPPED BY THE POLICE

The travellers' grapevine is littered with tales of tourists being stopped by the police; 'no licence', 'no helmet' or 'dangerous driving' can all be reason enough for the police to demand on-the-spot payment of a 'fine' – baksheesh by any other name. The simplest answer is to keep away from areas where you are likely to bump into the police – avoid the national highways and the Zuari and Mandovi Bridges where there are often police checkpoints. Many people get away

without any hassle, however, so there's no point in worrying too much about it. In recent years Goan police have been pulled into line and extortion of foreigners is on the decline.

THE HELMET ISSUE

Whether or not helmets should be obligatory for two-wheeler riders has been an issue for decades. On 29 July 2004 the government unanimously decided (…drum-roll please) to establish a committee to study the issue. Finally, it was decided that helmets should indeed become mandatory as of 15 August 2004. And yet the issue rages on. The Motorcycle Action Group (MAG) strongly opposes the law. Their argument (in addition to the fact that carrying a helmet is inconvenient, women's hair may become dishevelled and helmets may cause dandruff) is that casualties would be decreased through less reckless, negligent and drunk driving, rather than more helmets. Never mind that of the 235 people who were killed in road accidents in Goa in 2003, 128 of them were drivers or pillion passengers, more than 100 of whom died of head injuries.

In practical terms, the decision is yours. Use your head and protect it or not as you wish.

ROAD CONDITIONS

Because of the extreme congestion in towns and the narrow, bumpy roads in the country, driving is often a slow, stop-start process. The only genuine highways are the NH17, running north–south and passing through Margao, Panaji and Mapusa, and the NH4A, which heads east from Panaji into Karnataka, bypassing close to Ponda.

The country roads away from these highways are much more pleasant for motoring, as there's very little heavy traffic and the countryside is scenic. Most main roads are in reasonable condition but are generally not well signposted – it's very easy to get lost if you don't continually ask directions.

ROAD SAFETY

Road safety is an important issue when you're out on a motorcycle. India has the worst record for road accidents in the world, and almost one person a day dies in a road accident in Goa alone. Inexperienced, helmetless foreigners on motorcycles

TRANSPORT

are extremely vulnerable. Each season more than a few tourists travel home in a box via the state mortuary in Panaji.

Watch out for 'speed breakers'. Speed humps are stand alone back breakers or come in triplets. The extra nasty ones are lined up in groups of fives, and none of them are particularly well signed. Sometimes you only get a couple of metres warning. Also look out for pot holes, sand, wandering livestock and other inexperienced, overenthusiastic drivers.

ROAD RULES

Road rules in India are applied mainly in theory. Driving is on the left, vehicles give way to the right, and road signs are universal pictorial signs. At busy intersections, traffic police are often on hand to reduce the chaos. Otherwise, make good use of your horn.

Never forget that the highway code in India can be reduced to one essential truth – 'Might is Right'. On a motorcycle you're pretty low in the rights hierarchy. On a scooter, you're roadkill waiting to happen. Goan drivers often try unexpected moves, and Goan pigs have an unnerving habit of dashing onto the road without warning. Avoid riding at night – road surfaces in some places are very bad and many roads are unlit.

Organised Tours

Peter & Friends Classic Bike Adventure (☎ 2254467; www.classic-bike-india.de; Casa Tres Amigos, Socol Vado No 425, Assagao) is an established German company that organises motorbike tours on Enfields through the Himalayas, Nepal, South India and Goa. The two-week Goa and South India tour costs €1190, including accommodation and meals, with full insurance and support. Peter and his friends also organise other trips around the area and have their own divine accommodation at Casa Tres Amigos. Check out their website.

Purchase

Buying (and later selling) a motorcycle during a stay in Goa is not as practical or economical as it is in other parts of the country.

If you do plan to buy a bike, there are plenty of second-hand machines around – check advertisements in the daily papers or head to the Anjuna flea market on Wednesday. Enfield has a presence at Ingo's Saturday Nite Bazaar, where it promotes shiny new models.

TRAIN

Goa has two railways. The South Central Railway has its terminus in Mormugao (past Vasco da Gama) and runs due east, through Margao and into Karnataka. This line is often used by tourists day-tripping to Dudhsagar Falls in the east of the state, and travellers heading towards Hampi in Karnataka (the nearest station is at Hospet).

The Konkan Railway runs from Mumbai (Bombay) to Mangalore (in Karnataka) through Goa. It's unlikely that you'll use the train much for travel within Goa given the ease and economy of bus travel. However, trains may be useful if you're planning to travel from one end of the state to the other, ie Arambol to Palolem, which would otherwise require at least three changes by bus. In the north the stations of Pernem and Thivim (Mapusa Rd) are not particularly convenient for the beaches, but in the south, Canacona station is only 3km from Palolem beach.

Konkan Railway stations in Goa, from north to south, are: Pernem (for Arambol), Thivim (for Mapusa), Karmali (for Old Goa and Panaji), Verna, Margao (for Colva and Benaulim), Bali, Barcem and Canacona (for Palolem).

For more information on the train system see p234.

There are reliable travel agents all over Goa that can book train tickets for you, or you can go directly to the reservation centres themselves:

Margao (☎ 0832-2712790; 1st fl, Madgaon railway station; ☺ 8am-8pm Mon-Sat, 8am-2pm Sun)
Panaji (☎ 0832-2438254; 1st fl, Kadamba bus stand, Patto; ☺ 8am-8pm Mon-Sat)
Thivim (☎ 0832-2298682; Thivim railway station; ☺ 8am-8pm Mon-Sat, 8am-2pm Sun)
Vasco da Gama (☎ 0832-2512569; Vasco railway station; ☺ 8am-8pm Mon-Sat, 8am-2pm Sun)

Health

The potential dangers of going anywhere can seem frightening, but in reality, few travellers to Goa will experience anything more than upset stomachs.

BEFORE YOU GO

Pack medications in their original containers. Also bring a letter from your physician describing your medical conditions and any medications or syringes you may need to carry. If you have a heart condition, bring a copy of your ECG. Bring extra medication in case of loss or theft; it can be difficult to find some newer drugs, particularly the latest antidepressants, blood-pressure medications and contraceptive pills.

INSURANCE

Don't travel without health insurance – accidents happen, especially, it seems, when you don't have insurance. Declare any existing medical conditions you have – you won't be covered for pre-existing problems that are undeclared.

Find out in advance if your insurance plan will make payments directly to providers or if it will reimburse you later for overseas health expenditures. (In many countries doctors expect payment in cash.) You may prefer a policy that pays doctors or hospitals directly. If you do have to claim later, make sure you keep all the relevant documentation.

Some policies ask that you telephone (reverse charges) to a centre in your home country, where an immediate assessment of your problem will be made.

VACCINATIONS

Specialised travel-medicine clinics are your best source of information; they stock all available vaccines and will be able to give specific recommendations for you and your trip.

Most vaccines don't give immunity until at least two weeks after they're taken, so visit a doctor four to eight weeks before departure. Ask your doctor for an International Certificate of Vaccination (otherwise known as the 'yellow booklet'), which will list all the vaccinations you've received.

Recommended Vaccinations

The World Health Organization (WHO) recommends these vaccinations for travellers to India (as well as being up to date with measles, mumps and rubella vaccinations):

Adult diphtheria and tetanus Single booster recommended if none in the previous 10 years. Side effects include sore arm and fever.

Hepatitis A Provides almost 100% protection for up to a year; a booster after 12 months provides another 20 years' protection. Mild side effects such as headache and sore arm occur in 5% to 10% of people.

Hepatitis B Considered routine for most travellers. Given as three shots over six months. A rapid schedule is also available, as is a combined vaccination with hepatitis A. In 95% of people lifetime protection results. Side effects are mild, usually headache and sore arm.

Polio Polio is still present in India. Only one booster is required as an adult for lifetime protection. Inactivated polio vaccine is safe during pregnancy.

Typhoid Recommended for all travellers to India, even if you only visit urban areas. The vaccine offers around 70% protection, lasts for two to three years and comes as a single shot. Tablets are also available but the injection has fewer side effects. Sore arm and fever may occur.

Varicella If you haven't had chickenpox, discuss this vaccination with your doctor.

HEALTH

These immunisations are recommended for long-term travellers (more than one month) or those at special risk:

Japanese B Encephalitis Three injections in all. Booster recommended after two years. Sore arm and headache are the most common side effects. Rarely, an allergic reaction of hives and swelling can occur up to 10 days after the doses.

Meningitis Single injection. There are two types of vaccination: quadrivalent vaccine gives two to three years' protection; meningitis group C vaccine gives around 10 years' protection. Recommended for long-term backpackers aged under 25.

Rabies Three injections in all. A booster after one year will then provide 10 years' protection. Side effects are rare – occasionally headache and sore arm.

Tuberculosis (TB) This is a complex issue. Adult long-term travellers are usually recommended to have a TB skin test before and after travel, rather than vaccination. Only one vaccine given in a lifetime.

Required Vaccinations

Proof of yellow fever vaccination is only required if you have visited a country in the yellow-fever zone within six days prior to entering India. If you are travelling to India from Africa or South America, check to see if you require proof of vaccination.

MEDICAL CHECKLIST

Recommended items for a personal medical kit:

- Antifungal cream, eg Clotrimazole
- Antibacterial cream, eg Muciprocin
- Antibiotic for skin infections, eg Amoxicillin/Clavulanate or Cephalexin
- Antihistamine – there are many options, eg Cetrizine for daytime and Promethazine for night
- Antiseptic, eg Betadine
- Antispasmodic for stomach cramps, eg Buscopam
- Contraception
- Decongestant, eg Pseudoephedrine
- DEET-based insect repellent
- Diarrhoea medication – consider an oral rehydration solution (eg Gastrolyte), diarrhoea 'stopper' (eg Loperamide) and anti-nausea medication (eg Prochlorperazine)
- Antibiotics for diarrhoea include Norfloxacin or Ciprofloxacin; for bacterial diarrhoea Azithromycin; for Giardia or amoebic dysentery Tinidazole
- First-aid items such as scissors, Elastoplast, bandages, gauze, thermometer (but not mercury), sterile needles and syringes, safety pins and tweezers
- Ibuprofen or another anti-inflammatory
- Indigestion tablets, eg Quick-Eze
- Iodine tablets (unless you are pregnant or have a thyroid problem) to purify water
- Laxative, eg Coloxyl
- Paracetamol
- Pyrethrin to impregnate clothing and mosquito nets
- Steroid cream for allergic/itchy rashes, eg 1% to 2% hydrocortisone
- Sunscreen and hat
- Thrush (vaginal yeast infection) treatment, eg Clotrimazole pessaries or Diflucan tablet
- Ural or equivalent if prone to urine infections

INTERNET RESOURCES

There is a wealth of travel health advice on the Internet. **Lonely Planet** (www.lonelyplanet.com) is a good place to start. Some other suggestions:

Centers for Disease Control and Prevention (CDC; www.cdc.gov) Good general information.

MD Travel Health (www.mdtravelhealth.com) Complete travel health recommendations for every country, updated daily.

World Health Organization (WHO; www.who.int/ith/) Superb, annually revised book *International Travel & Health* is available online.

FURTHER READING

Lonely Planet's pocket sized *Healthy Travel – Asia & India* is packed with information including pretrip planning, first aid, immunization, diseases and what to do if you get sick on the road. Other recommended references include *Travellers' Health* by Dr Richard Dawood and *Travelling Well* by Dr Deborah Mills – check out the website **Travelling Well** (www.travellingwell.com.au).

IN TRANSIT

DEEP VEIN THROMBOSIS (DVT)

Deep vein thrombosis (DVT) occurs when blood clots form in the legs, chiefly because of prolonged immobility. The longer the flight, the greater the risk. The chief symptom is swelling or pain of the foot, ankle or calf. If a blood clot travels to the lungs it may cause chest pain and difficulty in

---

HEALTH ADVISORIES

It's usually a good idea to consult your government's travel-health website before departure, if one is available:

Australia (www.dfat.gov.au/travel/)
Canada (www.travelhealth.gc.ca)
New Zealand (www.mfat.govt.nz/travel)
South Africa (www.dfa.gov.za/travelling)
UK (www.doh.gov.uk/traveladvice/)
USA (www.cdc.gov/travel/)

---

reathing. Travellers with these symptoms ould seek medical attention.

To prevent DVT on long flights, walk bout the cabin, contract leg muscles while tting, drink plenty of fluids, and avoid al-ohol and tobacco.

ET LAG & MOTION SICKNESS

et lag is common when crossing more an five time zones; it results in insom-ia, fatigue, malaise or nausea. To avoid et lag drink plenty of nonalcoholic flu-ds and eat light meals. Upon arrival, seek xposure to natural sunlight and readjust our schedule (for meals, sleep etc) as soon s possible.

Antihistamines such as dimenhydrinate Dramamine), promethazine (Phenergan) nd meclizine (Antivert, Bonine) are the rst choice for motion sickness. Their main de effect is drowsiness. Ginger works like charm for some people.

N GOA

VAILABILITY & COST OF EALTH CARE

lthough there are reasonable facilities in anaji (Panjim), Margao (Madgaon) and asco da Gama, Goa does not have the qual-y of medical care available in the West. The est facilities in Goa are at the **Goa Medical Col-ge Hospital** (☎ 0832-2458725, 2458700) at Bam-olim, 9km south of Panaji on the National ighway (NH) 17. In the event of a serious ccident this is the best place to go; it has a rain scanner and most other facilities.

In north Goa you'll also find **Mapusa Clinic** ☎ 0832-2263343, 2263346; Mapusa Clinic Rd, Mapusa), nd in Margao, the **main hospital** (☎ 0832-705664; Padre Miranda Rd).

Goa's **ambulance service** (☎ 102) can be un-reliable; it may be quicker to get a taxi.

There are well-stocked pharmacies in all Goan towns selling drugs manufactured under licence to Western companies; you can buy more over the counter here than you can in the West. The small size of Goa means you're never too far from a major town with a decent hospital. Upmarket ho-tels often have a reliable doctor on call.

INFECTIOUS DISEASES
Dengue Fever
This mosquito-borne disease is becoming increasingly problematic. As there is no vaccine available, it can only be prevented by avoiding mosquito bites. The mosquito that carries dengue bites day and night.

Symptoms include high fever, severe headache and body ache (dengue was pre-viously known as 'breakbone fever'). Some people develop a rash and experience diar-rhoea. There is no specific treatment – just rest and paracetamol. Don't take aspirin; it increases the likelihood of haemorrhaging.

See a doctor so you can be diagnosed and monitored.

Hepatitis A
This food- and water-borne virus infects the liver, causing jaundice (yellow skin and eyes), nausea and lethargy. There is no spe-cific treatment for hepatitis A, other than time for the liver to heal. All travellers to India should be vaccinated.

Hepatitis B
The only sexually transmitted disease that can be prevented by vaccination, hepati-tis B is spread by body fluids. Long-term consequences can include liver cancer.

Hepatitis E
Transmitted through contaminated food and water, hepatitis E has similar symptoms to hepatitis A, but is less common. It is a severe problem in pregnant women and can result in the death of both mother and baby. There is no vaccine; prevention is by follow-ing safe eating and drinking guidelines.

HIV
India has one of the highest growth rates of HIV in the world. HIV is spread via con-taminated body fluids. Avoid unsafe sex,

unsterile needles (including in medical facilities) and procedures such as tattoos.

There is a **helpline** (☎ 0832-2431827) in Goa for people with HIV. Contact the **Goa State Aids Control Society** (☎ 0832-2422519) for more information about HIV in Goa.

Japanese B Encephalitis

This mosquito-transmitted viral disease is rare in travellers. Vaccination is recommended for travellers spending more than one month in rural areas. There is no treatment; one third of infected people die while another third suffer brain damage.

Malaria

Malaria is caused by a parasite transmitted by the bite of an infected mosquito. The most important symptom of malaria is fever, but general symptoms such as headache, diarrhoea, cough or chills may also occur. Blood samples are used to diagnose.

Antimalaria medications should be combined with the following mosquito bite prevention steps:

- Use an insect repellent containing DEET. Natural repellents such as citronella must be applied more frequently.
- Sleep under a mosquito net impregnated with pyrethrin.
- Choose accommodation with screens and fans (if not air-conditioned).
- Impregnate clothing with pyrethrin in high-risk areas.
- Wear long sleeves and light-coloured trousers.
- Use mosquito coils.
- Spray your room with insect repellent before going out for your evening meal.

Many medications must be taken for four weeks after leaving the risk area. There are various options on the market.

- Combination of Chloroquine and Paludrine – limited effectiveness in parts of South Asia. Common side effects include nausea (40% of people) and mouth ulcers.
- Doxycycline – broad-spectrum antibiotic taken daily. Potential side effects include photosensitivity (a tendency to sunburn), thrush (in women), indigestion, heartburn, nausea and interference with the contraceptive pill. More serious side effects include ulceration of the oesopha-

gus. Must be taken for four weeks after leaving the risk area.

- Lariam (Mefloquine) – weekly tablet. Rare but serious side effects include depression, anxiety, psychosis and fits. Should not be taken by those with a history of depression, anxiety, other psychological disorder, or epilepsy.
- Malarone (Combination of Atovaquone and Proguanil) – side effects are mild and uncommon, and usually nausea and headache. Best choice for scuba divers and those on short trips to high-risk areas. Must be taken for one week after leaving the risk area.

Rabies

Around 30,000 people die annually in India from rabies. This fatal disease is spread by the bite or lick of an infected animal – most commonly a dog or monkey. Seek medical advice immediately after any animal bite and commence post-exposure treatment. Pretravel vaccination means postbite treatment is greatly simplified.

If you are bitten, gently wash the wound with soap and water, and apply iodine based antiseptic. If you are not vaccinated you need to receive rabies immunoglobulin as soon as possible, and this is almost impossible to obtain in much of India.

STDs

Sexually transmitted diseases most common in India include herpes, warts, syphilis, gonorrhoea and chlamydia. People carrying these often have no signs of infection.

Condoms prevent gonorrhoea and chlamydia but not warts or herpes. If after a sexual encounter you develop any rash, lumps, discharge or pain when passing urine, seek immediate medical attention.

If you have been sexually active during your travels, have an STD check on your return home.

Tuberculosis

While TB is rare in travellers, those who have significant contact with the local population (such as medical and aid workers and long-term travellers) should take precautions.

Vaccination is usually only given to children under five, but adults at risk are recommended pre- and post-travel TB testing.

e main symptoms are fever, cough,
ight loss, night sweats and tiredness.

phoid

read via food and water, this bacterial in-
ction gives a high and slowly progressive
ver, headache and maybe a dry cough and
omach pain. It is treated with antibiotics.
ccination is recommended for travellers
ending more than a week in India. Vacci-
tion is not 100% effective; still be careful
th what you eat and drink.

RAVELLER'S DIARRHOEA

raveller's diarrhoea is defined as the pas-
ge of more than three watery bowel ac-
ons within 24 hours, plus at least one
her symptom such as fever, cramps, nau-
a, vomiting or feeling generally unwell.

This is by far the most common problem
fecting travellers – between 30% and 70%
people suffer from it within two weeks of
arting their trip. In over 80% of cases it is
used by bacteria, and therefore responds
romptly to antibiotics.

Treatment consists of staying well hy-
ated; rehydration solutions like Gastrolyte
e best. Antibiotics such as Norfloxacin,
profloxacin or Azithromycin kill the bac-
ria quickly.

Loperamide is a 'stopper' and doesn't ad-
ess the problem. It can be helpful for long
us rides, though. Don't take Loperamide if
ou have a fever or blood in your stools.

Seek medical attention if you do not re-
ond to antibiotics.

moebic Dysentery

moebic dysentery is rare in travellers
t it is often misdiagnosed. Symptoms are
milar to bacterial diarrhoea: fever, bloody
arrhoea and generally feeling unwell. Al-
ays seek reliable medical care if you have
ood in your diarrhoea.

Treatment involves Tinidazole or Met-
onidazole to kill the parasite and a sec-
nd drug to kill the cysts. If left untreated,
omplications such as liver or gut abscesses
an result.

iardiasis

iardia is a relatively common parasite
travellers. Symptoms include nausea,
loating, excess gas, fatigue and intermit-
nt diarrhoea. The parasite eventually goes

away if left untreated, but can take months.
The treatment of choice is Tinidazole with
Metronidazole.

ENVIRONMENTAL HAZARDS
Diving & Surfing

Divers and surfers should seek specialised
advice before they travel to ensure their
medical kit contains treatment for coral
cuts and tropical ear infections. Divers
should also get specialised dive insurance
through an organisation such as **Divers Alert
Network** (DAN; www.danseap.org) and have a dive
medical before they travel.

Heat

For most people it takes at least two weeks
to adapt to the hot climate. Swelling of
feet and ankles is common, as are muscle
cramps caused by excessive sweating. Prevent these by keeping hydrated, and taking
it easy when you first arrive. Rehydration
solution and salty food helps. Treat cramps
with rest and rehydration with double-
strength rehydration solution.

Dehydration is the main contributor to
heat exhaustion. Symptoms include weakness, headache, irritability, nausea, sweaty
skin, a fast, weak pulse and a normal or
slightly elevated body temperature.

Treatment involves getting out of the
heat, fanning the sufferer and applying cool
wet cloths to the skin, laying the sufferer
flat with their legs raised and rehydrating
them with water and salt (¼ teaspoon per
litre).

Heat stroke is a serious medical emergency. Symptoms come on suddenly and
include weakness, nausea, a hot dry body
with a body temperature of over 41°C, dizziness, confusion, loss of coordination, fits
and eventually collapse and loss of consciousness. Seek medical help and get the
person out of the heat, removing their
clothes, fanning them and applying cool
wet cloths or ice to their body, especially
the groin and armpits.

Prickly heat is a common rash in the
tropicsl regions, caused by sweat trapped
under the skin. The result is an itchy rash
of tiny lumps. Treat prickly heat by moving
out of the heat and into an air-conditioned
area for a few hours. Cool showers also
help in treating the rash. Creams and oint-
ments clog the skin and should be avoided.

HEALTH

HEALTH

LIFE'S A BEACH

Outside of the monsoon season, the warm Arabian Sea off the coast of Goa is one of the safest waters in the world. That said, there are a few dangers to be aware of.

Swimming

Every year there are drowning deaths along the coastline. Undertows and currents can be strong, even close to the beach, especially early and late in the season. Don't swim immediately after eating, and definitely don't go in the water if you have been drinking alcohol. The underwater slope is not always even – the beach may suddenly drop leaving you in deep water. Despite the romantic temptation, it's not wise to take a midnight dip, especially if you've been out partying.

In the monsoon, swimming in the sea is out of the question. Also be careful in October and November; sand bars are still in a state of transition. During the monsoon large volumes of sand get swept inshore and are gradually eroded as the sea normalises. There are only a few channels through the sandbanks, which generates strong rips.

Jellyfish

Although they generally stay in deeper water, it's not unheard of for jellyfish to drift into shallower water, particularly during the early and late months of the season (October to November and March to April). A jellyfish sting won't kill you, but it will hurt like hell.

If you are stung, calm down and wash off the tendrils with sea water. Then use an acid solution to soak the sting – if you're near a beach shack ask for vinegar or lime juice. Then subject the sting to heat treatment. Protein toxins of the venom break down in temperatures between 43°C and 45°C. If you can't find a heat pack (ask divers), fill a basin with hot water and immerse the affected area, gradually adding more hot water until the temperate is as high as possible. Do *not* use an ice pack – it makes symptoms worse.

Other Sea Creatures

Although you may see the occasional dead sea snake (called *kusada* in Goa) on the sand, you are extremely unlikely (or unlucky) to spot a live one; they're extremely timid and try to avoid swimmers.

Scorpion fish (sometimes known as stonefish) and lionfish inhabit areas of the Goan coastline. They prefer the shelter of rocks and stones so you're unlikely to find them on the sandy bottom of the main swimming beaches. They are found in shallow waters around one or two of the small islands off the coast of Goa. Both types of fish have poisonous dorsal fins, and if stepped on, understandably inject venom into the offending foot. As with jellyfish stings, heat treatment breaks down the toxins. Medical treatment should be sought as soon as possible.

Locally purchased prickly heat powder can be helpful.

Tropical fatigue is common in long-term expatriates based in the tropics. It's rarely due to disease and is caused by climate, excessive alcohol intake and the daily demands of a different culture.

Insect Bites & Stings

Bedbugs don't carry disease but their bites are itchy. You can treat the itch with an antihistamine. Lice inhabit various parts of your body but most commonly your head and pubic area. Transmission is via close contact with an infected person. They can

be difficult to treat and you may need nu merous applications of an antilice sham poo with pyrethrin. Pubic lice are usuall contracted from sexual contact.

Ticks are contracted after walking i rural areas. Ticks are commonly found be hind the ears, on the belly and in armpit See a doctor if you get a rash at the site the bite or elsewhere, fever or muscle ache The antibiotic Doxycycline prevents tick borne diseases.

Bee and wasp stings mainly cause prob lems for people who are allergic to them adrenalin injections (eg Epipen) should b carried for emergencies.

Skin Problems

There are two common fungal rashes that affect travellers in humid climates. The first occurs in moist areas such as the groin, armpits and between toes. It starts as a red patch that slowly spreads and is usually itchy. Treatment involves keeping the skin dry, avoiding chafing and using antifungal cream such as Clotrimazole or Lamisil. Tinea versicolour is also common – this fungus causes small, light-coloured patches, mostly on the back, chest and shoulders. Consult a doctor.

Cuts and scratches become easily infected in humid climates. Wash wounds in clean water and apply antiseptic. Be particularly careful with coral cuts, which become easily infected. If you develop signs of infection (increasing pain and redness) see a doctor.

Sunburn

Even on a cloudy day sunburn can occur rapidly. Use strong sunscreen (at least factor 30), making sure to reapply after swimming, and wear a wide-brimmed hat and sunglasses. Avoid lying in the sun during the hottest part of the day (10am to 2pm). If you become sunburnt, apply cool compresses and take painkillers. One percent hydrocortisone cream applied twice daily is also helpful.

DRINKING WATER

- Never drink tap water
- Bottled water is generally safe – check that the seal is intact
- Avoid ice
- Boiling water is the most efficient method of purifying water
- The best chemical purifier is iodine. It should not be used by pregnant women or people with thyroid problems
- Water filters should also filter out viruses; ensure your filter has a chemical barrier such as iodine and a small pore size, ie less than four microns

---

TRAVELLING WITH CHILDREN

See p213 for more information on travelling with children.

WOMEN'S HEALTH

In most places in Goa, sanitary products (pads, rarely tampons) are readily available. Birth control options may be limited, so bring adequate supplies of your own form of contraception.

Heat, humidity and antibiotics can contribute to thrush. Treatment is with antifungal creams and pessaries such as Clotrimazole. A practical alternative is a single tablet of Fluconazole (Diflucan). Urinary tract infections can be precipitated by dehydration or long bus journeys without toilet stops; bring suitable antibiotics.

Pregnant Women

Pregnant women should receive specialised advice before travelling. The ideal time to travel is in the second trimester (between 16 and 28 weeks), when the risk of pregnancy-related problems is at its lowest.

Ensure that your travel insurance policy covers all pregnancy-related possibilities, including premature labour.

Malaria is a high-risk disease for pregnant women, and WHO recommends they do *not* travel to areas with Chloroquine-resistant malaria. None of the more effective antimalaria drugs are completely safe in pregnancy. Traveller's diarrhoea can quickly lead to dehydration and result in inadequate blood flow to the placenta. Many drugs used to treat various diarrhoea bugs are not recommended in pregnancy. Azithromycin is considered safe.

TRADITIONAL MEDICINE

You've come to the right place if you're interested in traditional medicine. There is a strong culture of holistic healing in Goa, from Ayurveda to reflexology to reiki. As with all medicine, some practitioners are better than others. Ask around and do your research before you commit to anything – be wary of people who offer treatments but have no experience or qualifications whatsoever.

HEALTH

Language

As a legacy of its unusual colonial history, Goa has inherited a mixture of languages. Portuguese is still spoken as a second language by a few Goans, although it is gradually dying out. The official language of India is Hindi, which children in Goa are obliged to learn in school. Konkani (which has five different scripts) is now accepted as the official language of the state, and Marathi is also taught as a standard subject.

Ironically the primary language used in many schools is actually English. Arguments about continuing or abandoning this policy of placing such importance on English rage on. How can Indians get away from their colonial past, many ask, if they are still forced to use the language of the colonisers? Others feel that continuing use of English is a distinct advantage to their children, who will need it if they are to find good jobs in the future. Meanwhile, children in Goa are taught three or four languages as a standard part of the school syllabus.

You'll find that English is widely spoken in Goa's tourist areas. For a comprehensive guide to Hindi, get a copy of Lonely Planet's *Hindi, Urdu & Bengali Phrasebook*.

HINDI & KONKANI
Useful Words & Phrases

There are many different ways of writing Konkani in the Roman alphabet, and the Konkani words included in this chapter are only approximate transliterations.

Beware of the Hindi *achaa*, an all-purpose word for 'OK'. It can also mean 'OK, I understand what you're saying, but I'm not necessarily agreeing' (such as when negotiating a price with a taxi driver).

	Hindi	Konkani
Hello.	namaste	paypadta
Goodbye.	namaste	mioshay
Excuse me.	kshamaa keejiye	upkar korchi
Please.	meharbani seh	upkar kor
Yes.	jee haang	oi
No.	jee naheeng	naah
Thank you.	danyavaad	dev borem korum

How are you?
aap (kaise/kaisee) haing? (m/f) (H)
(kosso/kos-hem) assa? (m/f) (K)
Very well, thank you.
bahut achaa, shukriaya (H)
bhore jaung (K)
What's your name?
aapka shubh naam kya hai? (H)
tuje naav kide? (K)
Do you speak English?
kya aap angrezi samajhte hain? (H)
to English hulonk jhana? (K)
I don't understand.
meri samajh men nahin aaya (H)
mhaka kay samzona (K)
Where is a hotel?
hotal kahan hai? (H)
hotel khoy aasa? (K)
How far is ...?
... kitni duur hai? (H)
anig kitya phoode ...? (K)
How do I get to ...?
... kaiseh jaateh hai? (H)
maka kashe ... meltole? (K)
How much?
kitneh paiseh? kitneh hai? (H)
kitke poishe laqthele? (K)
This is expensive.
yeh bahut mehnga hai (H)
chod marog (K)
What is the time?
kitneh bajeh hain? (H)
vurra kitki jali? (K)

	Hindi	Konkani
big	bhada	hodlo
small	chhota	dhakto
today	aaj	aaj
day	din	dees
night	raat	racho
week	haftah	athovda
month	mahina	mohino
year	saal	voros
medicine	dava-ee	vokot

Numbers

Where we count in tens, hundreds, thousands, millions and billions, the India numbering system goes tens, hundreds, thousands, hundred thousands, ten millions. A hundred thousand is a lakh, and 10 million is a crore. These two words will almost always used in place of their English equivalent. Thus you'll see 10 lakh rather than one million and one crore rather than 10 million. Furthermore, the numerals are generally written that way too – thus three hundred thousand appears as 3,00,000 not 300,000, and ten million, five hundred thousand would appear numerically as 1,05,00,000 (one crore, five lakh) not 10,500,000. If you say something costs five crore or is worth 10 lakh, it always means 'of rupees'.

When counting from 10 to 100 in Hindi, there's no standard formula for compiling numbers – they are all different. Here we've just given you enough to go on with!

To complicate matters further, there are two different counting systems in Konkani. Hindu Goans use the system shown in the list below, but for Catholic Goans there are differences: – *vis-ani-ek* rather than *ekvis* for 21, for example.

	Hindi	Konkani
1	ek	ek
2	do	don
3	tin	tin
4	char	char
5	panch	panch
6	chhe	sou
7	saat	saat
8	aath	aat
9	nau	nov
10	das	dha
11	gyaranh	ikra
12	baranh	bara
13	teranh	tera
14	chodanh	chouda
15	pandranh	pondra
16	solanh	sollah
17	staranh	sottra
18	aatharanh	ottra
19	unnis	ekonis
20	bis	vis
21	ikkis	ekvis
22	bais	bavis
23	teis	tevis
24	chobis	chouvis
25	pachis	ponchis
26	chhabis	sovis
27	sattais	satavis
28	athais	attavis
29	unnattis	ekontis
30	tis	tis
35	paintis	posstis
40	chalis	chalis
45	paintalis	ponchechalis
50	panchas	ponnas
55	pachpan	ponchavan
60	saath	saatt
65	painsath	pansatt
70	sattar	sottor
75	pachhattar	ponchator
80	assi	oichim
85	pachaasi	ponchalsh
90	nabbe	novodh
95	pachaanabbe	ponchanov
100	so	chembor
200	do so	donshe
1000	ek hazaar	ek hazaar
2000	do hazaar	don hazaar
100,000	lakh	lakh

LANGUAGE

Glossary

The following are terms you may come across during your Goan travels. For definitions of Goan and Indian food and drink, see p58.

Adivasi – tribal person

amrita – immortality

autorickshaw – small, noisy, three-wheeled, motorised contraption used for transporting passengers short distances

avatar – incarnation of a deity, usually *Vishnu*

Ayurveda – ancient study of healing arts and herbal medicine

babu – lower-level clerical worker (derogatory term)

baksheesh – tip, bribe or donation

balcao – shady porch at front of traditional Goan house, usually with benches built into the walls

bandh – general strike

betel – nut of the areca palm; the nut is mildly intoxicating and is chewed with *paan* as a stimulant and digestive

Bhagavad Gita – Hindu song of the Divine One; *Krishna*'s lessons to Arjuna, emphasising the philosophy of bhakti (faith); part of the *Mahabharata*

Bhairava – the Terrible; refers to the eight incarnations of *Shiva* in his demonic form

bhang – dried leaves and flowering shoots of the cannabis plant

Brahma – source of all existence and also worshipped as the creator in the Hindu *Trimurti*; depicted as having four heads (a fifth was burnt by *Shiva*'s 'central eye' when Brahma spoke disrespectfully)

Brahmanism – early form of Hinduism that evolved from Vedism (see *Vedas*); named after the *Brahmin* priests and the god *Brahma*

Brahmin – member of the priest caste, the highest Hindu *caste*

bund – embankment or dyke, used in Goa to protect *khazans*

caste – four classes into which Hindu society is divided; one's hereditary station in life

Chandra – moon, or the moon as a god, worshipped particularly in Goa at the Chandreshwar Bhutnath Temple, on Chandranath Hill

charas – resin of the cannabis plant; also referred to as hashish

chillum – pipe of a hookah; used to describe the small clay pipes for smoking *ganja*

communidades – traditional system of land management in Goa

crore – 10 million

Dalit – preferred term for India's casteless class; see *Untouchable*

deaknni – traditional Goan dance

deepastambha – lamp tower, a prominent and distinctive feature of many temples

devadasi – temple dancer

Devi – *Shiva*'s wife

Dhangars – tribe of Goa's indigenous people

dharma – Hindu and Buddhist moral code of behaviour; natural law

dhobi ghat – place where clothes are washed

Dravidian – member of one of the indigenous races of India pushed south by the Indo-Europeans and now mixed with them; languages include Tamil, Malayalam, Telugu and Kannada

dulpod – traditional Goan dance

durbar – royal court; also used to describe a government

Durga – the Inaccessible; a form of *Shiva*'s wife *Devi*; a beautiful but fierce woman riding a tiger; major goddess of the Sakti cult

fado – type of song popular in Portuguese colonial era, delivered in operatic style

Ganesh – Hindu god of good fortune; elephant-headed son of *Shiva* and *Parvati*; also known as Ganpati

Ganga – Ganges River; also the Hindu goddess representing the sacred Ganges River

ganja – dried flowering tips of cannabis plant; highly potent form of marijuana

gaon – village

garbhagriha – inner sanctum of a Hindu temple

ghat – steps or landing on a river; range of hills, or road up hills; Western Ghats are the range of mountains that run along India's west coast, effectively forming the eastern border of Goa

GTDC – Goa Tourism Development Corporation

Hanuman – Hindu monkey god and follower of Rama; prominent in the *Ramayana*

Harijan – name given by Gandhi to India's *Untouchables*; the term is no longer considered acceptable (see *Dalit* and *Untouchable*)

Indra – most important and prestigious of the Vedic (see *Vedas*) gods of India; god of rain, thunder, lightning and war

Jainism – religion and philosophy founded by Mahavira in the 6th century BC in India; its fundamental tenet is nonviolence

ji – honorific that can be added to the end of almost anything; thus babaji, Gandhiji

Kali – the Black; terrible form of *Shiva's* wife *Devi;* depicted with black skin, dripping with blood, surrounded by snakes and wearing a necklace of skulls

Kama – Hindu god of love

karma – principle of retributive justice for past deeds

kell tiatr – form of *tiatr*

khadi – homespun cloth

khazans – low-lying areas alongside Goa's rivers, reclaimed by building *bunds;* the flow of salt and fresh water is regulated to allow the land to be used for a variety of purposes

Krishna – *Vishnu's* eighth incarnation, often coloured blue; he revealed the *Bhagavad Gita* to Anjuna

Kshatriya – Hindu *caste* of warriors and administrators

KTC – Kadamba Transport Corporation; Goa's state bus company

Kunbis – Descendants of Goa's first inhabitants, and among the state's poorest groups; sometimes called 'Goa's aborigines'

kusada – sea snake

lakh – 100,000

Lakshmana – half-brother and aide of Rama in the *Ramayana*

lathi – bamboo stick often used by police

lingam – phallic symbol of *Shiva*

Mahabharata – Great Vedic (see *Vedas*) epic poem of the Bharata dynasty

Mahadeva – Great God; *Shiva*

Mahadevi – Great Goddess; *Devi*

mahatma – literally 'great soul'

Maheshwara – Great Lord; *Shiva*

maidan – open grassed area in a city

mandala – circle; symbol used in Hindu and Buddhist art to symbolise the universe

mandapa – pillared pavilion of a temple

mando – famous song and dance form, introduced originally by the Goan Catholic community

Manguesh – an incarnation of *Shiva*, worshipped particularly in Goa

mantra – sacred word or syllable used by Buddhists and Hindus to aid concentration; metrical psalms of praise found in the *Vedas*

Manueline – style of architecture typical of that built by the Portuguese during the reign of Manuel I (1495–1521)

Maratha – warlike central Indian people who controlled much of India at various times; fought the *Mughals*

marg – major road

masjid – mosque

Moghul – *see Mughal*

moksha – liberation from the cycle of rebirth

monsoon – rainy season between June and October

Mughal – Muslim dynasty of Indian emperors from Babur to Aurangzeb (1526–1707)

Nanda – cowherd who raised *Krishna*

Nandi – bull, vehicle of *Shiva;* his images are usually found at *Shiva* temples

Nataraja – *Shiva* in his incarnation as the cosmic dancer

niwas – house, building

paan – mixture of betel nut and various spices, chewed for its mildly intoxicating effect, and as a digestive after meals

panchayat – local government; a panchayat area typically consists of two to three villages, from which volunteers are elected to represent the interests of the local people (the elected representative is called the *panch;* the elected leader is the *sarpanch*)

Parasurama – sixth incarnation of *Vishnu,* and the 'founder' of Goa

Parvati – the Mountaineer; a form of *Devi*

pousada – Portuguese for hostel

prasad – food offering

puja – literally 'respect'; offering or prayers

Puranas – set of 18 encyclopaedic Sanskrit stories, written in verse, relating to the *Trimurti;* dates from the period of the Guptas (5th century AD)

raj – rule or sovereignty

raja, rana – king

Ramayana – story of Rama and *Sita;* one of India's most well-known legends, retold in various forms throughout almost all of Southeast Asia

ramponkar – traditional Goan fisherman; fishes the coastal waters from a wooden boat, using a hand-hauled net (rampon)

ratha – temple chariot or car used in religious festivals

reredos – ornamented screen behind altar in Goan churches

sagar – lake, reservoir

saquão – central courtyard in traditional Goan houses

Sati – wife of *Shiva;* became a *sati* (honourable woman) by immolating herself (although banned more than a century ago, the act of *sati* is occasionally performed, though not in Goa)

satyagraha – literally 'insistence on truth'; nonviolent protest involving a fast, popularised by Gandhi; protesters are *satyagrahis*

Scheduled Castes – official term for *Dalits* or *Untouchables*

Shiva – also spelt as Siva; the Destroyer; also the Creator, in which form he is worshipped as a *lingam*

shri – also spelt sri, sree, shree; honorific; these days the Indian equivalent of Mr or Mrs

Sita – in the *Vedas* the goddess of agriculture; commonly associated with the *Ramayana,* in which she is abducted by Ravana and carted off to Lanka

sitar – Indian stringed instrument

Sudra – caste of labourers

susegad – Goan expression meaning relaxed or laid-back

sutra – string; a list of rules expressed in verse, the most famous being the *Kamasutra*

swami – title given to Hindu monks meaning 'lord of the self'; a title of respect

tabla – pair of drums

taluka – administrative district or region

tank – reservoir

tiatr – locally written and produced drama in the Konkani language

tikka – mark devout Hindus put on their foreheads with *tikka* powder

toddy tapper – one who extracts toddy from palm trees

torana – architrave over a temple entrance

Trimurti – Triple Form; the Hindu triad *Brahma, Shiva* and *Vishnu*

Untouchable – lowest *caste* or 'casteless' for whom the most menial tasks are reserved; name derives from the belief that higher castes risk defilement if they touch one (formerly known as *Harijan,* now *Dalit* or *Scheduled Castes*)

Upanishads – esoteric doctrine; ancient texts forming part of the *Vedas* (although of a later date)

vaddo – also spelt as waddo; section or ward of a village

varna – concept of *caste*

Varuna – supreme Vedic god

Vedas – Hindu sacred books; a collection of hymns composed in preclassical Sanskrit during the second millennium BC and divided into four books: *Rig-Veda, Yajur-Veda, Sama-Veda* and *Atharva-Veda*

Velips – traditional forest-dwelling people

vimana – principal part of a Hindu temple

Vishnu – part of the *Trimurti* with *Brahma* and *Shiva;* the Preserver and Restorer

wallah – man or person; can be added onto almost anything, thus dhobi-wallah, taxi-wallah, chai-wallah

Behind the Scenes

THIS BOOK

This 4th edition of *Goa* was written by Marika McAdam. The Health chapter was written by Dr Trish Batchelor. Bryn Thomas, with assistance from Douglas Streatfeild-James, researched and wrote the 1st and 2nd editions, and Paul Harding updated the 3rd edition with assistance from Lucas Vidgen and Susan Derby. This guidebook was commissioned in Lonely Planet's Melbourne office, and produced by the following:

Commissioning Editors Carolyn Boicos, Janine Eberle, Lucy Monie, Marg Toohey, Sam Trafford
Coordinating Editors Barbara Delissen, Victoria Harrison, Laura Stansfeld
Coordinating Cartographer Valentina Kremenchutskaya
Coordinating Layout Designer Cara Smith
Managing Cartographer Shahara Ahmed
Assisting Editor Andrea Dobbin
Cover Designer Gerilyn Attebery
Colour Designer Yvonne Bischofberger
Project Manager Sarah Sloane
Language Content Coordinator Quentin Frayne

Thanks to Imogen Bannister, Sally Darmody, Jennifer Garrett, Nicole Hansen, Kate McDonald, Celia Wood

THANKS
MARIKA McADAM

The opportunity to embark on the indulgent adventure of Goa came from the fine people at Lonely Planet. Thanks in particular to Lucy Monie, Shahara Ahmed and Janine Eberle for their patient and steadfast support.

Sincere gratitude to the nonchalantly noble people of Goa, who gave me a laugh or gave me a hand without ever realising how much help they were. Thank you to the travellers who took the time to write in.

Christian and Todd gave me fine conversation and festive spirit; Claire, Matt and Grant gave me holiday – thank you! Many thanks too to Deepti for making our 'office' such a sociable place to be. The German Bakery in Anjuna couldn't possibly be a nicer place to sit and write about Goa; thanks to the staff there for never throwing me out.

Back at home, thanks to my family for time, space and support, and to friends who remain so even though I'm never there. Finally, to Jo Aigner, the greatest adventure of all my adventures…thank you for all the sacrifices you make to be with me, and for your unwavering love and support, even when you can't.

OUR READERS
Many thanks to the travellers who used the last edition and wrote to us with helpful hints, useful advice and interesting anecdotes:

A Malika Anderson, Shaine Arison, **B** Frank Bacon, Roman Bansen, Ricky Batra, Clive & Sue Beck, John Beevers, Majlin Bienz, Jack Birch, David Bloch, Graham Boulding, June Bradley, Steve Braithwaite, Jill & Michael Brough, Geoff Bullock, **C** Juliet Cairns, Debbie Carnegie, Marta Ceriani, Boucaud Claude, Jean Constable, Ann Cooper, Yvonne Cousins, Paul Cullen, **D** Ketan Dalal, Sara Daly, Charlotte Day, Catherine Diggle, Heli Donaldson, Barry Donnan, **E** Silvia El Sayed, **F** Jon Farkas-Blake, Sarah Fernandes, Lynn Fickenscher, **G** Lee Fen Goh, **H** Karen Hahnel, Olli Halikka, Simon Hall, Nada Hankin, Jennifer

Hayes, Pirkko Heikkila, Katrina Henderson, Felix Heubaum, Elizabeth Horne, **I** Rachel & Martin Ive, **J** Lee Jhonson, Pernilla Johansson, Louise Jones, **K** Michelle Kanes, **L** Mark Langley, Sallie Latch, Per Lauritsen, Yolanda Lobo, **M** Patricia Maier, Laura Mcclelland, Andy McQuade, Steve Meldrum, Paulina Mennez, Anne Myles, **N** Sahadev Naik, Anna Nathanson, Christiane Nepel, P Nielsen, **O** Michael Owen, **P** Shekhar Pagi, Laura Paukkunen, Nancy Peckford, John Pemberton, Ken & Olove Philcox, Jay Priebe, **R** Laura & John Read, Peggy Richards, Sheila Robinson, Sheila & Clive Robinson, Anne Rohan, **S** Rudi Scobie, Mark Scott, Claire Sedge, Tegan Shohet, Max Sieber, Erik Sorensen, Clare Spencer, Michael Spice, Jakob Sprickerhof, Diane Strong, **T** Dea Turner, **V** Chris Vaughan, Dierk Vorwerk, Tatjana Vucanovic, **W** Kat Waldschmidt, Caryle Webb-Ingall, Golbarg Wedin Bashi, Nicole We Gordon & Ginette Westerman, Sharon Williams, **Y** F J Yates

ACKNOWLEDGMENTS

Many thanks to the following for the use of the content:

Globe on back cover ©Mountain High Map 1993 Digital Wisdom, Inc.

Index

INDEX

INDEX

12am 1am 2am 3am 4am 5am 6am 7am 8am 9am 10am 11am 12pm

International Date Line

Mon / Sun

ARCTIC OCEAN

Queen Elizabeth Is *(Can)*

Ellesmere Is *(Can)*

BAFFIN BAY

9am Greenland *(Denmark)*

11am

GREENLAND SEA

NORWEGIAN SEA

CHUKCHI SEA

BEAUFORT SEA

Banks Is *(Can)*

Victoria Is *(Can)*

Baffin Is *(Can)*

Iceland

NORTH SEA

United Kingdom

Russia

Alaska *(US)*

3am

4am

5am

Canada

HUDSON BAY

LABRADOR SEA

8am

Ireland

NORTH ATLANTIC OCEAN

BERING SEA

2am

GULF OF ALASKA

6am

7am

8.30am

Azores *(Port)*

Portugal

Spain

NORTH PACIFIC OCEAN

1am Midway Is *(US)*

United States

Bermuda *(UK)*

Morocco

Canary Is *(Sp)*

Mauritania

Mali

Hawaii *(US)*

Mexico

GULF OF MEXICO

The Bahamas

Cuba

Haiti

Eastern Caribbean Islands

Cape Verde

12pm

Senegal

Guinea

Burkina Faso

Ghana

EQUATOR

Guatemala

Nicaragua

CARIBBEAN SEA

Panama

Venezuela

Guyana

Suriname

Liberia

GULF OF GUINEA

Kiribati

Galapagos Is *(Ecuador)*

Colombia

Ascension *(UK)*

Samoa

2.30am

Ecuador

Peru

7am

8am

Brazil

9am

Tahiti

French Polynesia *(Fr)*

Bolivia

SOUTH ATLANTIC OCEAN

Tonga

12am

Cook Is *(NZ)*

1am

2am

Pitcairn Is *(UK)* 3.30am

Easter Is *(Chile)*

Paraguay

New Zealand

12.45am

Chatham Is *(NZ)*

SOUTH PACIFIC OCEAN

Chile

Uruguay

Argentina

Tristan da Cunha *(UK)*

Gough Is *(UK)*

Falkland Is *(UK)*

South Georgia & South Sandwich Is *(UK)*

Bouvet Is *(Norway)*

12am 1am 2am 3am 4am 5am 6am 7am 8am 9am 10am 11am 12pm

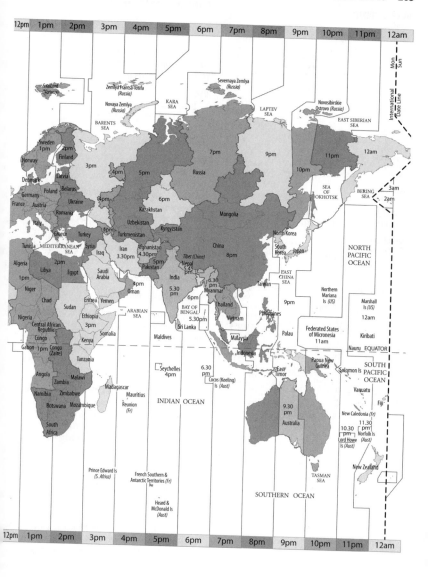

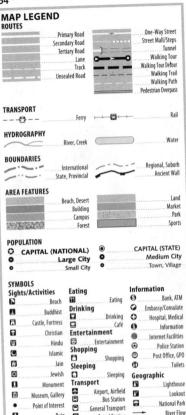

MAP LEGEND

ROUTES
- Primary Road
- Secondary Road
- Tertiary Road
- Lane
- Track
- Unsealed Road
- One-Way Street
- Street Mall/Steps
- Tunnel
- Walking Tour
- Walking Tour Detour
- Walking Trail
- Walking Path
- Pedestrian Overpass

TRANSPORT
- Ferry
- Rail

HYDROGRAPHY
- River, Creek
- Water

BOUNDARIES
- International
- State, Provincial
- Regional, Suburb
- Ancient Wall

AREA FEATURES
- Beach, Desert
- Building
- Campus
- Forest
- Land
- Market
- Park
- Sports

POPULATION
- CAPITAL (NATIONAL)
- CAPITAL (STATE)
- Large City
- Medium City
- Small City
- Town, Village

SYMBOLS

Sights/Activities
- Beach
- Buddhist
- Castle, Fortress
- Christian
- Hindu
- Islamic
- Jain
- Jewish
- Monument
- Museum, Gallery
- Point of Interest
- Ruin
- Zoo, Bird Sanctuary

Eating
- Eating

Drinking
- Drinking
- Café

Entertainment
- Entertainment

Shopping
- Shopping

Sleeping
- Sleeping

Transport
- Airport, Airfield
- Bus Station
- General Transport
- Petrol Station
- Taxi Rank

Information
- Bank, ATM
- Embassy/Consulate
- Hospital, Medical
- Information
- Internet Facilities
- Police Station
- Post Office, GPO
- Toilets

Geographic
- Lighthouse
- Lookout
- National Park
- River Flow
- Waterfall

LONELY PLANET OFFICES

Australia
Head Office
Locked Bag 1, Footscray, Victoria 3011
☎ 03 8379 8000, fax 03 8379 8111
talk2us@lonelyplanet.com.au

USA
150 Linden St, Oakland, CA 94607
☎ 510 893 8555, toll free 800 275 8555
fax 510 893 8572
info@lonelyplanet.com

UK
72–82 Rosebery Ave,
Clerkenwell, London EC1R 4RW
☎ 020 7841 9000, fax 020 7841 9001
go@lonelyplanet.co.uk

Published by Lonely Planet Publications Pty Ltd
ABN 36 005 607 983

© Lonely Planet Publications Pty Ltd 2006

© photographers as indicated 2006

Cover photographs by Lonely Planet Images: The Trippy musician by the sea, this gentleman will read your fortune for a few coins on Anjuna beach, Paul Beinssen (front); People, motorcycles and palm trees silhouetted at sunset, Peter Ptschelinzew (back). Many of the images in this guide are available for licensing from Lonely Planet Images: www.lonelyplanetimages.com.